PALMERSTON

The Uniform Edition of the Works of
PHILIP GUEDALLA

"A writer who is son of Ariel and the nephew of Puck."—*Sir Edmund Gosse.*

"Mr. Guedalla writes his history not as one who consults and transcribes documents, but as one who has so lived in the period that fact, comment, gossip, quotation, simply flow from the tip of his pen."—*Punch.*

THE DUKE

PALMERSTON

THE SECOND EMPIRE

IDYLLS OF THE QUEEN

RAG-TIME AND TANGO

VISCOUNT PALMERSTON, 1850
From the painting by F. Cruickshank, at Broadlands.

PALMERSTON

PHILIP GUEDALLA

" But in spite of all temptations
To belong to other nations,
He remains an Englishman!"

H.M.S. PINAFORE; OR, THE LASS
THAT LOVED A SAILOR.

LONDON
HODDER AND STOUGHTON

PALMERSTON BY PHILIP GUEDALLA WAS FIRST
PUBLISHED IN NOVEMBER, 1926.

IT WAS REPRINTED IN DECEMBER, 1926, AND
JANUARY AND DECEMBER, 1927.

IT IS NOW REISSUED IN THIS UNIFORM EDITION
OF THE WORKS OF PHILIP GUEDALLA IN
SEPTEMBER, 1937.

PRINTED AND BOUND IN GREAT BRITAIN FOR HODDER AND STOUGHTON, LTD.,
BY RICHARD CLAY AND SONS, LTD., BUNGAY, SUFFOLK.

TO

THAT UNWEARIED BAND OF WORKERS, COPYISTS,
AND FRIENDLY (BUT NOT TOO FRIENDLY) CRITICS,

MY WIFE

LET me explain the scope and purpose of this book and my design in writing it.

The life of Palmerston was the life of England and, to a large extent, of Europe in the last sixteen years of the Eighteenth and the first sixty-five of the Nineteenth Centuries. Perhaps its magnitude accounts for the fact that the task has been so rarely undertaken. For he covered an amazing span. Stated in terms of art, his life unites an almost legendary past to our own time : when he was born, Reynolds was painting Mrs. Siddons, and Mr. Swinburne published Atalanta in Calydon in the year that he died. A Regency beau, he spoke in debate when Mr. Pitt and Mr. Fox had not long fallen silent, and he was Secretary at War against Napoleon. He moved in the candle-light of the drawing-rooms where Mr. Creevey told his stories ; and men still living have conversed with him. For he lived to be fifteen years Foreign Secretary and twice Prime Minister in the gathering gloom of a later age. His first diplomatic duels were fought with Talleyrand and Metternich, his last with Mr. Lincoln and Prince Bismarck. For he had a positive genius for survival ; perhaps the reason why he left no disciples was that he had survived them all. Did he not accept office from Mr. Spencer Perceval and live to offer it to Mr. Cobden ? So it is not surprising that his long journey across the English scene has startled biography into one of its rare silences.

He had his epitaph, of course. Within twelve years of its close the rich curves of that long career had been pressed into the more decorous outline of a Victorian statesman, and the slightly rakish figure was gravely mummified in five volumes by pious, contemporary hands. But epitaphs are frequently deficient in perspective, and monumental masonry can rarely be mistaken for portrait sculpture. One feels that something more lifelike

*would have been more to his own taste ; and marble is scarcely
the medium in which to catch a statesman of whom Victor Hugo
wrote after meeting him at dinner,* lord Palmerston appartient
un peu à l'histoire et beaucoup au roman. *This liveliness
disqualifies him almost equally for the no less glacial treatment
which we customarily accord to our distinguished dead. So
much of him is lost, if we approach him with the pins and
killing-bottle of normal academic method. Yet I have always
felt that there is a Muse, no less than a method, of history ; and
using (though, I hope, concealing) the full apparatus of research
and documents, I have done my best to paint his portrait, to
catch something of the movement of his world, and to bring back
the dead without sacrifice either of accuracy or of vividness.
For I conceive that both should be pursued with equal ardour by
any historian who is not prepared to leave half his work undone.*

*In this task I have been fortunate in receiving unusually
generous assistance. The key of Palmerston, as Lord Beacons-
field would have said, is at Broadlands ; and friendly access to
the house, the portraits, and the papers lays me under the deepest
obligation to the Right Hon. Wilfrid Ashley, M.P., and to
Mrs. Ashley, whose kindness is responsible for the greater
number of the illustrations, and for such aid as the narrative
derives from such sources as the unpublished letters of Lady
Palmerston, the Melbourne correspondence, and the long series
of Palmerston's early letters to his mother, as well as innumerable other inédits. I am no less obliged to the Marquess of
Lansdowne (through the kindly intervention of the Earl of
Kerry) for access to the unpublished Palmerston letters in the
Bowood Papers, and to the Earl of Clarendon for the full and
important series of Palmerston's letters to his grandfather.
These unpublished papers have often enabled me to state
Palmerston's policy in the easy terms of letters exchanged
with colleagues rather than in the formal language of despatches.
For his early career at the War Office I have made use of the
departmental papers (largely unexplored) at the Public Record
Office ; and the British Museum contains a miscellaneous
collection of his public and private papers, upon which I have*

drawn largely.   I am also indebted to the India Office for the sight of a portion of the unpublished Broughton Papers relating to his influence on Afghan policy ; to Dr. H. W. V. Temperley, of Peterhouse, Cambridge, for an unpublished fragment relating to Palmerston's tenure of office under Canning ; and to the Rev. F. A. Simpson, of Trinity College, Cambridge, for the kindly gift of an original letter of Palmerston.   Three scholars, Dr. C. F. Strong, Mr. W. F. F. Grace, and Mr. D. Dawson, have assisted with rare unselfishness by placing at my disposal the unpublished results of their researches on Palmerston's policy in Italy, Poland, and Mexico.

The figure that emerges from these pages may be found to differ in certain respects from the traditional effigy of Lord Palmerston.   More Liberal (he was a Free Trader before Bright or Cobden, and an untiring worker for slavery abolition), more cosmopolitan (his French was faultless), and more assiduous in the performance of his public duties (I have laboured through the alarming mass of his speeches in the House of Commons), he was no less engaging than the smiling figure that endeared ' Cupid ' and ' Pam ' to three generations of Englishmen ; and perhaps, in his long passage from the certainties of 1784 to the certainties (how different, but not less certain) of 1865, he may be counted—since he was, beyond doubt, the last of the Canningites, and Mr. Canning was the very last of the Pittites—the last fragment of the Eighteenth Century.

1926.

A writer who revisits his own work after ten years does so at the risk of his own peace of mind, if not of his self-respect.   But unless he can resist the impulse to reconstruct it, he will be sentenced to waste valuable time in rearranging lights and colours on an already overcrowded canvas or in perfecting by his later standards something that he made as well as he knew how ten years before.   These exercises, though great masters have succumbed to them, always strike me as peculiarly futile. From a literary point of view there is really no excuse for tampering with finished work, since the hand that made it is no longer there to touch it up. For mind and method both change far too rapidly for a writer to be the same to-day as he was ten years ago ; and any drastic rearrangement of his predecessor's work is little more than a collaboration of two ill-matched partners. For that reason there is little to be said for doing more to his completed text than smoothing a sentence here and there to clarify the sense or to eliminate an error.

But from the point of view of scholarship it is not altogether unpleasant to survey the field in which this work was done more than ten years ago. Nothing, I think, has yet transformed the Palmerstonian landscape. But its familiar features have been admirably accentuated by the patient labour of Professor Herbert C. Bell, of Wesleyan University, Middletown, Connecticut, whose friendship is (for me) one of the pleasanter consequences of our common interest in a British statesman ; and I cannot doubt that Professor C. K. Webster's thorough excavation of the Broadlands Papers will one day make serious additions to our knowledge. Meanwhile the central figure of the tale stands very much as I was privileged to leave him in 1926, and my subsequent encounters have only served to emphasize the portrait. For what could be more Palmerstonian than his cheerful plea (in a letter which had somehow strayed to a bookseller's at Los Angeles) with a duchess who entertained some doubts about a youthful relative's political début that " the Duke objected that his Brother is young, but I told him that six months in the House of Commons would go further to form a young Man than two ordinary years rolled over his Head, and as to his being only a Cornet of Cavalry, Lord Chatham was first known in the House of Commons as ' that terrible Cornet of Horse ' " ? And a later chance put me in possession of the manuscript (and richly illustrated) Palmerstoniana of Richard Cockle Lucas. That gifted sculptor, whose scarlet waistcoat subsequently dismayed official Germany by its startling recrudescence in the interior of a charming bust which the combined learning of Dr. Bode and his Kaiser had attributed with

Teutonic dogmatism to Leonardo, was a devotee of Palmerston. Indeed, his slightly overheated worship has a good deal in common with poor Haydon's feeling for the Duke of Wellington. The devoted artist studied the object of his adoration from an eyrie in convenient proximity to Broadlands and, on occasion, with the gratitude reserved for public benefactors by the objects of their benefaction. For, like Haydon, Lucas had his awkward moments ; but, more fortunate, he found a friendly rescuer in Palmerston. His glimpses of the statesman vary from a domestic invitation to " put our toes on the fender and be cozy " and his confession after the summary dismissal of 1851 that " I am out at grass, and grass to an old horse is like mother's milk to a baby," the sharper comment that " common report is a common liar and the newspapers are uncommon ones " and the Prime Minister's genial enquiry, " What amount of pension do you wish ? " to the apocalyptic vision of his crest bristling like a Homeric hero's as he drafted something at his standing-desk in the rousing days of the Pacifico crisis, or the Romsey post-boy getting the cryptic order " The owl flies tonight " and duly meeting the London mail at Winchester, where Lord Palmerston alighted somewhere round 3 a.m. to transfer to a chaise and pair and drive in sight of the mail's lights until the chaise turned off to Broadlands and the guard of the departing mail saluted it with " Oh come cuddle me " on the post-horn.

The enthusiastic Lucas was fairly drunk with hero-worship ; and the same emotion in a milder form inspired the elegy of a Dissenting Minister encountered among Gladstone's papers. For his Muse, which had been stirred by the Prince Consort's death, was moved again by Palmerston's to mourn, as he wrote with a strange failure to appreciate the facts,

> *The loss of one whose life has truly been*
> *A source of comfort to our Widow'd Queen.*

It was not surprising that the poet in this rosy mood hazarded an even stranger summary of the Prime Minister's career :

> *The various nations of the earth around,*
> *In him a constant friend they ever found :*
> *Since Amity his maxim always stood—*
> *And loving others, he himself was loved.*

The sad event was then surveyed in its various aspects —

> *No longer will his powerful voice be heard,*
> *No longer will his counsel be observed,*
> *No longer will he fill the place of state —*
> *Since reckless death has laid him quite prostrate.*

Nor was Lady Palmerston forgotten by the Southampton elegist, since

> *His valued Partner whom he loved so dear,*
> *O'er his mausoleum oft will drop a tear,*

while the electorate, whose care was now transferred to John Russell, was left to

> *trust he whose called to fill thy place*
> *May prove like thee, a blessing to our race.*

But Mr. Gladstone, who received a copy at the Treasury, endorsed it with admirable self-restraint, " Thanks for his courtesy."

1937.   PHILIP GUEDALLA.

CONTENTS

PRELUDE

B

I

THE child was born on the full tide of the Eighteenth
Century. The world lived by candlelight; Mr. Pitt was
minister; and at the Pump Room the lawful successor
of Mr. Nash dictated the last elegance of 1784. The Prince,
in the first flush of that manly beauty which had so long,
so golden, so positively Turneresque a sunset, was at the
feet of a plump young widow from Richmond, whose religious
opinions were in alarming conflict with the Act of Settlement; and while Fitzherbert fluttered, Siddons sat to
Sir Joshua in the becoming green and brown of the most
imposing Muse that ever strayed from Helicon into the
studio of a President of the Royal Academy. Mr. Walpole
still watched the world behind the battlements of Strawberry. A twinge in the shoulder and the dreadful tale of
fifty-six nieces and nephews served to remind him that he
could not look on for ever. But his eyes were still sharp;
and he followed the *ton* most creditably for his years. The
balloons, which bobbed perilously over London, intrigued
him immensely. But he failed, somehow, to catch the
general fever for the noble savages just disclosed in Captain
Cook's miraculous *Voyage*. Flat noses, palm trees, and red
feathers were altogether too unpolished for a person of such
refinement. And when Miss Hannah More retailed to him
the poetic marvels of the Bristol milkwoman, he grimly
prescribed for that humble daughter of the Muses an ascetic
diet of Dryden and Prior. The solemn perfection of the
Eighteenth Century seemed to stretch symmetrically away
to the farthest limits of the European horizon. That year
Mr. Gibbon, well into his fifth volume, was walking on his
terrace at Lausanne with the accomplished, if voluble,
daughter of M. Necker; and at the Essex Head tavern it

3

was credibly reported that an enlightened Empress had
ordered the *Rambler* to be translated into the Russian
language, a circumstance which afforded considerable satisfaction to its author, because " I shall be read on the banks
of the Wolga. Horace boasts that his fame would extend
as far as the banks of the Rhone; now the Wolga is farther
from me than the Rhone was from Horace."

It was a cheerful, factious time, when little girls were
heard to say, ' Pray, Miss, of which side are you ? ' or
' Mama and I cannot get papa over to our side ! ' The
cause of progress was represented by the intermittent
talents of Charles Fox. But England was, for the most
part, content to ingeminate that

> Chatham, thank heaven ! has left us a son;
> When *he* takes the helm, we are sure not undone ,
> The glory his father revived of the land,
> And Britannia has taken Bill Pitt by the hand.

The civic virtues of ' Immaculate Master Billy ' seemed
full of agreeable promise; and his countrymen settled down
with gusto to the scurrilous horseplay of the Westminster
election. There was even a vague stir of politics across the
Channel, where the stout young King and his advisers
were studying without enthusiasm the Dead Sea fruits of
one of those bankrupt victories that appear to be the
favourite objects of French policy. It was a lively age,
which retained most of the colour that had gone before.
Something, perhaps, had faded. One no longer found, if
one was detained in a pretty fellow's dressing-room, ' a
neat little chamber hung round with Indian paper and
adorned with several little images of pagods and bramins,
and vessels of Chelsea china, in which were set various
coloured sprigs of artificial flowers ' or a ' toilette with
everything intended to be agreeable to the Chinese taste '
and ' a looking-glass enclosed in a whimsical frame of
Chinese paling.' Mr. Chippendale was dead; and Mr.
Hepplewhite was dying fast. But Mr. Sheraton was still
upon the town; and ladies hung their walls with puckered
blue satin, whilst the shapes of chairs were borrowed with

light-hearted impartiality from antique lyres, from Gothic shields, from Grecian urns, from posies, from Prince of Wales' feathers.

There was a cold, wet summer. But the world, in spite of floods and burglaries, swung into a lively autumn. Siddons was hissed at Drury Lane for stinginess; Dr. Johnson drove down to Lichfield after a notable visit to Oxford, on the occasion of which he " seemed to feel himself elevated as he approached that magnificent and venerable site of learning, orthodoxy and Toryism "; and Mr. Romney was painting hard in Cavendish Square. One dreadful morning four gentlemen fetched the shrinking Fitzherbert to her Prince, who lay, a horrid spectacle, ' pale and covered with blood,' supposed the victim of his intolerable despair. The wound was later disclosed to privileged eyes and variously attributed to the dagger, the pistol, or the meaner agency of a royal table knife. The startled lady believed the dreadful evidence of her eyes, saw that the noble sufferer had brandy, and fled to Aix.

The tide of the Eighteenth Century seemed at the flood that autumn. Sir Joshua, in his twelfth Discourse, was warning the young gentlemen of the Royal Academy against the sad example of M. Boucher and the *pittori improvvisatori* ; Mr. Gibbon was assuring a noble correspondent that Lausanne was " full as good as Bentinck Street "; and Dr. Johnson was translating Horace. One Wednesday (it was October 20) he wrote from Lichfield to his printer, expressing with a rare courtesy his regret that he was unable to conduct him round his native town. Further to the south that morning, at ten o'clock, a mild young gentleman was sitting to Mr. Romney in Cavendish Square; the portrait had a red curtain in the background, and the young gentleman in a plum-coloured suit grew up to be Earl Grey and pass a Reform Bill. Further, still further to the south, beyond the utmost limits of Mayfair, a child was born on the same day at Lord Palmerston's in Park Street, Westminster. In the square outside Queen Anne reigned decorously in stone over the trim Augustan house-fronts,

and the stone masks frowned and grinned above the door-
ways. Park Street prolonged that elegant line; and there
was a stir at No. 4, where the child was born. The big
door opened and shut between its iron flambeaux; and
from the low windows of the room upstairs they would see
a gleam of chilly water between the bare October trees.
Life seemed to beckon him on to a crowded and pleasant
stage; since it was, it would always be, the Eighteenth
Century. Elegance, *bon ton*, King George and King Louis
were surely perpetual. Was it not the year 1784? Even
in five years' time it would still be only 1789.

II

THEY lived between the sea and the New Forest, when
they were not at Sheen or in Park Street or travelling in
search of the antique in Italy. The house (its name was
Broadlands) watched the slow eddies of a running river;
the little town of Romsey crept respectfully almost up to
the lodge gates; and the aspect of the mansion was impressively columnar. But the family title was an Irish
peerage. Their main connection with that island was
limited to a graceful consent to adorn its nobility and live
upon its revenue, since the Temples came from Warwickshire. One of them, a person of some literary distinction,
had been secretary to Sir Philip Sidney, forced by the
exigencies of late Elizabethan politics to decline upon
Trinity College, Dublin, as a convenient retreat. His
grandson, Sir William Temple, made a great name in the
world of cyphers, periwigs, and mystery, which constituted
diplomacy under King William, emitted those "classic
lucubrations," which formed *Endymion's* recollection of
"the statesman-sage who, it is hoped, will always be
remembered by a grateful country for having introduced
into these islands the Moor Park apricot," and left a younger
brother in Ireland, whose son was created Viscount Palmerston by Walpole. The first Viscount sat in Parliament for
several English boroughs, and presumably repaid his ennoblement by faithful voting. He was succeeded by his
grandson, who followed him into the House of Commons
and, in a Parliamentary career of forty years, once seconded
the Address.

The second Viscount held minor office under several
ministries of varying political complexions. His celebrated
intervention in debate, on a June afternoon in 1765, had

reference to " important occurrences " in America, for which
Mr. Grenville, always pedantic, moved to substitute the
unpleasant word " rebellion."   But the senate seemed hardly
to afford a favourable theatre for the display of his accomplishments, which lay in a more elegant direction. This
nobleman, who was early left a widower, had a turn for
verse. Verse was, indeed, his element. For his first
marriage had attracted a genteel epithalamium from
Colonel John Burgoyne of the Light Dragoons, that intrepid
versifier, who set *As You Like It* to an air of Mr. Gay and
marched through the dripping woods to Saratoga.

> While, Palmerston, the public voice
> Displays in comments on thy choice,
>   Praise, censure, and surprise. . . .

The Dragoon was arch. But the bridegroom answered, if
he answered at all, in prose; and whilst his Fanny lived,
his Muse was silent. But bereavement tuned his lyre;
and the lyric Viscount, after adorning Fanny's monument
in Romsey Church with appropriate reflections, attracted
the favourable attention of the polite world at Bath. Perhaps his lines *On Beauty* were a trifle sententious. The
opening apostrophe,

> Enchanting nymph of heavenly birth,
> Celestial beauty, sent on earth
> To soothe our cares, our toils, our strife,
> And gild the gloom that saddens life . . .

reflects, aptly enough, the wistful widower. But his more
formal eloquence—

> To gain thy praise, his valour's meed,
> For thee the hero dares to bleed,

or the more voluptuous note of

> A cheek that shames the vernal rose,
> A breast that vies with mountain snows;
> A mouth that smiles with matchless grace,
> Like pearls within a ruby case,

is, it must be confessed, a little trying. His lines written
in the Album at Crewe Hall—

Here, in rude state, old chieftains dwelt,
  Who no refinement knew—

were much admired. And upon one occasion the lyrical
nobleman was inspired to a copy of verses entitled *Cupid
Jealous* by the pleasing spectacle of " a Young Lady, Miss
F——s, who was dressed in the Habit of a Judge at a
Masquerade at Southampton." On the occasion of the
plays at H—— he even spoke a Prologue in heroic couplets
of his own composition, in which the eternal problem of
finding a suitable rhyme for ' *Fête-champêtre* ' was solved
by a sudden and singularly happy introduction of the word
peut-être. But his loftiest poetical achievements were
reached in a more rarefied atmosphere. The air of Bath
was always peculiarly propitious to his Muse. Had he not
enquired (according to one tradition on the very tomb of
his lamented wife),

> Whoe'er like me with trembling anguish brings
> His heart's whole treasure to fair Bristol's springs?

So, when Captain Miller's lady—" a beauty, a genius, a
Sappho, a tenth Muse, as romantic as Mademoiselle Scudéri,
and as sophisticated as Mrs. Vesey "—propounded a new
poetical contest, it was hardly surprising that the accomplished Viscount was among the most eager competitors.
The lady was blessed with a husband whose Italian travels
had so profoundly affected him that his fingers " are loaded
with cameos, his tongue runs over with *virtù* "; and
adjacent to their home she had erected " a new Parnassus,
composed of three laurels, a myrtle-tree, a weeping-willow
and a view of the Avon," which was hastily renamed Helicon
for the solemn occasion. On this auspicious spot they held
a Parnassus fair every Thursday, at which competing lyrics
were shyly dropped into " a Roman vase dressed with pink
ribbons and myrtles," and kneeling poets were crowned by
the presiding Muse herself. They made, to be precise,
bouts-rimés. The Duchess of Northumberland made some
on a buttered muffin; accomplished Miller's were found to
" have no fault but wanting metre "; a French gentleman

wrote some lines upon *La Belle Assemblée au Château de Batheaston*; and Palmerston struck a more idyllic note than was habitual with his Muse. He fluted of returning Spring, of shady groves and Nature's warblers. He even exclaimed that

> Flora's sweet treasures enamel the ground,

and generally comported himself in a fashion befitting a troubadour of the court of Mrs. Miller. These " innocent and liberal Amusements " were all printed in a book and sold for the benefit of the Pauper-Scheme. No record exists of the extent to which the march of poverty was arrested by Mrs. Miller's poetical friends. But Palmerston's pieces seemed " very pretty " to Mr. Walpole, although the snarling Tickell exclaimed a few years later that

> With chips of wit and mutilated lays,
> Here Palmerston fincers his *bout-rhimés*.

The embittered poet even hinted that the Viscount, who was now a member of the Board of Admiralty, like Ariel wrecked navies with a song. But the jealousy of genius is proverbial.

Poetry was not the sole accomplishment of this man of taste. He had travelled widely upon a system approved by Mr. Gibbon; and in case his recollection should omit any particular, he travelled with a painter, who took views for him. His companion was admirable in wash and assisted the Viscount's recollection of Switzerland with renderings of its horrid grandeur in this medium. The fortunate painter was introduced to the polite world by his patron, made several drawings of Strawberry for Mr. Walpole and, taking subsequently to oil and portraits, left for Italy to improve himself. But this was not Lord Palmerston's sole contact with the graphic arts. He sat intermittently to Sir Joshua for his portrait; but as he rarely, if ever, sat twice in the same year, the picture was never painted. He was a cheerful creature, moving easily in the world where Mr. Burke exhibited his brogue and Mr. Boswell made his little notes. One sees him walking in Paris with Mr. Wilkes,

where an indignant Scotsman recognised his outrageous
companion by his squint and challenged him to a duel for
the honour of Scotland. He was at Mr. Topham Beau-
clerk's on Muswell Hill one evening a week or so before the
rebellious Americans declared their independence, when
Mr. Burke and Garrick the actor and the preposterous profile
of Mr. Gibbon were there; Mr. Walpole looked in and found
that they made such a prodigious noise with talking " and
Lord Palmerston so much more noise with trying to talk,"
that he could pick up no news for Lady Ossory. One catches
a glimpse of him in the crowded winter of 1779, when the
King's troops were campaigning in the Carolinas and General
Eliott at Gibraltar was staring across the Straits at the blue
bulk of Africa and reflecting upon the valuable qualities of
red-hot shot. It was at one of Sir Joshua's parties in
Leicester Square; and the portentous Mrs. Cholmondeley,
sister to Mrs. Woffington the player, was quizzing little
Burney a shade heavily upon the authorship of *Evelina*.
The young lady te-he'd and sought refuge by the card-
table. But her tormentor pursued, with Sir Joshua and
Lord Palmerston in tow. She was even a trifle arch with
the noble widower; and he, in return, was rather dry with
his host about a pamphlet. He was at the play at Ham
Common one night in the year after Yorktown to see the
three Miss Hobarts entertain their mother's guests with
genteel comedies. Lord North sat smiling in his seat; and
as the company went home, they were so well protected by
the blunderbusses of their domestics that "when the
servants were drawn up after the play, you would have
thought it had been a midnight review of conspirators on
a heath." And on the winter day when Garrick dead
' eclipsed the gaiety of nations' and the Club walked
solemnly behind him to the grave, Palmerston helped to
bear his pall in the Abbey.

So, between Bath and London, the accomplished Viscount
cut quite a figure. His friends, his verse, his pictures passed
an agreeable life. *Ton* and the Muses cheered the widower;
and he held on his elegant course, always the man of fashion,

sometimes (but at longer intervals) a Lord of the Admiralty
or Commissioner of the Treasury. But now he was turned
forty, and romance was waiting. A riding accident unseated
him outside a hospitable house in Dublin. His host possessed a daughter; and the languid gaze of the reviving
nobleman rested upon the pleasing features of Miss Mee.
Since the young lady's father (described by later malice as a
hatter) had been at Harrow and she was closely related to a
director of the Bank of England, she was scarcely a beggar
maid. But the exigencies of romance were amply satisfied
by their unpremeditated meeting. The afflicted Viscount
soon revealed the impetuous widower; and early in 1783
they were united at Bath. Since the bride's family came
from the West of England, the bridegroom's, as has been
told, from Warwickshire, there was little danger of exposing
any small sprig of the Irish nobility (should there be one) to
the imputation of Irish blood. So his new lady played
hostess with eager aptitude, and portraits of smiling Mees
hung gratified among dark Temples on the wall at
Broadlands.

Their marriage did not withdraw the Viscount from the
world. He was, he had always been a man for clubs.
Early a member of the Catch Club, he had once entertained
Mr. Gibbon at "a great dinner of Catches." But in the
first summer after marriage he sustained a grave reverse.
One evening at Hampstead his name was proposed to The
Club at dinner and, *contradicente* Samuel Johnson, was
rejected. Perhaps the Viscount never knew it; since
shortly afterwards his tremendous supporter overcame all
opposition, the ban was removed, and he became a member.
In the next year he came to town to give his annual sitting
to Sir Joshua Reynolds, and on an autumn day in 1784 the
Viscount had his heir.

III

THEY named the baby Henry John—Henry after his father, and John as a pure flight of fancy. There was a christening ball at Winchester, and the Mara came down from the Opera to sing at a concert for them in her thin voice. After that the world went on much as before. Mr. Fox continued to denounce Mr. Pitt as an obstacle to progress, and Mr. Pitt persevered in unmasking Mr. Fox as a menace to his country. The Prince fell deeper in love with his pretty widow and then fell out again. Disrespectful drawings began to appear in Mrs. Humphrey's window in St. James's Street of improvident Princes keeping Whig company (with Mr. Burke as a most alarming Jesuit) and dancing with attractive, but slightly aquiline, ladies; of Princes reduced in circumstances to the humblest domestic shifts; of prodigal Princes, Princes indigent, and Princes in rags; and finally of Princes reconciled and restored to royal favour, while Dido Fitzherbert mounted her sacrificial pyre and handled, more aquiline than ever, the dreadful emblems of her Popish faith. The world wore tiny portraits of a lovely eye, that dangled from its buttonhole on a riband, and challenged enquiring friends with a 'Lord! don't you know it?' One still talked balloons or passed disparaging remarks on Johnson's biographic zany, who printed such egregious anecdotes of his master and brawled with Mrs. Thrale and was deliciously castigated in the new eclogue of Bozzi and Piozzi. Next year, when Cipriani's drawings were the vogue and Lady Di was painting whole rooms at Richmond with peasants and children in little rounds and squares 'chained together by wreaths of natural flowers,' the talk was all of India and Mr. Hastings and the strange story of the Queen of France's diamonds; and a gentleman who

13

looked in for half an hour at Lady Palmerston's toilet,
noticed when the baby was brought in " a fine, eager, lively,
good-humoured boy," aged one.

The bland procession of the Eighteenth Century went
slowly on.   The old King of Prussia faded out into history;
and they kept Handel's Jubilee with chorales and kettle-
drums in Westminster Abbey.   Mrs. Jordan came upon the
town; Miss Burney went to Court; and the child in Hampshire began to grow behind the far too Grecian portico of
Broadlands, although one visitor found him a trifle " washy."
The little town beyond the gates enjoyed the interminable
leisure of a small country market, and the park was majestic
with that irregular interruption of green grass with large
English trees, which indicates a stately dedication to complete uselessness.   Sometimes they were at Sheen, where
the house was large and the garden was full of little streams
and tiny mountain ranges.   But they were much in London.
For his mother was a lively lady, who nicknamed an uxorious
neighbour in Park Street " Sir Bashful Constant," kept late
hours, and went a great deal to the play.   Delighted that
an injured Viscount had been carried in to hospitable Mr.
Mee's, she laboured indomitably in pursuit of pleasure,
" was yesterday morning at Sheen, gave a great dinner in
town, went to a great assembly, thence to Ranelagh, came
home at one o'clock and dressed for a guinea masquerade
at the Opera House, where she went with Lord Palmerston."
They played a part in the Whig world, gave dinner to Charles
Fox and Mr. Sheridan, and supped with Mrs. Crewe.   Indeed, she was almost inseparable from that voluble Egeria,
" so extremely communicative of her own secrets and of
other people's."   But their politics were always a shade
epicurean.   For they seemed to find the Ridotto more
diverting than Westminster Hall; Mrs. Crewe's principles
were almost endurable on a water-party; and Mrs. Sheridan,
who " sang like an angel, till two o'clock," was vastly more
entertaining than her husband's long-suffering Begums.   So
the cheerful round went on in Park Street, while she perpetually urged her Viscount to remove " to a more central

situation" and forced him at last into a corner house in
Hanover Square, which led the mode in smokeless chimneys
constructed upon a wonderful new system; and a neighbour
" never saw any two people make such a toil of pleasure as
both he and she. She seems completely worn down by her
raking, but is always eager for the next labour." There
was the Opera, and animal magnetism, and the philosophical fireworks (a most genteel performance without
noise or smoke, but retaining a strikingly unpleasant smell,
and highly fashionable), and Ranelagh so conveniently
poised at Chelsea, halfway to London from the rustic delights
of Sheen, and Sir Joshua, with niece and ear-trumpet, to
dine and sleep, and a masquerade at Hammersmith at
which the Prince of Wales and his two brothers gave way
to their hereditary weakness and appeared in kilts, and
another at Vauxhall where Mr. Windham and Miss Burney,
escaped from Windsor, were in the party. It was a discreetly riotous progress, indubitably correct, but cheerful.
Even rustic surroundings had no power to sober them, since
" the life at Sheen is certainly not over rural, being very
junkety, but that cannot be avoided in Surrey or Middlesex,
much less in any place inhabited by the Palmerstons or any
of their family." Sometimes, indeed, the note was strained
almost beyond decorum. Three wild young gentlemen
came drunk one evening to Mrs. Crewe's and began to " talk
so plain that Lady Francis and Lady Palmerston fled from
their side-table to ours, and Mrs. Sheridan would have followed them, but did not make her escape till her arms were
black and blue and her apron torn off"; and there is a
pleasant raffishness in the arrival of Mrs. Cholmondeley at
Park Street after dinner, stout, redolent of old green-rooms,
and calling " in one of her high-spirited humours " for a
bottle of champagne. Such were the cheerful noises of the
house, which floated up the big well of the stairs to Harry's
nursery.

In the world around him Mr. Pitt was exhibiting his
public virtues a trifle primly; and one summer evening
in 1787 Mr. Gibbon laid down his pen and took a turn in

" a *berceau*, a covered walk of Acacias, which commands
a prospect of the country, the lake and the mountains."
It was a still evening; and he was feeling sedately uplifted, because that night " between the hours of eleven
and twelve " he had finished his *History*. The world went
on, and zealous persons were far too eager paying fifty
guineas for places in Westminster Hall, where Mr. Sheridan
denounced the atrocious Hastings, to feel misgivings about
France. Yet France was uneasy. King Louis still smiled
his empty smile; and the perspicacious Mr. Young, whom a
grateful country rewarded with the dual gift of a merino
ram and a Secretaryship of six hundred pounds a year,
found good temper everywhere in his travels. But a strange
leaven was working below that amiable surface. No word
of it reached England; and Paris remained the elegant,
slightly scandalous goal of polite travellers, until the *Parle-
ments* faded into the States General and the States General,
on a summer day in 1789, could hardly be heard talking
for the sudden crackle of musketry round the Bastille.
Then Mr. Fox threw himself into paroxysms about liberty,
and even Mr. Walpole interrupted *Les amusemens des eaux
de Straberri* to raise an enquiring eyebrow. Perhaps the
Eighteenth Century was ending eleven years before its time.

But before that happy date, whilst a hard winter still
delayed the hot summer of 1789, Lady Palmerston had put
her Viscount's heir into breeches. The boy was above four
years old, " quite stout, with a fine high colour "; and he
came down to dessert now in the solemn dining-room at
Broadlands, where the sideboard that lived so kindly in
Sir Joshua's memory stood in its long recess between the
two grave urns on their pedestals. The deep drawing-
room, where his mother sat in a soft gleam of satinwood,
was still sacred; and he rarely kept still enough to watch
the visitors, as they commented with polite ecstasy upon
' Mr. Adam's ' (or was it Mr. Kent's?) ' gingerbread and
sippets of embroidery,' and medallions by the accomplished
Kauffmann looked down on them from the bright gilt of the
ceiling. The boy was growing; and his first scrawls strayed

cheerfully across the lines they ruled for him. There were
two little sisters and a small brother now, and a black pony
with an alarming reputation.

The strange doings in France went on; Mr. Burke was
provoked to *Reflections* on the subject; and society was
gravely divided over the propriety of his metaphors. The
dawn of liberty was a distasteful spectacle, and Mr. Walpole
was left lamenting over "the most *Iroquois* of nations."
When the boy was six, with interests that (to judge from his
earliest letters) were mainly dental, his papa went on his
travels again and ventured his person on French territory.
At Calais the intrepid Viscount sported a national cockade;
and on the road to Paris the evident break-up of large
estates caused him to be assailed by melancholy reflections;
it was in the dusty, glaring weeks after the King and his
scared people had been caught at Varennes; and Lord
Palmerston, accustomed to Park Street, found "the white-
ness of everything about Paris (except the complexions and
linen of the inhabitants)" a grave drawback. He walked
in the Palais Royal and found the *ton* sadly deteriorated,
although the English society at his hotel afforded some
compensation. A peer, a captain in the Navy, one of the
Egremonts, and Mr. Windham were gravely studying the
singular proceedings of the French. Colonel Hew Dalrymple
was there, reserved by fate for a long pause in the wings, a
hurried landing after Vimeiro, and the dismal proceedings
of a Court of Enquiry at Chelsea Hospital; and before
Palmerston left Paris, the Hamiltons on their amazing
honeymoon passed through, *en route* for Naples. Sir
William, whose interest in volcanoes was perennial, studied
Paris with the eye of an expert from Vesuvius. But his
Emma, wifed at last, was a less eager student than Lord
Palmerston. He "rode through the Champs Elysées, which
consists of a wood of young trees planted in rows with an
excessive broad strait road thro' the middle of it." Their
politics, it must be confessed, slightly bewildered him; and
their painters, "all in the historical line," singularly failed
to rouse his enthusiasm. It was all lamentably unlike Bath;

c

and although he alleviated his situation by breakfasting
with Gouverneur Morris and going as frequently as possible
to the play, it is to be feared that he returned to Broadlands
with a poor opinion of his neighbours.

He came back to find his country slightly disturbed by
the proximity of France. There had been a dangerous
release of political ideas; and even the century of unbroken
felicity, which had succeeded the Glorious Revolution,
hardly rendered England immune from the contagion. It
was necessary for the King, in the same week as he proclaimed his neutrality in the war between the Most Christian
King and the King of Hungary, to denounce the dangerous
flow of wicked and seditious publications, which threatened
to disturb his country's intellectual peace; and it forthwith
became the pleasure of his leading subjects to meet in shire-
halls and corn exchanges and meeting-houses and even upon
licensed premises in order to affirm in loyal addresses their
detestation of all foreign notions and their unalterable
devotion to the existing institutions of their country. Lord
Palmerston's neighbours at Southampton and Lymington
took the loyal fever and warranted by their votes that the
Revolution should never come up-stream to Broadlands,
where the children were still playing on the black pony
under the great trees.

His heir, at seven, corresponded profusely with his mother,
although a fastidious eye at home once judged his letters too
bad to send. His zeal for correspondence even impelled a
formal acceptance of her invitation " to goble up mince-
pyes or whatever else there is for dinner " on Christmas
Day, addressed to " Viscountess Palmerston in her dressing
room up stairs, Broadlands," and sealed in glorious, if
slightly grubby, emulation of a grown-up seal. Early in
1792 Lord Palmerston enjoyed the melancholy satisfaction
of walking in Sir Joshua's funeral. The portrait could
never be finished now; and, consoled by the second choice
of a picture from the deserted studio in Leicester Square,
the Viscount carried his pall with three dukes, two mar-
quises, and three earls. In the next year he took the road

again for Italy. This time he carried his family with him;
and his eldest son retained a loving memory of cheap and
plentiful oranges and of miracles of *charcuterie* at Bologna,
which put all English sausages to shame. Such were,
conceivably, the simple fountains at which he imbibed his
earliest sympathy with Italian aspirations. But his father
was a more serious traveller. It was not, perhaps, for
nothing that Mr. Gibbon had said of him that he had " a
very right notion of travelling." Such persons are rarely
satisfied with the mere amenities of the country through
which they drive. Their quest is for higher, deeper things;
and, true to the memory of Mr. Gibbon, Lord Palmerston
pursued the antique. He purchased extensively the more
sober relics of Roman antiquity. He had a fancy for a
frieze. He did not disdain the blind eyes of a goddess or
so. But tomb-stones, altar-stones, mile-stones were added
to the steadily swelling bulk of his baggage; and when they
returned to Hampshire, these austere trophies were exhibited
in the entrance-hall at Broadlands, which became at once
impressive to callers and faintly reminiscent of the Catacombs.

In this home the boy was growing, while the world
changed slowly round him. The French king was beheaded
by a dreadful machine; and King George went to war with
the nameless multitude of Frenchmen which had usurped
his place. Mr. Pitt hastily beat his ploughshare into a
sword; and the fleet put to sea. The Guards campaigned
without enthusiasm in Flanders; and Mr. Gillray incited
his countrymen to detestation of their enemy with wild
representations of his silly savagery. But the war, it must
be confessed, failed singularly to interrupt the even flow.
Mrs. Damer persevered with the elusive art of sculpture,
while distracted generals prepared to besiege French fortresses *en règle*. Exquisite young gentlemen affected zebra
waistcoats, as Carnot's ragged infantry, with an outrageous
disregard of the more decorous rules of military deportment,
attacked with the bayonet. And while the French, in utter
ignorance of the art of war, pursued the Allies out of Holland,
Walpole, an earl at last, refused a dedication. The age of

common-sense and couplets was ending; and the candles
fluttered in a strange wind, which blew from France. But
London still went on. The Prince of Wales observed his
royal bride and faintly asked for brandy; and feminine
taste, in its eternal oscillation between the rival ideals of
the bell-shaped and the mushroom-shaped, alighted upon a
momentary distortion of the figure which inspired a poet to
exclaim,

> Shepherds, I have lost my waist,
> Have you seen my body?

At nine the boy was touring on the Continent with an
Italian master. They fetched a wide circuit into Switzerland by way of Munich; and from Berne he sent the anxious
intelligence that a double-tooth had lost its ' stoping.' In
the next year he was home again at Broadlands in charge
of his Italian and a French governess, whose ministrations
soon bore fruit in terrifying letters all in French and signed
" *Henri Temple*." The pony pawed; sometimes a pony
phaeton rolled behind; and the boy kept house for his
little sisters with Signor Gaetano and Mademoiselle. But
there were seasons when they came to London. His mother
was at Bath, and her eager correspondent sent the family
news. The complete letter-writer wrote in French; he
wrote in Italian; he even wrote, in more alarming tones,
that he had read with grave concern " in the debate of last
night " about the tax on hair powder. But on the next day
he turned with obvious relief to the less trying intelligence
that the Park Street cat had kittens. At this moment,
early in 1795, Lord Palmerston began to concern himself
with his son's education. It had been commenced by an
Italian refugee. What form of knowledge he imparted or
from whom, at this happy stage of Italian history, he sought
a refuge is unknown. But it was hardly fitting that a
Viscount's heir should be entertained with foreign notions.
Something more truly British was plainly his destiny; and,
by a happy inspiration, they sent the boy to Harrow.

IV

Harrow in 1795 reflected accurately the educational ideals prevalent in the reign of Queen Elizabeth. An alarming Doctor dispensed stray fragments of Renaissance learning; scared prize-winners declaimed short, petrified portions of classical eloquence; and there was an exquisite aloofness from the vulgarity of contemporary ideas. To this pleasing retardation British institutions owe much of their stability. For the leading men have always been largely bred in the great schools; and there is small danger of unwholesome innovations under a system which reared young Elizabethans to govern the subjects of King George III., multiplied young Georgians to administer the world for Queen Victoria, and in a more exacting age produces still a delightful crop of young Victorians.

His parents' choice was guided by one of those family accidents to which the education of all children (except foundlings) is strangely exposed. His grandfather Mee had been at Harrow, had even won a prize for archery. Encouraged by this bright example (for it is the modest aim of English education to model its pupils on their grandfathers) his parents committed him without misgivings to Dr. Drury; and as the boy scaled the steep road which climbs to Harrow Church, his grandfather's Silver Arrow gleamed hopefully before him up the hill. Quite soon a cheerful pen informed his parents that "I like the Scool very much," then, in greater (if slightly sententious) detail, that "I am very well and hope to continue so, for I am in a very healthy place." A cake, it seemed, was "very much liked—what I liked best in it was that at top it was plain and at bottom plumb, and then the sugar was so rich." One can hardly wonder

that a whole week elapsed before he found that a Prayer
Book had been left behind. A strong, but waning, passion
for cross-bows ruled in the school, and led him to deplore
the price of whalebone; and the loss of a ferret engaged
him deeply. That he was still something of an urchin is
evident from the glee with which he noticed that "a man
came here to-day with a nest of hedgehogs. If I had
known where to have put it, I should certainly have bought
one to keep Fanny's guinea-pig company, for he must be
very solitary." But the passion for promiscuous livestock
fades all too early; and he was soon absorbed in those
more occult processes of mind and body, which are believed
to minister to the formation of character. He fought with
his fists, proceeded with becoming pauses through the
various Removes of the Fourth Form, wrote Latin verses
on Lord Nelson's victory at the Nile, assisted in the execution of the "boy whom we tossed in a blanket for stealing
four shillings," and played his part in an unheroic mutiny
which collapsed completely before a judicious threat of
expulsion. Sometimes he fought "the Clods," sometimes
his peers. One catches a glimpse of an anxious housemaster's wife fluttering round him, as he returned, black-
eyed and bleeding at the nose, from a battle with "a great
boy called Salisbury, twice his size." It was waged (as
such battles should be) on the ledge of grass ' behind school,'
conveniently adjacent to the Crown and Anchor, from
which respectful seconds brought two pots of water and
a lemon. His gigantic adversary, succeeding later to a
baronetcy, buried his ferocity in the Church. But Palmerston never lost a faint air of the Milling Ground.

More adult interests were soon aroused by a seat of
learning where visiting parents of distinction still tended
to arrive behind four horses with stars gleaming on their
coats, and young noblemen out shooting secured "three
skylarks, two titlarks and two sparrows." Promoted to
the Remove and dignified with the title of Temple senior
by the arrival of a younger ·brother, he discovered the
easier Latin writers and corresponded with a young friend

in Italy. Professing a deep, if slightly inaccurate, enthusiasm for Homer and an unnatural eagerness to read
Cervantes in the original, he still retained a wistful memory
of warmer climates : ". . . when I am sucking a sour
orange, purchased by perhaps eight biochi, I think with
regret upon those which I used to get in such plenty in
Italy; and when eating nasty things misnamed sausages,
envy you at Bologna, who perhaps now are feasting off
some nice ones." The poignant vision faded; and he sat
writing in the cold light of Mr. Bromley's house at Harrow,
concurring in his correspondent's stern censure of " drinking and swearing, which, though fashionable at present, I
think extremely ungentlemanlike; as for getting drunk I
can find no pleasure in it." The jaded pleasure-seeker was
thirteen. His friend, of the same age, went still further;
and—prefacing his austere opinions with " a kiss to each
of your two amiable sisters, but particularly to Fanny,
and tell her to write me a letter whenever you answer
mine "—persisted in " never marrying, and I suppose you
think the same, as you must have read as well as myself
of the many faults and vices of women." But Temple
senior was more cautious, and " cannot agree with you
about marriage, though I should be by no means precipitate
about my choice." That year a little Melbourne danced
in a children's ball at Sheen, with whom in forty years he
verified his sage prediction.

In the holidays he went to the play, although he missed
the children's ball when the house was full of small Caven-
dishes and Lambs. Sometimes he practised his Italian
with a tutor; and once, when he saw the King and Queen
with five Princesses, he lost (as eager youth so often loses)
all his illusions about royalty—" as they were in mourning,
it was not very brilliant; the Queen gives me the idea of a
housemaid, and the King is a good-looking man." The
family found him rather quiet. Perhaps his indomitably
cheerful father—" no schoolboy is so fond of a breaking-up
as he is of a junket and pleasuring "—was a little trying in
the home. But this sober reputation hardly followed him

to Harrow, where he chased his friends with bolsters, and
provoked a harassed housemaster to call them, with the
gloomy levity of his profession, "young men of wit and
pleasure." His name progressed sedately up the school.
But there is evidence of other interests in his urgent appeal
for "two pair of stumps for cricket, and a good bat."
They were required in May, 1796, for what may well have
been the earliest fixture of a famous contest. For "we
have accepted the challenge sent us by the Eton boys, who
have challenged us to fight, not with cannons and balls,
but with bats and balls in the Holydays, 18 of our best
players against 18 of theirs." He reached the Sixth Form
at last, a master of fags, messing gravely with Althorp and
Duncannon, reading the war news, and enjoying the solemn
music of Dr. Drury's exhortations. The deep charm of
that diapason lived in his memory as a positive temptation
to do wrong; but from the fact that he was selected to be
a Monitor, it may be conjectured that he resisted it in
part. In his last term he figured heroically on every
Speech Day of 1800. At the first he declaimed Tacitus;
at the second he denounced Catiline; but at the third he
confronted the greater difficulties of the vulgar tongue.
An angular boy named Haddo, whom he was later to help
into war with Russia, had quavered through the complaint
of Dido forsaken by the cold Æneas; and Temple senior,
with pleasantly ruffled hair, scaled the dithyrambic heights
of Gray's *Bard*, one of those alarming compositions which,
from their total lack of love, or any other, interest except
perhaps that of bloodshed, have always been considered
suitable for juvenile study—

> " Ruin seize thee, ruthless King !
> Confusion on thy banners wait ! "

The young voice came clearly down the long Dancing
School, as Temple senior gallantly impersonated the im-
passioned prophet in his painstaking indication (in nine
Pindaric stanzas) of the future course of English history.
At length he soared to a climax, prophesied Queen Eliza-

beth, and resumed his seat to the respectful applause,
which upon such occasions has more reference to cricket
or pugilism than to successful elocution. That term he
carved his name on a corner panel in the Fourth Form
Room and left, a few months before the austere arrival
of a blue-eyed boy named Peel.

Emerging from Harrow at sixteen with a pleasant smile
and limited classical attainments, he seemed to have escaped
from both horns of that angry dilemma which prescribed
that private schools make poor creatures and public schools
sad dogs. But in 1800 the next stage of a gentleman's
education presented special difficulties, since the Grand
Tour was sadly interrupted by the Great War. Although
the Mintos, impressed by his " good sense and good humour,"
had invited him to the Embassy at Vienna, the Continent
was almost closed to young travellers in pursuit of learning.
For the French roads were obstructed by the republican
excesses of Buonaparte's egregious followers. Italy was a
tangle of new republics with trying classical names; the
groves of Bipontinum were offended by the impending
tricolour; and even Leyden, haunt of elusive jurisprudence,
lay in the highly questionable jurisdiction of a Batavian
Republic. In this predicament aspiring students were
confined to the British Isles; and Scottish ingenuity had
evolved a fair substitute for foreign travel. Learning,
profundity, slightly incomprehensible sages, and a sufficient difference of language to try the young enquirer
were to be found in Edinburgh; and English students
flocked to its University before entering their own. To
this seat of learning the Palmerstons next exiled their
son and lodged him with Professor Stewart. There, for
four hundred pounds a year, he enjoyed the conversation
of a mathematical philosopher and his agreeable wife.
This lady, who was slightly inclined to gush over the
resident pupils, corrected her husband's lectures, wrote
verse, and (as became a poetess) was afflicted with perpetual headaches. Her mate, whom a daring addiction
to French philosophy endeared to the Whigs and a monu-

ment of alarming classicism commemorates on the Calton
Hill, lectured enormous classes with that amazing rhetoric
which impressed James Mill with his superiority to Fox
and Pitt and, combined with his asthma, elicited the more
vivid comment that there was " eloquence in his very
spitting." Under these tremendous auspices the young
gentleman played a sober part on the Scottish scene, where
Mr. Scott was training with the volunteers at Musselburgh
or riding through Ettrick in pursuit of Border ballads,
whilst in a cottage at Ecclefechan a fierce, bare-footed
urchin watched his parents darkly.

Once he debated in defence of Mary, Queen of Scots,
and once, improvidently, in favour of a short life. He
afterwards attributed " whatever useful knowledge and
habits of mind I possess " to his three years at Edinburgh,
where he enjoyed unlimited lectures without the sordid test
of examination. Sometimes he read; sometimes he explored the marvels of chemistry, learning to " burn our
fingers and tables with acids most delightfully," or studied
drawing with a pupil of Allan Ramsay; sometimes he sat
in crowded lecture-rooms taking copious notes in his clear
handwriting. Dugald Stewart was lecturing in his first
winter upon the new, but already fashionable, science of
Political Economy, established with startling erudition its
connection with Natural Jurisprudence, and even seemed to
approve in part the gloomy speculations of Mr. Malthus.
The omniscient Scot boomed inexhaustibly upon Money,
the unwisdom (as established by Mr. Smith in his *Wealth of
Nations*) of restraints on the corn trade, the desirability of
a police force, and " the Effects which might be expected
on the Morals of the Lower Orders from a Systematical
Attention to their Instruction and to their early Habits."
He quoted Franklin, Lucretius, Arthur Young, and the
Abbé Raynal; nor were Sir William Petty and even Mirabeau disdained. He was a most enlightened person; and
the young disciple filled attentive notebooks. Such assiduity
earned the highest praise; the Professor found his talents
" uncommonly good " and had never " seen a more fault-

less character at his time of life, or one possessed of more amiable dispositions." He was seen at the Mintos' (they had taken a house in Edinburgh for their son); and these members of the lively world of Sheen and Hanover Square noticed his "diligence, capacity, total freedom from vice of every sort, quiet and kind disposition, cheerfulness, pleasantness and perfect sweetness." Somewhat oppressed by such perfection, he displayed at times a certain "want of spirits." He even read Miss Edgeworth and copied a passage from the *Lay of the Last Minstrel*. But that the mood was intermittent is evident from the meditated purchase of a "learned Poodle" and his accident in spraining a leg by jumping over a Gothic couch, which was the glory of the Professor's drawing-room. His family remembered him beyond the northern mists; even his brother, still at Harrow, found time for a thought of "Harry . . . thinking of setting off for England" in a letter written at the end of term to urge his family to "send for me very early, as there will hardly be one of the boys left after ten or eleven o'clock."

One day in April, 1802, he was fetched southwards by alarming news of his father. He drove off with a young Minto; and to spare him the sudden sight of drawn blinds in Hanover Square, they met him on the North Road at Barnet, where a tactless servant spoiled the kindly plot and told him suddenly. The old Viscount (he was sixty-three) had died at home, indomitably frivolous almost to the end; and Harry Temple was an Irish peer at seventeen. His mother's gaiety was quite extinguished. They let the house at Sheen to Lord Castlereagh; and the young Viscount (still known to a disrespectful younger brother as "old Harry") after a voyage of exploration to Cambridge, went to stay with the Mintos before returning to the intellectual breach at Edinburgh. He seemed depressed by his promotion. The northern climate (there was "a good deal of gentle rain") was scarcely calculated to raise his spirits; and he wrote almost wistfully to a proud father of his acquaintance, hoping that the new baby might long enjoy what he

had lost, and signing himself a little awkwardly in his
new style as "H. Palmerston." His hosts in Scotland
found him "entirely silent and at present dejected," and
lamented rather strangely that "he has had too little
spring for his age." This sad deficiency was scarcely
made up by his remaining months with Professor Stewart;
and even Lord Minto's kindness in reciting *The Lay of
the Last Minstrel* can hardly have brought much sunshine
into his life. Yet he recovered sufficiently to enjoy his
first flirtation; and in the summer a "giggish plan"
resulted in a driving tour through the Highlands, where
he made the most improving observations of a geological
character. But Scotland could not last for ever; even
Professor Stewart's *Outlines of Moral Philosophy* had an
end; and soon the long pursuit of education beckoned
him to a milder air.

Cambridge lay in the pale autumn sunshine of 1803,
thrusting spires and gables into the slight mist which is
inseparable from the older seats of English learning. The
young gentleman, freighted with the accumulated wisdom
of Harrow and Edinburgh, alighted at a great gate in a
narrow street where friendly monsters ramped cosily across
a warm background of red brick, and saw the mild, domesticated battlements of St John's. He was already admitted
a nobleman of the college and now, a Johnian at last,
assumed the ample gown, the tufted cap of noble birth.
These glories, lovingly described in his first letter home,
consoled him; and he could awe his sisters by signing
"Your affectionate Brother, Cantab." The Master, whose
varied attainments included the classics, mathematics, a
Chair of Arabic, and a published sermon *On the Evidence
of a future state of Rewards and Punishments*, confided him
to two tutors, whose efforts were seconded by a private
coach; and his studies proceeded, pleasantly punctuated
by college examinations. He furnished hard through the
first autumn, and sent at once for six dozen of port with
two dozen of sherry, promptly supplemented by a further
appeal for two dozen of Madeira, with the reassuring

note that "no body is ever pressed to drink more than they chuse." His rooms, in a corner of the First Court, faced a little church across the busy street; and from the back he looked into college, past a fine new stone building that quite shamed the old, unfashionable brick, towards the windows where thirteen years before a gaunt youth named Wordsworth had moped above the college kitchen. He dined, as his birth demanded, at high table; where, wigged like *Doctor Syntax*, high-coloured, and high-nosed, the Master presided over a respectful company. His tutor, halfway to his deanery already, smiled his perpetual sardonic smile under a long upper lip among the Fellows; but Palmerston sat with a more cheerful group in gold-laced gowns. These exquisites, the sons of peers, composed a little world. Abstaining wisely from matriculation in the University, they escaped proctorial discipline, and thus prepared themselves to govern England, unhindered by restraints appropriate to humbler persons. He joined "a kind of sporting club of a dozen members." A horse, a masquerade, and concerts seemed to fill his letters home, together with the acid comments, usual in brothers, upon their sisters' *début* and a knowing hint or so on politics from one who seemed to move already in that exalted world ("A friend of mine was in company with one of Fox's intimates the other day . . . I thought Canning would come right again and not quarrel with his bread and butter. It never answers . . . only one objection to the plan of blocking up the Boulogne Harbour, which is that it is wholly impracticable "). He could put Napoleon so neatly in his place with the cheerful admission that he "certainly has got the start of Cromwell and has probably made a better bargain with the Sooty Monarch." But once he was gravely agitated by a friend's demand for his sister's portrait, "as it is not a usual thing for a man to have the picture of a woman unless she is a near relation."

The vacation brought a round of gaiety in London which included the Dome of St. Paul's and Grassini at the Opera. But his home in Hampshire was very quiet now. The

sisters danced in London (Fanny was seen at Mr. Thellusson's
fancy ball, where that magnate left his counting-house and
dressed up as a most comical lady of fashion); and his
brother William soon followed him to St. John's.   But
their mother failed through the winter months of 1804;
and early in the New Year Palmerston sat at Broadlands,
answering letters of condolence. The loss was real. For
his bright temper answered hers, and there was a strong
love between them.   The gay lady had rushed to Harrow
when he fainted at school, and kept every line of his writing,
even docketing his letters. The boy responded, wrote
everything to her; and in this age of dully dutiful sons
they made little friendly jokes together. For he adored
his "dear M. P." and threatened her lovingly with "two
red-haired young Welsh ladies" for daughters-in-law, when
he took his brother for a tiny Grand Tour through Wales.
Perhaps he had from her the liveliness that never left him;
and so the cheerful Miss Mee lived on for sixty years in
Palmerston.

His vacations now were spent with friends. At school
and Edinburgh he had made a second home with the
Mintos, who breathed a comfortable Whig air and rated
him as "another son of mine."   But in the Cambridge
years he was increasingly assiduous with his guardian at
Park Place, where the deaf Lord Malmesbury dispensed
inexhaustible wisdom on foreign affairs, together with the
perilously Tory doctrine of reconciliation with Mr. Pitt.
This view, indeed, was scarcely a novelty to the young
gentleman, since his father had discovered an attachment
to the minister so early as 1798. Referring with distaste
to former loyalties as "connexions since dissolved," the
eager Pittite renewed a previous request and asked, without
circumlocution, for an English peerage. The elderly recruit
was pressing; but the minister was cold. The fountain of
honour refused to play, and Palmerston escaped the House
of Lords. But the family had swung from Whiggery to
Mr. Pitt; and the young gentleman could listen without
disloyalty to Lord Malmesbury. His host and guardian

was an 'old Whig,' one of those sober statesmen who,
scared halfway to Toryism by the revolution in France,
had abandoned Mr. Fox to his heresies and rallied to
Government; and the Mintos looked on aghast, as the old
man (they called him 'the Lion' for his blazing eyes and
mane of white hair) formed the young mind for politics.
Until he came of age, Palmerston was his ward; and the
young gentleman could learn his Europe from a retired
ambassador, who had been on mission to King Frederick
and Empress Catherine, earned compliments from Mirabeau,
and sat in conference with the Jacobins. The quality of
his wisdom appears in the advice vouchsafed a few years
later to a young diplomat : "*To listen, not to talk*—at least,
not more than is necessary to induce others to talk. . . .
To be cautious in *any* country, or at *any* court, of such as,
on your first arrival, appear the most eager to make your
acquaintance . . . our reserve and *ill manners* are infinitely
less dangerous to the stranger than these premature and
hollow civilities. . . . It is scarce necessary to say that no
occasion, no provocation, no anxiety to rebut an unjust
accusation, no idea, however tempting, of promoting the
object you have in view, can *need*, much less justify, a
falsehood. Success obtained by one is a precarious and
baseless success." The old man had lived in a diplomatic
world of nods and whispers and deft disguises, where policies
were played like hands of cards. It was a strange initiation; and perhaps he left something of his firm adroitness
in his pupil. Deaf and retired, he was now the oracle of
Mr. Pitt and his official friends; and at Park Place Palmerston learned to be a Pittite.

Cambridge still claimed him at regular intervals; the
young gentlemen of his college aired themselves in tufts
and gold lace, whilst a poetical solicitor's clerk named
Kirke White wooed his brief Muse and died in a sizar's
room,

> The struck eagle stretch'd upon the plain.

The Cambridge Volunteers defied the invader; and Palmerston learned his infantry exercises, became a captain and, martially cross-belted, drilled the college company in the top-hat and tight pantaloons of that heroic corps. But these stern distractions scarcely served to interrupt his education. The studious Viscount made it " a rule always to be in bed by one o'clock, as I am regularly up at seven," and condescended twice a year to the vulgar scrutiny of a college examination. Valuing " the habit of mind acquired by preparing for these examinations," he held no high opinion of the system ; since " the knowledge thus acquired of details at Cambridge was worth nothing because it evaporated soon after the examination was over." But he was placed invariably in the first class, was even commended for the general regularity of his conduct. Awed by this unusual record, his coach, a married Fellow with a stronger grasp (one feels) of mathematics than of politics, " more than once observed to me that . . . it would not be amiss to turn my thoughts to standing for the University whenever a vacancy might happen." The University was represented at the moment by the spare figure of Mr. Pitt ; and Mr. Pitt, unlike the bright young gentleman at St. John's, was head of the King's Government. But when that austere statesman died of gout and Austerlitz in a darkened room at Putney, he left a vacancy at Cambridge, which a brisk Viscount of twenty-one, who had heard him debate with Mr. Fox the year before, offered obligingly to fill. He promptly joined the University which he desired to represent, matriculated, and proceeded on the same day to a Master's degree *jure natalium*. This tribute to his birth, paid with " a very short buttering " and without any sordid preliminary of examination, gave him the necessary standing to aspire to Mr. Pitt's succession. Then, twenty-one, a Master of Arts, and candidate for the University in the first weeks of 1806, Palmerston was a public man at last.

V

HE emerged at twenty-one into a changed world. As a child, he had played in the trim garden of the Eighteenth Century, where dim statues gleamed in green perspectives and bright skies looked perpetually down on little shifting groups of gentlemen and ladies. His mother smiled in the sunshine; his father made his jokes and laughed; and their little world fluttered discreetly round them. Beyond the gates there was a vague murmur from a name-less crowd, which pressed, pressed sometimes a trifle menacingly, to watch the pretty show. But few ears caught it; and no sounds came down the neat alleys except light laughter, rustling silk, the tap of heels, and a squeal of fifes where King George and King Louis drilled their Guards to the roll of drums. The world has rarely known a more delightful interlude. But before the boy was of age, the garden was lost. In France, indeed, it had faded before he went to Harrow. The fiddles played bravely on in England across a deeper note, which first sounded from the French guns above Toulon; but as it swelled and rose, they checked and, one by one, died out. It echoed among the hills at Montenotte, came faintly down the wind from Egypt, rang out again in Italy, and came clear across Europe in the full diapason of the First Empire. The air was changing fast, as the boy walked the steep streets of Edinburgh; and when he entered public life at Cambridge, the little quavering note of English politics was scarcely audible above that thundering melody. For the world, in 1806, was quite transformed. The scene had darkened, and under winter skies the long columns of the Emperor's armies moved slowly across the grey plains of Central Europe to the conquest of the world. There was a bright

D   33

gleam of bayonets, as the marching lines wound homewards
from Austerlitz; the Guard went heavily in their tall bearskins, and the guns rumbled and clanked behind them.
All Europe seemed to stand at doors to watch the conquerors
go by, except where Russia moved uneasily behind the
mists in Poland and on the edges of the world the King's
cruisers rode sedately on the tide and watched the coasts.

Cambridge, with three candidates at a by-election, was
in a pleasant flutter. Little Lord Henry Petty, the new
Whig Chancellor of the Exchequer, split the Trinity vote
with Althorp; and Palmerston, safe in his Pittite orthodoxy,
canvassed the smaller colleges. Significant handshakes,
nods from learned men were continually exchanged behind
college doors; and the candidates " run foul of each other
perpetually." But it was a friendly business, since he knew
Lord Henry and had messed with Althorp at Harrow. Mr.
Creevey, the Whig manager in London, moved his battalions,
and his anxious candidate reported that Palmerston " has
130 secure." A member of the Scottish Bar named
Brougham, who had seen him at Edinburgh, warned
Macaulay's father that he was unsound upon the slavery
question. The modest lawyer found the young man " devoid
of all qualifications for the place " and vitiated by an unwholesome appetite for preferment, unknown to lawyers—
" His maxim is that of all the objects of ambition in the
world the life of a courtier is the most brilliant." A young
gentleman of Trinity College, recently from Harrow, struck
the satiric lyre—

> Then would I view each rival wight,
> Petty and Palmerston survey:
> Who canvass there with all their might
> Against the next elective day—

and found, with that scorn which Lord Byron reserved for
all efforts except his own, that

> One on his power and place depends,
> The other on the Lord knows what.

The weight of Carlton House was thrown into the opposite

scale by 'our fat friend,' zealous for his Whigs; and an embarrassed chaplain, favoured with "your Royal Highness's commands that I give my Interest to Lord Henry Petty," was reduced to a stammering confession that he was already promised to Althorp. But the young Johnian compiled his promises, reckoned on at least four Heads of Houses, and bravely entertained " strong hopes of success." His hopes, alas ! were shipwrecked and left him " at the poll where a young man circumstanced as I was could alone expect to stand; that is to say, last, and by a large interval the last of the three. It was an honour, however, to have been supported at all, and I was well satisfied with my fight."

Fortified by this exemplary philosophy, he withdrew to London and sought another vacancy. But none occurred; and for a few months he was reduced to confiding to his Journal impeccable sentiments upon the events of the day. A peace negotiation with Buonaparte filled him with grave suspicions of "the tyrant." Fox died; and the young Pittite dropped a generous, but a Tory, tear, reflecting that " with this impetuosity of temper it is less to be wondered at than regretted that, in the general delirium produced by the French Revolution, he should have been infected with the disorder, and have connected himself with the most frantic of the reformers." These stern convictions were refreshed by further draughts of Lord Malmesbury's wisdom at Park Place. He went to Scotland in the summer; and later in the year he drove out from Cambridge to dine at Wimpole with the Hardwickes. His host, whom Mr. Cobbett remembered rather rudely as " a gentleman chiefly distinguished for his good library in St. James's Square and understanding the fattening of sheep as well as any man in Cambridgeshire," was not enlivening; but he was High Steward of the University and might be helpful to Palmerston, if he stood again. A General Election came in November; and he stood for a Sussex borough with Lord Malmesbury's heir, while the strong flow of the French tide swept over Prussia in the grey weeks that followed

Jena. A sum of fifteen hundred pounds secured the affections of the Horsham electors for each candidate. But the return was challenged. He wrote ruefully to Fanny that he had passed "two days in a hot, high-flavoured Court," and on petition an unsympathetic Committee of the House of Commons seated their Whig opponents. So the two young gentlemen had paid their money "for the pleasure of sitting under the gallery for a week in our capacity of petitioners."

Resigned once more to private life, he sat among his trees at Broadlands, while the French fumbled across the snow at Eylau and lay staring into Russia. The long columns wound slowly eastwards over the pale ground under dark winter skies. They seemed to move more slowly now; and it was a faint echo of French cheering, a distant tap of the French drums that drifted back into Europe. But the King's ministers startled their sovereign's conscience with a hint of justice for his Catholic subjects. The outraged Gillray filled his plates with Popish emblems, and Mr. Canning celebrated the happy moment

> When the Broad Bottomed junto, all nonsense and strife,
> Resigned, with a groan, its political life;
> When converted to Rome, and of honesty tired,
> It to Satan gave back what himself had inspired.

The Whigs were out; and England, herself again, defied her enemies under the more restful direction of the Duke of Portland.

The sagacious Malmesbury begged a small place for his young friend at Broadlands. The Duke approved; Lord Mulgrave found him a seat at the Admiralty; and at Easter, 1807, Palmerston, not yet in Parliament, became a Junior Lord. He came to town, dined with his benefactor, and three days later kissed hands for his first office. His colleagues on the Board were three old sailors and two minor politicians, of whom one indulged a strange fancy for writing novels. This entry into official life was an honourable, but—since "at that time lay Lords of the

Admiralty had nothing to do but sign their name "—scarcely
an arduous initiation.   At a General Election in the summer
he tried again to come in for Cambridge.   Once more he
knocked at college doors and noted the nods of learned men
in his canvass books.   His Tory colleague for the double
seat was the Attorney-General, an ungenial person of vast
professional attainments, who had made a name as Erskine's
junior in the treason trials of 1794, and was " quite intolerant
and quite sincere."   These rich endowments manifestly
fitting him to represent a University, he stood in the Senate
House and watched the polling hopefully.   But Palmerston's
friends displayed an awkward tendency to plump for
Palmerston, in spite of an understanding that their second
votes should go to Gibbs.   Late in the evening, as the last
electors were straggling in, the anxious lawyer protested to
his colleague; and that straightforward young gentleman,
who was standing with his coach, proposed to check his
impetuous friends.   But the faithful coach, conscious that
his advice had launched the young man in politics, demurred.
His friends objected; but Palmerston insisted, and walked
to " the bar through which the voters went up to poll, that
I might beg each man as he went by to vote for Gibbs as
well as for me."   His pressure prevailed; four graduates,
who had wished to plump for him, parted with their second
votes to the Attorney-General; and by four votes he lost
the second seat to Gibbs.   His fastidious honour was much
praised; and as the exulting lawyer went sedately on his
way towards the Bench, Palmerston returned to the
Admiralty, with a gratifying sense of virtue, but without
a seat in the House of Commons.

But a few months later that assembly was enriched by his
return for Newport, Isle of Wight, which had given his
first chance to Mr. Canning.   Since the proprietor of that
placid borough had stipulated that he " should never, even
for the election, set foot in the place," his candidature was
not exacting; and in later years he even mistook the name
of his first constituency.   The long French columns were
moving southwards now.   There was a gleam of bayonets

between the hills in Spain, as they moved slowly down the
curving roads in the dusty sunshine.   So the young gentleman went to Parliament; and while Junot's infantry stared
at the streets of Lisbon, he voted with Government in a
respectful silence.   He broke it on a winter evening in 1808,
when the Opposition challenged Mr. Canning's heroic impropriety in bombarding Copenhagen and capturing a neutral
fleet in time of peace.   An Irish member moved for papers;
Mr. Canning retorted with considerable eloquence and two
classical quotations; the Opposition, burned by that sense
of justice which consumes Oppositions in time of war,
alluded to the law of nations and pressed for the secret
information, upon which ministers had taken their drastic
action.   The debate trailed on; and late in the evening
Palmerston got his chance.   Closely prepared, but " not . . .
so much alarmed as I expected to be," the young gentleman
" conceived it improper to disclose the information which
ministers had received on the subject, because their honour
was pledged to preserve secrecy.   In another point of view
. also, he conceived it improper . . . because it would, in
all probability, destroy the future sources of information.
. . . Much had been said by a right honourable gentleman
on the law of nations, on right and policy; he was as ready
and willing as any man to pay his tribute of respect to them,
and to recommend their application whenever circumstances
would permit it; he was afraid, however . . ." His simple
argument proceeded to an accompaniment of polite applause.
French wickedness, Danish impotence, and British rectitude
were triumphantly established; and the young gentleman
resumed his seat.   He had spoken for the first time in
debate on February 3, 1808; and at frequent intervals he
spoke again for fifty-seven years.   When he opened his
papers in the morning, he found (as maiden speakers often
find) that " they have not been very liberal in their allowance
of report to me."   But his world was profuse in congratulations; and a proud sister received a full *précis* of his speech,
which amply compensated for the deficiencies of the press.
Recognised by ministers as a safe young man, he was almost

transferred to the Foreign Office in the summer, to serve as
Mr. Canning's Under-Secretary.   Lord Malmesbury favoured
the prospect of his disciple.   But Mr. Canning was bound by
an earlier promise of the place; and as the smoke of the French
guns drove across Saragossa, Palmerston continued, in the
intervals of quadrilles, to sign his name at the Admiralty.

After a bachelor interlude in the Albany, he made a
home with his sisters, sometimes at Broadlands, sometimes
bringing them to town for a dull winter season, when parties
were scarce, the Opera was on the point of closing, and
society was devastated by the two monotonous enquiries,
' Do you belong to the Argyle, and have you read " Mar-
mion "? '—" and before you have pronounced the first to
be bad and the second inferior to the ' Lay,' you are called
upon to answer the same interrogation to a dozen other
people."   A town house was hard to find, if one was unwilling to follow the preposterous expansion of the capital
into unfashionable regions; and they were almost forced to
seek refuge in the remote recesses of Manchester Square,
" to be sure, sadly out of the way."   He kept a watchful
eye on the house in Hampshire, redecorated the saloon and
bookroom with " curtains of the suppressed green " and
" carpets less likely to show stains than the present," applied
the drawing-room curtains to mend the chairs and sofas,
replaced them with " new curtains of sarsnet . . . hanging
down by the side of the windows in the modern style," and
pronounced the result " exceeding smart for the present."
His brother was still at Cambridge; and in the Long Vacation following his *début* in the House of Commons, whilst
Wellesley's men were feeling for the French in the hills
beyond Vimeiro, they made an expedition to his estates in
Ireland.   There were lakes and landlords and large houses
in bad repair and one efficient person, " just the sort . . .
of whom, could one put down one in every thirty miles
throughout Ireland, it would in forty years' time become as
much civilised as England."   But the roads were bad; the
rivers were worse; the climate exhibited its most lamentable
failings; and Palmerston inspected his Sligo property in the

driving rain. The estate, which cannot have been looking its best, was managed by a clergyman, and the young land-lord rode bravely round, stared at his swarming tenants, and formed heroic plans for road-making, for schools and teachers—" I fancy they must be Catholics, for the people will not send their children to a Protestant "—for land improvement, even for that ultimate object of all Irish aspirations, a stone pier. He was full of generous notions about " a little manufacturing village in a centrical part of the estate," the elimination of intermediate landlords, and a Scotch farmer who should be imported to instruct his people in the elements of agriculture. Then (for he was an Irish landlord) he returned to England.

The world went on, as the young gentleman signed his name to Admiralty papers. That winter the Emperor was in Madrid; and Moore saw the heaped cupolas of Sala-manca come up against the eastern sky, plunged across Leon to the north, and broke away towards the sea, as the Army of Spain pounded after him in the teeth of a Spanish winter to meet his bayonets on the bare hills above Corunna. Then the long columns turned eastwards again and wound slowly across Europe in the spring sunshine of 1809, down the long valley which leads to the tall spire above Vienna. Twice they drew out to fight; and the sound of gunfire drifted across the town from Aspern-Essling. Once they were checked; but in the long summer days they fought again in the broad valley by the Danube and wrote upon French standards the name of Wagram. The King's cruisers still swung slowly with the tide on every coast; and in Portugal there was a faint gleam of distant red-coats. But at home Mr. Gillray made desperate drawings of the Corsican ogre; the Duke of Portland presided wearily in Cabinet; and Mr. Canning despised Lord Castlereagh and resigned, whilst Lord Castlereagh resigned and abominated Mr. Canning. These indignant patriots preserved their honour, drove with their seconds through the autumn mist to Wimbledon, and standing their distance on the Common, shot with pistols like gentlemen. Then their distracted leader died; and England, still at war, passed to the rule of

Mr. Spencer Perceval, K.C., M.P. This shadowy figure, which gleams uncertainly in the flash of Bellingham's pistol, emerged from the Treasury to govern his country. He was (the inventory is not exhilarating) a sound financier and a good debater, with those vaguer attributes of mind which Englishmen agree to describe in public men as honesty. His supporters could express a faintly patronising determination to " fix this honest little fellow firmly in his seat "; and in October, 1809, he formed his Government. His task was sadly complicated by the fact that so few patriots were on speaking terms; and, with a choice that borders on desperation, he invited Palmerston to join as Chancellor of the Exchequer. He had fluttered the young gentleman, just returned from three days' sailing in the bright, gusty weather of early autumn, with a summons to London, which he found at Broadlands on an October day. He posted off; and here was the Prime Minister positively asking him to be his Chancellor. The Treasury, in an age when most ambitions were fixed on the Foreign Office and the Service Departments, was not quite the impressive thing that it has since become. Finance in 1809 was a secondary affair; and even on finance the Chancellor was apt to be subordinate to the First Lord. But it was more dignified than the Board of Trade, less passive than Privy Seal; and it carried a seat in Cabinet. The young gentleman's Parliamentary experience was limited to a single half-hour speech delivered more than a year before on a plain topic, whilst his official training had been confined by Admiralty practice to the simple act of frequent and legible signature. But the obliging Perceval offered to " take the principal share of the Treasury business, both in and out of the House "; or, if his young friend preferred it, to leave him for a few months " fagging at the business " as a Lord of the Treasury, in training for promotion to be Chancellor; or, if the prospect of finance in any form alarmed him, to make him Secretary at War. The boy (he was twenty-five that week) gasped and took two days to consider. He wrote his doubts at length to Lord Malmesbury—" my inexperience in the details of matters of finance, and my want of practice in public speaking." His oratory,

it seemed, left him with no illusions : "All persons not
born with the talents of Pitt or Fox must make many bad
speeches at first . . . and a bad speech, though tolerated
in any person not in a responsible situation, would make a
Chancellor of the Exchequer exceedingly ridiculous, particularly if his friends could not set off against his bad
oratory a great knowledge and capacity for business."
There was a quiet air of determination to get on. But,
more clear-eyed than most beginners, he seemed to know
his limitations. He wished to choose his moment, to be
unhurried in his career—" Of course one's vanity and
ambition would lead to accept the brilliant offer first proposed; but it is throwing for a *great stake*, and where much
is to be gained, *very much* also may be lost. I have always
thought it unfortunate for any one, and particularly a young
man, to be put above his proper level, as he only rises to
fall the lower." The wise young man concluded that it was
best to be Secretary at War. " From what one has heard
of the office " (it was engaged at the moment in a war with
Napoleon) " it seems one better suited to a beginner." The
sage concurred, though Mulgrave, with a soldier's reckless-
ness, had been for acceptance; and Mr. Perceval searched
elsewhere for a Chancellor, whilst Palmerston looked sedately
forward to the War Office, confiding to his sister that it
would be " a very great confinement and Fag." He rejoiced
soberly over the splendid offer; but, with a curious control
of impulse, he had turned away. He even declined a seat
in the Cabinet, since " people in general, so far from expecting to see me in the Cabinet by taking the War Office, would
perhaps only wonder how I got there." Caution could go
no further; and in the last week of October, 1809, whilst
Mr. Creevey gathered angry gossip from disconsolate Whigs
and the London crowds stood half the night in Whitehall to
stare at the Jubilee illuminations, cheer the carriages, and
pull the coachmen's hats off as they passed the blazing
crowns over the Admiralty gate, with which Their Lordships
celebrated their sovereign's survival, the wise apprentice
dined with Mr. Perceval at Ealing and drove back to London,
a minister of state at twenty-five.

WAR OFFICE

I

THERE is an ineptitude about the War Office, which it has never lost; and it confronted the First Empire at the very height of its absurdity. On one side of the Channel an incomparable figure, in the white and green of the *Chasseurs* of his own Guard, surmounted an exact and towering hierarchy. On the other the gentlemen of the War Department sat with dignity in one of those labyrinths which are the glory of British administration. Housed in becoming state above an archway in Whitehall, they wrote sedately at the Horse Guards, shared the pleasing prospect of St. James's Park with the back windows of the Admiralty, and in these dignified surroundings led an administrative life of exquisite confusion. A Secretary for War, who divided his official life with the Colonies, directed operations and attended Cabinet. A Secretary at War controlled finance and explained the Army Votes to Parliament. A Commander-in-Chief, with headquarters at the Horse Guards, reigned with unchallenged supremacy over the cavalry and infantry. But the artillery, with sturdy independence, acknowledged no other authority than that of the Board of Ordnance in Palace Yard, with separate rates of pay and even, through their own chaplains, with a distinct theology. Bewildered Engineers, who owed allegiance to the Master-General of Ordnance, had by a pleasing anomaly no authority whatever to command their own subordinates, the Military Artificers, and competed briskly with a Staff Corps formed by the Commander-in-Chief for the performance of precisely the same duties. But this splendid anarchy hardly sufficed to gratify the national appetite for decorous disorder, since two further branches of the King's forces were controlled by two totally distinct departments. The Home Office still exercised a vague, but warmly challenged, authority over

a mixed array of Fencibles, Militia, Volunteers, and all the
martial figures that drilled and drummed and trumpeted in
bold defiance of the foreign invader; while the Treasury,
amongst its ledgers, kept a distracted eye upon the services
of transport and supply, commanded a vague host of store-
keepers and master-bakers, and through its Commissaries
governed the Commissariat.

Such was the labyrinth which Palmerston, at twenty-five,
elected to enter at the height of a European war. He felt
it to be " suited to a beginner "; and as Secretary at War
he took his seat at the Horse Guards, where one hundred and
forty-four clerks sat writing round him. The sound intelligence of Lord Liverpool discharged the functions of Secretary
of State; and as Commander-in-Chief one of Chatham's
young men still trailed a scabbard round the corridors.
Known from inveterate addiction to the drill-book as " Old
Pivot," he retained professional respect and, not yet eighty,
founded his ripe decisions upon experience culled from the
Seven Years' War. Beyond the Channel a less venerable
instrument operated with unbecoming rapidity. Unhallowed by such antiquity and with less consecrated usage the
Emperor, at forty, dictated inexhaustibly to the ranged
obedience of France. Brusque to Foreign Affairs, always a
trifle peremptory with the Interior, he was never curter than
with War; and notes, directions, stabbing enquiries, sudden
commands, sharp orders fell in a steady rain upon the
splendid backs of Clarke, Duke of Feltre, Minister of War, of
Marshal Berthier, Major-General of the Army of Spain and
Prince of Neuchâtel and Wagram, of Marshal Bessières, Duke
of Istria, commanding the Imperial Guard, and all the long
perspective of docility which bent over littered tables, jingled
spurs on palace stairs, or lounged among tall shakoes in hot
ante-rooms. The French sentries in their bearskins stiffened
to salutes, as Marshals clanked by in blue and gold; and
three hundred miles away Lord Palmerston, fresh from Cambridge, touched a civilian hat to the mounted sentries in
Whitehall and climbed a dark staircase to plumb the mysteries
of the War Department.

II

HE signed his first official letter on October 30, 1809. There was a lull in Europe; and for a moment after Wagram the Empire seemed to sit with folded wings. But between the mountains and the sea the guns still boomed through the dusty Catalan sunshine outside Gerona; and whilst Lord Wellington watched gloomily from Portugal, the Spanish armies stumbled towards disaster at Ocaña. So the new Secretary at War signed his first official letter : it dealt, without undue originality, with the topic of regimental accounts.

On the next day he exercised his powers to commit a Guardsman's demented wife to Bedlam, attending a week later to perform the same sad office for a private of the Line. At first the brunt of his correspondence was borne by his Deputy. But soon he was assiduous at the office, where his life became a decorous whirl of greatcoats, sealed patterns, forage, and finance, relieved by rare flickers of reality when a constable called down official thunders by obstructing the Foot Guards or a zealous press at Liverpool was positively caught diverting soldiers to the baser uses of the Admiralty. He signed Militia circulars and explored the mysterious recesses of the Compassionate List; he was prolific in minutes upon homely affairs of inn-keepers and billets; and his pen grew strangely familiar with absorbing problems of pay and allowances, occasionally troubling the General commanding the forces in Portugal with detailed inquiries of that meticulous class, which is the delight of Departments and the despair of soldiers in the field. He discovered with a pleased surprise that the Commander-in-Chief " has a strong national propensity to a job "; and once he was solicited to find an Army medical appointment for Dr. Knighton, " accoucheur," as Mr. Creevey wickedly notes, " to Poll Roffle, Wellesley's

Cyprian.'' So he walked an interminable minuet in corre-
spondence with the Secretary of State for the Home
Department and the Lords Commissioners for His Majesty's
Treasury, while the less familiar figures of the Apothecary-
General or the Clothing Board sometimes wove into the slow
dance.

As the year waned, he plunged into the departmental
delights of the Estimates for 1810; and on a winter evening
he introduced them with becoming modesty under twenty-
one heads. He claimed indulgence and led a drooping House
into a maze of figures. But those Service members, whose
professional grievances are annually revived by Army
Estimates, displayed their knowledge. General Tarleton,
speaking from a rich experience of unsuccessful operations
in America, was especially severe upon the senseless luxury of
a Waggon Train, since, in that sage's view, the British Army
'' would always get waggons enough.'' Palmerston, in reply,
referred with some humility to the contrary opinion of Lord
Wellington, might, indeed, have added that transport was
the sole lesson of Talavera, and abstained by a laudable effort
from any reference to the campaign of Yorktown. A fierce
attack upon the Manx Fencibles was successfully repelled;
and when an angry earl pelted him with abrupt questions on
the medical service, Mr. Spencer Perceval strode to the table
and, in the chivalrous attitude of Achilles above the body of
Patroclus, rescued his young subordinate. The debate
trailed on for two days more; misgivings were expressed
about Martello towers; General Tarleton emitted the sagacious judgment that ' where ever gentlemen could hunt, there
could cavalry act '; and Palmerston secured his Vote.

But, apart from these somewhat arid exercises, he was not
heard in Parliament; and whilst his elders endlessly debated
the Expedition to the Scheldt in gloomy retrospect, he read
his drafts and signed his letters in the War Office. In front
of Wellington the slow surge of a French advance was gathering on the upland, which parts the high prairies of western
Spain from the tumbled rocks of Beira. Masséna saw the
brown cupolas of Salamanca; and at Ciudad Rodrigo Ney
watched the red tiles and the big brown church across a wide,

green valley. Far to the south bewildered Portuguese were
digging on the tumbled skyline above Torres Vedras; and
in the War Office Lord Palmerston embarked sedately on the
absorbing topic of Militia epaulettes. The misbehaviour of
some Irish recruits engaged him deeply; and he handled the
case of an obstructive constable on the Portsmouth road with
laudable firmness. At midsummer, as Ney counted his
casualties and Crawford's Light Division scrambled back
from the Coa, he was adjudicating upon the claim of a clergyman for spiritual ministrations to the troops at Dorchester
Barrack; and shortly afterwards his desk was enlivened by
an assault upon a Lifeguardsman at Putney.

The leaves of 1810 were falling. The War Office was
busy that autumn with a grand promotion of Drum and
Trumpet Majors. Masséna made his slow lunge across
Portugal; and France came roaring up the slope, across the
heather to the heights of Bussaco. Then, as the lines filed
westwards, the big, bare hills of Torres Vedras climbed slowly
up the sky. The French, who lay in a dun wilderness, surveyed that obstacle with marked distaste. Supply was
difficult; and advertised assault upon prepared positions was
uninviting. So Wellington sat waiting in the Lines, until
Masséna, stared out of countenance by that impenetrable
blend of geography with fortification, turned sharply eastwards to the Spanish border. Then the campaign ended,
and Wellington had won his game without a victory.

Lord Palmerston had his triumphs also. The eager novice
seemed to enjoy his post, and trusted with the hopefulness of
youth that " much may be accomplished in arranging the
interior details of the office, so as to place it on a respectable
footing." The topic of Army clothing presented an almost
unlimited field for ingenuity. It lay between the Horse
Guards and the War Office in one of those devastated areas of
administration that are familiar to students of departmental
differences. Controlled by a Board of Generals, it was paid
for by an obscure system of deductions from the soldiers'
pay, which formed a regimental fund administered by each
colonel. This minor perquisite of the military was for long
the object of envious glances from the civilian side of the

E

Department, since public money was involved and finance was sacred to the War Office. With unworthy stealth a Bill was introduced to transfer control from the unconscious soldiers to the Secretary at War; and Parliament, intent (as usual) upon other things, sanctioned the change. Not without glee, Lord Palmerston announced it to the Commander-in-Chief. That veteran, whose military experience included almost every unsuccessful engagement fought in Europe for the past fifty years, was strangely moved by the news. The base civilians of the War Office encroaching on the Horse Guards, a schoolboy tampering with the rights of colonels—here was an outrage upon Sir David Dundas, which almost robbed his official pen of language. Lively visions of the contumacious Secretary at War opening " this Masked Battery on the Colonels " danced before his angry eyes. But he replied with laudable restraint. Then, with the weary gesture of a nurse complaining to the indulgent parent of a refractory child, he appealed to the Prime Minister; and Mr. Perceval was made aware of the rash proceedings of his young colleague. The angry veteran wrote with increasing frequency and at growing length; the weary minister, excusably less interested in Army clothing than in Portugal, restrained his junior; and as the French advanced, grave conferences in Downing Street had almost lulled the storm.

But the bland young man persisted in his sadly provocative courses. Demure in Downing Street, he was almost truculent at his table in the War Office; and shortly afterwards he defied the military lightning once again by calling upon the army for a duplicate of a monthly return of bread and forage, evincing at the same time a dangerous tendency to vary the form of pay-warrant in use for Generals. Doom followed swift on the heels of these revolutionary proceedings. Once more the guilty youth was caught trespassing on strictly military ground; and the Horse Guards rang with protests, while Palmerston explained indulgently that the Commander-in-Chief was " a little irritable and hasty in transacting business and apt to take up a matter somewhat warmly before he is quite in possession of all the facts of the case." The mine exploded; the Prime Minister poured

quantities of oil on waters, which disobligingly refused to subside; the calm young gentleman stood his ground; and in a
formal reference to the Prince Regent the indignant soldier
appealed to Cæsar. Somewhere beyond the sea the distant
war went on. But at Carlton House the royal brow was knit
over a graver problem. For the Horse Guards, at war with
Napoleon, were at war still more profoundly with the War
Office. The disputants approached the judgment-seat;
the Regent reflected; and after a becoming interval his
pleasure was made known in an impressive instrument, which
traced the administrative limits of the War Office under the
Sign Manual itself.

The soldiers breathed again; and the official career of
General Dundas, like that of General Wolfe, closed in a happy
certainty of victory. But a spirited Department is not so
easily deprived of a cherished grievance. As the French
drew off to Spain, the timbrels of the Horse Guards welcomed
the Duke of York, Commander-in-Chief once more after an
interruption due to the lively Mrs. Clarke. A decorous
oblivion now veiled the house in Gloucester Place, where the
Grecian lamp had vied with the Duc de Berri's plate and the
list of promotions pinned with artless grace to the royal bed-
head. But quite soon he was exchanging broadsides with
the War Office on the familiar topic. Lord Palmerston
displayed a terrifying erudition, drew fine distinctions between the authority of a Commander-in-Chief and a Captain-
General, and was eloquent upon departmental practice under
Queen Anne, while St. John, Craggs, and Pulteney smiled
ghostly approval of his precedents. Once more the
collective intellect of England wrestled with the problem.
Law was invoked; Lord Eldon wrote opinions from the
Woolsack; and a committee of the Cabinet drafted a full
report, to which Sir David in the cool shades of Chelsea
Hospital appended offensive *marginalia*. As the slow tide of
war crept into Russia, he was still drafting memoranda.
Moscow burned; the sudden hand of death withdrew Mr.
Perceval; and at the War Office hopes were distinctly enter-
tained of a decision. The flames of war burned lower;
Dresden, Leipzig, the Rhine—all the grey milestones of de-

feat passed slowly by; and as the Emperor fell back fighting across France, it was confidently felt that the long debate in Whitehall was " drawing to a close." Europe might hope that the powers of the War Office were defined at last. But nine years away, in 1823, when war lay buried under a stone at St. Helena, it still left an echo.

This lingering debate exhales the authentic air of the War Office. Savoured with protracted gusto for the best part of thirteen years, it delighted the participants with its asperity, its adorable irrelevance, its cheerful disregard of the war that had provoked it. The administrative life glows with such ardours; and in these tourneys, where no trumpet sounds, no Queen of Beauty smiles, Palmerston rode happily to break his lances. The work confined him. Once a bout with the Clerical Establishment (for Army chaplains were among his subjects) postponed a country visit; and even when he got away for Christmas, he found grave employment among the Fellows of St. John's. He was still nursing Cambridge, where University votes were to be secured over hands of learned whist and bowls of clerical punch. The snipe-shooting at Broadlands was left to his brother, who rode his hunters for him and was even permitted by a more touching attention to " wear any of my comical hats if he likes them."

But Palmerston was not quite submerged by the grey waters of the War Office. There was a little Lady Cowper with the most attractive eyes (Lawrence had painted them). She had danced at Sheen in children's parties with a contingent of small Lambs; and now she was married to a handsome earl whose family, by a graceful admission, " was illustrated by the great Poet of his blood still more than by the title of Prince of the Holy Roman Empire." Cowper, who brought her Panshanger, was nine years older and far from lively. Even a friendly pen draws a depressing picture —" I don't know why they call Cowper dull; I never saw a man less dull in my life, but he has a slow pronunciation, slow gait and pace." Palmerston was nearer to her age and far nearer to her spirits. So they were much seen together. They called him ' Cupid ' for his bright eye and boyish air; and he sketched a Cupid for her in her Album—a not wholly

successful *amorino* upon a wine-press. He even wrote a
verse :

> Cease, mortals, to consume your Prime
> In vain attempts at killing Time.
> For Time, alas, whate'er you do,
> Is sure to end in killing you.

She esteemed her husband, who was soon in trying health.
But she still had Almack's and her babies. Moreover there
was a young Secretary at War; and Palmerston's career
was watched by the bright eyes of Lady Cowper. He missed
some dances at the Malmesburys' that year; yet it appeared
from an order for a new pair of pumps that the Secretary at
War was not quite inseparable from his desk, and he got a
day's shooting in Epping Forest when the French were before
the Lines. The Lambs were there, William a little sleepy-
eyed and his ' Cherubina ' as gusty as the weather, reserved
to flutter in the wilder gales that swept before *The Corsair.*
An Essex spring-gun caught him by the leg and almost
ended him; but the charge was damp, and he returned to
the War Office in order to array his country's forces against
the Emperor at the eccentric salary of £2,280 a year.

His world proclaimed in 1811 that " Harry is doing very
well—with a clear head and a good understanding. He will
never be a great man because he has no great views—but he
is painstaking and gentlemanlike to the highest degree, and
will always swim where greater talents might sink. Nothing
can be more amiable." These tepid praises were the highest
that Lady Minto could find. The young man was amiable
and knew his limits. Had he not declined the Exchequer,
to sit industriously in the War Office and minute papers
about medical stores? Yet there were gleams. The hand
that played Sir David like an angry trout had a touch.
Hardly apparent in his annual exposition of the Army
Estimates, which erred, if it erred at all, on the side of
blamelessness, it glimmered faintly in his departmental
correspondence. It was, one feels, a slightly sardonic
Secretary at War of twenty-six who insisted drily that religious books supplied to convalescent soldiers should have the
" specific approbation of the Prelates "; for even tracts
might be unblest and cause official scandal. In Parliament

he read out his figures audibly and obtained his Vote.
Docked of a Drum Major, the Manx Fencibles still figured in
his papers. But that threatened unit was triumphantly
disbanded; while General Tarleton dwelt with gloomy
satisfaction on retreats in the Peninsula, pointed a warning
finger at the unprotected state of Sicily and Ireland, alluded
meaningly to Carthage, and enlivened his eighteenth con-
secutive column of *Hansard* with a poetical quotation.

The war crept slowly on. The French still lay behind the
Spanish frontier; and in May, 1811, as Palmerston prepared
himself to speak on the interchange of English and Irish
Militia, the rain was beating on the hill of Albuera. Bewildered brigadiers watched the French lancers charge.
There was a storm of grape, in which the red-coats seemed to
melt; and through the drifting smoke a dismounted colonel
roared unforgettably "Fifty-seventh, die hard!" That
month the Secretary at War referred to the Clothing Board
a new process for rendering greatcoats water-proof. Im-
pulsively, perhaps, he expressed a desire that they should
test it. But those judicious warriors, with a nicer sense of
official propriety, were powerless to act without a direction
from the Commander-in-Chief and referred with perfect
justice to a binding precedent, which dated from Queen Anne.
This decorous atmosphere, unfriendly to any undue sense of
the urgency of war, ranged the long struggle neatly with the
French wars of Mr. Pitt, of Chatham, Newcastle, and Marlborough. So Palmerston, far from reality, signed innumerable letters; whilst Wellington seemed to fumble a little
with the Spanish fortresses, and Prinny, "very fat . . . in
his full Field Marshal's uniform," watched the Pavilion
footman taking round iced champagne punch and sandwiches,
or sat in the Music Room and thumped a royal leg in time to
the band. The guns roared in Paris for the King of Rome;
and Palmerston explored the varied administrative problems
presented by a deaf and dumb private of the Line or smoothed
a Dean and Chapter, ruffled by sounds of drilling in too
audible proximity on the Green at Gloucester.

The world swung into 1812; and his official charges played
their varied parts. His War Department stores rode slowly

up the Tagus, heaped the dusty quays at Lisbon, and wound
through the Peninsular sunshine on creaking ox-waggons.
His bayonets stormed up the breach at Badajoz, gleamed in
the flashes of French guns, or lay rusting in the ditch below
the tall lunettes. His tunics reeled through the shuttered
streets of the stormed town; gesticulated at shawled women
who screamed and scattered; and lurched, limp but happy,
into impenetrable oblivion of Spanish sunshine, beauty,
sieges, wines, and the Provost-Marshal erect beside his
gallows in the Plaza. Hospitals bewildered him with demands for drugs in strange Portuguese measures; Army
chaplains, bound for that field of genteel simony, flitted
through his correspondence; and soldiers' children stared at
the tortured stones of Belem, as they learned their letters from
alphabets of his providing.

There was a false gleam of victory in the Peninsula that
year. The strong places of the frontier went down before
them; and they marched briskly eastwards into Spain,
having the red earth underfoot and a long line of mountains
watching from the right. They saw the wheeling dust of
Marmont, as he circled in the plain of Salamanca; and those
heaped brown cupolas looked down from a summer sky. The
hunt swept northwards; and they tramped through the
Spanish dust into Valladolid. South through the dancing
heat Madrid was shrill with welcome. A scared French
remnant cowered at the Retiro. The streets were throbbing
where, high-nosed and silent, an English rider sat above the
roaring, whilst his horse picked a cautious way between the
black *mantillas* across a floor of flowered shawls. But they
were checked in the north. A grey cathedral watched them
file through Burgos under the moon. The infantry went at the
trail, and the guns clanked heavily down the empty streets with
muffled wheels. So the gleam faded; and that winter they lay
once more on the windy hills which look down into Portugal.

It was a quiet season at the War Office. The Estimates
were almost dull, though Palmerston thrilled with quiet
pride at official generosity to the veterans at Chelsea, and a
bold defence of flogging in the army secured the rare support
of General Tarleton. In the spring Mr. Perceval dropped to a

madman's pistol in the Lobby.   Prospects of office made a
pleasant stir among the Whigs.   But high-minded Oppositions are frequently incapable of concerted action.   There
was an interlude of brisk intrigue; and Mr. Creevey said the
most amusing things about all his friends.   His jokes upon
Wellesley were in great request, and in the drawing-room
after dinner Lady Holland graciously desired the naughty
jester to " come here and sit by me, you *mischievous toad*."
Whig magnates whispered endlessly in corners.   But they
failed to discover even the small degree of unanimity which
was required of official colleagues in 1812; and with almost
audible relief the Regent turned back to the Tories.   The
cloak of Mr. Perceval fell upon Lord Liverpool, who wore those
somewhat meagre folds for fifteen years.   He had worked
with Palmerston at the War Office, and invited him to become
Chief Secretary for Ireland.   Had he not land in Ireland,
even visited the country?   But that wise young man preferred a simpler path and retained his post.

A sudden election in the autumn brought fruition to his
interminable sippings of college port; and he returned to
Westminster, member at last for Cambridge.   Late in the
year he established the great principle that the widow of a
Chaplain-General should be pensioned at the rate appropriate
to the widow of a colonel.   Somewhere across the world
Napoleon hung like a thundercloud on the edge of Russia.
There was a faint tap of distant drums, and the side-arms
gleamed in the pale Baltic sunshine, as the long columns
wound across an interminable plain towards the haze.
The mists enclosed them.   Sounds came faintlier now out
of the north—the quick receding jingle of cavalry, a sudden
trumpet, the thud of guns, French cheers that died upon the
distance.   The war seemed almost still behind the mists.
But they were lit with a strange, reflected glow, where something flamed suddenly.   The sky was paler now; and as it
darkened into winter, the plain was white beneath it, a never-
ending white that stretched unbroken to a black horizon,
except where something trailed uncertainly across it.   So
France stumbled through the white silence out of 1812.

In the next year a conquered world prepared for the

unaccustomed exercise of victory. A strange shadow had
fallen on the Empire. The Czar appeared in the white
radiance of his new character as Liberator; Austria struggled
weakly with the last scruples of a neutral; Prussia propelled
its king into heroic attitudes; and as the thrill of 1813 ran
agreeably through Central Europe, Lord Wellington, in the
new dignities of Marquessate and Garter, followed the
hounds on the bare hills above Ciudad Rodrigo and waited for
the spring. An anxious Government bought Spanish dollars
and shipped drafts to Lisbon. But before his annual performance upon the Estimates Lord Palmerston made a slight
incursion into home politics. Early in 1813 there was a
three days' debate upon the Catholic question. Mr. Grattan
moved for a committee and provoked a flood of Protestant
eloquence from private members. Lord Palmerston, dissenting from some of his colleagues, supported the motion
with unusual emphasis. Declining sturdily to be intimidated
by the deluge of Protestant petitions, he took his line. His
reasoning was quaint, since he refused to admit the Catholic
claims as a matter of right—" if I thought the Catholics were
asking for their rights, I for one would not go into the
committee." He was rarely interested in abstractions;
and this peculiar logic was plainly his own. The problem
appeared to him a mere question of expediency, an attempt to
bring a neglected section of the community into the public
service. Avoiding higher flights, he closed upon a modest
refrain of " Is it wise . . .? " He said little of liberty;
but pausing to speculate on events " if it had unfortunately
happened that, by the circumstances of birth and education,
a Nelson, a Wellington, a Burke, a Fox, or a Pitt, had belonged to this class," he perorated with unusual practicality
upon " the means of national prosperity and public wealth."

From this rare excursion he returned to the War Department. The Estimates were a less arduous exposition, though
Mr. Creevey attacked a sinecure and some frivolous Whig
found that the Life Guards looked like " the Rinaldos of
an epic poem " in their new uniforms, which their critic
thought " worthy of Grimaldi or D'Egville." Lord Palmerston maintained his departmental gravity in reply, found

something wise to say upon the utility of helmets to cavalry in the field, and resumed his interminable correspondence. That year he drove a firm of agents to distraction with a fine distinction between the Invalids and the Royal Veteran Battalions. They claimed, and he disputed, a right to issue pay to retired officers. As Wellington moved slowly forward into Spain, the solemn battle was joined with the full courtesies of official correspondence. At midsummer, when the French broke in the plain of Vittoria and ran for the Pyrenees, there was an appeal to the Treasury. For a short time his official life seemed to be lived to a running accompaniment from his voluble correspondents at the Invalid Office. But the *motif* was soon engulfed in the melody; the bright thread vanished in the big tapestry of the War Department; and the broad stream of his varied duties flowed slowly by. His nights were social; but his days brought him innumerable letters for signature—to colonels, to the Treasury, one to acquaint Lord Wellington of his promotion to be Field Marshal, and one (for he had a strange familiarity with exotic units of Maltese Fencibles, Royal Corsican Rangers, *Chasseurs Britanniques*, Dillon, the King's German Legion, and the Sicilian Regiment) to authorise a new regiment of Greek Light Infantry with clothing and accoutrements " in the Albanian fashion." Once more he defended flogging against fanciful Whigs; and later in the year the House of Commons heard him, in a tone familiar to all students of British war ministers, on the superiority of volunteers to " a band of slaves, torn from their homes by force."

The war crept slowly northwards. Spain lay behind them now. They heard the sea in San Sebastian bay, and through the high passes they looked down into the green distances of France. Europe rolled westwards. Incredulous Russians, Prussians, and Austrians tasted the strange flavour of victory, as the long rearguard action flickered before Paris. In the south the guns came nearer; and as the Emperor trailed off to Fontainebleau, they hunted Soult along the Pyrenees. A closed carriage drove down the long road to Fréjus; a cruiser sailed for Elba; and, in a world at peace, Lord Palmerston introduced the Army Estimates for 1814.

III

THERE was a hush in Europe like the deep silence after thunder. The last trumpet died on the air; and in the stillness a receding drum throbbed faintly. The armies had passed by; and Spain lay empty in the sunshine. There was no dust stirring on the long road to the north. No convoys wound across the great plain beyond Vittoria, no couriers clattered into Valladolid. At San Sebastian the sea swung idly below the silent guns of Urgull, and in the dusty south Badajoz slept in the shade of broken walls. There was a gleam of peaceful rivers—of Seine, of Beresina, of Tormes in its slaty gorge, of the deep windings of Mondego, of Tagus gathered in the hollow beneath Toledo to flow past Talavera or spread to take the Portuguese sunshine beyond the arches in the white square below the straight and sheltered streets of Lisbon. The world was almost still; and as the deep peace pervaded Europe, summer was undisturbed. The birds wheeled over Eylau; Friedland slept. The fields were empty beyond Leipzig; whilst on the glaring, sunlit plain outside Vienna, where the tall cathedral looked halfway into Hungary, Wagram danced in the silent heat, and nothing stirred between the dusty trees that line the road to Aspern. Germany was still; France scarcely moved; and somewhere beyond the edge of Italy Elba hung in the summer haze.

Peace came to England in a pleasant flutter. Allied monarchs, inclining gracious heads or raising royal hands to big cocked hats, rode, reviewed, and dined interminably, sat through operas, and inspected troops. The big, blonde Czar wore his tight uniforms and deplored the length of dinners; de Staël, not quite so ugly as Mr. Creevey had feared and with a notable arm, was seen at Lady Jersey's, where she shocked a peeress by her religious opinions and complimented

59

Mr. Sheridan upon his moral principles; and, wronged but ridiculous, the Princess of Wales intruded inextinguishably upon her shrinking consort, storming royal pews, blockading Drawing-rooms, and supplying a cause of delicious inde-corum to eager Whigs in Opposition. There was a brisk return of politics. But these diversions seemed to miss the War Department. The Army Estimates lacked their usual fire in the prevailing air of peace and national thanksgivings; and Palmerston was heard with greater interest in the new problems of demobilisation and reduced establishments. He had a correspondence with the Prime Minister upon half-pay. But in the new year, whilst Europe sat in Congress at Vienna and dutifully remade itself in the Czar's image, he found a livelier means of expression than War Office drafts. The Whigs were pelted with a hail of squibs. Some came from the War Department, some from the room where the red head of Mr. Peel bent over a table in the Irish Office, and some from the solemn hand of Mr. Croker at the Admiralty. First printed in the *Courier* newspaper and assembled by later piety in *The New Whig Guide*, these cheerful fruits of official leisure exhale an air of 1815, of

> Bad faith with Murat—and the low price of Corn,
> The American Lakes—and the Duchy of Thorn,
> The Legion of Honour—the trading in Blacks,
> Baron Imbert's arrest—and the Property Tax,
> Colonel Quentin's Court-martial—and Spain's discontent,
> The Catholic claims—and the Treaty of Ghent!

This was politics set to an air of Mr. Mackworth Praed. Perhaps a familiar voice may be detected in the more sporting items. The air of sweepstakes and bottle-holders was always congenial to the Secretary at War; and more than a trace of him seems to linger in a political race-card filled with the most diverting names of Whig sires and dams, and in the narrative of a terrific battle at which " the fancy mustered very strong " to watch Lord Castlereagh punish an Opposition bruiser, and within the space of two rounds it was " Lombard-street to a China-orange against Sam." A more authentic echo of Army debates seems to ring in the account of a Whig

conclave among the Elgin metopes (still at Burlington House),
where some member moved to "revert to the ancient and
constitutional practice of making our artillery of leather,
instead of following the Continental fashion of having them
of iron or brass," whilst another economist "should never
think the Constitution safe till he saw the Foot Guards exchange their gaudy equipments for the modest garb of Special
Constables, and what was termed in the modern phrase, the
Household Cavalry, assume the appearance of the Surrey
Patrole." There were parodies of Mr. Moore's *Irish* and of
Lord Byron's *Hebrew Melodies*; and one lyric, in its
invocation of a member who

> Moved the Committee of Supply
> On Ordnance votes,

bears faint traces of the same departmental bias. The Muse
had visited his father; and perhaps her wing brushed
Palmerston. Such were the achievements which, in later
years, enabled Mr. Croker to add his name to the Athenæum
as "patron of the arts, and to my knowledge a person of
literary powers."

The silence deepened. At Vienna gentlemen in stars
discussed the affairs of Switzerland with gentlemen in ribbons;
Beauty averted her face from Carlton House, where the
Prince was "positively ordered . . . to give up his stays,
as the wearing them any longer would be too great a sacrifice
to ornament"; and Mrs. Creevey, in pursuit of health,
enjoyed the tranquillity of Brussels. The winter of 1815
faded into spring. Then something stirred; and across the
silence Europe heard the faint tap of a distant, solitary drum.
The night was still, when the brig *Inconstant* stood out of
Elba. Voices came across the water, and the white houses
in the town all turned to face the moon. The rest lay in deep
shadow. But as they sailed a trifle after midnight, the big
moon and the little houses watched them go; and Elba
faded into the dim blue behind them. They were at sea all
night, and on the next day they passed a cruiser. As it
hailed them and the tall masts slid by, the Guard lay close

behind the bulwarks without their bearskins, and the ship
from Elba had a most unmerited air of innocence. That
night they rowed ashore and marched in the moonlight down
the white road to Cannes. The War Office was deep that
week in those problems of pay and allowances which evoke
its highest qualities. Lord Palmerston assuaged the anxiety
of an earl as to an allowance for coals and candles in the
Governor's Office at Portsmouth with an assurance that the
Barrack Board, after consultation with the Commander-in-
Chief, would refer the matter to the Treasury. There was a
sudden recrudescence of the old debate upon the pay of the
Royal Veteran Battalions, which had seemed to slumber
since he countered a legal point in the previous year. The
distracted agents appealed through a private friend; and
Palmerston, resenting this intervention a little stiffly,
enunciated the sound conviction that " the most satisfactory
mode of discussing an official question is by letter." There,
for two years, the matter rested; until it came before the
Prime Minister, and the papers were lost.

This decorous calm enfolded the War Office, as the drums
began to beat down the long road to Paris and a *vivandière*
at Grenoble sang cheerfully :

> *Bon ! Bon !*
> *Napoléon*
> *Va rentrer dans sa maison !*

It filed assiduously; it minuted papers; it drafted with
consummate skill; it submitted innumerable letters to the
Secretary at War for signature; and at intervals it stared
out of its windows across the Horse Guards Parade or became
faintly aware of a world beyond Whitehall. On the day that
Monsieur, eager captor of the Corsican ogre, fumbled with
his troops at Lyons, there was some effervescence in the
streets of London connected with the price of corn. An attack
on Stanhope Street was feared, and Lord Palmerston instructed a neighbour on the defensive virtues of strong
boarding nailed " behind the fanlight over the street door."
Then he returned sedately to his papers. The drums were
throbbing nearer now; but his official work was soothingly

retrospective.   He settled claims and sanctioned payments;
he even reinstated a garrison chaplain at Curaçoa.   The
Emperor drove with half-closed eyes through the roaring
into Paris; and Lord Palmerston was assuring an officer at
Brighton of the propriety of certain expenditure incurred
in the prevention of smuggling off the coast of Sussex.   The
guns spoke across Paris for the *Champ de Mai*; and with
departmental unconcern Lord Palmerston occupied himself
with an issue of pay-warrants to officers serving in the
Channel Islands.   There is a magnificence about routine,
which borders on heroism.   At grave moments it aligns
assiduous clerks in Government offices with Casabianca and
the sentry of Pompeii; and as Europe darkened under the
sweep of a familiar wing and scared kings huddled into Belgium, the Secretary at War introduced with his accustomed
sobriety the Army Estimates for 1815.

The slow summer passed; the marching drums came
north; and in the Park at Brussels the Duke informed
enquiring Mr. Creevey that, by God! he thought Blucher
and himself could do the thing.   A private of the Line was
staring at the foreign statues under the foreign trees.   His
commander pointed a long finger and opined a little grimly
that " it all depends upon that article whether we do the
business or not.   Give me enough of it, and I am sure."
The world was not so sure.   But as it wondered and the last
army of the Empire massed behind the frontier, Lord Palmerston conveyed to an officer in Canada the welcome intelligence that he had earned some back-pay in Sicily a year
before and handled with his usual firmness the legal, almost
religious, complications resulting from the enlistment of a
recruit at Newbury in the peace of a Berkshire Sunday afternoon.   That day a dusty carriage rolled into Laon, and
Grouchy's troopers saw a squat, familiar figure, white-
breeched and booted.   They trotted across the frontier in
the summer dawn; and far away the War Department was
stung by a sudden passion for embarkation returns.   In the
evening Lord Palmerston spoke in the House of Commons
on the Mutiny Bill.   The debate turned imperturbably upon a

professional grievance of 1801 and the livelier concerns of a
hilarious court-martial, whose members "instead of per-
forming their judicial functions, after publicly betting on the
result of the trial . . . chiefly amused themselves throughout
with cutting papers and sticking them in the hair of the
President." That night the marching bayonets went down
the empty streets of Brussels; and Mr. Creevey, writing late,
entered in his Journal : " *Friday morning, ½ past two*—The
girls just returned from a ball at the Duke of Richmond's."

The trumpets sounded across the corn at Quatre Bras;
and as the lancers wheeled and Brussels strolled on the
ramparts to hear the faint thudding of the guns, the Secretary
at War unravelled one more recruiting trouble. On the
next day he was deep in a question of pay, as the summer
rain drove down and the armies changed ground on the
Brussels road. The long wall of La Haye Sainte watched the
gleaming *pavé*, and there was a sound of hammering among
the trees at Hougomont. Then a pale dawn broke over
Belgium. The guns opened across the sodden fields; and
at the War Office the sun slanted in on littered tables. A
faint sound of bells hung in the air; and as the sunshine
crept across the heaped papers in the empty rooms (for it was
Sunday), nothing stirred. They heard the guns all day in
Brussels, where Mr. Creevey watched the crowds and asked
his questions. The firing died away; and as the moon came
up, the pounding hoofs drove southwards into the summer
night. The Duke took his tea and toast, rode into Brussels,
and acquainted Creevey that it had been a damned nice thing
—the nearest run thing you ever saw in your life. Far to the
south a white face stared at Paris, stared at the flowers at
Malmaison, stared at the sea; and, in a world at peace once
more, Lord Palmerston defended flogging.

IV

PEACE dawned again with something of·an anticlimax; and
the sails of a tall ship gleamed faintlier, as the *Northumberland* went down a sunlit avenue into the South Atlantic.
The world resumed its normal movement. Gentlemen in
ribbons returned with gusto to their protocols. Gentlemen
in stars exchanged significant nods in the deep corners of
conference chambers. Gentlemen in Garters resumed their
contemplation of themselves in the still mirror of English
politics. Abroad frontiers were traced and fortresses
changed hands, as M. de Metternich tripped neatly about
Paris, the Duke demurred, and Lord Castlereagh made his
reservations. At home Tories swelled with pride and
attended patriotic banquets; Whigs muttered darkly and
resolved to badger Prinny. Mr. Cobbett denounced his
betters; and his betters, for want of a graver menace,
denounced Mr. Cobbett. The Regent's tilbury spun by on
gleaming wheels, and his lady trailed equivocally about the
Continent. His subjects drank hock and soda-water,
gamed, read the *Morning Chronicle*, paid taxes, and prepared
for peace.

Parliament was not sitting; and in the pleasant turmoil
of an Allied occupation, whilst his office compiled muster
rolls of ' Waterloo men ' and distributed an unprecedented
largesse of one shilling a day to subalterns of five years'
service, Lord Palmerston went to France. The packet
sailed; the sea, as befitted England's last defence, was
rough; and the Secretary at War noted with a certain schoolboy glee " a very constant and general requisition for the
Steward." But at sight of a foreign coast he stiffened into
the more impressive attitudes of *Milord*, observed that
Havre—" this extraordinary place "—was picturesque, and

F   65

commented with professional severity upon the fortifications.
Yet he seemed to talk to everybody, to the old pilot who
brought them in, to the men in the Custom House, to small
boys in the street; and " with all my prejudice against the
French, I must own that there is a great deal of natural good
manners and civility among the lower classes and particularly
the women, which one does not meet with in England."
The white flag of King Louis was flying already, and the
Douaniers wore a shred of white in their preposterous French
hats.   But their conversation showed strong traces of former
loyalties in a tendency to dwell on British perfidy towards
Buonaparte; and his late designs had left an unpleasant
echo in a street urchin's song—

> *Bientôt plus de Guerre*
> *Tous les Rois sont morts.*
> *Il n'y a que l'Angleterre*
> *Qui résiste encore.*
> *Tiggi riggi Dong Dong La Beauté,*
> *Tiggi riggi Dong Dong ah c'est beau !*

The big Englishman pursued this Anglophobe of eight,
demanded all the verses, and received from the " lying
little dog " an unreliable assurance that his song began
with *Vive le Roi*.   Then he gave a seat in his carriage to a
Cambridge friend, whose attainments included religious
architecture, and drove to Rouen, where they saw sights and
interrogated beadles, barmaids, postillions, hairdressers,
boatmen, carters, and National Guards, receiving those
unbounded praises of British troops and even hopes of British
annexation, which are the current coin of occupied territories.
These duties performed, they took the road for Paris.

It was in the confused, hot weeks that followed Waterloo,
when peace walked the streets in strange international
disguises. Uhlans, Austrian dragoons, Life Guards, and
Chevauxlegers clanked by ; egregious Cossacks stared at the
buildings; generously frogged hussars jingled past in
dolmans; shakos of every shape met *schapskas* tilted at
every angle; and variegated, tasselled, plumed, and crested,
the victorious helmets swarmed on the crowded pavements.

The Bois was full of Guardsmen; English bivouacs improved
the monotony of foreign avenues by felling trees; and
Prussian bandsmen fished under the solemn windows of St.
Cloud.   Even Mr. Croker had been amused " to see the old
Life Guards patrolling the Boulevard last night, as they used
to do Charing Cross during the Corn riots "; and the strange
scene greeted Palmerston.   He watched a great parade of
Prussians in the Champ de Mars.   Their dismal King rode
slowly down the lines with his little moustache and his
harassed air; and as the files went stiffly by, the tall dome of
the Invalides looked down, and the watching Englishman
judged the Uhlans " with their little black and white striped
flags at the end of their lances " to have " a very singular and
pretty effect at a distance."   On the next day he went to
Grenelle and saw them in manœuvres.   The Duke was there;
and they had some talk upon the superiority of line to
column, with instances from Bussaco and Albuera.   Something was said about the army of Waterloo—" that he
started with the very worst army that ever was got together;
but that four or five regiments who had been in the Peninsula
soon gave a tone and character to the whole army."   They
touched on the Prussian discipline, on the impolicy of
requisitions, the virtue of smartness in the private soldier,
and the unequalled sense of honour among British officers.
There was a manœuvre and march past of Austrian cavalry,
with a display of Polish lancers and big cuirassiers charging
in tall helmets.   But the greatest day of all was the morning
of the British review, when the Duke mimicked Salamanca
in graceful reminiscence across the open fields between
Montmartre and St. Denis.   The Prussians had rehearsed
their performance for two days, and their ground was pegged
" with little posts with bunches of straw on the top of them."
But Wellington's men moved with precision through a
brilliant impromptu.   The Blues charged imperturbably
across open ditches;   the Highlanders excited feminine
admiration with their swinging kilts;   and two Emperors
and the King of Prussia took the salute as, sixty thousand
strong, the scarlet lines swung past.

His evenings took him to Lady Castlereagh's or to the theatre, where loyal audiences applauded every reference to Henri IV. with the monotonous fervour of recent converts. He was an eager tourist, talking interminably to Frenchmen, Allies, diplomats, and total strangers; and his sightseeing took the affable Viscount over the Invalides and into the Louvre, where British sentries guarded workmen at the congenial task of removing Napoleon's stolen pictures. He even reached the top of the arch outside the Tuileries, whilst busy Engineers were lowering the big bronze horses, bound once more for Venice; and he ventured as far as Champagne to see a Russian review. All along the white road *sotnias* of Cossacks were lying in the shade and waiting for the Emperor of Austria to pass; and he found the traffic strangely mixed—" here a Prussian barouche, with forage and baggage tied in every out-of-the-way manner; there an English travelling carriage; at one place a French diligence, which resembled a caravan theatre at a fair more than any other machine; at another, a tandem with two English aides-de-camp and their groom; at one moment a great French cart; at another a little Russian waggon with four ponies abreast." The sharp eye watched the Russians under the broad, pale skies of Champagne; and he dined with the Czar, that singular compound of Romanoff and Methodist who, short-sighted and a little deaf, refreshed his principles with the nightly draughts of a Livonian evangelist irreverently diagnosed by Castlereagh as " an old fanatic who had a considerable reputation among the few high-flyers in religion that are to be found at Paris." Then they all drove back; Lord Palmerston dined at Malmaison with the Combermeres and saw the Emperor's round-backed chair at the end of the deep, pillared library, whilst a few miles away Alexander, flushed with moral purpose, elevated in an impulsive hand the strange torch of the Holy Alliance, announcing with richly Scriptural allusions the approaching union of the human race in a single family with Russia, Austria and Prussia for elder brothers and the Prince Regent as a likely relative. The sudden act promoted Christianity into foreign

policy; and for a splendid moment Holy Writ seemed almost
to acquire the validity of a treaty. As her imperial acolyte
murmured this singular incantation over the *status quo*,
Madame de Krüdener clasped delighted hands; M. de
Metternich tried hard to be respectful and hoped that what
looked like religion might be only philanthropy; and Lord
Castlereagh, with greater candour, wrote a little grimly that
"the Emperor's mind is not completely sound." Lord
Palmerston, unconcerned with these high matters, strolled
round picture galleries and buhl shops, until the War
Department claimed him. Then he took the road once
more, saw sights at Chantilly, clattered through Boulogne,
talked, still expansive, to the postboy and went on board the
packet at Calais. Respectful winds conveyed the Secretary
at War to Dover. His Odyssey was ended; and soon he was
safe again in Stanhope Street among his papers. South of
the Line a ship sailed on through sunny weather, until in the
failing light of an October day a black island stood up out of a
leaden sea.

V

THE war was ended. Ended, it left (like other wars) the
fond illusion of a possible return to pre-war. Memories
reached backwards; and, as always, there was a vague,
half-conscious craving for normal times. Unformed and
mainly unexpressed, it reached towards the past, towards
the vanished life which men still recalled from the days
before the war. But the past had faded somehow. It
was so distant now, as it lay twenty years away behind
the pleasant mists of the Eighteenth Century; and it
beckoned with the faint, receding gesture of a remembered
dream. Something, perhaps, remained—Lord Liverpool,
macao, the Regent, Almack's, the hunting field, watch-
men, and the fancy. Corinthians sustained the *rôle* of
Mohawks; Mr. Cruikshank plied Mr. Gillray's pencil;
poets still scanned couplets, although Lord Byron praised
his dark Zuleika in the most disordered metres and Mr.
Wordsworth expressed an unnatural preference for landscape. Yet so much had faded. The Regency might
be a lingering echo of the Eighteenth Century. But the
old air came softly now over a muted instrument; and
other, newer voices seemed to break in upon it. Harsh
commands were spoken by new masters; and there was
a rising murmur above the droning wheels in the raw
northern towns. The new voices crowded unrestfully in
the growing stir. A nation trooped to work; and strange
figures moved across blackened fields, strange eddies through
the still air. The stir deepened; and flame began to spout
from chimneys, and the skies were smeared. Trade found a
voice in the dull clang of workshops and the shrill creak of
winding-gear; and when Mr. Huskisson informed the
startled Commons that City merchants were arriving in the

squares at the west end of the town and took their dinner, not at two o'clock, but at six or seven, it seemed that politics might almost cease to be a genteel alternation of well-connected persons. The old air persisted; but new voices rose across its unchanging melody. Within doors the candles of the Eighteenth Century still burned. But in the little wind that runs before the day they flickered; and outside the sky was pale with the dawn of the Nineteenth Century.

In these uncomfortable and remote beginnings of the modern world, when shy steam-engines drove infrequent mills in sylvan Lancashire, Lord Palmerston sat at the War Office between two centuries. Formed by the Eighteenth, he still seemed to linger in it. Perhaps, indeed, a lifelong citizen of that polite republic, he never left it; and where he took his way through the deepening shadows, the glowing ardours of the Nineteenth, Palmerston walked always by the clear and regulated light of the Eighteenth Century. He had his manners from his cheerful mother and the little world of Sheen, that lively echo of Bath junketings. He had his notions of policy from old Lord Malmesbury, who dispensed his leonine wisdom in interminable reminiscence of a vanished Europe where England, France, and Prussia, untroubled by principles, walked an unending minuet of varying alliances. And had he not grasped the succession of Mr. Pitt in his first candidature at Cambridge? This fresh young man, who formed a part (though scarcely a vital part) of Lord Liverpool's administrative apparatus for perpetuating the past, belonged inevitably to his own beginnings, to the clear-eyed generation which knew in a happy time before knowledge had become difficult. His century did not ask questions: it answered them. Lord Palmerston was always ready with an answer; and rarely tortured by the speculations which drove his contemporaries to doubt, to test-tubes, or to Rome, he dwelt secure among the certainties of the Eighteenth Century. His age had formed him; and through the thickening air of the new century he retained its clarity and its poise, a cheerful *revenant* from that bland, unhurried world.

His career, in 1815, was curiously arrested. The rising
hope of Mr. Spencer Perceval, he had been summoned almost
from the nursery and thought of in mid-war for the Treasury.
All but Chancellor at twenty-five, this self-appointed
successor of Mr. Pitt might have seemed to rival his master.
He had grazed success.   But a cautious refusal relegated him
to the War Office, judged "better suited to a beginner";
and for nineteen years that vortex in its slow rotation drew
him down.   The apprenticeship became a habit, and his
brief initiation was dangerously prolonged.   Lulled by the
rhythms of routine, he graduated interminably in office
forms; he learned to weigh a precedent and acquired a
creditable command of that majestic diction in which
Departments clothe their lightest fancies; and innumerable
controversies, conducted with the elaborate etiquette of
strict administrative decorum, exercised his strong natural
powers of contention.   Yet this long imprisonment failed
signally to impair him.   The assiduous minister was always
alert, and sometimes sprightly.   Drugged with official
detail, he retained his spirits with a bright observant eye for
Paris and the *beau monde*.   His style survived his drafting;
and for nineteen years Lord Palmerston sustained without
ill effects the blameless *rôle* of the Industrious Apprentice.

His office, it must be confessed, was not enthralling.
The War Department, when a war is over, assumes an air
that is at once bellicose and unheroic; and it presided a
little fussily over the conquerors of Napoleon, whom it
alternately exasperated by ingenious reductions of pay
and consoled with tremendous excesses of sartorial magnificence.   Coatees grew tighter in the shade of stupendous
busbies; plumes brushed the sky; and the Prince Regent
offended Whigs in their most civilian scruples with his invariable Field-Marshal's uniform and an immense cocked hat.
The Secretary at War discoursed on pensions and reduced
the Irish staff.   He listened respectfully, whilst Lord John
Russell enjoined economy with copious historical allusions
and a citation of Blackstone.   Then, refusing blandly to
reciprocate Mr. Brougham's accusation that he very seldom

troubled the House with his observations, he eschewed general principles and addressed himself to the Estimates for 1816, enunciating *à propos* of the Canadian border a sturdy conviction that " there was no better means for securing the continuance of peace and tranquillity to any country than to have it known that any possessions in the neigh-bourhood of a foreign state were in a condition to repel attack. He was firmly persuaded that among nations weakness would never be a foundation for security." Whigs might be scandalised by the nascent militarism displayed in the formation of the United Service Club, " where military men alone are admitted and where of course the general topics of conversation must be of a military nature," and by the sentries who offended British eyes outside Somerset House and the British Museum. But the Secretary at War was unperturbed. That autumn he resumed his travels and saw the Loire at Tours, the Rhone at Lyons, and a great part of central France. In the next year he had his Estimates again and grappled with the grave problem of the liability of marching troops to bridge tolls. Once, with a sudden reminiscence of his Churchmanship and his electors, he gratified Cambridge with a word on tithes; and in a copy-right debate he upheld the privileges of the University Library. He found time for an offer, made in his character of Irish landlord, to oblige the Chief Secretary by the creation of " from 280 to 290 votes by giving leases to tenants who were now holding at will." But he was mostly bound on the slowly revolving wheel of the War Department, reducing establishments and adjusting claims in its grave idiom, whilst Wellington hunted the country round Cambrai with the senior pack of the Army of Occupation, and at the Horse Guards the Duke of York, in whom young Mr. Greville detected " the feelings of an English gentleman " although " the men with whom he lives most are *très-polissons* and *la polissonnerie* is the *ton* of his society," fulfilled with vigour the more exacting *rôle* of the Soldiers' Friend.

The world went on. The Prince approached the dreadful year in which a startled Whig acquainted Mr. Creevey that

" Prinny has let loose his belly, which now reaches to his
knees." It had its terrors for Lord Palmerston as well;
since an officer, maddened perhaps by correspondence with
the War Department, lurked on his office stairs and shot at
him. The wound was slight; the escaping minister paid the
costs of his assailant's defence; and whilst the impulsive
critic went to Bedlam, Lord Palmerston pursued his departmental way. This year the Estimates were enlivened by his
rather brutal comment on a Whig that his speech " was
entirely made up of threadbare references to the establishment of 1792, and it really appeared to him that an allusion
to the period of the Saxon heptarchy would be as applicable
to the present circumstances "; and he paid a tribute (for
it was the year 1818) to the value of the army in civil
disturbances. That summer he engaged in a curious dispute,
insisting on his right to direct reproof by the Prince Regent
rather than by intervention of his secretary, for the grave
offence of sending in mere triplicate a document of which the
Crown was entitled to four copies. It contained the monthly
watchword of the London sentries, supplied (as Palmerston
irreverently conjectured) " in the event, I suppose, of the
Sovereign wishing like Haroun Alraschid to perambulate the
streets incognito." The point was fully argued; and,
this duty solemnly discharged, he sailed again for France to
visit the Army of Occupation in its last phase.

Once more he saw the slow climb of the coast to Grisnez;
and the Calais windows, where Mr. Brummell kept his
exile, watched the mail-packet anchor in the dusk of an
October evening. Twelve hours had brought him from
Stanhope Street to Dover, twelve more to Calais; and a
final twelve took him to Cambrai. He dined at headquarters and, until the Allied reviews began, employed
himself in instructive sightseeing. He observed the landscape, viewed canals, studied the battlefields of 1814,
and noted the startling silhouette of Laon. Then he
vanished into a whirl of military brilliance. A borrowed
troop-horse carried him to watch twenty thousand Russians
march stiffly by in the early light of a late autumn morning;

and he trotted off to see the grand review outside Valenciennes, where British, Russians, Hanoverians, Saxons, and
Danes performed a martial charade prettily composed by the
Duke, who felt (as he confessed apologetically to Palmerston)
" that he was writing a Harlequin Farce." There were
dashing charges of assorted cavalry, cannonades, and German
infantry in line of columns which reminded somebody of
plantations in a gentleman's park; the whole crowned by
complete victory over a phantom enemy and the triumphant
exhibition of a new pontoon bridge, the pride of the British
service, " supported by large long casks." Palmerston, who
rode with Marshal Beresford, saw the red-coats and exclaimed " How beautiful ! " and heard " that Hurrah !
which can never be heard by an English heart without
emotion." There was an official dinner complicated by
awkward problems of the precedence of kings and emperors
and adorned by the Duke's " perfection of manner " in this
exalted company. Then they drove to Maubeuge, " a dirty
filthy hole, fit only for a Russian army," and ungratefully
regarded with the sceptical eye of Allies " two servants who
. . . wanted only to be tatooed and covered with a mat to
pass for South Sea Islanders." In these austere surroundings they attended a state ball. The drive went on along
the frontier. Travelling in the Duke's wake, they jolted
slowly behind French post-boys, behind ploughboys on
cart-horses, behind Russian artillery drivers who, taking
them for Russian artillery, drove them into ditches. Then
an angular line of ramparts came up against the night sky,
and they clattered past dark houses into a strange little town
of woollen mills. It was Prussian headquarters; and
perhaps a distant omen lurked in the name. For in the
morning they watched Ziethen put his army through its
carefully rehearsed paces in the ring of green hills, which
make a trap of Sedan.

That day the Duke was almost voluble. Eloquent as ever
upon the superiority of line to column, he pointed, thumped
his fist, and explained how the French columns used to
waver from the rear, until one saw them " huddling together

and running to the right and left . . . so that at a little
distance they went waddling like ducks." He had a vivid
memory of one British line, which he had re-formed at
Waterloo " about twenty yards from the flash of the French
column." The Prussians gave them dinner in a riding-school
tastefully festooned with lengths of white military trousering
ornamented with scarlet material for facings, " none of which "
(as Palmerston noted with a departmental eye) " were cut so
as to be less useful afterwards." Having dined and danced,
they drove into the Ardennes. Their road was complicated
by "swarms of Grand Dukes and Generals, &c."; and
with assiduous flattery they coaxed a song out of the un-
attractive daughter of a post-house on the frontier. The
Russians were in Givet, and they saw the new works at
Namur, where a prophetic Belgian engineer " seemed to
think rather too much of the principle of fear in fortifications." The road to Brussels took them past Quatre Bras
and Waterloo. They thrilled with pride, cut sticks at
Hougomont, picked up the usual bullets, and " bought a
French sword which probably never saw the battle." Then
the tour was over.

An ungrateful country drifted uneasily through the
new century, stoning short-tempered Yeomanry, reading
Don Juan, puzzled by Finance Committees, and hooting
ministers. A new Princess rejoiced the Duke of Kent and
narrowly escaped the name of Georgina. Lady Jersey
paraded her mechanical singing-birds, Prince Leopold his
bereavement. Lord Palmerston had the Estimates for 1819,
and saw a lively riot in the Westminster election, that
brought out the Life Guards and almost engulfed pretty
Lady Cowper on her way home from the Ladies' Committee
of Almack's. He loyally recommended Cambridge men for
choice incumbencies, and even proposed the daring experiment of promoting to the Bench a law lecturer, who had long
been a rewarding object of undergraduate humour and died
soon afterwards " in the full vigour of his incapacity." But
his own political paternity was plainly acknowledged in
his praise of this eccentric's devotion to " those constitutional

principles upon which the administration of this country has
been fortunately conducted by Mr. Pitt and those who have
succeeded him.'' The eager Pittite shrank, with Lord Liverpool, from the ferment of the age; and, at a threat of political
meetings in Hampshire, he stiffly signed a counter-requisition
to the high-sheriff. For he was disinclined to bring the
conflagration to the gates of Broadlands. Then the old
King, alone at Windsor in his dream of Bute and Pitt and
Mr. Wilkes, faded out of a world which he had long forgotten,
which had forgotten him still longer. The Regent reigned at
last; and Carlton House, superb with Gothic dining-room,
rose satin drawing-room, and fringed velvet throne-room,
became a palace.

VI

A NEW reign dawned on the learner at the War Department. He was nearing forty now, and the ageing apprentice
was still in his indentures. His Corinthian monarch was
proclaimed, a trifle unwell, behind the Ionic splendours of his
palace. Corinthian as well, a world top-hatted and pro-
digiously lapelled heard the news, looked over vast cravats,
and stared from between the stiff, enclosing wings of monumental collars. And, no less Corinthian, Lord Palmerston
administered the army.

His files engaged him deeply, and twice a year he spoke in
Parliament. But he was much seen in the bright world
where Lady Cowper danced and *Tom*, *Jerry* and *Logic the
Oxonian* looked on respectfully at Almack's—

> To give their graceful motions scope,
> Now, *tightly stretched*, the barrier rope
> Hems in quadrillers, nymph and spark,
> Like bounding deer within a park;
> Now *dropped*, transforms the floor again,
> For waltzers, to an open plain.

Once safely past the scrutiny of the Ladies' Committee,
a stylish company leaned out from the gold bar of this
social Heaven, parading nightly under the stern eye of
Mr. Willis and the cold stare of the lady patronesses. A
frequent ornament of this assembly, Lord Palmerston
quadrilled and watched its elegant inmates—" the *imperious*
Duchess, the *proud* Marchioness, the *stiff* Countess, the
starched-up Lady, the *consequential* Honourable Fair One,
the *upstart* Mrs., the *contemptuous* Beauty, the *pert* Coquette,
the *turn-up-nose* Demure Creature, the *squeamish* Miss, and
the *fastidious* Patronesses "—to say nothing of the dark
divinity of the Whigs, who fascinated Mr. Creevey and, like

one of her own mechanical singing-birds, " begins to sing at
eleven o'clock, and, with the interval of the hour she retires
to her cage to rest, she sings till twelve at night without a
moment's interruption . . . changes her feathers for dinner,
and her plumage both morng. and eveng. is the happiest
and most beautiful I ever saw," or the more substantial
charms of that " fine tall lady " who awed *Corinthian Tom*,
" a noble mistress to her servants, a perfect lady to her
tradespeople and dependents, an honourable acquaintance
with an enlarged mind, and her mansion near the Regent's
Park, to all her visitors, is a complete picture of magnificence
heightened by hospitality."

His modish leisure passed among such social pinnacles.
Like *Tom*, he knew the pleasures of

> charming sights,
> On gala nights;
> Masquerades,
> Grand Parades.

The sharp eye of Madame Lieven, busy at Almack's among
' vouchers ' and ' single tickets,' saw him with her pretty
friend, Lady Cowper.   For him " a *turn* or two in Bond
Street, a *stroll* through Piccadilly, a *look-in* at Tattersall's, a
ramble through Pall Mall, and a *strut* on the *Corinthian Path*,"
or the wilder charms of

> Four-in-hand
> Down the Strand;
> Funny gigs
> With knowing wigs;
> Baxter's hats
> That queer the flats;
> Flashy whips
> With silver tips;
> Leathern breech,
> Pretty stitch !
> High-bred cattle,
> Tittle-tattle.

He could see Vestris dance and Saqui fly and the Saloon at

Covent Garden and Sadler's Wells and the fireworks at
Vauxhall, could even

> Hear Kean speak,
> Grimaldi squeak !

Nor was he unknown to those "fox-hunting clericals,
sprigs of nobility, stylish coachmen, smart guards, saucy
butchers, tidy helpers, knowing horse-dealers, betting
publicans, neat jockeys," who composed Pierce Egan's
inventory of the sporting world. It was a brisk and cheerful
scene, where impulsive persons were apt to wager ' Carlton
House to a Charley's shelter ' and the learned were "as
familiar with the odds upon all events as Chitty in quoting
precedents." He moved easily among " the *pinks* of the
swells, the *tulips* of the goes, the *dashing* heroes of the
military "; and sometimes, like Tattersall's auctioneer, he
found that " the nod from a stable-keeper is quite as important, if not more so, as the wink of a Right Honourable."
For the complete Corinthian was equally at home at Almack's,
Tattersall's or the War Department.

So royal mourning brought in the year 1820; and Mr.
Croker gravely studied Admiralty practice on a demise of
the Crown and drove down to Windsor on a raw winter
night for the King's funeral, to hear the dismal note of horns
in the Great Park. His sovereign was severely indisposed;
and while the surgeons bled him, the public mind regarded
his array of brothers with grave distaste and dwelt without
enthusiasm upon the prospect of the rapid succession of King
Frederick I., the egregious William, and the Regent Ernest.
The fretful patient faced a graver problem. He had a
Queen; he had a Church, whose loyalty impelled it to pray
weekly for both its sovereigns. Such fervour was embarrassing, since solemn gentlemen argued that if she was
fit to introduce to God, she might be fit to introduce to man;
and the Defender of the Faith, surrounded by Prayer-Books
of all sizes, studied the awkward syllogism. It preyed upon
his mind; but timely bleeding saved him, and he recovered.
His ministers, secured from the avenging blades of Thistle-

wood by an extremely illegible letter handed to someone in
the Park and a dark scuffle in a back street off the Edgware
Road, plunged into the tumultuous delights of a General
Election. Their country, assisted by an eccentric franchise,
affirmed its continued devotion to Lord Liverpool; and
Palmerston retained the War Department. His loyalty to
Cambridge was burnished by this fresh contact with his
constituents; and that year he got a deanery for his late tutor
and ran a candidate for the Master's Lodge at Trinity. One
night in March he dined at Mr. Croker's with his sister Fanny,
fluttered by her approaching wedding, to meet the gifted
Mr. Scott. The Arbuthnots were there—she with her looks
and he with his buttoned, Treasury air. But the poet, in
town to kiss hands for his baronetcy, was the *clou*. He was
looking older now; and no one liked to tell him that *The
Monastery* was not half so good as *Ivanhoe*. So he went on
to give his sittings to Sir Thomas Lawrence and to have his
audience—" I shall always reflect with pleasure on Sir
Walter Scott's having been the first creation of my reign "—
and they went home to Stanhope Street.

That year the Army debates were scarcely more enthralling
than usual. But an attack upon the Military College elicited
a familiar note from Palmerston, who " wished to see the
British soldier with a British character, with British habits,
with a British education, and with as little as possible of
anything foreign." He had his Estimates in June. A
passing faintness interrupted him; but he resumed on the
same evening. Four days later his Queen (for she was still
his Queen) stepped heavily ashore at Dover; and his
sagacious observations in the adjourned debate died on the
uproar. He spoke in praise of the military in civil disturbances and dilated on the beauties of the unreformed
Constitution in contrast with the depravity of " those self-
called but misled reformers." Meanwhile his countrymen
hunted a livelier covert. The Queen was home, pursuing
her reluctant consort with an odd blend of menace and appeal.
This insistent figure, half-dragon and half damsel in distress,
filled the whole stage with movement. Crowds cheered

G

along the Dover road; women waved handkerchiefs; and
men of feeling thought of her wrongs, repressed their swelling
hearts, and went out to break carriage windows, while
mysterious symptoms of insubordination were even noted in
the Guards. Malicious Whigs presided with broad grins
over a carnival of chivalrous disorder, which rose to a
crescendo when ministers, abandoning liturgical niceties,
moved to deprive their victim of her title and her husband.
The august divorce engaged the House of Lords for months.
The heroine, who supported her tragic *rôle* a trifle inadequately, made a surprising entry in black figured gauze and
thickly veiled, with big lawn sleeves, in which she " popped
all at once into the House, made a *duck* at the Throne,
another to the Peers, and a concluding jump into the chair
which was placed for her." Safely alighted, she startled
Mr. Creevey close behind with the undulations of her ample
back and the distasteful spectacle of " a few straggling
ringlets on her neck," while Lady Cowper found on the royal
sufferer's face an unseasonable hue " of brickdust." This
Queen of Beauty watched an interminable tournament, in
which the forms of law were exquisitely protracted by the
forms (no less majestic) of Parliamentary debate. Tried by a
jury of two hundred, the case became a legal nightmare.
Each juror was an advocate as well, and each pleaded
at becoming length with his two hundred colleagues.
Counsel submitted to the House; the House debated;
*Judges advised on points of law; and then, the point decided,
counsel submitted once again. The seasons passed; exasperated peers, detained in town, mourned their deserted
coverts; Newmarket was a wilderness that autumn; and
the unending argument went on. Charges ramified and
shifted; an inglorious procession of preposterous foreigners
perjured themselves with inexhaustible resource, as ' *Non mi
ricordo* ' passed into proverb; and outside the people of
England joyfully hooted remembered faces in Palace Yard,
cheered Radicals for their white top-hats, wore favours
chivalrously inscribed *Protection to the Innocent*, purchased
memorial bottles in the image of Mr. Brougham and his

Queen, or marched five abreast in lock-step through
Piccadilly to cheer the injured lady. The autumn faded into
winter; and there was an end at last. The year went out
on a receding shape in black figured gauze; and a retreating
echo of distinctly ribald songs came faintly up the wind.

But these uproarious standards were scarcely maintained
by 1821. A slight exhaustion settled on the delirious scene.
Yet decorum seemed to tarry, and a vociferous playgoer at
Drury Lane could still address the royal box with the
stentorian enquiry, "Where's your wife, Georgy?" The
War Department pursued its sober path, and Lord Palmerston continuing his cautious wooing of economy pressed in
private for reductions at Heligoland and the Isle of Man.
But in the House of Commons he insisted bravely upon the
inadequacy of pre-war establishments and turned a deaf ear
to Mr. Creevey, when that angry veteran, shocked by a
salary of £1,400 a year, enquired at what hour the War
Office clerks attended and whether they arrived in curricles
or tilburies. His repertory of Whig inanities received a
rich addition from Lord John Russell, who publicly deplored
the lamentable prevalence at the Military College of military
education and (scarcely less reprehensible) of instruction
in the French language. Little Lady Cowper, with a bright,
attentive eye for his career, avowed herself "very glad to
find Lord Palmerston has done himself such credit by the
talent, discretion, and temper he has displayed during all
this time, and if Hume has not managed to reduce the
Estimates, he has at least reduced the Secretary at War,
for he is grown as thin again as he was." The belle, who
reigned at Almack's with Madame Lieven, found her husband's ailments more trying now, although she gratified her
brother with a dutiful avowal of "Lord Cowper's kindness
and good nature to me, which is so very great that I really
do not know how sufficiently to show my gratitude for it."
The reference was a trifle stiff, and so was Cowper. But
Palmerston was less exacting. That year, encouraged by
the bright gaze of Lady Conyngham, his sovereign was
crowned in an ecstasy of tailoring. The town nodded with

plumes, muffled itself in ermine, and trailed unaccustomed
robes; even the ornamental water in St. James's Park wore
Chinese bridges for the occasion. A grateful public stared
and was rewarded by the unusual spectacle of an angry
Queen alighting at the Abbey and tramping from door to
door without a ticket. The unhappy lady had her cheers,
but missed the Coronation. Inside, the organ peeled, the
bishops prayed, and George received the sacred oil. But in
the summer streets his indefatigable mate trailed her eternal
sorrows before a thinning crowd. In three weeks a voice
behind her bedcurtains exclaimed, faintly apologetic, " I
am going to die, Mr. Brougham; but it does not signify."
She spoke the truth at last, and died; and it did not
signify.

   There was a shift of offices that autumn. Lord Liverpool,
perennially Prime Minister, offered a peerage and the Post
Office to his industrious Secretary at War. But Palmerston,
still faithful to the War Department, disdained these
glories and declined the elevation. His loyalty to this
impassive goddess survived a further offer of ennoblement in
the next year. Mr. Huskisson was growing a trifle restless
at the Woods and Forests and pressed for more active
employment. The War Office seemed a likely opening; and
the Prime Minister, anxious to create a vacancy and feeling
that, perhaps, in thirteen years its charms might have faded
for Palmerston, dangled a coronet once more. But he
declined and sat on immovably amongst his files; whilst
young Mr. Peel, his junior by four years, passed above him
to the Home Office. That year the Estimates went still
more smoothly, though startled Whigs referred to the
innocent orphans of the Military Asylum as " artificial
Mamelukes," and Palmerston was forced to urge, as pathetic
evidence of the industrious habits prevailing in his Department, that since 1810 twenty-six clerks had died in their
prime of pulmonary and other disorders due to their sedentary
lives. But large reductions silenced the Opposition; and
even the indefatigable Mr. Hume, who was to Palmerston's
unfriendly eye " so dull and blunderheaded a fellow, not-

withstanding all his perseverance and application," plied a
feebler oar against the stream. A blow fell in the summer,
when Castlereagh quite scared the Duke with his odd fancies.
That " splendid summit of bright and polished frost which,
like the travellers in Switzerland, we all admire, but no
one can hope, and few would wish to reach," was strangely
clouded. He started at chance words; his head was an
unhappy whirl of wild escapes from illusory dangers; and
left alone, the hunted man escaped one summer morning,
as Castlereagh lurched forward under a startled doctor's
eyes, clutching a little knife.

There was a grim frequency of such ends in that hurried,
anxious time—" an awful period," as it seemed to Sydney
Smith—when Europe still pitched on the long swell that
followed Waterloo and the clouds of disorder hung low over
England. The burden, which had already broken Romilly
and Whitbread, was heavy. Wild politics, long hours, and
port did something to increase it; and it was scarcely
lightened by a medical faculty which bled mercilessly and
mistook debility for rest. So Castlereagh, whom six months
before Mr. Croker had found " *better* than ever, that is,
colder, steadier, more *pococurante* ", was gone. A London
mob cheered horribly at sight of the coffin, and the waiting
group inside the Abbey thought that it was a shout for the
Duke. His death left an awkward gap on the Treasury
Bench; and there was an anxious flutter among the Tories.
The names of Mr. Canning and even of Mr. Peel were canvassed for the lead in the Commons. But there was a sad
dearth of competent lieutenants. Mr. Robinson was thought
of, and Lord Palmerston spoke highly of his talents and
eloquence. Many preferred Palmerston himself, judging
him to be " as powerful in intellect as Robinson and much
more to be relied on in readiness and nerve." Scarcely,
perhaps, a lofty compliment, it marks a considerable advance
on Lady Minto's tepid praise of him eleven years before for
being " painstaking and gentlemanlike to the highest degree."
But Mr. Croker, although he found him by far the ablest
of the departmental ministers, doubted his possession of

" that *flow* of ideas and language which can run on for a couple of hours without, on the one hand, committing the Government, or, on the other, lowering by commonplaces or insincerities the station of a Cabinet Minister." Once more, as Mr. Canning impended, promotion passed him by. His sovereign, fortified by the cheering presence of Lady Conyngham, took the distasteful draught. He sang his trios " not so much from the notes as from recollection," made his royal contribution (in a hearty bass) to *Life's a Bumper*, *The Friar of Orders Grey*, and even *Glorious Apollo* ; and, refreshed by these exercises, the King swallowed Mr. Canning.

VII

THE advent of Mr. Canning in 1822 was, perhaps, the dawn of modern politics. Almost by premonition he waited for the summons in a large house at Liverpool, where a small Etonian named Gladstone kicked his heels; and far away a youth, who startled the other articled clerks with a black velvet suit and ruffles and the red clocks on his stockings, sauntered daily from Mr. D'Israeli's house in Bloomsbury Square to a solicitor's office in Old Jewry. For the first time since Mr. Pitt high office was held by a minister unconvinced of the perfection of the existing order. It was a daring change, since hitherto England had clung with a desperate persistence to the men who (in a more recent idiom) had won the war. The impulse was natural; but it tended inevitably to perpetuate the tense air of 1815, to wave off with angry gestures the altered facts of 1822. The little group of ageing men had lived too long with the sound of the French guns in their ears. They had, in the consecrated formula, saved England by their exertions; and having saved her from Napoleon, they persisted from sheer force of habit in saving her from herself. Few characters, perhaps, are more exasperating than a persistent rescuer; and as his country swam, it was considerably embarrassed by the hail of life-belts which Lord Liverpool rained angrily upon it. Yet the mistake was natural in men who had spent twenty years in watching the red glare on the sky over Paris and straining to catch the tramp of the armed and marching Revolution, which echoed down the streets of Europe until it rang a trifle hollow from the shuttered fronts of Moscow. Such vigils are not easily forgotten; and having saved England once, they went on saving her in their uneasy dream of pikes and tricolours and guillotines. Such visions are

unfriendly to reforming instincts; and at the first hint of
change they looked nervously behind them. Pilots who
weather storms of such severity frequently prefer to navigate
with hatches battened down and half the crew below, if
not in irons. Accustomed for twenty years to adjourn
reforms by ingeminating ' Revolution ' or ' Invasion ' or
' Let us beat the French first,' they retained the habit,
confronting the slightest change with an expression of tight-
lipped negation. England must still be saved; and her
perpetual saviours muttered their cautious incantations in a
magic circle traced by the Yeomanry and the Six Acts.
The throne, the franchise, even the fiscal system acquired an
almost religious sanctity; and they referred with ritual
frequency to the blessed memory of Mr. Pitt. There was a
steady drone of old tunes; and heads nodded to the litany of
reaction in a steam of Tory incense. But Mr. Canning broke
the spell.

That smiling figure, whom the angry memory of Mr.
Brougham embalmed as ' the Merryman,' presents a less
forbidding front. He talked; he wrote revealing letters;
he positively joked. In an age, when to be brief was to be
misunderstood and Canning by speaking intelligibly incurred
a dangerous reputation for unparliamentary flippancy, he
made no effort to conceal his wit. No less engaged in the
long duel with the Empire, he seemed to face it in a less
Æschylean mood than his portentous colleagues, to escape
the prevalent conviction that the world would be well-
advised to retain its present posture, since it was shortly
coming to an end. He preferred to feel that it had a future,
although his ranging mind was curiously uneven in its forecast. He called no less frequently than his contemporaries
upon the name of Mr. Pitt, claiming indeed that his political
allegiance lay buried in his grave. But, unlike the majority
of Pitt's worshippers, he did not confine his knowledge of
him to these invocations. Rare among Pittites, he took up
the tasks which Mr. Pitt had dropped when the war caught
him. For until the war Mr. Pitt had been a reforming
minister; and when the war was over, his reforming impulses

lived on in Mr. Canning, who resumed his interrupted tenderness for Roman Catholics with his distaste for restrictions
upon trade and even for negro slavery. This pious application of the liberal notions of 1784 to the widening demands of
1822 made an odd patchwork; and his dutiful executor
performed the codicils without a particular regard for consistency. The friend of Catholic Emancipation and Free
Trade suspended Habeas Corpus and opposed Reform. But
even these eccentricities scarcely impaired the novelty of
Mr. Canning, as he intruded blandly on the Tory mysteries.

Perpetually subordinate, Lord Palmerston sat on sedately
at the War Department. Attuned by thirteen years of
office, he sounded a decorous official note. But he could
regard the new minister with unusual sympathy, since he,
like Mr. Canning, inherited the opinions of Mr. Pitt. With
Mr. Pitt, he sat for Cambridge; with Mr. Pitt, he favoured
Catholic Emancipation. Mr. Canning had bravely sustained
that banner even in war-time; and Lord Palmerston, after
speaking in his independent vein upon the question in 1813,
had voted, silent but faithful, with those enlightened
minorities which Grattan and Canning led year by year
through the lobbies. This strange bias inclined him to
Mr. Canning, since on the Catholic question he had voted
steadily against his Tory colleagues for nine years. The
assiduous subordinate, who even shared his eccentric
opposition to Reform, shared his Catholic opinions. It
was a bond between them, Pittites both, which might make a
Canningite of Lord Palmerston.

A leg at Almack's or a gun at Chatsworth, much seen
in the fine world where ladies dressed in rich cashmeres,
" Lady C.'s a white and Lady E.'s a scarlet, the wide borders
of the shawls making the flounce of the gown," he was no
less sedulous at the War Office. As the last echoes of his
great dispute with the military died away after thirteen years
of rich reverberation, the files of 1823 rejoiced in a brisk
revival of the conflict. An incautious discharge of army
clerks by the civilian branch provoked the battle. The
Duke of York, with prompt discourtesy, challenged the

Secretary at War and cancelled the discharges. Lord
Palmerston requested the Horse Guards to transmit his
" most respectful but strongest Protest " against his
epistolary manner, together with his " humble but decided
opinion " that the Duke was wrong; and the Horse Guards
concluded gloomily that " a state of warfare with the War
Office forms an unavoidable though a very disagreeable
ingredient in the composition of the Military Secretary."
Lord Palmerston received the imputation with a cheerful
promise that " the War will be carried on with as much
courtesy as a State of Contest in its nature admits."   Matters
had reached this point, when the indignant Duke cancelled
a second order of his civilian colleague upon the vexed topic
of travelling expenses; and Palmerston turned wearily to
defend himself upon a new front.   The battle raged; both
combatants threatened vociferously to resign; and the
whole correspondence was referred with heavy annotations to
the Prime Minister, who read with more than his customary
bad temper Lord Palmerston's truculent demand that the
offending orders should be formally removed from the files
at the Horse Guards.   Refreshed by this heroic conflict,
he made his usual appearance on the Estimates.   The
milder temper of the age was reflected in his defence of a
court-martial upon a colonel for awarding twenty-five lashes
to a private guilty of the unblushing offence of keeping in his
pocket two blank cartridges, which should have been in his
cartouche box, and supporting his firelock with the angle of
the arm rather than with the palm of his hand.   But the
year was notable for his first utterance on foreign policy.'
France had marched into Spain to defend reaction; Mr.
Canning, declining to intervene, wrote that " a menace not
intended to be executed is an engine which Great Britain
could never condescend to employ "; and his subordinate
echoed the sentiment in the House of Commons—" To have
talked of war and to have meant neutrality, to have
threatened an army and to have retreated behind a state
paper, to have brandished the sword of defiance in the hour
of deliberation and to have ended with a penful of protests

on the day of battle would have been the conduct of a
cowardly bully." It was an echo of Mr. Canning; but one
seems for the first time to catch the voice of Palmerston.

He was still Tory enough at a pinch, when Mr. Cobbett
threatened the Game Laws and deplored the execution
of some poachers for shooting two of the Broadlands keepers;
and he could speak with the voice of Cambridge upon church
construction, lamenting the spread of Dissent in the most
becoming tones. It was a distant age, when Mr. Croker
studied wine-lists for the infant cellar of the Athenæum, and
Railway Committees angrily obstructed "this infernal
nuisance—the loco-motive Monster, carrying *eighty tons* of
goods and navigated by a tail of smoke and sulphur, coming
thro' every man's grounds between Manchester and Liverpool." Innocent of the approaching menace, the monarch
took the field at Ascot in a black cravat and scratch wig, with
a plain brown hat cocked over one eye and Lady Conyngham
just behind him, "hardly visible but by her feathers."
Yet the dreadful change impended; and his Secretary at
War (he was turned forty now) was not untouched by
more modern cravings. Had not ministers already laid
sacrilegious hands upon the fiscal system? Vansittart,
whom the Peerage knew as Lord Bexley and Mr. Creevey
by the less impressive name of 'Mouldy,' had left the
Treasury; and Mr. Robinson reigned in his stead. In his
first Budget, which closed with a remarkable sentence
fourteen lines in length, he fell into his familiar vein of
optimism, quoted poetry freely upon trade prospects, and
reduced taxation. He even shed scalding tears over his
tenderness for Ireland—"whether it arises from the circumstance of my having at one period of my life resided there
for nearly two years . . . I know not "—and lowered the
Irish spirit duties. But he announced the bold design of
"sweeping away the useless lumber of antiquated prejudices
and restrictions"; and in the next year, when Austria
struck him almost dumb by the repayment of an Allied loan
he employed the surplus in abolishing a number of duties.
While these destructive tendencies raged at the Treasury,
Mr. Huskisson at the Board of Trade made threatening

gestures at the no less venerable fabric of the Navigation
Acts; and, encouraged by Mr. Canning, Lord Liverpool
seemed to his startled countrymen to preside over a positive
Walpurgis of economic reform.

Untouched as yet by these commercial questions, Lord
Palmerston confined his progressive instincts to the Catholic
problem and expressed in the House of Commons a sober joy
in the advance already made towards Emancipation. He
had a thin House for the Estimates of 1825, although his
system of linked battalions was an ingenious provision for
the needs of foreign stations and anticipated by almost half a
century the reforms of Mr. Cardwell. A rare excursion
from War Office matters led him to advocate the construction of a Thames Embankment in relief of the congested
traffic in the Strand; and he reminded members that the
bad appearance of the foreshore was noticeable to them on
their way down the river for those whitebait with which
Greenwich consoled exhausted legislators. But a more
significant act was his presentation in unbroken silence of a
petition from his constituency against the Catholic demands.
Cambridge was growing restive under the Whiggish pre-
dilections of its member, and he was generally expected to
lose the seat at the next election. He was at the Castle for
Ascot with a royal summons to the race-course. But his
summer was darkened by a depressing tendency in his
stable to go lame precisely on the dates of his most cherished
country meetings, although he won five races out of eight at
Salisbury that year and one horse brought him two cups and
several stakes in the season. He went to his property in
Ireland, where he satisfied tradition by building a pier and
even projected "an iron railroad of about six miles in
length." Returning, he inspected a Welsh quarry, in which
he had some money, and felt similar longings for " a railroad
to the sea." Then he struck across to Yorkshire and viewed
a property of his, where the lime-works were getting into
order and he had hopes of coal. From these industrial
ardours (he even exasperated Mr. Canning that year by a
flutter on the Stock Exchange after a grave official warning)

he returned to Broadlands; but the birds were wild, and he
was soon at his desk in London, sending envious felicitations
to a friend who was " pursuing the wild Fox." Late in the
year he got a week at Brighton and stared respectfully at the
new lodging-houses "upon a grand style of architectural
decoration." So he strolled along the front and wondered
where enough lodgers to fill its Ionic splendours were coming
from, whilst young Mr. Disraeli, fresh from Abbotsford, sat
in the London mail and learnt from the tremendous publisher
opposite that a recent article of merit in the *Edinburgh* came
from the pen of " a young lawyer of the name of Macaulay."

But in the winter he settled down to a gloomy canvass
of the University in preparation for the General Election
of 1826. The skies were darkened by "the three C's—
Corn, Currency, and Catholics "; and the prospect, although
he faced it cheerfully, was not inviting, since the Cambridge
Tories actively resented his Catholic opinions, and in that
ancient seat of learning Tories abounded. The local flames
were fanned by his more Protestant colleagues—by Eldon,
who disliked his Popish leanings, and by the Duke of York,
who viewed without regret the possible removal of a contentious Secretary at War. In this predicament he still had
hopes " of a great many Protestants, from a coincidence of
opinion on other questions; and of many Whigs, from an
agreement on the Catholic question." The balance was
precarious; and in the cautious terms of his election address
he walked with the unaccustomed gait of Agag. For he
intended that "the Protestants will support me as a Tory,
and the Whigs as a Catholic "; and in this laudable ambition
he proffered Catholic Emancipation a trifle gingerly, adding
defensively that he could hardly hope that each of his
opinions would find equal favour with each elector. But in
his private appeals he unequivocally claimed to be supported
by all enemies of country clergymen and bigots; and whilst
the Whigs responded, the bigots pardonably looked elsewhere. The Tories left him; and he became, almost imperceptibly, Whig candidate for Cambridge. The Whig
world of Lady Cowper felt that he stood " on very ticklish

ground . . . he has all the Whigs and Radicals warm in his
favour." Even his appearances in Parliament that year
had quite a Whiggish flavour. When he presented a Cambridge petition against slavery, he made a little speech;
and his annual defence of flogging was more temperate than
usual. But he was mainly left to his electoral labours.
His straiter colleagues worked actively against him; and
when he protested to Lord Liverpool, he " acted as he always
does to a friend in personal questions—shabbily, timidly and
ill." The fissure widened, and he remembered it in later
years as " the first decided step towards a breach between
me and the Tories." But the Whig battalions saved him—
" the Whigs supported me most handsomely, and were
indeed my chief and most active friends "—and he was left
with lively memories of Tory hostility and Whig support.
Such services are not forgotten; and that summer he was
writing gratefully of their conduct. William Lamb had
stayed up to vote for him, and Lady Cowper had an anxious
eye for the contest. Indeed, he even told her that he felt
like a character in *Freischutz*, quite afraid that Lord Grey
would " come with his long arm and claim him as his own."
It was a strange confession for a Tory minister.

But in 1826 his Toryism was oddly diluted, and he could
write disparagingly of " the stupid old Tory party, who bawl
out the memory and praises of Pitt while they are opposing
all the measures and principles which he held most important." For the eager Pittite was slowly turning Whig.
He regarded his leaders with increasing disrespect—" old
women like the Chancellor, spoonies like Liverpool, igno-
ramuses like Westmoreland, old stumped-up Tories like
Bathurst "—and his mounting note of progress accorded
strangely with the more restful harmony of the benches
behind him : " on the Catholic question; on the principle
of commerce; on the corn laws; on the settlement of
the currency; on the laws regulating the trade in money;
on colonial slavery; on the game laws, which are intimately
connected with the moral habits of the people; on all these
questions, and everything like them, the Government will

find support from the Whigs and resistance from their self-denominated friends.'' So the perfect Canningite was half-way to Whiggery already.

Colleagues preceded him on other roads. The Board of Trade announced a bold intention '' to remove as much and as fast as possible all unnecessary restrictions upon trade.'' Mr. Huskisson turned an unfriendly gaze upon '' the old and helpless system of prohibitory protection '' and insisted that '' the rule of free competition is the best for all trades.'' Even the Treasury, where Mr. Robinson rolled his eloquent eye, reduced the price of sugar, although it met a demand for cheap bread with the kindly, but unwholesome, concession of cheap tobacco. The War Department did not present a favourable field for the display of liberal opinions. But Palmerston revealed his temper as an Irish landlord. He boldly rejoiced that Emancipation must result in '' the breaking loose of the Irish tenantry from their landlords ''; and after a satisfactory racing season (he ran four horses and beat '' some tolerable nags ''), to say nothing of a sober interruption occasioned by the purchase of a Methodist chapel to make a national school at Romsey, he went to Ireland. His harbour was most impressive now, and he was sighing for a railroad. He watched potatoes, had a critical eye for oats and barley, and was full of land-reclamation. His bogs were drained and planted, and his sand-hills kept in check. Two schools, a linen market, and a lime-kiln fell from his kindly cornucopia upon the thirsty ground of Sligo; and he had '' a great mind when I go to Cambridge at Christmas to see if I cannot find some zealous Simeonite who would curb the ardent enthusiasm which would impel him to the banks of the Ganges, and might content himself with winning his Jerusalem spurs by a campaign in the parish of Ahamlish,'' since '' a very great deal might be effected by a well-informed man who would talk to the people . . . even if he did not make Protestants of them, he might make them Christians.'' The easy landlord faced his bold conclusion— '' the days of Protestant ascendancy I think are numbered. It is strange that in this enlightened age and enlightened

country people should be still debating whether it is wise to
convert four or five millions of men from enemies to friends,
and whether it is *safe* to give peace to Ireland."

Freighted with these convictions, he returned to England,
to Lady Cowper and his slow drift towards Whiggery, and to
the Army debates. Twice that year he refused promotion
and even preferred his War Office files to the glories of a
Governor-General of India. The weary minister still
struggled with the intelligence of Mr. Joseph Hume, "so
deeply obtuse as to require these numerous repetitions and
explanations—repetitions and explanations more numerous
even than those in which the honourable gentleman was in
the habit of indulging." Then, leaving his tormentor "to
that impenetrable darkness which dwelt within the interior
of his brain," he turned with a snort that almost penetrates
the page of *Hansard* " to the House of Commons, not to the
honourable member for Aberdeen." The departmental
round continued in the shortening days of 1826. The
drafts, the files, the grievances were still the same; the
solemn stream of empty letters flowed without interruption
through the War Office; and the same figures that had
shadowed official life since the Peninsular War remained
immovably in place. The Duke of York still traced his
tremendous " Frederick " on General Orders; and Lord
Liverpool, in his sixteenth year of office, alarmed his
sovereign with the increasing sharpness of his temper.

But the official landscape was strangely altered in the
new year. For the Duke died in the first week of 1827
after ten thousand days, in Mr. Peel's alarming calculation,
as Commander-in-Chief. There was an exciting interlude
of three weeks, in which General Orders bore the civilian
name of Palmerston, while the King had some strange design
of wielding the thunderbolt of war himself. But a greater
Duke succeeded. Five weeks later Lord Liverpool collapsed
in his room; and Mr. Croker found " not only no grief, but
not even a decent pensiveness " at the Speaker's dinner.
Fluttered, perhaps, by this stupendous happening, Lord
Palmerston introduced the Estimates for 1827 in a tone so

hurried and suppressed as to be almost inaudible to the
reporters and to an accompaniment of members leaving the
House.   Two months of glorious manœuvre followed.   The
King demurred;   the Duke resigned;   the Tories left *en
masse*;   and when Mr. Canning made a Government of his
friends, Lord Palmerston entered the Cabinet at forty-two.

VIII

He was to have the Exchequer at last. It was nearly eighteen years since Mr. Spencer Perceval had offered it, a few months after Wagram, to a boy who preferred the long apprenticeship of the War Department. But he had served his time; and here was Mr. Canning on an April afternoon in 1827 asking him to be Home Secretary or Chancellor of the Exchequer. His anxious sovereign, in the intervals of whispering sporting intelligence behind his hand to Mr. Greville, insisted upon an anti-Catholic at the Home Office; and finally he was to have the Exchequer. Mr. Canning had his doubts, had even hinted to Madame Lieven that Palmerston's speculations were scarcely becoming in a Chancellor. But one night at Downing Street the Prime Minister asked him after dinner to take the office at once and go down to Cambridge for his by-election. But Mr. Croker, who had developed an unpleasing tendency to mutter in corners with Mr. Peel and the seceding Tories, suggested slyly that if he delayed until the autumn, he might be returned unopposed. The advice was taken; and, promoted to the Cabinet, he waited at the War Office for the end of the session, while Lady Cowper gleefully recorded that he was " very well pleased." The work was heavy, since the Duke was out and the Secretary at War commanded the army once more. That bland civilian made all military appointments and signed the General Orders; he even incurred irreverent comments by attending a review of Guards in uniform and taking the salute. But whilst he placidly awaited his elevation to the Treasury, the wind was changing. His sovereign, who disliked his views, even disliked his manner, confessing to a lady that there was *" quelque chose en lui qui me déplait—il a l'air toujours si fier."*

98

Besides, he was rebuilding Windsor in an expensive ecstasy
of feudal architecture, and there were awkward questions
about royal palaces and Crown estates, which the Chancellor
might meddle with; and Palmerston was always truculent.
It resulted that whilst his pretty friend at Panshanger was
still expecting him to go to the Exchequer in the autumn,
an embarrassed Prime Minister withdrew the offer. The
pill was gilded, since for the moment he had all the Army
business; and Mr. Canning offered him a peerage or anything else that he might desire, when it should revert to a
new Commander-in-Chief, together with a profusion of those
" general assurances which mean nothing at all." A little
later he tendered a yet more meagre solace to his follower
with the surprising statement that the King had said to
him that he had good reason to know that the thing of all
others which Lord Palmerston should like would be to
succeed the Duke of Manchester as Governor of Jamaica.
The royal divination was strangely at fault; since Palmerston, whose laugh was hearty, laughed so loudly that Mr.
Canning was quite put out. His gravity was less disturbed,
but he was equally unmoved, by a further offer of the
Governor-Generalship of India. He had refused it twice
before and now declined with a graceful reference to the
climate and (less credibly) to his health.

So, while the tropics called in vain, Lord Palmerston
remained immovably at the War Department, and Mr.
Creevey ungratefully reported that " everybody's language
is that the Army is going to the devil under Palmerston."
But in the summer, after that August night when the cloaked
gentleman of *Endymion's* heated recollection " emerged from
a club-house at the top of St. James's Street and descended
that celebrated eminence," the brief light of Mr. Canning
flickered out; and Lord Goderich, in whom ennoblement had
effaced few traces of Mr. Robinson, assumed the burden.
The strange amalgam of Whigs and Canningites was continued, although the Duke returned to the Horse Guards.
The indefatigable apprentice at the War Department was
thought of for the highest positions. Earlier in the year

Mr. Croker had fancied him for Foreign Secretary; and now his name was even mentioned as a possible Leader of the House. But he was eloquent upon the superior qualifications of Mr. Huskisson. Lacking the taste for promiscuous debating (Canning had deplored his inability to bring "that three-decker Palmerston" into action), he felt himself "quite unequal to it. To go no further than one point, the person so placed must be in a perpetual state of canvass; and of all irksome slaveries there is none more difficult to me than that; besides the character of the Government is, as it were, identified with the debating success of the individual." But he felt equal to the Exchequer and promptly accepted it. Once more the official sky mysteriously clouded. The Cottage frowned; Lord Goderich whimpered; and whilst Jove thundered, Palmerston stayed chained, like Prometheus, to his departmental rock. But there were consolations, since he was in the Cabinet now and could read the despatches and dabble in foreign affairs. Lady Cowper always had an informing stream of international anecdote. It came to her in the voluble, slightly gasping letters of Madame Lieven to her *chère chère, amie*, whose interest in Nesselrode and Pozzo was so temperate that they were meant, one feels, for manlier eyes. Tutored, perhaps, by this Egeria, Palmerston breathed a Russian air, mistrusted Austria, but added something of his own in his distaste for "Metternich's absolutism," when that slightly spiral pillar of the European system seemed to the novice to prefer "the tortuous to the straight course where the option is before him." A gleeful ear received "the smash at Navarino," when "the mere circumstance of our having made a bonfire of the fleet of our good ally . . . was not a declaration of war, but only a slight act of remonstrance struck parenthetically into unbroken friendship." One begins to catch the familiar echo of a jocular voice. He even scared his colleagues with a dashing project for a British landing in Greece to expel the Turks. Such were, in 1827, Lord Palmerston's lively variations on a theme of Mr. Canning.

So, as the perfect Canningite settled comfortably in among his Whig colleagues, watchful Lady Cowper (who had, perhaps, a hand in his conversion) noted him as " quite a late convert "; and he dreamed of a time when " Whig and Tory will soon be erased from our vocabulary." Such moods of toleration frequently precede a change of allegiance. That autumn he went to Ireland again, gazed proudly at his harbour, and made a concordat with his bishop which filled his schools with children. But soon he was back amongst his papers, disbanding Yeomanry and fixing retired allow-ances with a wary eye upon the country gentlemen in the House of Commons, " inclined to think that if upon Army Estimates the Yeomanry were to make good muster and charge us gallantly we could scarcely make head against a proposition in favour of some of these old adjutants." Mean-while the ' transient and embarrassed phantom ' of his Prime Minister pursued its brief and lachrymose course, wringing spectral hands over Cabinet dissensions and dis-appearing from view in the first days of 1828 behind a royal pocket-handkerchief.

A trim figure in a tight frock-coat succeeded. Greeted at Windsor by a strange, turbaned form in a dirty silk jacket, which called cheerfully from the depths of a royal bed, " Arthur, the Cabinet is defunct ! " the Duke was in. His advent, watched with curiosity, was remembered by Mr. Disraeli as " a dictatorship of patriotism." But hopes, in 1828, were less exalted; a Tory crew with a slight leaven of Canningites might steer a tolerable course between the whirlpools of Reform and Catholic Emancipation. The Duke approached his new allies, and Mr. Huskisson was asked to Apsley House. There was a brief transaction; the Catholic question was to be left open and Mr. Huskisson's principles of trade maintained, together with a posthumous respect for the principles of Mr. Canning. Sometimes elusive in his life, these had descended to his heirs in a rigid, almost a canonical form. The inheritance was shared between Lord Palmerston, Lord Dudley, Mr. Huskisson, Lady Cowper's brother, Mr. William Lamb, and a few more;

and when the terms arrived, the group conferred. Careful
comparison disclosing no serious departure from the faith,
they accepted. In Palmerston's words, " we joined as a
party; as a party "—to reveal the fatal sequel—" we
retired." While Mr. Canning's banner was unfurled by
Lord Dudley at the Foreign Office and Mr. Huskisson at
the Colonial Office, Lord Palmerston, eternally denied
promotion, kept his faith pure at the War Department. His
terms—freedom of action on the Catholic question and a
neutral Lord-Lieutenant and Chief Secretary for Ireland—
were carefully defined. He even explained them to the
Duke, who was a little gruff and seemed indifferent. For
that warrior felt only the slightest sympathy with the fine
shades of politics, when Mr. Croker found him in that week
confronted with a formidable heap of red boxes and green
bags and remarking angrily, " There is the business of the
country, which I have not time to look at—all my time being
employed in assuaging what gentlemen call their *feelings.*"
But the laborious compound was effected; and Mr. Huskisson
could assure the Liverpool electors that " the presence
in office of such men as Lord Dudley, Lord Palmerston, Mr.
Grant and Mr. Lamb is the most satisfactory of all guarantees
that the general principles of our foreign and commercial
systems will remain unchanged, and that Ireland will be
governed with the strictest impartiality in respect to the
Catholic question"; whilst Palmerston exulted that it was
not to be " a pig-tail Tory Government," resigning himself
a little sadly to his task of leavening the Tory lump and
casting longing eyes in the direction of the receding Whigs—
" I very sincerely regret their loss, as I like them much better
than the Tories and agree with them much more." Such
were the sorrows of a Canningite in 1828.

The stormy voyage opened. Officiating temporarily as
Leader of the House in the debate on the Address, Palmerston paid a loyal tribute to the Duke and defended Canningite
consistency. In the next month he introduced the Army
Estimates for the last time, and a few days later he made his
last defence of flogging. A vote against the repeal of the

Test and Corporation Acts was justified by the somewhat eccentric reflection that " for the last eighty years they had virtually and practically been repealed." For Palmerston relief of Dissenters was a question of merely academic interest, until the graver realities of the Catholic question had been faced. But such broad issues rarely came before the Cabinet, which lost itself in the varied excitements of Greece, Portugal and the Corn Bill. He was increasingly attracted by the bright world of diplomacy. Mr. Canning's principles of policy must be preserved; and to preserve them he frequented the Russian Embassy, where Madame Lieven shook her curls and, already recognised by his hostess as " *our* minister," he learned to thrill with the nobility of insurgent Greece and the depravity of Metternich. So he corresponded actively upon foreign affairs, made a brave effort for the Greek slaves in Egypt, settled despatches, and determined the convenient limits of intervention; although his departmental eye was still attracted by the Militia, and when Mr. Huskisson despatched to Broadlands a voluminous correspondence on slavery, he protested that he had sent " more leaves than are to be found in the whole of the New Forest. This may be the road to manumission for the Blacks, but in the meantime it is something very like slavery for the Cabinet."

So they laboured at their various oars. But gradually, through the spring, an uneasy temper began to mar their harmony and set them swinging out of time. The breach very nearly came upon corn; and someone's scruples startled the Canningites into talk of resignation. But a tender conscience yielded just in time, and they remained. So the unhappy Cabinet continued, " differing upon almost every question of any importance that has been brought under consideration :—meeting to debate and dispute and separating without deciding." They differed, amongst other matters, upon the disposal of East Retford. Disfranchised for corruption, that borough was disputed between industry and agriculture, since the Whigs sought to transfer its member to Birmingham, while more cautious minds preferred to add him to the county members. Mr. Huskisson incautiously committed himself to the Whig view, voted against his Tory colleagues, and resigned. His resignation, in slightly uncertain terms, was promptly accepted by the Duke, who acted with a touch of that tortuousness which sometimes infects military men in civil life. Aghast, the Canningites endeavoured to withdraw the resignation. But the Duke, rare master of defence, clung to his ground. Palmerston, familiar with the uncertain moods of " our Imperator," walked with him for half an hour in the Long Gallery of the House of Lords. He plied him hard : he even made a pleasing use of metaphors drawn from military discipline; but the angry warrior refused to " go upon all fours to Mr. Huskisson," hoped that his friends would " get out of the scrape," and " begged to decline . . . taking a *roll in the mud* with them." When Palmerston told him that he must resign as well, the Duke stared sharply at him. But they parted without a solution. For four days there was a decorous scuffle. The Canningites conferred : the Duke was stiff; Mr. Huskisson wrote long letters and received short replies; and by the end of the week he was out. His friends surveying the unpleasing prospect— since they shared his fidelity to Mr. Canning, the harsh voice of resignation called. There had even been talk of it at Almack's. Lord Palmerston was clear upon the point, and so was Mr. Lamb. But Lord Dudley, who had enjoyed the Foreign Office, was an unwilling listener, " stroked his chin, counted the squares of the carpet three times up and three times down, and then went off in the agony of doubt and hesitation." They met that night at Mr. Huskisson's in Downing Street, and the three men left together. As they walked away (it was a fine night at the end of May, and their cabriolets followed), Dudley said, " Well, now we are by ourselves in the street, and nobody but the sentry to hear us, let me know, right and left, what is meant to be done— ' in ' or ' out '? " Lord Palmerston said ' Out,' and Mr. Lamb repeated it. With those words, quietly spoken under the London sky of 1828, the Canningites left office. An eager world received the news; the fair *Zenobia*, flushed by the exotic splendours of a garden *fete* at Wimbledon, exlaimed in the memory of Mr. Disraeli, " We have got rid of Liberalism for ever "; and for the first time in twenty-one years Lord Palmerston was out of place.

INTERLUDE

I

THE Canningites were out; the bright hues of office faded; and, out of his indentures at last, Lord Palmerston surveyed the world at forty-three. It was the uneasy, changing world of 1828, which danced on summer nights at Almack's and observed without undue exhilaration the new palace at Pimlico. The Duke charmed deputations; whilst at the Cottage Majesty indulged a rustic taste, went fishing on Virginia Water, stopped out late, and caught royal colds, or crept into London after dusk, " when nobody could see his legs or whether he could walk," especially (it seemed) to annoy Mr. Creevey. That watchful elder, inscrutable even to Mr. Greville, toured Whig country houses with an attentive eye for statuary, a ready ear for the rich particulars of Mr. Lamb's *crim. con.*, and the most irreverent doubts of his host's title to the Renaissance fountain at Woolbeding; whilst his fellow-subjects huzzaed for Catholic Relief or (no less vociferous) for Protestant ascendancy. A deeper murmur announced the growing appetite for Reform in a world where poverty picked pockets without a shirt, and wealth, in " 500 pair of white satin shoes from Paris to counteract the damp of the green turf," paraded a Boyle Farm for the *fête champêtre*, to sip its Roman punch and marvel politely at roads watered with Eau de Cologne. For Dives and Lazarus were oddly juxtaposed in 1828.

Lord Palmerston walked for the last time down the War Office stairs and savoured his unaccustomed leisure, a trifle strange—" quite comical "—after twenty-one years of official bondage. Prometheus hardly left his rock with more surprise. Released at forty-three, he could survey his long apprenticeship—the drafts, the grievances, the Estimates, the interminable letters, all the solemn round

which composed the War Department. He was reputed
" a handy clever man who moved his estimates very well,
appeared to care but little for public affairs in general, went
a good deal into society, but never attracted any other
remark but one of wonder . . . that he had been so long
in the same office." An angry pen described him later as
" a second-rate official for twenty years under a succession
of Tory Governments," with a Disraelian fling at " this acme
of second-rate statesmanship . . . the Great Apollo of
aspiring understrappers."

Yet, even in 1828, something more had been achieved.
For this easy, smiling man of forty-three, with hair beginning
to recede from a broad forehead, had learnt the mysterious
arts of government. He could frame a devastating letter,
laugh down an Opposition unduly avid of economy, or engage
a sinewy arm in the slow wrestle of official controversy.
Controversy was, indeed, his *forte ;* and the cheerful dexterity,
which he had used with such gusto upon the Commander-
in-Chief, might serve against other foes. Brisk and contentious, he seemed to derive infinite pleasure from affairs ;
though ' Cupid ' Palmerston was not unmoved by other
pleasures. Since eyes were bright, he danced at Almack's ;
and it was pleasant to watch his horses on the turf of country
race-courses or to shoot the Broadlands coverts. He
hunted when he could ; and there was always Lady Cowper
to adore. For his life was not bounded, like Mr. Croker's,
by the green top of an official desk. But born, as someone
said, for a bureau, he had lived too long with affairs to live
without them.

He had his views as well, strange fruits of his political
Odyssey. Park Place and Cambridge had made a Pittite
of him ; his reason and the crowding tenantry at Sligo made
him a Canningite ; and now the Canningites veered towards
Whiggery. But whilst they drifted in the shallows of
domestic policy, his eye was caught by a line of taller summits.
Home politics were well enough ; but something loftier was
demanded by a statesman. Were not foreign affairs the
crown of public life? This was the true arena for a Can-

ningite who had travelled and spoke foreign languages. His old guardian at Park Place had taught him the rudiments of diplomacy; and now the grey eyes of Madame Lieven seemed to beckon towards wider regions, where the principles of Mr. Canning might be applied to the respectful sovereigns of Europe. So Palmerston, at forty-three, was much at the Russian Embassy, sought the society of diplomats, and began a little hopefully to finger protocols.

II

THERE were few tears for the Canningite evictions. Such groups are rarely popular, since the public mind vaguely resents such posthumous loyalties. Engendering a slightly invidious orthodoxy, they repel recruits and tend to create a sect whose phylacteries are often unpleasantly in evidence. Their hieratic airs are distinctly unbecoming and often fatal to the sorrowing friends of deceased statesmen. For obtrusive mourning is always irritating to the casual spectator. Political bereavements are the least durable of afflictions; and there is little room in public life for groups of political widows, who droop in the attitudes of perpetual mourning above an honoured urn. Their airs, their weeds, their sadly shaken heads begin to pall; and soon a hasty world resents their dutiful reference of all questions to the unforgotten words of a single oracle. Few things are more paralysing to the intelligence than a Canon of ideas; and this Talmudic subservience to a sacred text tends to exasperate a wider public. It cannot hope to share their thought—the one, the inconsolable thought of Mrs. Gummidge; and finding them slightly sanctimonious, it excusably seeks brighter company. There is, perhaps, no future for political widows except political *suttee ;* and the fatal pyre awaited the Canningites, as it was to await the Peelites and still more recent relicts.

Such groups (one sees the cause) are rarely popular; and when the friends of Mr. Canning were suddenly marooned upon the lonely rock of their principles, the brutal act caused few regrets. The Tories grinned; the Whigs were strikingly unsympathetic; and the Duke rejoiced his countrymen with an exhibition of sturdy temper, which gave general pleasure and was understood to be soldierly in the extreme.

Even Mr. Creevey found talent, and, stranger still, plain
dealing in ' the Beau,' and hurled a final curse into the darkness after the tall, receding form of Mr. Huskisson. The
group was lonely, though patient enumeration showed a
fair Parliamentary strength for the ejected ' Liberals,' who
affected this odd, foreign name that aligned them, halfway
between plain Whig and honest Tory, with the raffish
Continental friends of Mr. Canning's policy. So Palmerston
was a Liberal before most of those who were to reproach him
with wanting Liberal principles. He expounded them at
some length in a debate upon their resignation, when he
expressed a definite preference " for transferring forfeited
franchises to large manufacturing towns " and protested his
undying fidelity to the principles of Mr. Canning in foreign
affairs and on the Catholic question. This vindication,
which was felt to be " manly and gentlemanlike," earned
him a hearty handshake from the eccentric William, while
Cumberland (as became a royal Tory) abused him for a
dangerous democrat. But the strange quality of his
democracy was oddly apparent in debate a few weeks later,
when he pressed for the transfer of a member " to a great
town, not because he was a friend to reform in principle, but
because he was its decided enemy. To extend the franchise
to large towns . . . was the only mode by which the House
could avoid the adoption, at some time or other, of a general
plan of reform. . . . When people saw such populous places
as Leeds and Manchester unrepresented, whilst a green mound
of earth returned two members, it naturally gave rise to
complaint. The House ought, therefore, to take advantage
of every case of delinquency, to apply a gradual remedy to
the defective state of the representation." It was a gallant
effort to reconcile common sense with his natural objection
to sweeping measures and with the general opposition to
Reform, which he had inherited from Mr. Canning. But such
an anti-Reformer came perilously near to being a Reformer.

The year went out on a Russo-Turkish war, a welter of
Portuguese insurgents and pretenders, and a protracted
argument as to the fitting limits of resurgent Greece, for

I

which Lord Palmerston was generously coached in Russian
views by Madame Lieven. Early in 1829 he was in Paris
with an attentive ear for Pozzo at the Russian Embassy,
although he made a healthy mental reservation as to the
sanctity of Turkey in Europe from Russian encroachments.
For Madame Lieven's pupil was not without his own convictions. His was almost the delectable Paris of Mr.
Praed—

> The cool *Café*, the *cabriolet*,
> Cigars and macaronis.
> And *Rouge et noir*, and *Eau sucré*,
> And conversaziones.

So he sat through enormous dinner-parties, went on to
soirées for further bouts of conversation, noted with gratification (and a faint reminiscence of Mr. Huskisson or, fainter
still, of Professor Dugald Stewart) that the Finance Minister
was " well versed in the true principles of commerce," and
listened with due solemnity to the opinions which reverberated from the vast cravats of MM. Casimir-Périer and
Royer-Collard. For it was the reign of Charles X., and
progress might dawn upon the world at any moment. But one
night he met two ghosts of an earlier age, and smiled politely
while Sebastiani declaimed upon the Rhine frontier and
Talleyrand, quite "sunk and broken," sat huddled in his chair.

He returned to a bright world, where Mr. Creevey was
shocked (and he was not easily shocked) to observe at Lady
Sefton's ' very small and early party ' for her daughters
a most unsuitable company including " by far the most
notorious and profligate women in London," as well as
Lady —— and Palmerston. The King had declined a shade
from *Ixion's* glowing vision of Jove—" Majestically robust
and luxuriantly lusty, his tapering waist was evidently
immortal, for it defied Time, and his splendid auburn curls
parted on his forehead with celestial precision, descended
over cheeks glowing with the purple radiancy of perpetual
manhood." But he still wore his " blue great coat all over
gold frogs and embroidery " on occasion. Yet though ' the
lovely Thais ' sat beside him, he was unhappy now. Indeed

he was generally in bed, ringing forty times a night for water, for the time, for anything. Brighton was faded; Windsor palled; even Pimlico lacked novelty. It was scarcely a consolation to dream that he had ridden Fleur de Lis for the Goodwood Cup or led the heavy dragoons at Salamanca. The light was fading from a world where one sat moodily designing uniforms, and one's successor danced— " a short, plain-looking child "—at children's balls. For the world, lit by a dreadful glare from the " Loco Motive machine," was changing too. This portent snorted almost within sight of Knowsley, filled Mr. Creevey with thoughts of sudden death and gave him a headache, left Lord Sefton gloomily convinced that some damnable thing must come of it, and after flinging an impudent spark at Miss De Ros's cheek, burnt a hole in Lady Maria's silk pelisse.

Even the Duke had modern leanings. He executed a brisk retreat upon the Catholic question with military promptitude. Almost ejaculating, in the cheerful forecast of one peer, " My lords! Attention! Right about face! March! ", the Great Captain issued his commands; and his startled battalions were invited to storm the lines of Protestant ascendancy, which they had held so long. The Catholic Relief Bill was introduced in March; and Palmerston conveyed his blessing in a slightly elaborate composition, which someone found " an imitation of Canning, and not a bad one." His own high opinion of it appears from a modest distribution, which he made, of printed 'copies. Opening upon an almost humble note—" I shall not go into any depth of historical research; I shall not lead the House into the mazes of theological disquisition; I shall rest my opinions upon the present situation of Ireland "—he was soon at large in the empyrean. He soared beyond King William, beyond the state of Ireland, to a region where he quoted the classics freely, spoke of earthquake and civil war, and sat down upon a line of Mr. Burke. But he was effective in ridicule of the Tory mind, which would admit Catholics to military command without a tremor, but was shaken by nameless terrors " if this man of divided allegiance were permitted to vote in a Committee of Supply "; ₄and he was always generous upon Ireland, " unfortunate and ill-starred Ireland."

He surveyed a broader field with still greater gusto in the summer, when an empty House was favoured with a dashing attack upon the Government's foreign policy; and once more his own estimate of its importance is fixed by a distribution of printed copies. A plea for vigorous intervention in Portugal was founded upon a scornful narrative of British inaction and Portuguese iniquity— " What followed ? any assertion of national dignity ? was Fort St. Julien laid in ruins ? was the Miguelite squadron burnt, sunk, and destroyed as per margin ? or was Don Miguel even treated with a courteous retort of one of his own favourite blockades ? Nothing of all this. . . . I say, that if the accounts which I have heard are correct, Buonaparte in the plenitude and insolence of his power never treated the humble representations of a petty German principality with more contemptuous disregard than that which our remonstrances have met with at the hands of Don Miguel." The policy might be the policy of Mr. Canning; but the voice was, beyond a doubt, the voice of Palmerston. Yet there was more in his mind than a programme of mere vigour; and he showed it at the close of a summary of the Eastern Question, which bore strong traces of Madame Lieven's drawing-room. The Russian was, for once, the generous line. For justice, as well as Nesselrode, required an ample trace for the Greek frontier; and there was almost eloquence in his dismissal of " a Greece which should contain neither Athens, nor Thebes, nor Marathon, nor Salamis, nor Platæa, nor Thermopylæ, nor Missolonghi." But his real thought, when it emerged, was larger than any frontier question. " There are two great parties in Europe; one which endeavours to bear sway by the force of public opinion; another which endeavours to bear sway by the force of physical control." The tyrant was Austria; the liberator—" the patron, no less than the model of constitutional freedom, the refuge from persecution, and the·

shield against oppression "—might, in his ideal, be England. Such was the prospect to which Lord Palmerston, with the noble (if slightly inconsequent) simile of the British line-of-battle ship controlled by the " puny insect at the helm," pointed the gentlemen of England in 1829.

These speeches operated a strange transformation in his political stature. For the slightly stilted declamations revealed an unsuspected statesman, and the industrious Canningite promptly became a man of note. Even Mr. Greville was surprised when the assiduous subordinate of twenty years emerged; and the clubs began to abound in sagacious gentlemen who had long observed his early promise. For the power of speech was singularly rare on the Front Benches, where Mr. Peel enjoyed an almost solitary pre-eminence. But Mr. Peel was cold. The impassive face, the buttoned manner chilled expansive squires; while Palmerston was a friendly presence who hunted, danced at Almack's, and ran horses at country race-meetings. Now (better still) he showed his political quality and became, at forty-five, the rising hope of either party. The Whigs watched eagerly; and one hopeful Tory made eccentric overtures to him over a plate of cutlets at the Travellers'. The squires had been startled by the Duke's *volte face* on Catholic Emancipation; Peel was an apostate, too; and there was a private move to replace them by something less accessible to ideas. Eldon seemed promising in this respect. But colleagues were required. Now, Huskisson professed alarming views upon trade questions. So would not Palmerston, the cautious gentleman enquired, consent to lead the Commons as Colonial Secretary? The advance was far too odd to be rudely repulsed. So Palmerston finished his cutlets and inclined a respectful ear, with a bland warning that he, too, was hardly free from opinions upon trade and currency. Had not the pupil of Professor Dugald Stewart learnt his enlightened lesson thirty years before at Edinburgh? The strange proposal left him reflecting upon his position as a Canningite, " free if I choose, because we have never met as a party, and have upon

no occasion voted as a body. We sit together, but upon
almost every question last session voted different ways."
Such groups are frequently fissiparous. For an exacting
orthodoxy always tends to produce heresies. Lady Canning
was understood to be denouncing schismatics on the ground
of some departure from her late husband's testament by his
less accredited widows. But Palmerston remained a Canningite of the Huskissonian shade. For Huskisson and he
frequented Lady Cowper at Panshanger, Melbourne at
Brocket, and Princess Lieven wherever those shaken curls
expounded Russian policy. She had sent discreet congratulations on his Portuguese speech and desired his news. Her
group, indeed, might bring him a more progressive alignment; since Wellington complained that if any point were
discussed with Lieven, " we should have a statement of the
case with Lord Grey, Lord Palmerston, and Mr. Huskisson,
as soon as the post would carry it." So Grey and the Whigs
were waiting. A few months later Grey even thought of
him as a possible Leader of the House in a Whig ministry.
But the cool detachment of the Canningites was, for the
time, more congenial to Palmerston; though he viewed a
Tory allegiance with evident distaste. Tory no longer, he
could write that " as to going to the Tory Party . . . to
belong to people you do not think with cannot answer."
So far from Toryism had Lord Liverpool's young subordinate
travelled in 1829.

He went to Ireland in the autumn; and before the year
was out, he was on the Continent again, the Continent of
1829, where Grisi sang and Thorwaldsen studied the antique.
He was in France as usual, and Paris was full of English.
Most well-bred travellers see little except their countrymen.
Some, indeed, draw even finer distinctions; for Mr. Greville
noticed no names in the little Roman cemetery under the
grey pyramid of Cestius except " the pretty Miss Bathurst."
But Palmerston although he harvested a golden store
of English gossip and sent home his sheaves to Lady
Cowper with a charming intimacy, had a watchful eye for
the Parisian scene. He went to Court, dined with Polignac,

and travelled the round of *soirées*. The Ultras were
grotesquely Tory, and there was a new brand of patriot who
" raves about *nos frontières* " ; but his martial intentions
were shrewdly diagnosed, since " while they have Chambers
who must levy taxes to carry on a war, nothing but egregious
folly on our part can bring on a war between the two
countries." It was a lesson in the hollowness of French
flourishes, which Palmerston was slow to forget. He found
an odd mood in Paris, which might lead (with a sound
prevision of 1830) to " a change of name in the inhabitant
of the Tuileries, and the Duke of Orleans might be invited
to step over the way from the Palais Royal." So the
observant Viscount sauntered round, paying his morning
calls, survived a trying opera named *Le Nozze di Lammermuir*,
and even endured a most improving course of lectures by
M. Guizot on the Progress of Civilisation, together with some
more upon the Origin of Modern Languages and the
Mechanical Arts and Industry of the Civilised World. We
sometimes underrate the fortitude of earlier generations.

Loaded with presents for Lady Cowper and the children
(and rewarded by a charming letter of thanks to her " dear
H."), he was back in England, when the House met in
February. There were hopes of an active Opposition led
by Melbourne and Palmerston in the two Houses; and he
was soon harrying Mr. Peel upon the Greek question. He
took, perhaps, a slightly Russian tone and betrayed a
suspicious intimacy with the course of negotiations. Scent-
ing the Lievens, Mr. Peel asked tartly in whose confidence
he was and whom he represented. The rash enquiry
provoked a deep-chested reply from Palmerston :—

> " My right honourable friend has told the House that he
> does not know whose representative I am. I will tell him.
> I stand here, humble as I am, as one of the Representatives
> of the People of England; and next, as the Representative of
> my own opinions—opinions, Sir, which I will never shape to
> suit the opinions of any other individual, let his situation be
> what it may, either in this House or out of this House. I
> stand here as the Representative of my own opinions. . . . I

also stand here, I trust, as one of that body which represents, or which at least ought to be the maintainers of the honour and interests of England; and I can assure the House . . ."

Lord Palmerston had found his voice; and in the reverberation one can almost catch an echo, twenty years before its time, of a resounding *Civis Romanus sum*.

The year went on. Ladies in large bonnets blustered on the steps of the throne to hear the Lords' debates; gentlemen in pumps, fur cloaks, and velvet waistcoats strolled out to evening parties; Miss Fanny Kemble charmed the town; Mr. Macaulay suggested to his editor that an article on Mr. Robert Montgomery might brighten the *Edinburgh;* and Palmerston gave ministers a brush on the Portuguese question. But there was a hush at Windsor in the summer; for the King was dying. He was nearly blind now, though he could sometimes summon spirit to mimic his ministers to their successors. A doctor found him " cheerful at times and very fond of talking about horses," and he was designing a new tunic for the Guards almost to the last. Always correct, he thought the prayer for his health in good taste; and, " very nervous but very brave," he waited for the end. It came at last; and Mr. Creevey recorded almost with awe that " poor Prinney is really dead—on a Saturday too, as was foretold." So there was no more laudanum and no more rouge. Innumerable coats hung limp in royal wardrobes. For there were no more parties at the Cottage; an empty Pavilion waited by the sea, a fishing-pagoda on the bright silence of Virginia Water. For he had walked his interminable minuet, and was beyond them all—beyond the memory of Fitzherbert and the avenging furies of Queen Caroline and the tired eyes of Lady Conyngham. The Regency had passed, and now the reign itself was over. His ministers, his vexatious ministers, had died—the glacial Castlereagh, Lord Liverpool with his tempers, and the irritating smile of Mr. Canning. They were all dead, as dead as Mr. Fox and Mr. Burke and Mr. Sheridan; and in a room at Calais Mr. Brummell sat among tarnished silver watching a green macaw on the back of a tattered silk chair of faded gilt.

III

So the King died, almost sublime at last; and the ridiculous succeeded. A ruddy old gentleman with short, white hair trotted about town on foot and displayed a most unroyal tendency to say what he thought. The Court looked on aghast; the Guards enjoyed the unusual spectacle of a sovereign long past riding " with a great pair of gold spurs half-way up his legs like a game-cock "; and Mr. Greville surveyed his royal master with the cheerful prediction that " if he doesn't go mad, he may make a very decent King."

His Parliament, obedient to a demise of the Crown, dissolved. But while candidates prepared for their exertions, strange news arrived from Paris. The streets had risen, swept by an unusual fervour for the Constitution. There was a roar of *Vive la Charte !* and, in hoarser tones, a *À bas les Bourbons !* and even of *Vive Napoléon II*. Stray carts and paving-stones became barricades. The King was shooting at Rambouillet. But the din rose on the still air of a French summer. There was a rattle of musketry; and as the raw smoke curled and hung above the city, old ghosts walked Paris on the uproar, where a Swiss Guard defended one more palace, and Lafayette, a little shaky at seventy-three, was hurried down the roaring streets to save mankind again at the Hôtel de Ville. The tumult deepened, and Marmont in the confusion quite forgot to betray his master. But the troops tired quickly in the hot streets. There was a sound of wheels on the road to Normandy; and as the dust receded, the King of France was halfway to England, whilst his unnatural cousin paraded the bland features of Louis Philippe before tearful crowds and reigned (by a subtle change) as King of the French.

The news was lively; and Lord Palmerston wrote grimly to a colleague : " Charles X. seems at last to have passed the Rubicon. How long will it be before he also passes the

Alps?" The mails came in from Paris; and, safely re-
elected for Cambridge, he paused in his triumph to inform
Lady Cowper that "we shall drink the cause of Liberalism
all over the world. Let Spain and Austria look to themselves; this reaction cannot end where it began, & Spain
& Italy & Portugal & parts of Germany will sooner or
later be affected. This event is decisive of the ascendancy
of Liberal Principles throughout Europe; the evil spirit
has been put down and will be trodden under foot. The
reign of Metternich is over & the days of the Duke's policy
might be measured by algebra, if not by arithmetic." This
was strange language for a University member in the week
of a revolution. But heads were quickly turned in 1830.
One cannot easily recover those raptures, since the leading
rôle was slightly miscast. Louis Philippe, by whom the
movement was adroitly captured, must always seem a
somewhat uninspiring emblem of revolt. For the imagination is slow to kindle at sight of a *père de famille* with six
children, who wore a wig, practised the domestic virtues,
and ingeniously satisfied all exigencies by a discreet retention
of the monarchical principle draped in a tricolour. A sly
duke, transformed into a wary king, had raised the torch;
but the torch was decorously shaded. The picture is scarcely
thrilling. Yet thrills were rare in 1830. The July Revolution, seen from 1848, was merely a depressing prologue; but
seen from 1830, it was the dawn. So the world thrilled;
and Palmerston, obedient to his instinct and the principles
of Mr. Canning, thrilled with it.

The Duke ignored his evolution. Needing recruits, he
was disinclined to study them too closely. Had he not
made men of Portuguese and Dutch-Belgians? Even
Canningites might serve at a pinch; and before the elections
he had made a move to re-enlist them. The sleepy Melbourne was approached; and no objection was raised to
Palmerston, though watchful Mr. Croker was already expecting to find him among the Whigs. But they never joined,
since Melbourne insisted upon bringing in Huskisson and
Grey. The Duke demurred, since both held views distasteful
to himself. That autumn Mr. Huskisson, always progressive,

fell under a train; and, this obstacle removed, the Duke's invitation was repeated. Lord Palmerston had been a trifle free with declarations of his goodwill and independence; and this time the approach was made to him. A friendly peer pursued him with assurances of the Duke's esteem, the similarity of their opinions, and the offer of " a high office, which, if he does not object to his colleagues, would I think be agreeable to him." He answered warily that he " could not singly join his Majesty's government, constituted as it now is," hinting that he must bring in his friends. The tactful peer withdrew to Apsley House and returned to ask their names. Palmerston named Melbourne and another Canningite; but since their views might well be overborne by Tory colleagues, he stipulated blandly for the inclusion of Lansdowne and Grey. Such terms dismayed the peer; the Duke had bargained for some Canningites, but he was hardly likely to accept two Whigs as well. Palmerston, set rather upon giving a Liberal flavour to the whole administration than upon a penitent return of prodigal Canningites to the Tory fold, insisted. For now his only possible allies were Whigs; and having made this grave confession, he escaped the tempters by a flight to Paris. Summoned to Apsley House on his return, he had six minutes with the Duke, repeated his awkward insistence upon a thorough reconstruction of the Cabinet, and dismissed himself politely. The Canningites were almost Whig now. The group consulted at his house and resolved to align themselves with Mr. Brougham upon Reform. So when Mr. Croker sounded him once more on a junction with the Duke Lord Palmerston confessed himself a Reformer, and the transaction ended. The Canningites had left the Tory lines and marched at last with the multitude of Whigs and Radicals, who menaced their country's peace.

The clamour for Reform increased. The Duke dilated bravely on the perfection of the Constitution—such excellence as was scarcely attainable by human institutions. There was a week of panic. The Whigs conferred; the New Police reaped a rich harvest of alarming leaflets and tricolour cockades; Francis Place cheerfully recorded " the first step in the British Revolution "; and cautious ministers declined

to risk their sovereign at a Guildhall banquet. Even the
Oxford Union resolved, by a majority of one, "that the
administration of the Duke of Wellington is undeserving of
the confidence of the country," and a Tory Secretary named
Gladstone added to its minutes in ribald parenthesis,
Tremendous cheering from the majority of one. The Government still lingered. But it fell at last, defeated with the
fine inconsequence of Parliamentary life upon a totally
irrelevant matter relating to the Civil List. The way was
clear; the King sent for Lord Grey; and for the first time
since Mr. Fox the Whigs were in—

> Go pluck the jewels from the Crown,
>   The colours from the mast,
> And let the Three per Cents come down—
>   We can but break at last.
> If Cobbett is the first of men,
>   The second is Lord Grey;
> Oh, must we not be happy, when
>   The Whigs are in to-day!

The Canningites came with them. Melbourne went to the
Home Office; the faint shadow of Lord Goderich governed
the Colonies; and Palmerston, who coveted the Foreign
Office, was pressing Princess Lieven for a word to Grey.
Egeria pondered. Was not Palmerston friendly, liked by
the diplomats, and apt at his lessons in Russian policy?
True, the pupil was already recognised as "somewhat
difficult to manage." But his cause was prettily pleaded by
Lady Cowper. So Egeria yielded and proposed him for
the Foreign Office. That dignity had been offered first to
Lansdowne; and while the prospect wavered, Palmerston
rode in suspense between the Russian Embassy and the
Lievens' house at Richmond. But he had a stronger ally
than he knew. For when Lansdowne at last refused, he
had enquired, "Would not Palmerston suit the Foreign
Office?" So Grey was free to accept Egeria's advice;
indeed, the graceful man left her in the belief that the
suggestion came from her. So the place which the Nestor
of the Whigs declined was offered to their Achilles; and
Palmerston, at forty-six, went to the Foreign Office.

FOREIGN OFFICE

IT was in the false dawn of freedom that followed the
Revolution of 1830. A king still reigned in France, although
in his tricolour, his National Guard, and his shrill challenge
to the unnatural frontiers of 1815 he seemed almost to
apologise for not being a republic. There was an odd
flutter of insurrection on the streets of Brussels, where a
Belgian crowd streamed out of a theatre in a sudden fever
of nationalism and showed to the startled Dutch clenched
Belgian fists, which had scarcely been seen in Europe since
they were clenched at Alva. In Italy the white-coats still
kept the peace, the peremptory and slightly guttural peace
of Metternich. Big Croats saluted stiffly in the Milanese
sunshine; Uhlans gave German passwords in the deep shade
of Lombard gateways; and the crash of Austrian bands
disturbed Italian echoes. But something was stirring in
Modena; an aquiline young man named Bonaparte (he was
really nothing like his uncle, but he had a charming mother)
rode about Rome and scandalised the Papal *sbirri* with a
quite shameless display of the tricolour on his saddlery;
and the Romagna was uneasy. Brunswick and Hesse-
Cassel was scared by sudden abdications; the broad and
pleasant streets of Hanover observed an unaccustomed riot;
and far to the east excited students ran through Warsaw in
an ecstasy of loyalty to that undying nationality, ' not so
much alive as surviving, which persists in thinking, breathing,
speaking, hoping and suffering in its grave, railed in by a
million of bayonets and triple-sealed with the seals of three
great empires.' It was still night in Europe; but the stars
were paler in the sky.

By this half-light Lord Palmerston went to the Foreign
Office in November, 1830. He had been learning his lesson
for nearly thirty years now. He had learnt something of it

from his own, his Eighteenth Century, when old Lord
Malmesbury sat at Park Place dispensing ambassadorial
wisdom to his ward. This sage, who as ' Excellency Harris '
had flitted through the vanished Potsdam, the long faded
Peterhof of Frederick and Catherine, was Palmerston's
earliest instructor in diplomacy, and left on his attentive
pupil some trace of the remote and irrecoverable age of
red heels. The old man's talk held little to encourage any
exaggerated belief in principles, in European systems, in
all the impressive apparatus of policy with which the Holy
Alliance and M. de Metternich had encumbered the world.
For he derived from the splendid anarchy of Europe before
the Revolution, when diplomacy had as few fixed principles
as a minuet and nations changed allies with the easy grace
of dancers setting to partners. Always unfriendly to general
ideas, Englishmen nurtured in the Eighteenth Century
regarded them with exceptional, if always well-bred, scep-
ticism. The Holy Alliance was a generalisation incarnate;
M. de Metternich was a succession of principles; and
Palmerston, apt pupil of the Eighteenth Century, viewed
them with a cool and sceptical eye, emerging with an inclina-
tion to murmur *Les nations n'ont pas de cousins* and an
instinctive sense that M. de Metternich was wrong. That
feeling led him far from the trim walks of the existing
European order into the winding paths of freedom; and
perhaps, when he challenged despotism and seems to
admiring eyes to lead in the Nineteenth Century with a
cheerful flourish, he was reaching backwards into the
Eighteenth.

Another tutor drilled him in distaste for Metternich.
For Princess Lieven, true to her Emperor, assiduously
warned her British aspirant against Vienna. He listened
eagerly and seemed to learn his lesson. But whilst the
lively Russian distrusted Metternich for being Austrian, her
pupil disliked him for himself—for his opinions, for his
absolutism of that impeccable brand which Mr. Canning
used to call "ultrageous," for the hieratic air with which
he presided in the international Areopagus, for the dull roll
of Austrian drums that seemed to drown at every moment

the rising voice of Europe. Such music was unpleasing to an English ear; and Palmerston, for all his easy French, his friendship with the Lievens, and his Irish land, was ineradicably English.

That lesson he had taught himself. It came to him from Harrow, from the white mist along the Cambridge backs, from the big trees at Broadlands and the doors in Stanhope Street; he caught it in the cheerful buzz of country race-meetings and the flutter of Almack's; and it spoke to him with the sharp note of shots in distant spinneys or the clear voice of hounds. Perhaps the War Department helped. It is a sound school of patriotism to spend nineteen years with Army files; and his later method owed something to the fact that he had got his training whilst England was at war. For war ministers frequently form a habit of mind which regards a frigate and a battalion of the Line as the normal messengers of British policy.

Such lessons prepared him to receive the teaching of Mr. Canning, who could write that " for *Europe* I shall be desirous *now* and *then* to read *England*," and summarised his policy in " the substitution of one word for another—for 'Alliance' read 'England.'" With his principles he even acquired his metaphors. For where the master had startled the electors of Plymouth with the splendid image of their warships " now reposing on their shadows in perfect stillness," the pupil roused a sleepy House of Commons with a vision, less eloquent but strikingly similar, of a line-of-battle ship as the embodiment of England. Metternich had deplored Mr. Canning (in terms more appropriate to Attila) as *ce fléau du monde*. Death relieved him from that menace. But Mr. Canning's dream remained—to " become the model of Europe. Let us hope for the interests of mankind that this model will be generally adopted—that all nations will endeavour to introduce that vital spirit, that germ of strength which has enabled so small a country to make such extraordinary exertions to save itself, and to deal out salvation to the world." He had dreamed a lofty dream of England—" a model, and ultimately perhaps an umpire." And for nearly forty years his dream lived on in Palmerston.

K

II

HE was appointed on November 18, 1830. That night he met his colleagues at Lansdowne House; and on the next day Princess Lieven asked her first official favour. There was some talk of a change at the British Embassy at St. Petersburg; the Czar was admirably suited with its present occupant; and perhaps Lord Palmerston might see his way . . . The obliging minister complied in a charming note. His French was excellent; but the composition cost him some pains. For the draft (which still survives) was carefully corrected; it closed with an arch insinuation—*Si l'administration du Duc avait duré encore quelque tems elle aurait pu entraîner dans sa chute, toujours inévitable, des choses même encore plus importantes que Herries et Goulburn.* Such was Lord Palmerston's first essay in diplomacy.

But business crowded on him, and he was soon complaining cheerfully that he was " like a man who has plumped into a mill-race, scarcely able by all his kicking and plunging to keep his head above water." In that congenial element, which immersed but never totally submerged him, he plied an easy stroke. Expected to be active in the Commons as well, where Mr. Croker with scant respect for Althorp's blameless qualities denominated Palmerston " prompter to the puppet," he made a single appearance as deputy Leader before the year was out. But Downing Street absorbed him; and he returned with obvious relief to the tortuous delights of foreign policy.

The skein was tangled. In France the dynasty designed by the collective wisdom of Europe to perpetuate the *status quo* had vanished; and while Charles X. explored once more the amenities of Holyrood, he was replaced at Paris by a monarch of the younger branch in quite dangerous sympathy with his subjects. The new king had spent à nervous autumn explaining himself away. At home he rolled ecstatic eyes at unfurled tricolours, spoke frequently of Valmy, or waved a royal forefinger in time to the slightly fevered throb of the *Marseillaise*. But abroad he hung a modest head, deplored his revolutionary origins, disclaimed designs against the treaties of 1815, and generally comported himself as an anxious *débutante*, receiving with appropriate emotion a diamond-mounted *tabatière* adorned with a miniature of William IV. Europe looked on; while Russia, more sceptical than the rest, began to mobilise, and uneasy Chancellors met to shake heads at Carlsbad.

The sudden change recalled the unhallowed age before the future of the race was fixed immutably by the Congress of Vienna. Had not the world devoted fifteen years to organising nervously against the memory of the Empire by providing France with a five-barred frontier and a dynasty of gaolers? The dynasty had vanished. But worse still remained; for a vital section of the frontier was promptly threatened by the collapse of its appointed guardian. The watch on the northern border had been entrusted to the composite Kingdom of the Netherlands, an ill-considered blend of Holland and Belgium. This strange amalgam, one of the less felicitous products of diplomatic ingenuity, ignored the Reformation, combined a Protestant with a Catholic state, and endured uncomfortably until in 1830 the sudden chemistry of revolution resolved it sharply into its component parts. For politics are rarely friendly to synthetic products. Brussels, reacting to the unusual stimulus of an Italian opera with obscurely topical allusions, flamed into insurrection. Excited Belgians cheered for independence; the Dutch appealed to force and, when it failed, to Europe; and Europe observed with mild alarm the disappearance of its northern barrier against the tide of French invasion.

A Conference sat hastily in London; and Lord Palmerston embarked with gusto on that heroic course of diplomatic composition which earned the name of 'Protocol Palmerston' from those exhausted Foreign Office clerks, whose weary pens had traced his splendid tale of seventy-

eight protocols on the affairs of Belgium. Nineteen years
of War Office drafting bore at last their sober fruit. Lord
Grey was at his elbow (malicious Mr. Creevey wrote crudely
that he " never signed a dispatch that had not been seen
and *altered* by Lord Grey "); and he met the glassy stare
of Talleyrand, where the old man sat deep in his chair
making, as someone said, " the cursedest nasty noises in
his throat," and an ashy face looked out of the lank, powdered
hair that hung (in Mr. Macaulay's horrified recollection)
" straight as a pound of tallow candles " to the padded
shoulders.

Before Christmas, 1830, they had agreed that Belgium
should exist, since a free Belgium was manifestly preferable
to a French one; and in the first weeks of 1831 they engaged
a grave debate to the accompaniment of unnumbered protocols, on frontiers, on forms of government, on (most delicate
of all) a suitable prince. Whilst Lord John Russell and
' Radical Jack ' Durham sat in the Committee of Four to
frame a Reform Bill, Palmerston fenced with French hints
that Luxemburg would be a welcome gift, that Belgium
would never miss a fortress or so. But Grey reported in
almost Palmerstonian tones that " there seems to be no
hope but holding a strong language to France, whose
Government, I think, would not like to run the risk of seeing
her whole commerce swept from the sea "; and his cheerful
colleague secured from Talleyrand the neutrality of an
undiminished Belgium " by the same means by which juries
become unanimous—by starving." Next, a galaxy of
princes was paraded for the new crown. A young Bavarian
was disqualified by his public opinions and his private life,
a Neapolitan by his youth and the fact that his aunt was
Queen of the French, a Leuchtenberg by the still more
fatal circumstances that his father had borne the name of
Beauharnais. Remained the Prince of Orange, distasteful
to the Belgians as an emblem of Dutch sovereignty, the
Duc de Nemours, for whom they showed a taste at once
delightful and embarrassing to his father, King Louis'
Philippe, and (discreet alternative) Prince Leopold of Saxe-

Coburg. Nemours was averted by a threat of war from
England. Grey and the Cabinet were firm; Palmerston
spoke amiably to " old Tally " of activity at Portsmouth;
and the French, inclined at first to put by the proffered
crown with something of Cæsar's gentleness, accelerated
their refusal. The field was clear at last for Leopold; and
fortified by the advice of Stockmar, the judicious widower
waited sedately at Marlborough House.

    The world was changing round him. On a March evening
' a little fellow not weighing above eight stone ' engaged the
attention of the House of Commons, when Lord John
Russell introduced the Government's Reform Bill. In the
long debate Whigs cheered incredulously, astonished squires
tore Tory passions to shreds, and Palmerston, who had
already made his Parliamentary *début* as Foreign Secretary
in a statement on Belgian affairs interposed rather inconse-
quently in an Army debate, defended Canningite consistency
on Reform. Had not Mr. Huskisson's career been sacrificed
to his reforming instincts upon the East Retford Bill?
The case of Mr. Canning was more awkward, since he had
quite notoriously opposed Reform; and, confronted with
his utterances, Lord Palmerston frankly confessed to a
change of opinion which, he boldly argued, would equally
have carried Mr. Canning into the ranks of the Reformers.
But his reforming ardour was distinctly temperate. He
was already pressing Grey to make concessions in the Bill,
and he had little taste for the heroic prospect of a General
Election upon Reform. His disquiet found expression in a
letter to Lansdowne, in which he stated his alarm at " Durham's violent and intemperate Counsels . . . he looks only
to triumph on a particular Measure, totally reckless of the
consequences, which may be produced by the Means he
would employ to gain his victory; or at least if he does
look beyond the Struggle of the Moment, he is much bolder
and more confident than I am. I confess I could not go
gayly and carelessly to a Dissolution in the present state of
England and Ireland. . . . In England at all events it would
array against each other in fine conflict in a contest upon
Principle great masses of the Community, and the different

classes of Society. I confess that of two evils I think the least would be to be driven to some Modification of our Plan, which I would have liked just as well, if it had not been so extensive; and upon the same principle upon which I told Ld. Grey before it was brought in, that I, for one, could not bind myself to the plan such as it is, in all its details to stand a fall by it, so also I should be very reluctant to be a party to a Dissolution, merely for the purpose of avoiding any modification in our measure."

Such were the hesitations of a Canningite fallen among impulsive Whigs. It was pleasant to find a little sympathy, when he met Melbourne and the Cowpers at Lord Sefton's under the eyes—observant constellation—of Mr. Greville and Mr. Creevey. As winter turned to spring in 1831, excited members watched the Reform Bill in Committee. But Palmerston, at his nineteenth protocol, had more pressing business. He harped manfully on Belgian neutrality, bent over maps of Luxemburg, and wrangled endlessly with the French upon the disarmament of Barrier fortresses. In April faint echoes of a Government defeat reached him among his papers. There was a nervous scurry; and as respectful Belgians asked their way to Marlborough House for an appointment with Prince Leopold, disorder reached the House of Lords. That day a marquis shook his fist; there was a flutter among the peeresses; and it appeared to *Hansard's* startled gaze that the peers were "almost scuffling." Brougham bounded on the Woolsack like an angry ball; and outside in the April afternoon King William drove to Parliament in state behind the royal creams. Their manes, in dreadful evidence of haste, were out of plait. But the sovereign, in a considerable hurry and wearing his crown slightly on one side, entered the Chamber and dissolved the Commons.

The dissolution of 1831 projected Palmerston into a Cambridge election. He went without enthusiasm, although he contributed to the Loyal and Patriotic Fund raised by the Whigs to finance the contest in the country. He made a speech which annoyed the Duke of Wellington by its professions of moderation, and his election address closed with a brave assertion of his loyalty to "the fundamental Principles of the Constitution." But his canvass was disheartening, and he reported gloomily to Grey that "I have scarcely met six people who approve of our Bill." Cambridge was restive in spite of a tactful offer of a living to an eminent Johnian. Shocked earlier by his Catholic opinions, it was frankly scared by the graver heresy of Reform. The Church, it seemed, was more than usually in danger; its anxious guardians trooped to the Senate House to vote; and he lost the seat. But ministers in combat enjoyed something of the immunity of Homeric heroes. With pleasing irony a rotten borough received the fallen Reformer, and the Treasury directed his return by the electors, few but obedient, of Blechingley.

In the summer it was seen that Reform had swept the country. But this rousing spectacle failed to increase Lord Palmerston's enthusiasm. Less perturbed, perhaps, than young Mr. Gladstone, who informed the readers of a newspaper with the rich eloquence of an undergraduate that "the day of our greatness and stability is no more and that the chill and damp of death are already creeping over England's glory," Palmerston warned the Prime Minister that he was moving too fast and pressed for an increase in the voter's qualification. But he was overborne and took no part in the interminable debates upon the second Reform Bill. In Parliament he became a model of official reticence, greeting questioners with the slightly irritable retort that "if Gentlemen expect that his Majesty's ministers are here to serve no purpose but those of a newspaper, I can assure them that they will find themselves greatly disappointed." He was at Windsor for two days in Ascot week, when royal William dozed after a hot dinner in a crowded room. It was Palmerston's first time at the Castle since an ampler figure sat beside Lady Conyngham where now a "plain, vulgar, hospitable gentleman" yawned at his guests or beamed (in Mr. Greville's indecorous phrase) upon *toute la bâtardise*. But he was soon back at his Belgian papers, tracing frontiers with a wary eye on France and cheerfully predicting "a most exemplary licking" for the Belgians, if

they were rash enough to fight the Dutch. At Marlborough
House Prince Leopold still struggled with his scruples;
Stockmar abounded in wisdom, despite an irritating
habit of addressing English peers in correspondence as
" My singular good Lord "; there was a vigorous exchange
of drafts and memoranda; and at length the cautious
widower accepted, waiving his British income with a gesture
which was only slightly marred by a sage reservation for
the maintenance of Claremont and the punctual payment
of all charities formerly allowed by himself or his lamented
Charlotte. Then he sailed from Dover and announced his
safe arrival to William IV. in a letter where it is strange to
encounter that eternal uncle as a " devoted nephew " : and
with the judicious monarch duly housed at Laeken the stage
seems set for the Nineteenth Century.

But his problem was far from solved. An angry Holland
hung on his northern frontier, while to the south the French
seemed dangerously inclined to rescue him in force.
Palmerston resisted Metternich's craving for a Congress—
" We ought to prevent any more congresses till we have
another French war in Europe, which, I trust, will not be
in our time "—and watched the smouldering flame in
Belgium. Protocols multiplied hopefully, and Eighteen
Articles became Twenty-four under the fruitful hand of
diplomacy. But the angry Dutch flung into Belgium; the
Belgians broke; and, surrounded by a defeated army, the
cautious Leopold enjoyed the precarious delights of monarchy
in a cottage outside Louvain. The French rushed to the
rescue and, their kindly task completed, discovered a
singular reluctance to evacuate the rescued kingdom.
While Palmerston had a brush with Mr. Croker on the
question and refused information with that solemnity which
never fails ministers (but without questioning the right of
members " to make remarks, however voluminous, and to
ask questions, however ill-timed "), the situation was
extremely grave. " One thing," he wrote, " is certain—the
French must go out of Belgium, or we have a general war,
and war in a given number of days." Even Lord Grey
wrote of " a flame which would make war inevitable."

But the French fell back behind the frontier; and as the summer of 1831 turned to autumn, the healing flow of protocols was resumed.

Reform still held the stage. The Bill had passed the Commons. But the Lords rejected it in the dawn of an October morning. Palmerston was pressing Grey for something less extensive in deference to "the great bulk of the gentry of the country." But his leader was firm; and even Melbourne, who was no zealot for Reform, urged him to conceal Cabinet differences for fear of a "general convulsion," although the faintness of his own enthusiasm appears in Lady Cowper's bland admission that "as for my brother William and others of the ministers they seem to me quite overjoy'd to have got rid of the Bill for the present." While Grey and Althorp struggled with Lord Palmerston's doubts, he shepherded the unwilling Powers into a Belgian treaty. The work was heavy; and since Broadlands was out of the question, he rode to Richmond for a night of quiet work at the " Star and Garter "—" people ought to be many months confined in London to know the value of even a few hours of fresh air and exercise." The Powers signed, when the tale of his protocols had reached the forties; and Europe blessed the Belgian kingdom. But at home uneasy Whigs surveyed a restless nation. Tempers were rising; and though Reform was past the Commons, King and Lords (both formidable in 1831) remained to be overcome. William had lost his ardour and repeated with mournful iteration what Peel described as " perhaps . . . the only poetry he ever made "—

> " I consider dissolution
> Tantamount to revolution."

Lord Grey felt equal to handling his sovereign alone; but for the Lords he made some use of Palmerston. Distasteful to the more ardent Whigs, who had excluded him from a Reform banquet, Palmerston was admirably fitted to make discreet approaches to the Waverers. These cautious peers were soon in touch with Grey. Drafts were exchanged, and Durham wrote angrily that " I see what Palmerston is driving at ! He does not mind the dis-

franchisement of rotten boroughs, or the enfranchisement of
great towns, provided he can get such an elective qualification as will make those large towns as little real representations of the people as the boroughs he has destroyed.
And as a thorough anti-Reformer (which he is) he is right."
The fling was hardly just, since Palmerston was loyal to the
principles of the second Bill, though he warned Melbourne
that " it would be infinitely better to break up the Government than to be party to a proposition more democratic
than the last. There would in such a case be danger of
convulsion, but there would also be the means of forming a
new Government." The tumult deepened. Parliament met
before Christmas; and like Sisyphus, Lord John introduced
the third Reform Bill. Palmerston " came in late, and
seemed " (to the eye of Mr. Croker) " to go to sleep." But
he was still busy with the peers. While Durham raged,
Grey soothed the Waverers and his uneasy Cabinet discussed the wisdom of making peers to pass the Bill through
the Lords. This prospect was unpleasing to Palmerston;
and as the argument proceeded, Lord Durham waited hopefully for his place. For that irritable young man was not
averse to the Foreign Office. Meanwhile the Bill was read
a second time in the Commons; and on this pleasing turmoil
the year 1831 went out.

But Belgium and Reform were not its sole concerns. A
livelier tumult fell upon the ear from Italy, where *Carbonari*
breathed mysterious passwords and raised Bologna against
the Pope. Ungrateful for an almost total absence of taxation and a profusion of police, the Romagnuols rose; and
cardinals, beneath whose scarlet Mr. Greville's disrespectful
eye detected " a wretched set of old twaddlers," gathered
their ample skirts in sudden agility and scampered off to the
comforting proximity of St. Peter's. Two fair young men
brought to the insurrection the rousing name of Bonaparte,
whilst their anxious mother fluttered about Florence and
an indifferent father remembered gloomily that no one had
ever paid the least attention to him, even when he was
King of Holland. The younger (and more aquiline) brother
designed a *coup de main* upon the sound lines prevailing in

the Swiss army. Such were the earliest battle-honours of
the hero of Magenta and Solferino. But they were induced
to leave the fighting, as the slow tread of an Austrian army
announced a sudden end to revolution. For Metternich,
enjoying the restrained rapture of his third marriage after
a honeymoon consisting principally of draft despatches and
interrupted at short intervals by Gentz, cast a wary eye on
the Legations; and the white-coats moved. Austria, the
blind, repressive Austria of 1831, marched heavily into
Papal territory. The Croats went by; and before the thud
and blare of those incomparable bands the Italian dream
began to fade. One forgets sometimes the dull brutality
of Austria. Was not Vienna one large, mild *cabaret*, where
names of exquisite frivolity—Pepi Esterhazy, Diamantine
Potocka, Lori Fuchs—rotated in a languid ecstasy of lilting
music? Was not the age of Metternich also the age of
Schubert? Yet such melodies could bristle with guns, flog
women, and fill prisons. For whilst one head was planning
reaction at the Congress of Verona, another throbbed with
the mysterious beauty of the Unfinished Symphony. So
the little songs wound to their tearful endings; heads jigged in
time to the slightly prancing ballet-music of *Rosamunde*; and
Vienna danced, as the Croats went by in the Italian sunshine.

Whilst one Empire raised the menace of its arm over
Italy, another was already at grips with Poland, where
the fighting swayed obscurely among the winter trees outside
Warsaw. Russia was held off for a breathless moment, and
the despairing Poles appealed to Europe. A nobleman
(Poland was rich in noblemen) appeared in London and saw
Palmerston. But the Foreign Secretary was almost agon-
isingly correct. Talleyrand had already noted his distaste
for embarrassing the Czar, and it distressed his Polish visitor.
Perhaps he had learnt it from Princess Lieven. The Pole
demurred, pleaded for independence, quoted the hopeful
instances of Greece and Belgium. But Palmerston was
stern, insisting that "we must stand upon our treaties;
and while, on the one hand, we should remonstrate if Russia
tried to depart from the Treaty of Vienna, on the other
hand, we could not do so ourselves by helping to make

Poland entirely independent." His visitor withdrew and
was succeeded shortly by a young man named Walewski, in
whom a familiar profile announced a singular descent; for
he was the son of a Polish lady and a Corsican, and it was
just ten years since his father had died in a great storm of
wind at St. Helena. But he fared no better, though Palmerston could scarcely stifle a sporting sympathy with the Poles
and found it " impossible not to wish them heartily success;
but the odds against them are still very great." When
France proposed a joint *démarche*, he was correct and chilly;
and he felt small enthusiasm for his colleagues' efforts to
extract from the terms of the Vienna Treaty a British
guarantee of the Polish constitution. Such views might,
perhaps, be natural in Whigs, who had endeavoured to
impose a precisely similar guarantee of a Spanish constitution
on Mr. Canning. But Mr. Canning had resisted; and in
1831 the faithful Canningite resisted also. For he still bore
a trace of Princess Lieven's lessons. Warsaw despaired, as
the long martyrdom dragged on and the grey columns
wound endlessly out of Russia. Late in the year the fighting
died slowly down, as Palmerston wrote, a little ruefully,
" So there is an end of the poor Poles ! I am heartily sorry
for them," and in Paris a minister defied an angry Chamber
with the grim announcement *L'ordre règne à Varsovie.*

Then 1831 was over; and he was at Panshanger in the
first week of the new year. Lady Cowper was there with
a smile and a length of flannel for the cottagers and her
engaging habit of rustling into church half an hour late.
Palmerston came down for two days, with Talleyrand and
the voluble grimace of Madame de Dino, and filled his
hostess with disquiet about Reform. For the Prime
Minister was still set on his peer-making, and Lansdowne
and Palmerston seemed to fight a losing battle in Cabinet.
His voice was scarcely heard in debate, and he watched
the struggle for Reform with obvious distaste. A colleague
found him " bored," and with Europe on his hands it was
not surprising. But he still found energy to traffic discreetly with the Waverers. Mr. Greville, slightly unnerved

by sitting next to " a common-looking man in black " at Holland House, who alluded in the course of dinner to Alfieri, Scaliger, and Loyola's wound at Pampeluna and was subsequently revealed as Mr. Macaulay, buzzed like a cheerful fly between the parties. The busy messenger ran delighted errands, called on judicious peers, looked in at the Home Office where Melbourne " in his lazy, listening, silent humour " gave little satisfaction, and found Palmerston at the Foreign Office " infinitely more alert . . . and more satisfactory to talk to, because he enters with more warmth and more detail into the subject." The subject was the eternal Bill, and Palmerston confessed himself a convert to the ten-pound franchise—" he had at first been disposed to consider it too low, but he had changed his mind and now doubted if it would not turn out to be too high." In this mounting temper of democracy he watched Reform pass for the third time through the Commons, whilst anxious colleagues counted peers and the cholera was in the Thames. The Cabinet framed lists of ' peerables '; and for a dreadful moment Palmerston was in danger of immersion in the fountain of honour. When the Bill was in the Lords, he was still busy among the peers, collecting doubters, making discreet appointments for the Prime Minister, disputing phrases in minutes of private conversations, and tasting to the full the questionable joys of negotiation.

But the pace was quickened when a Tory amendment carried against the Government drove them to their last decision—the King must make fifty peers, or they must resign. The bold proposal came from Palmerston, who drew their minute; and that afternoon in May, 1832, the King saw Grey and Brougham, and refused. For seven amazing days the Government was suspended, whilst England was abandoned to an ecstasy of public meetings. A long stream of delegates poured into London; memorials showered on the King; and while the indomitable Duke struggled to make a Tory Government, there was a run on the Bank, and cheerful placards announced " No taxes paid here until the Reform Bill is passed." At last the Tories wavered, and Lord Grey returned to office. The King had yielded; and as Doyle's agreeable pencil depicted a cheerful Grey exclaiming on a mounting see-saw, " Here we go up up up," the Bill resumed its progress.   But no peers were needed, since an angry Opposition drove home to sulk or lurked in clubs; and on a day in June the Commons trooped to the bar of the House of Lords to hear the Royal Assent recited to the red hangings, the cheerful Whigs, and the empty benches of the Tories.

That month the Duke rode slowly from the City on a familiar date.   It was June 18, and four policemen walked by the horse's head.   For they had tried to drag him from the saddle in Fenchurch Street, and some stones were thrown in Holborn.   He turned down Chancery Lane into Lincoln's Inn; and as his angry countrymen waited hopefully at the gate, the stiff horseman rode slowly back to Apsley House. A lively pen at Craigenputtock revived the scene for a shrewd mother—" the cast-metal man riding slowly five long miles all the way like a pillar of *glar !* "   The Bill was passed; and before midsummer, 1832, a new world opened; a new, ungrateful world that had forgotten Waterloo and left the Duke predicting gloomily that " we shall never again see a government in England "; a world (so time advanced) that even found Mademoiselle Mars a shade mature for playing *jeunes amoureuses* at Covent Garden.   Was it an omen that Mr. Creevey boarded his first omnibus in the same year and found it " really charming "?   An age was passing; Goethe died that season, and Walter Scott was dying.   It was a world that owed almost its whole being to Grey's incomparable judgment, but something (more rarely recognised) to those interminable talks of Palmerston with the Waverers.

For the Canningite had learnt his lesson.   He freely confessed to the House of Commons that " I have no difficulty in saying that I have changed my sentiments, and that I have done so from having become wiser," and Mr. Praed responded in indignant stanzas—

> There was a time when I could sit
>   By Londonderry's side,
> And laugh with Peel at Canning's wit,
>   And hint to Hume he lied;

> Henceforth I run a different race,
>   Another soil I plough,
> And though I still have pay and place,
>   I'm not a Tory now.
>
> *   *   *   *   *
>
> If Harvey gets Brougham's seals and seat,
>   My friend will Harvey be;
> If Cobbett dines in Downing Street,
>   He'll have my twice times three;
> If Hunt in Windsor Castle rules,
>   I'll take a house at Slough;
> Tories were always knaves and fools.
>   I'm not a Tory now !

Converted to Reform, he made in the same year a more striking concession to progress. A debate upon the silk trade elicited a bold statement of those principles in which he had been instructed thirty years before by Professor Dugald Stewart—" What were called protecting duties were in fact disturbing duties . . . for the interest of the country to cast off the fetters with which ignorance had bound it. It was monstrous to suppose that commerce could be all on one side, or that nations could sell without buying. By repealing what were called protecting duties and acting on Liberal principles we should compel other nations to follow our example." The full Cobdenite doctrine rings strangely from Palmerston in 1832. But he retained his Edinburgh lessons and repeated them, while Mr. Cobden was still innocent of such opinions and before Mr. Bright had startled the Rochdale Literary and Philosophical Society with his wild surmise.

The year was no less crowded in the more congenial field of foreign affairs. Belgium persisted—" these never-ending Belgian affairs," as he wrote wearily to a colleague, " which will be settled whenever the Cabinet take a vigorous Resolution to order Malcolm to sea, but not till then." The affair was exquisitely complicated by the almost inexplicable provisions of a loan made by the Dutch to Russia during the French war, which Palmerston expounded endlessly to his sceptical supporters and a weary House. But the Powers had not yet ratified the treaty. Metternich and

Nesselrode had little taste for Belgium, born of a revolution
and cherished by such Jacobins as Casimir Périer and
Palmerston; and they adroitly delayed the ratifications in
hope of a change of Government upon Reform. British
importunity prevailed at last; and a week before the ' Days
of May ' the treaty was ratified. So Belgium existed in
public law; and a beam of felicity seemed to gild its prospects, when Leopold resigned his cherished weeds and,
almost with a smile, married an Orleans princess at Compiègne. The infant kingdom had recognition and a dynasty.
But these blessings scarcely sufficed, while Dutch troops,
still obdurate, surveyed the roofs of Antwerp from the
Citadel. Through the autumn there was uneasy talk of
coercion, and diplomats surveyed an alarming document
severely termed *le thème de Lord Palmerston.* Louis Philippe
ached for the inexpensive heroism of a march on Antwerp;
and his fleet arrived at Spithead in spite of King William's
' Jack Tar animosity,' which was raised to fever by the dreadful prospect of the Union flag contaminated by alliance with
the tricolour. The royal slumbers, broken at irregular
intervals after dinner by the courtly obligation of saying
with startling irrelevance " Exactly so, ma'am ! " and
dropping off again, were strangely troubled; but a drunken
sailor, who shared his sovereign's opinions, enjoyed a brief
police-court martyrdom for expressing them. The Powers
scowled (and Wellington wrote gloomily of " our Jacobin
course "), as France and England rushed to the rescue of
their revolutionary *protégé.* But Palmerston sat at his
papers, and his countrymen were slightly bewildered—

> We'll carry poor Palmerston through, Charles,
>   Whatever the country may say;
> But his Lordship, between me and you, Charles,
>   Behaves in a very odd way;
> He's clever at jesting and joking,
>   Which surely we might do without;
> But he won't—it's extremely provoking—
>   Explain what the war is about !

The combined squadron sailed for the Scheldt; French
drums were beating in the northern towns; the big shakos

moved; and Marshal Gérard took six divisions across the
frontier into Belgium with a pleasant flavour of old campaigns (but with a comforting absence of risk). They
headed straight for Antwerp, where the Dutch, commanded
by an officer with the inauspicious name of Chassé, waited
behind their guns. The Belgian army, by a wise precaution,
was detailed to watch for an invasion which was unlikely to
arrive. Whilst Europe waited, England plunged into the
questionable delights of a General Election; and when the
first reformed Parliament was elected, Palmerston, deserting
the uneventful shades of Blechingley, wooed his country
neighbours, drove out to Ringwood, and came in by the new
dispensation for South Hampshire. At Antwerp Gérard
besieged the Dutch *en règle*. Trenches were opened and
fascines filled under a dropping fire; a lunette was stormed;
and, Dutch honour satisfied, the place surrendered. So, to
an accompaniment of " chuckling at Brookes's and great
exultation among the Whigs," Belgium was completed in
the last week of 1832.

The year was lively under milder skies, where Austria
marched stiffly down the white Italian roads. His problem
had been simpler in Belgium, where Palmerston was merely
concerned to secure the integrity and independence of a
territory vitally important to Great Britain. In Italy his
objects were more complex, since his main anxiety was to
avert an Austrian invasion, which might provoke the French
and would certainly diminish the slender liberties of the
Italians. Such intervention must be checked; and to check
it he was prepared to intervene in the name of non-intervention, which Talleyrand defined with wicked glee as *mot
métaphysique et politique qui signifie à peu près la même
chose qu'intervention*. That had been Mr. Canning's mood;
and Palmerston had already joined a Conference in 1831,
"not to assist either the French or Austrian influence in
Italy, but to endeavour to restore tranquillity and order in
the Papal States in such a manner as not to increase in those
states either the one of these influences or the other." The
Powers conferred, while Palmerston held France and Austria
apart, warning the French that it was scarcely worth their

L

while " to risk involving all Europe in war for the sake of protecting the revolutionists in Romagna. If we could by negotiation obtain for them a little share of constitutional liberty, so much the better. . . ." These mild ambitions were almost satisfied, when a cautious project of reform was embodied in a Papal *Motuproprio*; and, society saved for the moment, the white-coats marched dustily back to Austrian territory. But the interval was brief. Early in 1832 Bologna was in disorder once again. A fluttered cardinal appealed to Austrian chivalry; and, sensitive as ever to the menace of freedom, the white-coats returned, and Radetzky held Bologna for the Pope. But this time the knight-errant was not alone. For two French battalions, moved with equal ardour, sailed from Toulon and rescued Ancona. From whom they rescued it was a shade obscure; but as their action took the rousing form of hoisting the tricolour and issuing (over a captain's signature) a singularly offensive proclamation against the Austrians, the cardinals between their two discordant friends assumed the innocent, but uneasy, posture of the Babes in the Wood, while British policy fluttered anxiously above the threatening scene with profuse assurances to both parties that neither meant the slightest harm. This nervous homœopathy prevailed; and peace was undisturbed, though Metternich was left shaking a rueful head over Palmerston's almost revolutionary proclivities, and warning an ambassador that London contained *un immense foyer de conflagration générale—vous aurez lieu de vous convaincre que nous dirigeons nos pompes vers ce foyer.*

A sharper conflict parted them upon a German question. The menace of the times, lamented by Metternich almost in *falsetto—' l'esprit* révolutionnaire *est venu s'infiltrer dans la paisible et sage Germanie '*—had provoked an attempt to centralise the German states for the common maintenance of the *status quo*. This innocent precaution elicited a sharp enquiry from Lord Palmerston, who scented a vague menace and was wholly undeterred from trespassing on German ground by the sacred duty of non-intervention. Indeed, he found the word distasteful—" for it was not an English word." The purist, fortified by a recent dinner at Holland House in the erudite company of Macaulay, preferred to speak of " non-interference "; and though he firmly repudiated all interference by force of arms, he reserved a perpetual right to interfere " by friendly counsel and advice." In this helpful mood he launched an enquiry as to Metternich's somewhat excessive precautions against the threatened march of progress into *la paisible et sage Germanie.* The Chancellor, though *Zampa* burst that year upon Vienna, was frosty, wrote an interminable despatch upon the Germanic constitution, accompanied it with appropriate reflections upon a comparison of British and Austrian methods of government (distinctly unfavourable to the former), and enclosed the whole in a circular to the German courts-which denounced with due asperity this unwarranted interference in German affairs. It was, perhaps, a triumph to have elicited from Metternich a rebuke of intervention.

1833 dawned in a faint atmosphere of farce, where his sovereign in transports over a Turkish ambassador in a red fez, whom Palmerston brought down to Brighton, indulged his fatal aptitude for after-dinner speaking. Indeed, the monarch so far caught the Turkish spirit as to urge a startled lady to introduce a daughter of Lady Jersey in Constantinople as " the daughter of one of his late brother's sultanas." So royal William danced the new year in with a breathless admiral of sixty-one and enquired of a gasping duke where he intended to be buried; while someone asked what you could expect from " a man with a head like a pineapple," and obliging Whigs governed his kingdom. The year wore on,

> As if the world of thirty-two
> Had been the world of thirty-three,

and as they abolished negro slavery, made grants of public money for education, chartered the East India Company (on condition that it listened to Mr. Macaulay), and passed a Factory Act to please Lord Ashley, the long shadow of Ireland—doom of progressive governments—fell across them. But these distractions scarcely reached the Foreign

Office, where Palmerston surveyed the world of 1833 with
an increasing tendency to turn indulgent eyes on France
and keep his sternest gaze for Russia. For France, with all
her faults, had scruples; even her prejudices were faintly
liberal; and, above all, she had tax-payers to restrain her
from unnecessary wars. That won him, since his first anxiety
was peace; and Palmerston informed the Commons that
" France and England could command the peace of Europe;
for France and England together would never make an
unjust war." In spite of Princess Lieven one could not
quite say that of Russia, which showed an awkward tendency to force embarrassing attentions on the shrinking
Turks. A terrifying Pasha of Egypt, who bore even stronger
traces of his early service in the Bashi-Bazouks than of his
earlier training in the tobacco trade, had invaded Syria,
passed the Taurus in 1832, and swept into Anatolia. When
Mehemet Ali threatened the Porte itself, the desperate Turks
appealed to Russia; for a drowning man, in the eloquent
image of the *Reis-Effendi*, will clutch at a serpent. The
Russians, prompt to save, sent warships to the Bosphorus
and marched an army-corps into full view of the indignant
British Embassy at Constantinople. This sudden chivalry
was most disturbing, since Palmerston, with little taste for
Mehemet Ali as " an occupier of the road to India," had still
less for Russia in that commanding situation; and his
anxieties were scarcely diminished when the Czar made a
secret treaty with the Turks, put off the British *chargé
d'affaires* with the unsatisfying assurance that he was
chevalier anglais and, pointing to his Garter, murmured
twice, " *Honi soit qui mal y pense.*"

These strange manœuvres cooled his friendship with the
Lievens. Indeed, he had already been something of a
disappointment to the exacting Dorothea. Designed to
play a docile part, he was revealed so early as 1830 as
" somewhat difficult to manage "; by 1832 he had become
" a poor, small-minded creature "; and the following
year disclosed him as a monster—" *un très-petit esprit,
lourd, obstiné* "—who left one marvelling how Lady Cowper
could endure so much of his company and positively ready

to "accept Mr. Cobbett as his successor without repugnance." The hateful man proposed to send Sir Stratford
Canning to the Embassy at St. Petersburg; there had been
talk of it before, but now the nomination was seriously
pressed. This person—*soupçonneux, pointilleux, défiant*—
was almost equally distasteful to Nesselrode and to his
master. But while their protests reverberated in the
Foreign Office, the unspeakable appointment was positively
gazetted. For Palmerston, with anxious eyes on Turkey,
was not inclined to leave his Russian business in inferior
hands, inclined still less to have his course dictated by a
long-necked foreign lady with (one must confess it) a reddish
nose. He had told Lady Cowper that he "thought both *she*
and her *Court* wanted to be taken down a peg"; he suspected her of having boasted that she could prevent the
appointment; and when she committed the double *gaucherie*
of appealing to the Prime Minister and employing Durham
to give noisy expression to her views, the rebellious pupil
at the Foreign Office held firm. Such unimaginable conduct
pricked the busy lady to pelt her Emily (and Palmerston's)
with angry letters, to pour her sorrows into the most receptive ear of Mr. Greville, and finally to leave with 'a back
somersault over the Baltic' and impart to a gravely nodding
Emperor her disappointment in Lord Palmerston.

That year his spring was enlivened by the influenza of
1833. A debate on foreign affairs was adjourned "because
my whistle was not . . . quite in tune"; and his letters
abound in calomel, quinine, and barley-water. He dined at
Kensington one night. The little Princess was in the saloon
with her rather overpowering mamma. She had dined early
with dear Lehzen, but came down to make her bows and
admire the manly, almost more than manly beauty of the
Duc D'Orléans and Talleyrand's queer leg and smiling M. van
de Weyer, whom Uncle Leopold trusted so much, and all the
gentlemen and ladies. Then they went in to dinner; and
she could hear the Coldstream Guards playing, while she and
Lehzen waited for the ladies to come back to the saloon.
That week Lord Palmerston was reassuring an anxious brother
in the Legation at Naples that "there is no truth whatever in

the Tory reports of a quarrel between me and Grey . . . I never met with anybody with whom I found myself so constantly agreeing." He corrected his Foreign Office drafts without much thought of the little girl in the saloon at Kensington, although he noted " a flight of German princes come over to us." A Brunswick, Solms, two Wurtembergers, and the luxuriantly hyphened Prince of Reuss-Lebenstein-Gera succumbed to sudden cravings for a sight of England; but Palmerston opined a trifle drily that " Princess Victoria is hardly old enough as yet to make it worth their while to come."

He drafted in his big handwriting through 1833. His callers waited, sometimes in the office and sometimes at Stanhope Street; and since he rarely kept them waiting less than two hours, his waiting-room was full. There was a slight, but intricate, revival of the Belgian problem to be discussed with a delightful Dutchman, who spoke perfect English and had been at Eton and St. John's; and there was always Metternich to watch, and the Italian antics of Grand-Dukes and cardinals, and Russia—" the only Power with which we are likely to come to a real quarrel, and even with her I trust we shall be able to keep the peace." Once he found time to appear again in an Army debate, speaking, with quite a pleasant reminiscence of old times, on flogging; and later in the year he gave another airing to his progressive opinions upon trade—" He could wish that the word ' Protection ' were erased from every commercial dictionary; for instead of protection it was disturbance, for it interfered with the operations of capital—it was an impediment upon industry—it was a bar to competition."

That autumn Lady Cowper took an ailing daughter to the Riviera; and, her guardian eye removed, Lord Palmerston's strayed towards Lady Jersey. The pursuer, if Princess Lieven could be believed, was the delicious Sarah. But Palmerston was " not a little touched by her enticing ways, paying her visits during his mornings of two hours' duration, and then little dinners with her, and then going to the theatre together." To an unfriendly eye he even looked love-lorn; and there was positively talk of an invitation to

Broadlands. The tale reached Mr. Creevey, though he was inclined to doubt it. But Sefton was a believer, and Princess Lieven quoted with gusto Lady Jersey's slightly fatuous announcement that " P. was never really in love with anybody but her." Such sweet distractions waited upon a Secretary of State, whose silk waistcoats were always in request for ladies to bind books of verse in, whilst Lady Cowper watched a blue and distant sea and Cowper lived obstinately on.

But that year a wilder music fell on his official ear, where Spanish and Portuguese pretenders whirled together in the stamp and thunder of an interminable *jota*. The dance was highly complicated, with European repercussions; and as the claimants wheeled, the Foreign Office seemed to catch a click of distant castanets, a throb of faint guitars. The Secretary of State might murmur the slightly fevered invocation uttered a few years later by Mr. Borrow, of the British and Foreign Bible Society, to Asturian *aquadores* lolling by fountains, to Valencian post-boys waiting languidly for fares and rolling cigarettes, to beggars from La Mancha huddled in blankets and asking charity indifferently at prison gates, to Basques, to Catalans and Andalusian *toreros* and, last of all, "genuine sons of the capital, rabble of Madrid, ye twenty thousand *manolos*, whose terrible knives . . ." For Spain invaded the despatches, odd and intractable, where Mr. Villiers at the British Embassy savoured the rose, the fan, the comb, the black *mantilla*, noting how well they walked in their silk shoes—" not pit-a-pat and in a hurry as French women do." Spain lounged in courtyards, humming *coplas* and sipping orangeade. But there was a stir among the empty hills, where cloaked muleteers jingled down mountain paths and the *contrabandista*, most national of figures, smuggled a contraband king.

It began in Portugal, where a girl Queen at war with a wicked uncle made an irresistible appeal to British chivalry. Indeed, it had begun in Mr. Canning's time, when a reactionary threat by Spain in 1826 against the constitution of Portugal provoked the most Palmerstonian of Mr. Canning's gestures—" It was only on last Friday night that this precise information arrived. On Saturday His Majesty's confidential servants came to a decision. On Sunday that decision received the sanction of His Majesty. On Monday it was communicated to both Houses of Parliament—and this day, Sir, at the hour in which I have the honour of addressing you—the troops are on their march for embarkation. . . . We go to plant the standard of England on the well-known heights of Lisbon. Where that standard is planted, foreign dominion shall not come." That lively intervention, executed with gusto in the sacred name of non-intervention, had struck the note; and British policy observed with a parental eye the infant (but not uniformly well-behaved) Liberalism of the Peninsula. So when a complex of abdications ranged the little Queen against a reactionary Regent, the British course was clear; and Palmerston frowned upon the Regent Miguel, endeared to Metternich by a Jesuit training and long residence at Vienna. The Queen's agents haunted London and Paris, raising loans and hiring troops. The Foreign Enlistment Act was cheerfully ignored; and a British officer commanded her exiguous fleet. But her prospects waned in a civil war of wild incompetence. All Portugal outside one starving city was held for Miguel, and Lisbon rang with the Miguelite song :

> *El Rey chegou—el Rey chegou,*
> *E en Belem desembarcou,*

although her scared supporters had a faint hope of sanctuary from Palmerston's hint to the British warships in the Tagus that " if any individual were really in danger of his life from unjust violence, we should not and could not find fault if such a person were to find his way on board our squadron." But there was a sudden turn in 1833. While Palmerston was writing hopefully that " it was anybody's race yet," the laws of strategy were violated with complete success, and for the first and only time in military history a besieged garrison conquered a kingdom. The Queen's forces emerged, less than three thousand strong, from the battered lines of Oporto, sailed for the south, made an eccentric landing, and overran the country; her fleet of five destroyed her uncle's fleet of ten; Lisbon collapsed; and Palmerston, still haunted by the turf, wrote gleefully that " she has won the race, though she has not got to the winning-post." For Miguel was still in the field, foiled and fresh from the nameless crime of burning large quantities of port, a sacrilegious act which wrung from the indignant squire of Broadlands the bitter cry, " There never was so atrocious an outrage." But at Lisbon they proclaimed the little Queen with her " sensible Austrian countenance."

That month a king died at Madrid; and a strange chance reproduced in Spain the same duel between a girl Queen and a wicked uncle. The uncle, to be sure, was not so wicked; but the Queen, at three, was still more girlish. The issues were identical, since Don Carlos, dull-eyed and prim, stood for reaction, whilst his innocent niece became an unconscious emblem of enlightenment. That cause was sustained for the moment by her mother, a lively lady of twenty-seven who ruled as Regent, consoled by a good-looking guardsman and supported by a minister of striking tedium, in whom Palmerston found that " the wine merchant and the consul predominated over the minister and the statesman." Worse still, he had a warped affection for the Portuguese pretender; and British policy in the Peninsula was unfriendly to Jesuitical uncles. This attitude had stronger reasons than a Whig taste for freedom or a merely frivolous desire to irritate Metternich; since Palmerston, like Mr. Canning, was primarily concerned to secure the independence of Spain and Portugal from foreign (and, mainly, from French) influence; and he retained a sound conviction that such influence " can best be exerted over the Court of a despotic monarch and becomes much weaker, if not entirely paralysed, when it has to act upon the constitutional representatives of a free people. The British government, therefore, perceived that, by assisting the Spanish people to establish a constitutional form of government, they were assisting to secure the political independence of Spain, and they had no doubt that the maintenance of that independence would be conducive to important British interests." Such reasoning inspired his activity in Peninsular affairs, his distaste for Don

Carlos and Dom Miguel, and his watchful eye upon the marriages of Spanish and Portuguese princesses. Meanwhile two little Queens were installed at Lisbon and Madrid; and a small Princess at Kensington, who asked through her mamma for the autograph of the Queen Regent of Spain to put in her collection, received the delicious embarrassment of a Spanish decoration. As the year waned, the wicked uncles stood back to back in Portugal, whilst the north rose against the Spanish Regency. Priests stirred their flocks, while *guerrilleros* sharpened knives or polished muskets that had last fired at French despatch-riders on lonely roads in 1810. Basques in their little caps marched behind the dark features of Zumalacarregui; an army moved against them; Carlists watched *Cristinos* across the Ebro; and on this pleasing uncertainty the year 1833 went out.

The new year opened on the Spanish turmoil. Mr. Villiers at Madrid, fortified by a promise of *Peter Simple* and Hood's *Comic Annual* for 1834, endeavoured to direct a minister who actively insisted during a civil war upon his diverse qualifications " as a poet, a statesman, a dramatist, a Lovelace, a financier, an orator, an historian," and gratified his versatility by simultaneously producing a Spanish constitution and a tragedy in verse —both, as a critic said, from French models. The war of the nieces against the uncles trailed obstinately on among the hills. But Palmerston, in spite of a rumour of his resignation, designed a speedier end. There was an awkward risk that France might give decisive aid to the two Queens and so become paramount at their two Courts. Now, poachers were an abomination. He had some trouble with them that spring at Broadlands; and European poaching was no less distasteful. He checked it most adroitly. Uniting England, Spain and Portugal in an agreement for the expulsion of the two pretenders, he fore-stalled the French. Then, deftly numbering the poacher with the game-keepers, he included France in the compact and so concluded the Quadruple Alliance of 1834. The Cabinet was carried " by a *coup de main*, taking them by surprise, and not leaving them time to make objections."

It was " a capital hit, and all my own doing." For England had flung a shielding arm over the little Queens; the Queens smiled gratefully; France had gained nothing; and " what is of more permanent and extensive importance, it establishes a quadruple alliance among the constitutional states of the West, which will serve as a powerful counterpoise to the Holy Alliance of the East. . . . I should like to see Metternich's face when he reads our treaty." No painter caught it; but a choking exclamation survives among his papers—*la Reine Isabelle est la Révolution incarnée dans sa forme la plus dangereuse; Don Carlos représente le principe monarchique aux prises avec la Révolution pure.* So he was inclined, perhaps, to vary his earlier judgment, *Lord Palmerston est un peu naïf en politique.*

But the high comedy of 1834 was played on a more lighted stage, where the polite world read *Philip van Artevelde*, discussed the strange proceedings of Edward Irving, and was inclined (in Holland House, at least) to value Wordsworth lightly, while Mr. Greville quoted Stendhal and thought of his wasted life. That year Lord Palmerston was talked of rather freely. For rumour married him to Mrs. Jerningham; a second whisper named Mrs. Petre; and an irreverent scribbler even wrote of " the venerable cupid," since he was nearly fifty now and it was hardly wise of him to exhibit his lovely trophy in the House of Commons. Mr. Praed was almost angry—

> If you, my dear lord, had been ever the worse
> 　For the profligate things you have done;
> If the title you bear were a scoff and a curse
> 　To the scribes of the *Times* and the *Sun*,
>
> Perhaps I might learn, in your sorrow and shame,
> 　Whate'er the Rotunda might say,
> To fancy consistency more than a name,
> 　And truth a good thing in its way.
>
> But you—when you've babbled your jests and your jibes . . .

　　*　　*　　*　　*　　*　　*

Indeed, a slightly florid contributor to the *Morning Post*, who had already fought High Wycombe as a Radical and

speculated as to his own political alignment under the
striking epigraph "*What is He?*" was shortly to depict him
"tilting with a lady's fan." But diplomats knew better.
Madame de Dino might deplore his manners (though Lady
Cowper pleaded loyally that they were due to his dreadful
over-work), might even find his eye pale and hard, his nose
retroussé and impertinent. But there was always his
"remarkable facility for speaking and writing French";
and Talleyrand esteemed him highly, although H. B. had
drawn him as a fly to Talleyrand's spider, as a blind man to
Talleyrand's dog, as cat's paw to Talleyrand's monkey.
A more rueful witness to his powers sat in the Russian Embassy, where Princess Lieven stared at her letters of recall.
So her Emperor had failed her, and from the brink of exile
she sent imploring messages to Palmerston—*Toute ma vie,
tout mon bonheur seront détruits.*

But the order was obeyed, and she spent one final season
in a depressing round of farewell parties. There was a dreadful evening at Lord Palmerston's, when he came down late
as usual to a large official dinner and sat between Dorothea
and the Dino in the square dining-room at Stanhope Street.
And after that they were all absorbed in the grave problem
of her presentation bracelet. Rubies were too expensive;
turquoises were Russian; sapphires she had; peridots were
common; she disliked opals; and the distracted committee
decided upon a large pearl. Then she departed—

> She is gone, as the *Herald* announces,
> To latitudes milder and colder;
> She is gone with her pearls and her flounces,
> She is gone with the bows on her shoulder.

The Lievens were recalled to the accompaniment of a leader
in *The Times* upon 'the *petit nez retroussé*'; and, mindful
of Almack's, Dorothea lived on beyond the Channel, stretching
out hands towards Panshanger like *Tannhäuser's* towards his
mountain. So Metternich called Palmerston a tyrant and
added, by a crowning irony, "The age of tyrants is over."

The year was lively in home politics as well, and he made
one or two appearances in debate apart from Foreign Office

matters. A proposal of complete Free Trade in corn, which
"staggered" young Mr. Gladstone, provoked a slight retreat
from his advanced opinions, though he was still in favour of
a gradual reduction of the duties; and in support of a
Cambridge petition for the admission of Dissenters to degrees
he gave a notable performance in his familiar vein of common
sense, enquiring "what could be so absurd as to require a
man to subscribe to the thirty-nine articles before you
will allow him to cure you of a fever," and laughing off the
solemnities, that were being talked on the subject of college
chapel, in the mocking question, "Was it either essential or
expedient that young men should be compelled to rush from
their beds every morning to prayers, unwashed, unshaved,
and half dressed; or, in the evening, from their wine to
chapel, and from chapel back again to their wine?" He was
less successful (Mr. Greville found it a "woeful exhibition")
in his own defence from charges of "perfect indifference,
flippancy of manner, aristocratic contempt." But the
Cabinet—' the mighty Reform Cabinet with its colossal
majority, and its testimonial goblets of gold, raised by the
penny subscriptions of a grateful people '—had other
troubles. The shadow of Ireland lengthened; and an Irish
Church Bill touched ministers upon their Anglican consciences.
There were four resignations, and even Palmerston's was
rumoured. But Mr. Praed was left lamenting—

> There's no foundation for the news,
> 　Whate'er the sanguine *Post* may say;
> England has commerce yet to lose,
> 　And friendships yet to cast away.
> Dead are her laurels, dim her fame;
> 　But destiny has yet behind
> A darker doom, a fouler shame;
> 　Lord Palmerston has not resigned!
> 　*　　*　　*　　*　　*
> A nation's sneer, a nation's frown,
> 　Might awe, might fire, a noble mind;
> Pitt would have flung his office down!—
> 　Lord Palmerston has not resigned!

There was, indeed, no very obvious reason why he should.
But he asserted sturdily that "it was his distinct and

deliberate opinion that it was the right of the State to deal
with the trust of the property of the Church." That month
a loaded cab rolled under a " damp-clouded kind of sky "
across Belgrave Square, plunged into Chelsea, and set down
a wide-eyed couple (with a canary and a multitude of
luggage) before a newly painted door in Cheyne Row.

Lord Grey, a trifle weary, repaired the gaps in his Cabinet.
There was even talk of sending Durham to the Paris Embassy; but Palmerston mistrusted that impulsive figure—
" I know him to be my enemy "—and demurred. The
ministry hacked manfully at the upas-tree. There were
interminable Irish debates and a Coercion Bill. But before
the summer was out, Althorp resigned over an indiscretion
and, his loss sufficing as a decent pretext, Grey followed him
with evident relief. The Tories cheered; the Whigs, dismayed, sought refuge beneath the languid banner of Lord
Melbourne. His sovereign summoned him to Windsor; and
the expectant minister informed a secretary that he thought
it a damned bore and that he was in many minds what he
should do. The eager secretary replied that, damn it, such
a position never was occupied by any Greek or Roman and,
if it only lasted two months, was well worth while. The
judicious peer reflected. " By God ! " he said, " that's
true; I'll.go." So Lord Melbourne became Prime Minister
of England.

The secretary had promised him two months : he lasted
four. There was little change at first, as the Irish shadow
grew and Palmerston sat drafting steadily. That autumn
they were burning old Exchequer tallies at Westminster.
An overheated flue resulted, and the old Houses of Parliament went up in flame. The new resident in Cheyne Row
stood in a London crowd to watch the blaze, heard how they
" whewed and whistled when the breeze came, as if to encourage it," and felt his Lowland ear offended by their shrill
misuse of honest Scots—" There go their *Hacts!* " and
" There's a flare-up for the House of Lords," and " A judgment for the Poor Law Bill."

But in November a peer died. Peers had died before;
but this was no ordinary casualty.

" It is an immense event," said Tadpole.

" I don't see my way," said Taper.

" When did he die ? " said Lord Fitz-Booby.

" I don't believe it," said Mr. Rigby.

Althorp succeeded, leaving an awkward gap on the Treasury Bench. Melbourne required a Leader in the Commons, considered names, even had a passing thought of Palmerston. Then he drove down to Brighton, to consult his sovereign. William was difficult, alluded to the Irish Church, produced (as monarchs, when making difficulties, do) his royal conscience, raised objections and, in fine, dismissed him. The easy minister drove back to London and left his colleagues to discover from *The Times* that they were out. The Tories buzzed; Peel was in Rome; the Duke " after much fumbling with his spectacles," was sworn in as First Lord and all three Secretaries of State *ad interim*; and eight days later Peel was asking a panting messenger why he had not posted faster, while Metternich beyond the Alps expended treasuries of scandalised surprise upon the deplorable tone of Palmerston's announcement of his resignation. For the extraordinary man had written, " We are out," adding the highly undiplomatic sentiment that Prince Metternich would be extremely pleased to hear it. He was; but such jocularity was most ill-timed, and the cheerful intimation left him officially appalled at *une preuve nouvelle de ce que l'esprit et le caractère du dernier principal secrétaire d'État renferment de haineux et d'inexplicable.* But Palmerston was out, at any rate.

III

IT was four years, almost to a day, since he drafted his first despatch; and Palmerston had made amazing strides. The House of Commons was not yet captivated by that bland defensive manner. But he was, at fifty, a European figure. Not yet, perhaps, the full glories of his later transfiguration, when pious Germans muttered in abhorrence,

> *Hat der Teufel einen Sohn*
> *So ist er sicher Palmerston,*

whilst Austrian *douaniers* detained a case of table-knives whose guilty blades bore the suspicious name of " Palmer & Son," and an excited colleague glared at a British passport and, catching the hated signature, struck it from a startled traveller's hand with the hysterical exclamation, *C'est un nom détestable.* But Mr. Borrow, hopefully leaving tracts in the ruins of a robber's den in Alemtejo, was soon to have a different colloquy over the same signature with one of Queen Cristina's *Nacionales.* Asked for his passport, Mr. Borrow, according to his habit, was expansive, produced it with a flourish, and made play with the signature (to say nothing of a casual promise that Palmerston would shortly end the Carlist war). The awed *Cristino* hazarded the opinion that this *Caballero Balmerson* must be a very honest man. The eager emissary of the British and Foreign Bible Society concurred with emphasis, adding the highly idiomatic tribute, *Es mucho hombre.* And so they parted, the National uncovering to look his deferential last upon the clear, the flowing, the incomparable signature of the Secretary of State.

Handwriting was, indeed, his *forte.* He early cautioned the young gentlemen of the Foreign Office against the twin iniquities of ill-formed letters and pale ink. But letters still continued to slope backwards, "like the raking masts of an American schooner" or stood in horrid rows "which can only be compared to Iron Railings leaning out of the perpendicular." His own flowed exquisitely in that faultless hand, which lived on in Mr. Gladstone's memory as one of the two perfect things that he had known, entitling Palmerston to be a trifle captious on points of caligraphy, to return a despatch to a distant consul for transcription in blacker ink, and even to issue acidly precise instructions that some reluctant pupil "should form his letters by connecting his slanting down strokes by visible lines at top or bottom according to the letters which he intends his parallel lines to represent."

He was not always so exacting, though his sovereign found him a stern master, when royal William made a light-hearted promise of a consulate and failed for weeks to secure from Palmerston official sanction of his kindly impulse. He had a highly inconvenient taste for finding someone always waking in the office when the House rose; and if business pressed, he declined to recognise the sabbath. In later years a Sunday absentee provoked a sharp explosion, barely checked by Lady Palmerston's timid explanation that "You see, my dear, some people go to church on Sundays." But when high-spirited administrators dazzled the pretty dress-makers across the street by manipulating mirrors from an upper window, a bland Secretary of State enquired, "Who are these unmannerly youths who have been casting Reflections on young ladies opposite?" And an impudent subordinate, who had sent up a draft in an enormous parody of his favourite handwriting, was once rewarded by the imperturbable comment that "the Writer of this Paper would write an excellent hand if he wrote a little larger." Such gleams might compensate for late hours and devastated Sundays; and even his sharpest critics in the office confessed to Mr. Greville that the Secretary of State "wrote admirably, and could express himself perfectly in French, very sufficiently in Italian, and understood German; that his diligence and attention were unwearied—he read everything and wrote an

M

immense quantity." The worst of their indictment was
that he missed appointments—" never caring for an engagement if it did not suit him, keeping everybody waiting for
hours on his pleasure or caprice "—and was disliked by foreign
diplomats. Four years of Palmerston had left Talleyrand
respectful and M. de Metternich puzzled and angry. So he
was, beyond doubt, a European figure.

But he was out in the last days of November, 1834, a
shade relieved to see a chance of a little hunting at last. His
sovereign reposed on Tory counsels and waited for Peel to
come from Rome, while the Duke in various incarnations
held every seal—" he has fixed his headquarters at the
Home Office, and occasionally roves over the rest "—and
an irreverent pencil depicted a Cabinet of ten Wellingtons
in ten different costumes assuring a contented monarch of
their perfect unanimity.

Then Peel returned—' the great man in a great position,
summoned from Rome to govern England.' Young Mr.
Gladstone got a post at the Treasury, and the town waited
in a delightful flutter for the elections. Mr. Tadpole wanted
a cry; Mr. Taper promised a title; Mr. Greville felt that
young Disraeli with his slightly fluid principles was hardly
the man to bring into Parliament; and Lord Palmerston
went down to Hampshire " to take the field and commence
itinerant spouter at inn meetings of freeholders, and to ride
about the country canvassing."

> Hard, very hard, the patriot's fate,
>   Whom Brooks's and the stars send down
> To be the Liberal candidate
>   For some extremely liberal town !
> Who quits his house in sweet May Fair
>   In vain regretting and repining,
> While Fashion in her glory there
>   Is fiddling, flirting, dancing, dining—
>
> *   *   *   *   *
>
> Who rattles from his country seat
>   When hounds are meeting all about him,
> Or steals away from Lombard Street
>   When business can't go on without him—

Who leaves, in short, by hurried stages
Whate'er amuses or engages,
And, hanging out a ponderous flag
On Crown or Castle, Star or Stag,
By speech and placard makes it clear
To all who see, and all who hear,
That he's the man to represent
The march of mind in Parliament.

But his persuasions failed, in spite of a lively mob at Ringwood; and early in 1835, while Princess Lieven rubbed
distant hands over "a great man greatly fallen," he was
writing ruefully to Lord John Russell that the seat was lost.
The Church, it seemed, was still in danger; the farmers,
"in arrear and looking for abatements, were more than
usually dependent on Landlords"; and the Whigs had done
something unpopular about spirit licences.   This shocking
result almost made him a convert to "that absurd plan,"
the ballot—" I am certain that under a System of Ballot
I should have had a very large Majority.   But exceptional
advantages cannot counterbalance inherent objections. . . ."
So he retained his principles without a seat; and there were
wicked rejoicings at the Foreign Office.

Peel governed uneasily through the first months of 1835.
Tory no longer, his reluctant followers responded to the spirit
of the age and called themselves Conservatives—" 'a sound
Conservative Government,' said Taper musingly.   " I understand : Tory men and Whig measures.' "   But the Whigs
were too strong for them, and they were out in the spring.
Melbourne lounged back to office; and in the middle of it all
John Russell married a widow (and was called ' the Widow's
Mite ').   There was a highly complicated interlude, with wild
manœuvres to keep Brougham off the Woolsack and a
respectful offer of the Foreign Office to Lord Grey.   Even
Palmerston consented to this arrangement, though it must
have resulted in his own exclusion; and Paris was startled
from its talk of the new homœopathy, of M. Hugo's plays and
Madame Sand's subversive novels by a lively rumour of his
speedy arrival as ambassador.   But Grey declined; and
there was talk of Lord John Russell, even of Durham, for

Foreign Secretary. Lord Palmerston, in this alluring programme, was to become a marquis and withdraw with dignity to be Lord-Lieutenant of Ireland or Governor-General of India. But the prospect failed to please; Calcutta, Dublin Castle, and the House of Lords were equally distasteful; and he informed Lord Melbourne—"distinctly, unequivocally, unalterably"—that without the Foreign Office he "had rather not engage in the administration at all." Melbourne consulted Grey, surveyed the field, and yielded. So Palmerston in April, 1835, was back at his standing desk in the Foreign Office.

IV

THE Whigs were in again; and that 'silly bustling old fellow,' their royal master, swallowed them as Palmerston had once seen him swallow an unpalatable appointment—" as a good child swallows a dose; quickly, though with some wry faces."

The world in 1835 was much what it had been six months before; and as the red boxes poured despatches on his table, Lord Palmerston surveyed a well-remembered landscape. Beyond the Channel Louis Philippe, eluding almost monthly assassins with inconceivable agility, retained his throne; beyond the Pyrenees the sound of Carlist gunfire still rolled along the Ebro; beyond the Alps Italians dreamed uneasy dreams and Austrian sentries, pacing slowly in white tunics, cast stiff shadows in the spring sunshine. East of the passes Metternich plied his perpetual pen; and still further to the east the towering outline of Russia climbed slowly up the sky. Those pinnacles, that bulk, those swelling domes melted at last so easily. But for a century they never failed to awe, though Palmerston had once confessed in his most clear-sighted mood that " the fact is that Russia is a great humbug, and that if England were fairly to go to work with her we should throw her back half a century in our campaign "; but in 1835 they shadowed British minds with a disturbing range of emotions, from pity for the Poles to a less platonic sentiment of apprehension for Turkey, for Central Asia, for India itself. King William himself was always warning ministers of Russian perfidy, of her insidious ambitions " notwithstanding all her professions of moderation and disinterestedness," and eagerly commended the sovereign specific of a strong British squadron in the Mediterranean. So Palmerston confronted Russia, confessing blandly that " we are just as we were, snarling at each other, hating each other, but neither wishing for war." There was, perhaps, one change in the European scene, where Louis Philippe, always the *père de famille*, pursued his laudable ambition for daughters-in-law with sound dynastic prospects. This taste inclined him to Vienna; and oblivious of the Quadruple Alliance, he studied with increasing deference endless homilies from Metternich upon *cette dissolution générale, qui se masque sous le nom de progrès* and that more delectable state—*le premier des bienfaits pour toute société humaine*—which Metternich described alluringly as *le repos*.

Such was the stage to which Lord Palmerston returned in April, 1835; and one critic was shortly disappointed by Lord Grey's report that " in the Foreign Office I am told everything is *couleur de rose;* that all the subordinates are delighted with the kindness of their chief; and that the foreign Ministers praise his manner of doing business. Pozzo in particular. . . ." But he was not unaided, since Melbourne took an active hand in foreign affairs; for the two men were old allies, almost (through Lady Cowper) brothers-in-law. That friendship had survived his aberrations of 1834; and Mr. Creevey, enumerating guests, could still " beg *Cupid* Palmerston's pardon ! he, too, was there, as also was Lady Cowper, if you come to that." The Prime Minister was not always in ' his lazy, listening, silent humour '; and Palmerston received a daily series of undecipherable notes in that angular handwriting, which tended to begin " For God's sake don't . . ." or " This is rather awkward . . ." and maintained Melbourne's effortless control of policy and even of Foreign Office drafting. This harmony was emphasised in the summer, when their unaccountable sovereign took sudden offence at a diplomatic appointment and put his curly signature to a remarkable command that Melbourne should transmit his royal censure to his Foreign Secretary. Melbourne complied, insisting sturdily that he " must by no means be considered as concurring in any censure of a Minister with whom he has entirely agreed, or of an act to which he has himself been a party." So Panshanger repelled with perfect courtesy Windsor's erratic thunders.

But, Ireland and home politics apart, their first anxiety was Spain, where Mr. Villiers still wrung anguished hands over "this cannibal war, these 2½ years of *lèse-humanité*." For the *gorras* still intoned the Carlist litany of *Dios, Patria, Rey* in the northern valleys, and the steady killing had shocked even Wellington into a humanitarian appeal. But the urgent problem was less to mitigate than to win the war; and Palmerston made ingenious use of his Quadruple Alliance. That instrument had failed (perhaps it never was intended) to create the league of "the constitutional states of the West," which had startled Metternich into an angry splutter in 1834. But it admirably averted all risk of a French *coup* in Spain. For French intervention under the treaty was strictly conditional upon British consent; and whilst a British fleet earned Spanish gratitude by blockading Carlist ports, Palmerston had declined to sanction on the part of France anything stronger than shipment of the Foreign Legion from Algeria, and even trumped that mild instalment of French chivalry by suspending the Foreign Enlistment Act and embodying a considerable British Legion in the *Cristino* forces. Indeed, Lord Melbourne had enquired with a sudden gleam, "Could nothing be done with the Poles whom we have here?" So British soldiers fought in a temporary allegiance to Queen Isabella; and this equivocal operation provided Palmerston with his main Parliamentary business. He had come in for Tiverton that summer; and he was back in his place, as bland as ever, refusing papers and waving off questions, as angry Tories asked whether their country was at war or not and whether it was true that a company of sappers and miners . . . Once, in a rare excursion into Irish matters, his distaste for Orangemen inspired the judicious comment that "the unyielding opposition of a minority to an important measure, without any valid reasons for such opposition being assigned, was a species of tyranny quite as objectionable as any other." But his normal exercise was on Spanish topics, among Pragmatic Sanctions and problems of blockade and points of neutrality and returns of arms furnished to Queen Cristina.

As the year waned, the war climbed unsteadily towards its crisis (and Mr. Borrow's chosen moment for evangelical effort. in the Spanish mission-field) ; and Spain reeled into 1836 in a *crescendo* of atrocities.

Six hundred miles away Lord Melbourne had been reading Dr. Arnold's sermons and thought them very able. Lacking the more obtrusive signs of industry, he tempted the vivacious *Runnymede* to consign him with Disraelian scorn to " the gardens of Hampton Court, where you might saunter away the remaining years of your now ludicrous existence, sipping the last novel of Paul de Kock, while lounging over a sundial." But the Prime Minister was less passive than might appear, and little notes in his angular script abounded on his colleagues' tables. Palmerston had one in the first week of the new year about a famous *énergumène* in the Diplomatic service, suspected (not without reason) of official indiscretions —" I think it would be well to get him off to his post. These active persons are better after all in the Levant." It crossed a letter in his colleague's round handwriting, which cheerfully complained of " what Mrs. Malaprop would call one of the many *ellice*inations " of Mr. Ellice, deep at that moment in the political oracles of Paris and highly communicative of good advice. But their correspondence was not always quite so cheerful; and soon Palmerston was sending a map to Melbourne, which indicated the sinister advance of Russia towards the Indian frontier. The Prime Minister urged hopefully that remoteness from St. Petersburg must always be a source of weakness to Russian extremities. But Palmerston was unconvinced, and in his laudable desire to raise obstacles in the path of Russia he even elicited a mild rebuke from Melbourne—" I would leave the Circassians to themselves. I am against exciting people to commit themselves to a warfare in which you cannot give them effectual support." The tone was easy; but Palmerston's most vulnerable point was never more sharply touched. Three months later the Prime Minister was still insisting privately upon " the extreme danger of taking strong steps." Such warnings lend an odd flavour of unreality to *Runnymede's* elaborate contempt for Palmerston, as " the Lord Fanny of diplomacy . . . cajoling France with an airy compliment, and menacing Russia with a perfumed cane." The satirist dealt faithfully with his Tory origins and the eviction of the Canningites " for playing a third-rate part in a third-rate intrigue." He was lively on his subject's manner of affecting " to smile and settle your cravat " and suitably scornful of his lack of fluency. Shocked by " a callow confidence of tone and an offensive flippancy of language," the indignant scribe denounced the Foreign Secretary a trifle shrilly for insignificance, for " silly articles in newspapers about justice to Ireland," and for the Spanish exploits of " your crimping Lordship." Then as that youthful ear caught " the ground swell of the coming tempest," that youthful eye detected " a mysterious dimness . . . stealing over the gems of our imperial diadem " and watched with studied horror how " the standard of England droops fitfully upon its staff," the last claims of irony were richly satisfied, and Mr. Disraeli discovered in Lord Palmerston " a want of breeding."

In Parliament he did little more that year than count out the small change of departmental problems. But his official life was anxious, with " this division of Europe into two camps." Russia and Austria were growing quite inseparable, where Metternich in constant fear of his eternal *conflagration générale* had assembled his international *pompiers*, and Louis Philippe displayed an awkward tendency to prefer enlistment in this unheroic corps to being extinguished by it. Lord Palmerston surveyed his " dear friend and ally " a little sadly, and reflected with becoming resignation that " so goes the world, and one must take men as one finds them, and make the best of what is, shut one's eyes to failings and faults, and dwell as much as one can upon good points." But the desertion of France scarcely simplified his action in Spain, much less in Poland, where the last embers of the dying fire were stamped mercilessly out at Cracow.

Europe in 1836 had an unsettled air. There was a sudden hint of change in the autumn, when the peculiar son of Queen

Hortense slipped through the streets of Strasburg in the darkness of an October morning to inform a barrack-square that he was Napoleon II. In spite of a poor appearance (Princess Lieven had seen him at Baden-Baden in the summer and found him *vulgaire au possible*) the French artillery seemed glad to hear it. But the Line was harder to please; and after this singular commotion he spent the night in the town gaol. Even England, where the old King's oddity began to exceed the permitted extravagance of royal persons, turned hopefully towards a new regin. There was a young Princess; and Melbourne gave a casual thought to the problem, which would soon be on him, of a Prince Consort— " Chance makes marriages; even royal ones, and perhaps better than Policy ! "—adding the sound reflection, " We have Coburgs enough."

So 1837 dawned in a mild air of expectation. Lord Palmerston was entertaining unmarried diplomats in the snow at Broadlands and lamenting the inconstancy of France; the latest Emperor of the French caught his first glimpse of the American coast; Mrs. Fitzherbert, strange shadow of an earlier age, died at Brighton; and the King insulted his ministers and his sister-in-law with perfect impartiality. The outlook from the Foreign Office was a shade disturbing. Spain had lived through another year of wild confusion, with the sour ferocity of the Carlists in front and the grimacing mask of anarchy behind. Russia loomed more alarmingly than ever against the eastern sky; whilst Austria, her natural counterpoise, confronted Palmerston with the unpromising expression of M. de Metternich, where that faithful *pompier* still stood to his buckets in Poland and Italy, and grinned maliciously when England discovered a new taste for Austrian support. The game was growing anxious; but Palmerston maintained a cheerful front, which sent the explosive *Runnymede* into transports of indignation over " that debonair countenance." Mr. Disraeli even struck his infrequent lyre and evoked him,

lounging, voluble and pert,
And greatly glorying in a gay check shirt.

He was at Kensington one night, delighting Princess Victoria with his " pleasant and amusing conversation." Once more he explained his Spanish policy to the Commons— " the object was that for the future there should be neither an Austrian Spain nor a French Spain, but a Spain which should be Spanish "—and he pressed his plans upon a slightly discouraging Prime Minister and a reluctant King, whilst H. B. portrayed him as St. Sebastian, demure and shot full of departmental arrows.

But in the summer, with Mr. Greville in the full enjoyment of his comforting reflection that " *nothing* will happen, because in this country *nothing* ever does," there was a change. The old King failed suddenly with a vague murmur about wishing to see the sun of Waterloo, saw it, and one night later died; and a scared girl was waiting in the first light of a June morning to hear that she was Queen of England.

V

ONCE more a new reign dawned. Lord Palmerston was a close witness of this decorous sunrise 'in a palace in a garden.' He was at the first Council in the red saloon at Kensington and saw his small sovereign, in her new mourning, colour to the eyes as her old uncles knelt; and on the next morning he had his first audience at St. James's. There was an endless line of bishops, and old Lord Hill had gratified his Queen with the martial intelligence that her proclamation fell on the anniversary of Vittoria. So she was Queen Victoria indeed. That evening Lady Cowper dabbed her eyes at Panshanger and, widowed at last, thought of a future life. Cowper had failed for months; even homœopathy brought no relief; and now, on the second day of a new reign, " the most benevolent and the kindest of men, the most strictly just and the most considerate of the feelings of others " was gone beyond her praises. A brother helpfully proposed distractions. But Palmerston, her sole distraction, was busy in London impressing a small royal lady, who fixed him with a slightly prominent stare, laughed at his jokes till the gums showed, and found him " a clever and agreeable man," and so " very clear in what he says." He talked to her at length about Russia and Turkey, ushered respectful diplomats into a stiff, diminutive presence, sent her little notes upon how to address them, and watched her manœuvre an enormous Sword of State with Melbourne's assistance above the bowed shoulder of Lord Durham, just back from St. Petersburg for his G.C.B. His evenings were no less exhilarating. Once, when royal visitors from Brussels descended upon Windsor, he spent an entire evening talking to Uncle Leopold, whilst on an adjacent sofa his delighted sovereign (with Lord Melbourne in comforting proximity) assured herself that Aunt Louise " is really *an*

angel "; and a few nights later the cheerful little lady was
playing chess under the collective advice of her ministers
and Household—" all gave me advice, and *all different*
advice . . . and *all* got so *eager* that it was very amusing;
in particular Lord Palmerston and Sir J. Hobhouse, who
differed totally and got quite excited and serious about it."
Such divided counsels led to disaster; but under the more
harmonious direction of Melbourne and Palmerston she
challenged the Queen of the Belgians again and *beat* her
dearest Aunt Louise, that paragon who seemed to combine
" the liveliness and fun of a girl of 16 with all the *sense* and
deep thought of one of 30 and much older even," to say
nothing of her sagacious husband, her angelic eyes, and the
less spiritual fact that " she dresses *so well*, morning and
evening." But these gaieties in such enchanting company
did not compose the whole duty of the Queen's ministers;
and on occasion Palmerston drew a rein in one of those
courtly cavalcades, which lent to Windsor Great Park an air
that was almost Maupinesque, as they jingled—half homely,
half romantic—through the trees behind a small lady in a
long riding-habit from a large castle. One afternoon she
wore a military cap to review her troops, saluting " like the
officers do, and was much admired for my manner of doing
so "; and as the Guards—her Guards—went stiffly by, the
small rider in her blue with the red facings " felt for the
first time like a man, as if I could fight myself at the head of
my Troops "—yet not so manly as to escape a thrill that
evening from the delicious circumstance that " Lord
Melbourne rode near me."

These idyllic exercises led in the new reign. But as old
Creevey, fast ageing now and finding two pairs of stockings
a rare comfort, cocked a receptive ear for new stories of " a
handy little Vic," the slow routine of public life resumed.
That summer the Whigs survived a General Election, and
Palmerston held Tiverton, though an indignant Tory
denounced him as " the encourager of the Free Trade
Mania "; as the leaves fell, Mr. Greville won the St. Leger;
and in the winter young Disraeli moved the Commons to
inextinguishable laughter with his startling, his unforgettable

epiphany, pale mustard from cravat to waist and bottle-green from waist to varnished boots. Lord Palmerston's official concerns were largely unchanged. He still eyed Russia coldly and watched Spain with solicitude, that was scarcely diminished by the slow drift of victory towards Queen Isabella's Anglo-Spanish forces. There was so much to explain to a small sovereign with bright, protruding eyes; and he explained it, in the easy manner which she found so very clear, in London, in the big rooms in Windsor, and even by the sea at Brighton. For she was at Brighton in the autumn, a strange, vivacious little figure among the Regent's stale *chinoiseries*. Lady Cowper was at Kemp Town and saw a chance of Palmerston in the shortage of men at the Pavilion. She wrote hopefully to him; and before the week was out, he had his invitation. It was a happy time, when Queen and ministers were intimates. The sovereign might be (Mr. Creevey had seen it already) " a resolute little tit." But as yet her resolution scarcely checked her kindly feeling for the nice old gentlemen with charming manners, by whom she was deliciously surrounded. They talked, they rode, they laughed together. She even took their opinions upon Uncle Leopold's letters, and sat smiling between them at a great dinner just before Christmas, when Lord Melbourne was " very clever and funny about education"; and 1837 went out upon these happy confidences.

That winter nipped an ancient flower where, almost unobserved, Mr. Creevey, with his last note unwritten, his last enquiry strangely answered—" Where shall I go next ? " —went no man knew whither, dying " very suddenly and none of his connexions . . . at hand." The crowded vision faded—Bruffam, the Doctor and the Beau, Mrs. P. with her antics and Madagascar with her conversation, and the distant royal forms of Our Billy, Prinny, and Old Nobs himself—all had receded now. But the world went on in 1838. It read the Duke's *Despatches* or the news of Lord Durham's last extravagance in Canada. An anxious Queen found her Prime Minister looking a little pale; that easy man, lounging no longer, sat bolt upright beside her at a large round table and explained that *Hamlet* was better than *King Lear*, that Louisa was a fastidious name, that Lord Palmerston had once been a High Tory, that *The Beggar's Opera* was coarse beyond conception, that Canadian rebels were extremely tiresome, that the public schools encouraged lying, that Richelieu and Mazarin were shocking fellows, that the Irish Poor Law Bill . . . Sometimes, indeed, the indefatigable exponent " fell asleep for a little while in the evening, which is always a proof that he is not quite well," and left his eager sovereign more concerned than ever.

His hold on office was, it must be confessed, increasingly uncertain. The Government lost steadily in public esteem as it engaged more deeply in controversy; and Brougham could refer with angry scorn to " Lord John this and Mr. Spring that," even naming them from the obscure wearer of a long forgotten hyphen " the Thomson Government." But Palmerston, who " never utters except on his own business," was largely untroubled by these excitements. Indeed, he had his diversions in his own department. The vivid personality of Mr. David Urquhart, whose anti-Russian fervour had been of some value at the Constantinople Embassy and in the calculated indiscretions of the *Portfolio*, entered his post-bag in a letter of which " the first 47 pages . . . relate to your difference with Lord Ponsonby, the last 21 pages . . ." This heroic controversialist deemed himself wronged by official reluctance to pursue his impassioned vendetta against the Czar as an incarnation of the Evil Principle in politics. He had undoubtedly been used; and when his employers showed an awkward tendency to disown him, he was somewhat disproportionately surprised, pursued Lord Palmerston with controversy, drew him into *The Times*, filled six of its columns, and carried into a long and active life the dark conviction that Palmerston subsisted mainly upon Russian gold. The Secretary of State drafted assiduously through the year, pausing one day in response to a royal enquiry to explain at tremendous length the meaning of the word " bureaucratic." He was still smiled upon at Windsor, advised on dinner-lists, went out riding, even " rode near

me on the other side for some little time and admired Tartar
very much "; and Uncle Leopold wrote with enthusiasm of
his " clever and well-informed friend Palmerston." But his
admiration waned that year before a vexatious resurrection of
the Belgian question; and the Queen herself confessed that
Palmerston "was a little apt to sneer sometimes and to make
it appear absurd what people said." For the wicked chuckle
of the Eighteenth Century was not always merciful; and was
it altogether kind, when M. Van de Weyer married the rich
Miss Bates, to say that money was a great thing in marriage?

The Foreign Office still kept its anxious eye on Spain,
where Carlist armies manœuvred a trifle wildly under the
exalted command of Nuestra Señora de Dolores, who was
now their *generalissima* by formal appointment, and the
more secular *Cristinos* won victories in accordance with the
less Scriptural directions of Espartero. But though the war
trailed on, the political danger was averted now, and no risk
of a French Spain survived to darken Palmerston's outlook.
Indeed, it almost seemed that France, the disingenuous and
slightly incalculable France of Louis Philippe, might not go
on for ever. For a horse-faced Prince, who lived in Switzerland and wore a small moustache, applied that autumn for
a British passport in a false name and elicited from Melbourne the languid comment that " he is a strange young
man and nobody knows what he intends to do or what he
may do." But he got his passport; and Carlton Terrace
was soon mildly intrigued by the Imperial eagle on the
bright doors of his barouche.

With Spain subsiding into peace, the line of Palmerston's
preoccupations had shifted eastwards, where the bright
domes and crosses of advancing Russia came up against the
sky. There was still the perpetual danger on the side of
Turkey—that the Turks would drift into some war at any
corner of their vague dominions, " that in such conflict the
Turkish troops would probably be defeated, that then the
Russians would fly to the aid of the Sultan and a Russian
garrison would occupy Constantinople and the Dardanelles,
and once in possession of these points the Russians would
never quit them." It was clear from Palmerston's lucid

diagnosis that opportunities for Russian chivalry must be averted, and he observed with grave concern a marked revival of the Egyptian threat to Turkey. Mehemet Ali's desire for independence grew on him with advancing years; his power had spread from the Nile valley until it included Syria and Arabia; and the French displayed an alarming tendency to flirt with the new Arab empire, which lay from Suez to the Persian Gulf across the routes to India. It was small wonder that Palmerston wrote firmly about fleet-movements and struggled to align the Powers in support of Turkey. For five rescuers were much to be preferred to one, since that one must be Russia. The simple problem was neatly stated in a letter to Lord Lansdowne :

> " The object now to be attained is to stop Mehemet Ali, and Mehemet Ali is weak, and England, France, Austria and Russia are, outwardly at least and professedly, agreed to stop him. If we let him go on, we shall have to stop Russia ; and Russia is strong, and Austria might not help us against her."

The alternatives were plain; and Palmerston continued to support the Sultan against his Pasha with perfect confidence. Besides, he had little patience with easy talk about the inevitable decay of Turkey—" In the first place, no empire is likely to fall to pieces if left to itself, and if no kind neighbours forcibly tear it to pieces. In the next place . . . I am inclined to suspect that those who say that the Turkish empire is rapidly going from bad to worse ought rather to say that the other countries of Europe are year by year becoming better acquainted with the manifest and manifold defects of the organization of Turkey." So he drafted on, while Turkish and Egyptian armies trailed slowly towards the Syrian frontier and Captain Helmuth von Moltke, still with romantic hair and a moustache, watched the Euphrates flow past a Turkish camp.

But further to the East the Russian menace was still. more direct; and for the first time in the century the British imagination watched the flitting shadows of Russian agents upon the mountain-wall of India. The slow drift of the Russian frontier towards the Caspian had already

N

alarmed Lord Palmerston. But when a Russian diplomat
guided the feeble hands of Persia in an attack upon an
Afghan fortress, he wrote almost excitedly to Lord John
Russell that "the Success of the Shah in Affghanistan
would be full of danger and embarrassment to us in India.
. . . He is in this matter acting avowedly as the Tool of
Russia; and the Proceedings of Russia in Affghanistan are
certainly as direct an approach to British India as it is *at
present* in her Power to make. She has opened her first
Parallels, and it would not be wise in us to delay defensive
measures till she has reached the glacis. . . ." When he
complained to Nesselrode, that judicious Chancellor disclaimed designs upon India and appealed to the vast distances involved and (like a later sage) to large-scale maps.
But Palmerston retorted bluntly that "the proceedings of
Russian agents in Asia had for some considerable time been
so much at variance with the professed policy of the Russian
Government"; although he wrote modestly to a colleague
that "if, indeed, we were disposed to answer him contro-
versially as one would do an opponent in the House of
Commons, one might eat him up unmercifully. . . . But that
would be useful only if we wanted to lay the ground for a
rupture; whereas what we want is to carry our points without
a rupture; and as the Russians are disposed quietly to
back out, it is not for us to criticise their gait in so doing."
But Calcutta had already alarmed Leadenhall Street with
a dark hint of Russian intrigues beyond the frontier; even
Melbourne wrote sharply of "no less than the question—
Who is to be master of Central Asia"; the Duke composed
a memorandum upon operations beyond the Indus and was
especially emphatic upon the utility of steamboats on that
river; and the little Queen, fresh from her Coronation,
asked for a map of the entire continent. In this enterprising
mood seven ministers assembled at Windsor, concurred in
advising an eager Governor-General to "take decisive
measures in Afghanistan"; Palmerston wrote cheerfully of
the excellent effect of "making Afghanistan a British and
not a Russian dependency"; and the long column of an
Anglo-Indian army wound hopefully towards the Bolan Pass.

1839 opened upon a small Queen "getting on in *Oliver Twist*" and discussing the painful realism of Mr. Dickens with her Prime Minister, who had sharp things to say of its tone—"It's all among Workhouses and Coffin Makers and Pickpockets"—and caused the wildest amusement with his eloquent plea for a more elevating purpose in literature.　Thus did the Eighteenth Century lay its restraining finger on the impulsive Nineteenth.　But he was anxious now—"looking pale and black under the eyes"—although he still took his two apples off the royal dish and kept them all in fits of laughter with his diverting views upon ear-rings and education and the impropriety of forcing flowers.　Lord Palmerston was there sometimes, with his cheerful confidence in Tory dissensions; and once he wrote her such a comical note about the Duke of Lucca, who must be invited "by note instead of by card.　Your Majesty may think this a small matter, but the Duke is a small Sovereign."　It was delightful to repose a royal confidence in such advisers, and sometimes she seemed to consult them for the sheer pleasure of consultation.　A Belgian treaty was much discussed that year, and the sovereign was slightly bewildered by the correct pronounciation of one word in it, that was to have considerable significance in the world of seventy-five years later. The word was 'guarantee.'　While Melbourne's 'g' was hard, Lord Palmerston, it seemed, pronounced it with an unexpected 'w.'　Melbourne, consulted by his mistress, referred the point to Palmerston; and their joint advice was gravely tendered to the Queen.　This problem solved, he signed the 'scrap of paper.'

The Government was in rough water, though Palmerston was slightly aloof, drafting Notes at home in his view of the Park trees from Stanhope Street, or insisting firmly to a colleague that it would be "very soft in us" not to annex Aden.　Mr. Praed, now sadly ailing, lashed him cheerfully—

> King George the Third in Cockspur Street
> Sits fast and firm upon his seat,
> Though wickedly the rabble chat
> About his coat and queue and hat.
>
> 　*　　*　　*　　*　　*

But we, my Lord, confess at last,
  Though you've your spiteful critics too
That quite as firm and quite as fast
  Upon the Treasury Bench are you
    *   *   *   *   *
And whether Fortune's smile or frown
Set Whig or Tory up or down,
We find your Lordship's public views
Precisely what the Dame would choose.

And Mr. Greville, at his most censorious, found that " the
most enigmatical of Ministers, who is detested by the *Corps
Diplomatique*, abhorred in the House of Commons, liked by
nobody, abused by everybody, still reigns in his little kingdom of the Foreign Office, and is impervious to any sense
of shame from the obloquy that has been cast upon him,
and apparently not troubling himself about the affairs of
the Government generally, which he leaves to others to
defend and uphold as they best may."

His sovereign was less indifferent.   But the eager little
watcher at the Palace, counting out Government majorities
with an anxious eye and vigorous exclamations—" *we* had
a majority of 22 . . . delightful and I feel that I can breathe
again.   Thank God ! " and " We had only a majority of 5.!
This struck to my heart and I felt dreadfully anxious "
—could scarcely save them from the House of Commons.
The blow fell in the first week of May.   Melbourne confessed
that " Palmerston will feel it, he likes his business so much."
Had he not said frankly, " I don't at all conceal that I
think it a great bore to go out; I like power, I think
power very pleasant " ?   And soon the Queen—after a
dreadful evening, a good night, no breakfast, and a morning
of revived distress—was penetrating the Duke of Wellington's deafness with a distinctly articulated request to form a
Tory Government.   The Duke demurred;   and when at his
advice she sent for Peel, " the Queen don't like his manner
after—oh ! how different, how dreadfully different, to that
frank, open, natural and most kind, warm manner of Lord
Melbourne."   A strange *imbroglio* ensued, reported in loving
detail to Lord M.   The buttoned gentleman submitted
names of ministers;   he even suggested changes in the

Household.   His small sovereign, " calm but very decided,"
clung to her Ladies as to a point of conscience.   Peel was
aghast; Lord Melbourne ran to the Palace and ran back
again to South Street, where his former colleagues met in a
pleasant flutter to advise the Crown of which they were no
longer servants.   He would have played for time.   But
Minto urged a flat refusal by the Queen of Peel's demands;
and his draft, revised by Melbourne, was adopted, whilst a
weary colleague sat drawing horses on the paper in front of
him.   They parted after midnight; and the draft, copied
by Melbourne for the Queen, was copied out once more by
a royal hand and sent to Peel.   The " cold, odd man "
with his stiff manner was successfully rebuffed; the Whigs
—her own delightful Whigs—were in again; and the small
Majesty enjoyed her Ball, with Lady Cowper smiling on a
seat beside her.

Once more at the Foreign Office, Lord Palmerston delightedly supplied an ambassador with a slightly fevered
narrative, in which the dauntless Queen, " alone and unad-
vised," survived this nameless outrage to " her youth and her
isolated position."   But, chivalry apart, the Cabinet " had a
long sitting of it " and upheld the sovereign's action—first
roundly, then with discretion, and finally in the distinctly
tepid language of a Minute, which Melbourne bore in triumph
to the Palace for a scene of brimming eyes and tender hand-
clasps.   Emotionally satisfying, the Whigs' return to office
had a darker side, since even Lady Holland found that they
had " nothing to rely upon but the Queen and Paddy."

> These tasks, these joys, the Fates assign
> To well-placed Whigs in 'thirty-nine.

But Palmerston amongst his papers was largely indifferent
to this cloudy prospect; and a reluctant diplomat confessed
that year that he " comes to any conference so fully and
completely master of the subject of it in all the minutest
details, that this capacity is a peculiar talent with him;
it is so great, that he is apt sometimes to lose himself in
the details."

His aptitude found rich employment, since the skies of

diplomacy were thickening above him. A gleam relieved
the West, where a last treachery ended the Carlist war and
uneasy peace descended upon Spain; though even in that
improving quarter Palmerston had already detected a fresh
cause for uneasiness in the first dawning of Louis Philippe's
ingenious ambition to marry a son to the small Queen.
There was a lull in Italy, where the Pope's rival rescuers
had finally withdrawn their troops; and Poland was quite
silent now. His main concerns (apart from the persistent
thinness of the Foreign Office ink) lay east of the Balkans,
where he watched Turkey and still hoped that " if we can
procure for it ten years of peace under the joint protection
of the five Powers, and if those years are profitably employed in reorganising the internal system of the empire,
there is no reason whatever why it should not become again
a respectable Power." He closed upon a sage reflection—
" Half the wrong conclusions at which mankind arrive are
reached by the abuse of metaphors, and by mistaking general
resemblance or imaginary similarity for real identity. Thus
people compare an ancient monarchy with an old building,
an old tree, or an old man, and because the building, tree,
or man must from the nature of things crumble, or decay,
or die, they imagine that the same thing holds good with a
community. . . . All that we hear every day of the week
about the decay of the Turkish Empire, and its being a dead
body or a sapless trunk, and so forth, is pure and unadulter-
ated nonsense." That breath of cheerful wisdom marks
admirably the difference between sound policy and good
journalism. But his hopes of peace were sharply disappointed. A frontier incident on the Syrian border
deepened into war; the Sultan's army, with its ' Russian
tunics, French drill-books, Belgian muskets, Turkish caps,
Hungarian saddles, and English cavalry sabres,' consulted
muftis and assumed a posture in closer accordance with the
Koran than with military requirements; Captain von
Moltke wrung his hands and, cross-legged on a carpet,
proffered superfluous advice. There was a Turkish rout at
Nisib; and the Egyptians swept towards the Taurus. The
Sultan died; his fleet, by French manipulation, deserted to

the Egyptians; and Mehemet's triumph threatened the whole precarious edifice of European peace. Turkey in danger might evoke the chivalrous impulse of the Czar, which had sent Russian troops to the Bosphorus in 1833; and Palmerston worked hard to avert it. At first he managed to align the Powers in support of Turkey. The French were reasonable; " Soult," he wrote gleefully, " is a jewel "; and a collective Note seemed to proclaim that Europe was united in a desire to save the Turks and (more important) to exclude the Russians from their lonely and lucrative trusteeship. But this harmony was brief, since the French displayed an awkward tendency to break away. Vague recollections of the Egyptian expedition of 1798, a hazy sentiment that the Pasha of Egypt was a Napoleonic figure, and a growing taste for North African dependencies drew them towards Mehemet. Had he not to his credit a usurpation and some victories? Perhaps (who knows?) he had a star. The din rose in the Paris newspapers; it even reached the Chamber; and Palmerston resigned himself to check the Egyptian advance on Constantinople with Russia, Austria, and Prussia, " *whether France joins or not.*" So the French must please themselves. At least he had averted the long nightmare of a solitary intervention by the Czar, which might leave behind a dangerous legacy of Russian garrisons in Turkey.

Far to the west a line of bayonets wound through the passes into Afghanistan; and one more Russian move seemed neatly forestalled, where Burnes and Macnaghten rode through the sullen streets of Kabul. A docile Amir was installed, and British sentries kept the Bala Hissar. There was still uneasy talk of a Russian march on Khiva across the steppes of Turkestan. But with Nott at Kandahar, Sale at Kabul, and Macnaghten writing delighted minutes from Jellalabad, India seemed to sleep in safety.

The shots at Ghazni had an echo further, still further to the East, beyond the fear of Russia and the reach of normal policies, where that year an ancient race exasperated England into a second war. Its most obvious cause resided in the singular fact, which has so often baffled European

statesmanship, that the inhabitants of China are Chinese.
These quietists preferred their isolation and repelled the
commercial embraces of the West with courtesy, which
deepened into firmness and then (through all its various
degrees) into violence. A lively British Superintendent at
Canton, irked by his almost menial situation, took a lofty
tone, produced a squadron off the port, and insisted on the
rights of traders. His cause was only slightly marred by
the favourite article of their commerce, which was (he did
not blush to state it) opium. The scuffle quickened; a
magnificent personage from Pekin seized and destroyed the
offensive imports. But when a happy afterthought suggested a demand for the decapitation of all traders in the
forbidden article, the narrower limits of Western courtesy
were reached and twenty-nine war junks were indecorously
scattered by two frigates in the first movement of the China
War, earliest of those expeditions—half punitive and half
marauding—which mark the onward march of culture in
lands reluctant to receive it.

Nor were these lively exercises the sole excitements of
1839. Even the Foreign Office was not undisturbed, when
it took fire one winter's morning and a small housemaid
kept the flames at bay, until the Guards arrived. Lord
Palmerston was on the scene; and someone—they never
caught him—popped an irreverent head round a corner to
shout, with a happy reminiscence of old office nicknames,
" For God's sake, take care of the protocols ! "   The minister
turned sharply; then he went upstairs, distinctly annoyed.
But he retained his blandness. For he found an old trans-
lator calmly at work in a distant room. " Have you,"
enquired the Secretary of State, " any valuable books in
this room, Mr. Huttner ? "   Deep in his papers, the old
man grunted, " And what if I have ? "   " Oh, nothing, if
you have," replied his bland superior, " but I suppose you
know that the house is on fire."   Then Palmerston withdrew,
shutting the door with care.

That year two hands were asked in marriage. The
sovereign ran a kindling eye over the varied charms presented by a faint moustache, a ' slight but very slight ' pair

of whiskers, and a perfect figure, and proposed to Albert.
Meanwhile impartial Cupid pricked his namesake, and Lord
Palmerston asked Lady Cowper to marry. Indeed, he was
always asking her. Even a brother's stony heart was
touched by " the excessive niceness of his steady perseverance," and advised her, " if she likes it, to do it, not to
potter about it." But there was Melbourne to be consulted;
and, slightly doubtful of his colleague's circumstances, he
was far from helpful. He even discussed it with the Queen,
explaining dubiously that Palmerston was said to be in
debt and so, if he went out of office, the imprudent couple
might be reduced without his salary to love in a cottage;
although the suitor was not strictly homeless, even owned
" a very nice place in the country with a nice house, something like Holkham." The Queen, savouring the delicious
secret but slightly damped by the lovers' ages, enquired
sagaciously if late marriages between persons of settled
habits were apt to be successful. Her thoughtful minister
replied that it would be a great change for Palmerston, who
was " accustomed to run about everywhere," and warned
his sister a trifle cheerlessly that she must take the consequences. This was cold comfort; besides, she had an
uneasy feeling that the Queen " may think it foolish in a
person of my age marrying." Another brother wrote from
Vienna the depressing apophthegm *In dubio abstine.* But
less chilling counsels prevailed; and before October was out,
Lord Palmerston was announcing his " future comfort and
happiness " to a relation, enjoining secrecy since " nothing
is so disagreeable as the congratulatory state." The
wedding, as became the union of a Foreign Secretary with
the Prime Minister's sister, was to be postponed to the
November Cabinets.

That month the Queen succumbed to Albert's fatal
beauty; and as her uncle Leopold sang (with far more truth
than he desired) his *Nunc dimittis,* another couple prepared
themselves for felicity. Victoria announced it with a slight
giggle to her absent Albert—" The *Second,* as you always
called Palmerston, is to be married within the next few days
to Lady Cowper, the sister of my *Primus.* . . . They are, both

of them, above fifty, and I think they are quite right so to act, because Palmerston, since the death of his sisters, is quite alone in the world . . . still, I feel sure it will make you smile." Perhaps he smiled in Coburg. But the news brought no smile to Princess Lieven, still lamenting in exile. To send her diamonds by a Foreign Office messenger for sale was cruel enough; but it was bitterness itself to lose her dearest friend to Palmerston, who had taken her embassy, her life, and now her Emily. She heard it from the bride herself and wrote a tearful letter, was almost sisterly, and sent a message of affecting reminiscence to Palmerston—". . . the good old times . . . I ask him once again for his friendship, and frankly promise him mine." So the days drew on, as Albert smiled and Dorothea dried her eyes in Paris. They married on a fine winter's day at St. George's, Hanover Square; and Melbourne signed the register with her son and daughter and Palmerston's brother from Naples and a brother-in-law. It was December 16, 1839, a year of wedding bells. For Mr. Gladstone had married his Catherine in a country church at midsummer; and young Disraeli led his cheerful widow to a more modish altar when the House rose. Windsor and Coburg shared the nuptial flutter; and the Palmerstons drove down to Broadlands with an uneasy fear of being called back to town by Turkish business. For the wooer of fifty-five had claimed his bride of fifty-two. Had he not told a small Harrovian forty years before that he should be by no means precipitate in his choice?

So he brought Em to Broadlands. They passed the gates and saw the big portico together. Her house was waiting. Then the carriage stopped. Perhaps the paved hall with its Roman antiquities was a shade severe. But soon Lady Palmerston (it had a delightful sound, even at fifty-two) could stand in a tall window to watch a stream that flowed across a park—her park. Somewhere beyond, the New Forest spread its brown foregrounds and mauve distances under the winter sky; and, in the house behind her, Palmerston was waiting among his own possessions

—pictures of Mees and Temples, his father's Reynolds, his billiard-table, and the big sideboard in the dining-room with the racing plate that he had won—while painted ceilings looked down at her with their dull gilt, and even the servants stared a little. For Broadlands, after more than thirty years, had found an incomparable mistress.

It was, this belated union, a perfect marriage, though it held few surprises for them. Had they not known and liked and, liking, loved each other since the distant days when a young Secretary at War, who danced at Almack's, paid his constant homage to a Lady Patroness with grey eyes and a brilliant smile? That was nearly thirty years away. The war had ended; Mr. Canning had come and gone; Reform had passed; three Kings had died; and all the time they had remained close to one another, inviting Mr. Greville's leer and Mr. Creevey's nudge, sharing hopes and policies and friends—first Lieven, then her brother Melbourne. Sometimes he strayed; for, as he lived in the memory of *Endymion*, the bluff man with his pleasant manner was " famous, and powerful, and fashionable, and knows how to talk to women." That slightly fevered social medium even evoked him with " the feelings of youth and the frame of age." For that reason, perhaps, it was still a thrill for him to bring her home, and he could write to someone with an exquisitely domestic air that " I want you to be well acquainted with my partner." They spent the honeymoon at Broadlands. Christmas came quickly; and, her flutters ended, the bride's diary recorded that New Year's Day was " very comfortable and cheerful," whilst an old friend was comforted to learn from her that " Lord P. is utterly and entirely devoted to me and so completely happy that it is quite a pleasure to look at him."

So it opened, the long, unhurried partnership of a smiling pair, in the first weeks of 1840. He had a hostess now, who could make adherents for him, with her deep voice and its prompt, perpetual " Stay ! we will have a party." Never, perhaps,

> A rebel in the softest silks,
> A kind of muslin Mr. Wilkes,

she was yet the best of Whigs and always the soundest of Palmerstonians. Palmerston had hung for years *en garçon* on the flank of other groups. But marriage gave him a new power; and the world began to talk of Lady Palmerston's parties. At first it seemed to rivet him more closely in Melbourne's circle and even in that other, graver circle where Melbourne, bolt upright, sat answering his sovereign's questions. For Lady Cowper had been much with the Queen; her daughters formed a staple topic in those slightly exhausting conversations; one of them, indeed, was a Lady of the Bedchamber; and her marriage with Palmerston made him more than ever one of the royal intimates. An eager pen had already confided to a queenly Journal that Lord Palmerston was " the one with whom I communicate oftenest after Lord Melbourne "; her uncle commended him most highly upon all questions which did not relate to Belgian interests; and now her faithful ' Second ' was safely married to dear Lady Cowper.

These happy stars presiding, they returned to town when the House met. Her new felicity (she felt " like a spoilt child ") agreed with her. For Melbourne found her looking uncommonly well in " rather a dashing gown." Even her sovereign thought that she was dressing better, although a gallant brother insisted that she was " always like a pale rose." Stanhope Street was too small now; and they moved to Carlton Terrace, where No. 5 saw the first of their entertainments. It was spacious, overlooked the Mall, and was near his office—so near, indeed, that it gave him no ride in the mornings. So that indomitable devotee of exercise made it a rule " to ride up to Hyde Park and round the Ring every day . . . it only takes half an hour."

It was a year of novelties, with the penny post and the new Assam tea and Mr. Carlyle lecturing on Heroes and the strange and almost totally disregarded incitements of a highly novel poet to hear Sordello's story told and (greatest novelty of all) the Prince. He came from Dover after a dreadful crossing; and Melbourne had languidly permitted the gentleman who fetched him to accept " the Order of Coburg, whatever it is." He came with his handsome,

rather empty face and " a little of his blue ribbon showing ";
and whilst the Reverend Edward Tauerschmidt delighted a
restricted public with a brief study of his ancestry and the
town was mildly fluttered by preparations for the wedding,
Lord Melbourne was deliciously funny at Court " about his
new Coat, which he said, ' I expect it to be the thing most
observed.' " The day arrived in torrents of rain. A small,
determined bride with ' a large searching eye, an open
anxious nostril and a firm mouth ' (to adopt the somewhat
cheerless inventory of her charms compiled by a Scotch
newspaper) endured the ceremony, remembered to praise
Melbourne's coat, drove down to Windsor, opened her
Journal, dipped a pen, and made the ecstatic entry " I and
Albert aloné." Lord Melbourne, Palmerston, the Cowpers,
Uxbridge, her Ladies, all the intimates receded before the
dawning of a greater intimacy.

Ministers had their troubles on an ebbing tide of popularity, and all hands were mustered in a last effort to with-
stand the Tories. Even Palmerston showed an increasing
tendency to participate in general business, slept at a
Cabinet dinner in full view of an observant colleague " in a
deep meditation upon the Scotch kirk "; although his
departmental affairs were more absorbing than ever, and
the news from China ruffled the waters of the House of
Commons. He crossed an experienced sword with the
moral indignation of young Mr. Gladstone and, with engaging
frankness, " put it to any man opposite whether he could
with a grave face say that he honestly believed that motive
of the Chinese Government to have been the promotion of
the growth of moral habits. . . . Why did they not prohibit
the growth of the poppy in their own country? The fact
was that this was an exportation of bullion question, an
agricultural interest-protection question. It 'was the poppy
interest in China . . ." Small wonder that excited Tories
whirled like dervishes at this bland puncturing of their
loftiest sentiments. His hands were no less full in other
quarters. A vague fear of French designs in Morocco, an
awkward tendency on the part of French missionaries to
invite martyrdom in the more eligible islands of the Pacific,

a wrangle with the Portuguese, and an interminable dispute
with Naples about concessions in the sulphur trade kept
him as busy as he could wish. He was particularly firm
with Naples; and since the British case was strong, he
supported it with the unanswerable argument of the Mediterranean Fleet. The Neapolitans saw the prompt capture
of their shipping; and their courage—never the strongest
point of Naples—evaporated; while Melbourne wrote
approvingly, "This is strong, but if we cannot obtain a
settlement, we must do something effective," and a nervous
private secretary added, "What with China, Portugal,
Naples, etc., we have a great deal of this sort of work upon
our hands at once." Clear views tend to enrich foreign
policy with 'incidents;' and Palmerston, whose views were
nothing if not clear, was not without a healthy appetite for
'incidents.' But Melbourne was a close collaborator in
policy and even in actual drafting, although his health was
failing, and one seems to catch a hint of increasing depen-
dence upon Palmerston in his slightly helpless enquiry
à propos of an impending question in the House of Lords:
"What does he mean, and what is to be said?" So
Palmerston pursued his course, although his colleagues were
informed of his proceedings and rarely refrained from
offering advice upon matters with which they were imperfectly acquainted, whilst he found time for endless exposi-
tions of the Foreign Office point of view in his round
handwriting. That year Lord Lansdowne was favoured
with a trenchant essay upon the absurdity of American
pretensions over the Maine boundary—"the outcry is a
factitious one raised by a few land jobbers and speculators.
. . . The States of the Union are in a condition of general
bankruptcy, and that does not give a fancy for maritime
war to a nation who live by commerce." Deep reverence
for the Union could hardly be expected of a statesman born
within three years of Yorktown; and Palmerston reserved
his shrewdest judgments for the martial intentions of others.

But his main preoccupations lay further to the East,
where the Egyptian problem raised its various heads. His
deft manœuvre of associating the Powers in defence of

Turkey had broken the Russian monopoly of noble intentions. The secret treaty of 1833 had vanished in the new
harmonies of the European concert. But the Pasha was
still in Syria; Turkey was still in danger; and the French
displayed a mood that required his close attention. Vaguely
ashamed of the domesticated Monarchy of July, Paris
became increasingly Napoleonic. Poets invoked the Emperor; artists filled leagues of canvas with the marching
splendour of his vanished armies; and innumerable actors
in grey overcoats pinched supers' ears before excited
audiences. The King himself, profoundly conscious of his
umbrella, was quick to gratify these cravings; and Ver-
sailles, hastily reconsecrated ' à toutes les gloires de la France '
and filled with battle-pictures, became a temple of the new
faith, whilst an *Arc de Triomphe* recited the splendid litany
in stone. This mood was friendly to heroic impulses, to
sudden clenchings of the fist, and to vague menaces breathed
at perfidious Albion; and when a turn of the revolving
wheel brought M. Thiers into power that spring, the mood
found an appropriate instrument. For M. Thiers was, in
the noblest sense, a patriot by profession. Had he not
unendingly narrated the Consulate and Empire? Did he
not burn with the unnatural bellicosity of a military historian? His star was bright; he would begin, like Bonaparte, with a campaign of Egypt; and he bent hopefully
over the long despatches in which M. Guizot reported on
the countrymen of Mr. Pitt. For that sage, in the unofficial
charge of Princess Lieven (widowed at last and captive now
to his erudite, if slightly Lutheran, charms), appeared in
London as ambassador. Palmerston had crossed swords
with the Princess before; and since his official career
included eight years of war against a real Napoleon, he was
not unduly alarmed by a synthetic replica. He was always
sceptical of martial professions. Even Russia, a more impressive belligerent, had provoked him two years earlier
to the cool reflection that " she is always pushing on as far
and as fast as she can go without war; but that whenever
she finds that perseverance in encroachment will lead to
forcible resistance, she will pull up." As to the French, he

could never forget a conviction formed at Paris so long ago
as 1829 that although " every Frenchman you meet raves
about ' *nos frontières* ' . . . all this, however, is mere froth and
vanity ; and while they have Chambers who must levy
taxes to carry on a war, nothing but egregious folly on our
part can bring on a war between the two countries." Paris
might gesticulate its sympathy for Mehemet Ali and the
' Napoleon of Peace ' protest his adoration of the *nouvel
Alexandre* in Egypt. But " would they hazard a naval war
for such an object ? Where are they to find ships to equal
or to contend with the British navy alone, leaving out the
Russian navy, which in such a case would join us ? What
would become of Algiers if they were at war with a Power
superior to France at sea ? Would they risk a Continental
war ? and for what ? Could they help Mehemet Ali by
marching to the Rhine ? And would they *not be driven back
as fast as they went ?* Is the interior so tranquil and united
that Louis Philippe would like to see the three military
Powers of the Continent armed against him, and the two
Pretenders to his throne, the Bourbon and the Buonaparte,
supported by foreign or domestic aid ? It is impossible.
The French may talk big, but . . ." It was cruel diagnosis ;
and whether Palmerston knew France or not, he knew his
mind and never wavered in a settled incredulity, when
M. Thiers assumed the *rôle* of Mars.

The problem still remained : Mehemet—" that aged
afrancesado freebooter," as the cheerful Palmerston described
him—must be driven out of Syria in spite of France ; and
while M. Guizot under the diplomatic tutorship of Dorothea
conducted mild intrigues with friendly Whigs and lectured
him, Lord Palmerston proceeded. The ingenious Metternich, assuming the wisdom of Solomon, proposed that Syria
should be halved between the rival claimants. Europe
reflected ; and whilst a slight lull overtook the Egyptian
question, M. Guizot enlivened the interlude in London with
a singular request. He desired, if understood correctly,
leave to translate the Emperor's body from St. Helena ;
Lord Palmerston suppressed a wicked smile, consulted
colleagues (with a naughty note to Russell about " the late

. Emperor Nap.") and consented; and the *Belle-Poule* sailed down into the South Atlantic to embark a nation's memories. That season Prince Louis Napoleon, more mysterious than ever, was still to be met at Lady Blessington's, alluding freely to his star and extending remarkable invitations to dine with him that day twelvemonth at the Tuileries. But Conneau was printing proclamations in a locked room, and a bewildered firm of London button-makers struggled to oblige its strange foreign customers by reproducing the patterns worn in French Line regiments.

In July the interminable debate on Egypt was resumed. The French, detected in a sly manœuvre to secure Syria for their *protégé* and wreathe Louis Philippe with more than Napoleonic laurels, provoked Lord Palmerston to sudden action. His colleagues were a shade reluctant, and he had some difficulty in communicating to Lord John Russell his indignant certainty that the question was " whether England is to remain a Substantive Power, or is to declare herself a dependency of France. In the event of the latter decision you had better abolish the office of Secretary of State for Foreign Affairs and leave in London an Under-Secretary for the English Department deputed from the Foreign Office at Paris." Appearing at a Cabinet, he casually informed his colleagues that " he thought it right to mention that he had been for a long time engaged in negotiation upon the principles agreed upon at the Cabinet at Windsor " (nine months before) " and that he had drawn up a Treaty, with which it was fit the Cabinet should be acquainted." The treaty contained an ultimatum to Mehemet and engaged the Powers (omitting France) to use their fleets against him, if he made further war on Turkey. The risk of a collision with the French was obvious, and there was a flutter of startled colleagues. He offered to resign; two colleagues, of the contrary opinion, did the same; Lord Melbourne, not without reference to his Maker, induced the dissentients to sink their differences and to continue; and Palmerston proceeded blandly to the public humiliation of the French, although he had few illusions about his new association with the Russians. For that month he wrote that " it seems

o

pretty clear that, sooner or later, the Cossack and the
Sepoy, the man from the Baltic and he from the British
Islands will meet in the centre of Asia. It should be our
business to take care that the meeting should take place as
far off from our Indian possessions as may be convenient
and advantageous to us. But the meeting will not be
avoided by our staying at home to receive the visit." Such
impeccable sentiments might almost have reassured Mr.
Urquhart, more darkly convinced than ever of Lord Palmerston's treason. For his veering against the French had, to
that fevered eye, a sinister look—he might, he positively must
subsist on Russian gold. So he signed his treaty with the
Powers, pledged England, Russia, Austria and Prussia to
stand by Turkey, and left Mehemet and Louis Philippe to
digest it as they could, expressing a polite curiosity " to know
how Thiers had taken our convention." Such were the
spirited antecedents of the Convention of July 15, 1840.

August was feverish. France effervesced; M. Thiers
exploded in cataracts of patriotic indignation; even the
King, after a cautious hint to Egypt not to go too far,
assembled a solemn conclave. That week, with the delicious
inconsequence of fate, a paddle-steamer left the Pool of
London; and the indomitable Prince Louis Napoleon
startled his elders by invading France with fifty men, nine
horses, and three proclamations. A brief scuffle in a
barrack-yard at Boulogne, an interrupted gesture under the
tall *Colonne de la Grande Armée*, a scamper down the hill to
Wimereux, and a damp rescue from the Channel closed his
account once more; and the King at Eu enjoyed the story,
while Palmerston denied with real conviction that he or
Melbourne had " set eyes upon Louis Bonaparte or upon
any of the adventurers by whom he was surrounded." One
more eccentric dawned upon his view that month. Marriage
had brought him a son-in-law, since Lady Cowper's Minnie
was married to Lord Ashley. That grave young man, whose
diverse sympathies were disputed by the beauties of revealed
religion, the ' climbing boys,' the insane, and all the dumb
victims of a blind industrialism, was strangely drawn towards
the Holy Land. The lack of Jews in that eligible region was

peculiarly distressing to his somewhat literal appreciation of the Scriptures; and the dispute about the territories which lay between Turkey and Egypt seemed to afford an almost providential opportunity to remedy this defect. One summer night he dined with Palmerston and, left alone with him after dinner, developed his strange project—the Jews restored to Palestine, a guarantee of the new state by the Great Powers, the prophecies fulfilled, and the Day of Judgment brought comfortingly nearer. His diary records the singular *tête à tête* :

> " Propounded my scheme, which seemed to strike his fancy ; he asked some questions, and readily promised to consider it. How singular is the order of Providence ! Singular, that is, if estimated by man's ways ! Palmerston has already been chosen by God to be an instrument of good to His ancient people ; to do homage, as it were, to their inheritance, and to recognise their rights without believing in their destiny. And it seems he will yet do more. But though the motive be kind, it is not sound. I am forced to argue politically, financially, commercially ; these considerations strike him home ; he weeps not like his Master over Jerusalem, nor prays that now, at last, she may put on her beautiful garments. . . ."

This was unfortunately true. For Palmerston, perhaps excusably, was less interested in accelerating the Day of Judgment than in defeating Mehemet Ali. But the strange scheme was not without mundane advantages, since it would neutralise a portion of the disputed territory and create a buffer-state on the Egyptian frontier. Besides, Lord Ashley with all his noble sympathies was a Tory, and the strange young man might be usefully employed securing Tory adherents for his Egyptian policy. He even—stranger still —had friends in newspaper offices, and Palmerston had always a taste for managing the press ; Mr. Greville once wrote of him that he " would see any newspaper writer who called on him," and he was invariably considerate to reporters. There was a glorious outburst of apocalyptic articles in *The Times*, which became unaccountably reconciled to Palmerston ; Lord Ashley delightedly recognised in one of his despatches "a prelude to the Antitype of the decree of Cyrus," and put his scheme in writing upon lines that bear a strong resemblance to a later Mandate and Declaration; and for an interval the splendid prospect, with which General Bonaparte had once made unconvincing play at Jaffa in 1799, gleamed before Jewish eyes. Then once again it faded, to reappear in eighty years.

But the Egyptian tangle was still unresolved in 1840. Late in August, with M. Thiers striking Napoleonic attitudes and Louis Napoleon safely lodged in a Paris cell, M. Guizot returned to his post, went down to Windsor, and struck Melbourne as "rather touchy and high, and like a man who thought himself called upon to support his dignity." The observant guest, however, found Palmerston "a little subdued." Indeed, he had abundant cause for thought, apart altogether from a queer little note from Broadlands, where Em was all alone, disliked her solitude, and signed herself his "affectionately (tho' with some *rancune*)," and confessed adorably how much she liked the place—"I do so admire it and enjoy it—and think myself so very fortunate to have a right in it—and love you for being the cause of all my comfort." His disbelief in French heroics was still unshaken —"France now is a very different thing from the France of the empire. Then war was the only way which anybody had of getting money; now war would put an end to most people's chance of getting money. A quarter of a century of peace does not pass over a nation in vain. But people say that Thiers is a dare-devil capable of anything, and therefore highly dangerous, and consequently a man whom one ought to give way to. Now I hold just the opposite doctrine. . . ." But whilst he watched the French with a fencer's eye, his colleagues' nerves were not so steady. John Russell, permeated with the purest milk of the Whig word, was most uneasy. Had not Mr. Fox always been partial to the French? Lord Lansdowne disapproved; Lord Althorp, deep in the House of Lords, emitted a sound of warning; and Lord Holland frankly regarded disrespect of France as an affront to Holland House. Even Melbourne shared the general uneasiness, confided to John Russell that he "could

neither eat nor drink nor sleep," and warned Palmerston that
Louis Philippe had " a good deal of Jemappe left about him
still." There was a most uncomfortable party at Windsor,
with .Guizot on his dignity and Palmerston on his guard
and Uncle Leopold in a positive fever for the safety of
Belgium in case of a war between France and England, to
say nothing of his agonised feelings before the spectacle
of this unnatural conflict between his father-in-law and his
favourite niece. The long duel was resumed in London,
where M. Guizot at the risk of becoming slightly wearisome
intoned interminable Notes and Palmerston retained his
bland conviction that " *Mehemet Ali cédera ; il ne faut pas
s'attendre qu'il cède à la première sommation ; mais donnez-lui
quinze jours, et il finira par céder.*" They gave him twenty.
But the magic failed to work. Mehemet was obdurate, and a
British squadron bombarded Beyrout. Paris stirred at the
sound ; and while journalists breathed fire, M. Thiers covered
his floor with maps and sprawled across them, moving his
conquering pins from point to point in the best Imperial
manner. Caught by the fever, an impulsive prince proclaimed his preference for dying on the Danube or the Rhine
rather than in a Paris gutter. The army was increased ;
Paris became a fortress ; and its theatres were loud with the
Marseillaise. The fever spread, and cautious Germany
began to sing her *Wacht am Rhein*, while de Musset retorted
hotly,

Nous l'avons eu, votre Rhin allemand ! . . .
Où le père a passé, passera bien l'enfant.

The European din grew almost deafening; but Palmerston
persisted, instructing his *chargé d'affaires* in Paris to convey
" in the most friendly and inoffensive manner possible that
if France throws down the gauntlet, we shall not refuse to
pick it up; and that if she begins a war, she will to a certainty lose her ships, colonies, and commerce before she sees
the end of it ; that her army of Algiers will cease to give her
anxiety, and that Mehemet Ali will just be chucked into the
Nile."
He played a steady hand; but his associates were far
from helpful. John Russell frankly winced at the prospect ;

and a group of startled Whigs, on whose slightly equivocal
errands Mr. Greville ran delightedly between the French
Embassy and the Privy Council Office, intrigued its hardest to
get Lord Clarendon substituted as Foreign Secretary. Late
in September there was an awkward brush in Cabinet.
John Russell nerved himself for resignation. Melbourne
informed the Queen, who initiated the habit of a lifetime
with an appeal to her health—" the Queen really could not
go through that *now*, and it might make her *seriously ill* . . .
she has had already so much lately in the distressing illness of
her poor Aunt to harass her." He had already warned
Palmerston that "never, I will answer for it, was a great
measure undertaken upon a measure of support so slender
and so uncertain," and he urged him now to handle the
French gently. His sovereign joined the chorus; her
watchful uncle, perpetually anxious for his beloved Belgium,
added his sagacious note; and the most earnest prayer of all
was contained in a memorandum, modest precursor of an
impressive line. For, laboriously written in English and
slightly misspelt, it emanated from Prince Albert.

The autumn was a lively alternation of news from Syria
and threats of resignation. First, John Russell's scruples
were allayed by a talk with Palmerston and an uneasy
Cabinet, where someone happened to look up in the heat of
the discussion and found the Prime Minister sound asleep.
These grave deliberations proving inconclusive, they met
again after a singularly uncomfortable dinner with Palmerston at Carlton Terrace and an evening of erratic conversation at Holland House. At the next Cabinet Melbourne gave
a cue; and Palmerston, by prearrangement that was a
trifle obvious, promptly volunteered a concession to French
feeling. His colleagues eagerly concurred, but were slightly
damped on the next morning to read a vigorous denunciation
of the agreed policy in a newspaper, whose sympathy with
Palmerston even carried with it a fair reflection of his style.
For that unwearied pen, which flooded Europe with state
papers, would not infrequently engage in humbler tasks.
His relations with the press were always intimate; and (sad
to relate) a plain denial of his authorship left Russell regret-

tably incredulous. Indeed, the angry little man told someone that "all his confidence in him was gone." But that week the news of Mehemet's first discomfiture arrived; and Mr. Greville, a little rueful after a glorious interlude of intrigue, found them at Holland House for dinner—" Palmerstons, John Russell, and Morpeth, all very merry, with sundry jokes about Beyrout and what not." The plots were over now. Melbourne had shown the judicious weakness of a Prime Minister with slightly incompatible colleagues. In August he had kept Russell in by the Queen's entreaties, and even prevailed on Palmerston to budge a little in September, though Mr. Greville wrote contemptuously that he "dreaded a breach partly official, partly domestic, with Palmerston, and only thought of keeping the rickety machine of Government together." Lord John had "submitted tamely, distrusted Palmerston, and didn't dare tell him so"; the leader of revolt had sadly failed to play his part. Nothing remained upon the disappointing scene except the smiling figure at the Foreign Office—" entrenched in a strong position, with unity and determination of purpose, quite unscrupulous, very artful . . . and able to communicate in whatever manner and with whomsoever he pleased." Even Clarendon admitted to his wife that " there is something grand in the way he braves everything in spite of all opposition from his colleagues—in spite of the Queen's fears—in spite of events at home and abroad—he goes steadily on." But it was all—to Greville, Clarendon, John Russell, Guizot and his Dorothea—most disheartening.

He played his last few cards with perfect calm, assuring a fluttered Queen (with voluminous enclosures) that " there never has been any real foundation for the alarm of war with France which was felt by some persons in this country." In the Levant the expulsion of the Egyptians proceeded smoothly, while Paris echoed with the expiring threats of M. Thiers. Melbourne was still a little nervous; and whilst other colleagues " worked away at the impenetrable Viscount," the adroit Prime Minister played a more skilful gambit and moved his Queen. The sovereign was advised to " seize this opportunity of stating strongly to Palmerston your wishes that this opportunity may be taken advantage of. . . . Your Majesty will see the necessity of at the same time not appearing too much to take the side of France, which might irritate and indispose." These soft approaches aiding, Melbourne retained his awkward colleagues through October. But before the month was out, he became almost Palmerstonian himself at a more than usually preposterous French threat and warned Louis Philippe through Brussels that, by God ! he wouldn't stand it. That cautious sovereign, promptly lowering the sword of France, dismissed his minister; and M. Thiers, replaced by M. Guizot, went off to write more history in Italy.

So Palmerston had won the trick. But the Tuileries still held a card or two; and the listening heavens were assailed with moving appeals from Louis Philippe for some concession which might salve, however inadequately, the wounded vanity of France. His ingenuity suggested the compelling plea that, in its absence, an indignant nation might engulf him in a new and more dreadful revolution. Lord Palmerston was frankly disinclined to sacrifice " important interests to appease the organisers of *émeutes* in Paris or to silence the republican newspapers "; besides, he had a shrewd suspicion that the French design was founded upon a perfectly rational desire to raise in Egypt a new and service-able ally in eastern waters. But France had more exalted friends. Was not Louis Philippe " the dear king " to Windsor and " the poor good king " to Brussels? Lord Palmerston might · be impervious to the anguish of this devoted man. Perhaps a squire could contemplate the fall of thrones with calm. But how could royal persons share this lofty indifference? How, above all, a son-in-law and his niece? Throughout the crisis Leopold's anxiety for his neutral kingdom had impelled him to a feverish activity in the cause of peace. Its earlier stages found his small correspondent unconvinced of the innocence of France and even mildly Palmerstonian. But with a throne in danger she dissented firmly from his customary argument that France would not fight and that " it is very natural that the French Government after having failed to extort concessions upon the Turkish Question, by means of foreign war, should now endeavour to obtain those concessions, by appealing to fears of another kind, and should say that such concessions are necessary in order to prevent revolution in France." Her dissent was conveyed at slightly greater length than usual in a letter, whose numbered paragraphs and inelastic phrasing suggest one of those memoranda of Prince Albert that had inspired his happy cry, " I always commit my views to paper, and then communicate them to Lord Melbourne. He seldom answers me. . . ." But a memorandum from the Queen was a different matter. She did not yet share Uncle Leopold's full distaste for " Palmerston, *rex* and auto- crat." But something had come between them.

Meanwhile, he outfaced the French. Where Thiers had bullied, Guizot whimpered. But neither made the least impression on the implacable man. He calmly quoted Sheridan, sent orders to the fleet, and waited imperturbably for news from Syria. John Russell made a second stand— this time upon the excellent ground provided by a wholly unauthorised refusal of Palmerston to refer outstanding questions to a Congress. Since he had got his way, Palmer- ston yielded gracefully; and the effect of his concession was promptly nullified by glorious news from the Levant. Acre, the *misérable bicoque* which had once stood between Napoleon and the conquest of the East and derived an unnatural prestige from that inexplicable event, succumbed to a brief attack. The sword was at Mehemet's throat; and he sur- rendered Syria, whilst Lady Palmerston in glee wrote, " This is of course nuts to us and a great lift to Palmerston." A rueful Dorothea wrote from Paris, " *Si vous étiez des Français, il y aurait des festons, des Cantates et des statues pour Lord Palmerston.*" For every single trick was taken now.

So 1840 closed upon his triumph—Egypt defeated, Turkey saved, the French outfaced, a victory in China, and the faint echo of a far success beyond the Khyber Pass. At home he had retained his hold on Melbourne and stifled the Whig grandees in Cabinet, though the year left John Russell sore and suspicious. The Queen still quoted

his opinions to Uncle Leopold, although a shadow (was it the
Prince or only Stockmar?) seemed to fall between them.
Even a hint from Melbourne as to the necessity of submitting
important despatches to the Queen before transmission left
no forebodings; and 1840 went serenely out on the Prime
Minister "like a boy escaped from school, in roaring spirits,"
and the Palmerstons sedately Christmassing at Broadlands.

The new year dawned across a tumbled sea of home
politics, with an angry Liberal exclaiming that " the Right
Honourable member for Tamworth governs England; the
honourable and learned member for Dublin governs Ireland;
the Whigs govern nothing but Downing Street "—and even
there, it seemed, their lease was rapidly expiring.　For the
Tory banners of *Coningsby's* heroic simile ' lowered on the
Whig forces, as the gathering h st of the Norman invaders
frowned on the coast of Sussex.'　The Queen still smiled;
Melbourne was no less absent-minded; but their strength
had gone.　Even Palmerston preached a whole leading article
in the *Morning Chronicle* from the rueful text,

> We are all sliding, slid, slid, sliding,
> We are all sliding, sliding fast away.

Their reforms, as reforms are sadly apt to do, had startled
their enemies and left their friends half satisfied; while
Palmerston's successive *coups* brought credit to no one but
himself, since even the envious Greville wrote that the diplomatic triumph of 1840 was " not looked upon as the work
of the Government, but as that of Palmerston alone—
Palmerston, in some degree, as contradistinguished from the
Government."　Had they not done their best to check him,
even inclined him to seek supporters for his policy among the
Tories?　Progressive parties are rarely equal to the more
exuberant forms of patriotism; and Palmerston's defiance
of the French was more in place among those less exacting
figures that trooped annually to the Duke's Waterloo dinner
or drank, with Mr. Tadpole, to ' Our Young Queen, and our
Old Institutions.'　He had a Tory past; worse still, he had
even acquired a Tory son-in-law; and someone overheard an

odd murmur from the Prime Minister himself, as he followed
his dreams aloud on a Windsor sofa—" . . . impossible the
Government can go on; Palmerston in communication with
the Tories—Palmerston and Ashley . . ." and then Melbourne swallowed his sentence. An eager colleague took
him up. Would Palmerston and the Tories come together?
A nod from Melbourne. His questioner proceeded. Which
would come to the other—Ashley to Palmerston, or Palmerston to Ashley? They never settled it. For Melbourne
chuckled, grunted, laughed, rubbed his hands and, turning
suddenly oracular, said, " Oh, I don't know."

But they were all still in together, though John Russell
had an awkward time at Broadlands avoiding foreign topics.
Christmas had been a riot of prize-givings and country
neighbours; and after that Lady Palmerston went visiting
and left him exposed once more to the perils of bachelor
life—" It is idle of the housemaids to leave your windows
open and fire out, and you should send and scold them for it,
for it might give you a very bad cold after coming from your
warm writing-room." Then she was off to the Continent,
and his perils increased—" I am so glad to think you had an
amusing dinner yesʸ, insteady of passing your evening all
alone. How glad L[ad]y J[ersey] will have been to get hold
of you without me. . . . But what a vile Man to go to bed
early now and get up early—to give the world an *impression*
that it is *I* who lead you astray—however, notwithstanding
this, I am glad to think you should have an early night, for
the sake of your eyes." His eyes, with France and Egypt
grown submissive, were less in use. There was still China,
where a fresh jewel was added to the Queen's crown and
provoked the Prince to the diverting suggestion (he was so
fond of jokes) that they should create the baby ' Princess of
Hong-Kong '; and a brisk ' incident ' with the United States
inspired Lord Palmerston to the spirited pronouncement that
American persistence would lead to war, " war immediate and
frightful in its character, because it would be a war of
retaliation and vengeance." But, this minor cloud excepted,
the skies were clear.

As winter turned to spring, their thoughts filled with

elections. Taper adored a Cry; Tadpole was all for Registra-
tion; even the Whigs grew confident; and Mr. Greville
observed that " the most decided for dissolution is Palmerston (who has never any doubts or fears, and is for fighting
everybody)." He wrote to Melbourne on the subject—
" the party are anxious for dissolution . . . the strong
feeling of the country with us." Four days later, he was
speaking on the last night of an interminable debate on the
sugar duties, insisting that " the question is between free
trade (and by free trade I mean trade open to competition)
on the one side and monopoly on the other." His Free
Trade plea on this occasion was distinctly qualified, since he
was urging the admission of Brazilian sugar to the British
market with a preferential duty of 50 per cent. in favour of
the British colonies. But the principles were admirably
stated, and he read Sir Robert Peel a sound lesson in the
elements of fiscal doctrine : Free Trade was defined as the
levying of import duties " solely for purposes of revenue;
let them not be laid on for what is called protection; that is,
to enable a comparatively small number of men to carry on a
trade in itself a losing one at the expense of the rest of the
community . . . a tax levied upon the industry and skill
of the mass of the community to enable a few to remain
indolent and unskilful. . . . Show me a trade that is free,
by which I mean open to fair competition and I will show you
a trade carried on with intelligence, enterprise and success.
Show me a trade that is highly protected, and I will show you
a set of men, supine, unimproving, and probably labouring
under perpetual embarrassment." He had forgotten none
of his Edinburgh lessons.

But they were beaten and dissolved in June; and whilst
a grave negotiation proceeded about the approaching change
of Ladies at the Court, Lord Palmerston went down to
Tiverton to meet his electors and Em went with him. It
was her first election; and she heard them laugh as he
described the old members before Reform—" no more the
representatives of the honest men and beautiful women in
Tiverton than were figures in a magic lantern of Jack the
Giant Killer or Gog and Magog "; and then they cheered,

as he spoke of their present members, "having tongues to
speak and legs to come among you and hands to shake your
hands with—and with an honest shake too," and cheered
again, as he proclaimed himself "an enemy to the system of
monopoly" and pledged himself to "support the principle
of extending freedom in our commercial relations."

Tiverton was faithful; but the Tories swept the country,
and ministers waited for their official doom. There was
no loss of royal favour. For Melbourne was at the Castle
in July, writing to Palmerston: "The Queen wishes you
to sit to a German artist who is here. Can't you give
him an hour Friday? I am to sit to him at two." Such
commands are rarely disobeyed; but no portrait of Palmerston is preserved at Windsor. Perhaps, in later years, a
royal hand turned it to face a royal wall-paper; perhaps a
ruder touch dismissed it into limbo. But all in 1841 was
royal smiles. Before the month was out, the exalted pair
stayed with the Cowpers at Panshanger and drove in summer
state for a delicious lunch at Brocket with Lord Melbourne.
Em rode in the royal carriage, while Palmerston trotted
alongside in a cavalcade adorned by the Prince himself, who
seemed to her excited gaze "like the Prince of a fairy tale
all perfection." It was still Maupinesque, perhaps, but with
a difference. Then they resigned and went to Claremont in
September for the last Council, where they found the
sovereign flushed, but composed. Lord M. departed. The
Ladies of the Bedchamber retired. This time there were no
tears.

VI

HE was nearing sixty now, an undoubted European figure.
In party politics he held a position that was a shade detached.
Denied the inner sacraments of the Whig communion by his
Tory origins, of which opponents in debate and writers of
squibs did not fail to give him frequent and forcible reminders,
he was even inclined to emphasise these imperfections.
The strongly national flavour of his foreign policy tended to
make him friends among the Tories rather than in his own
party. Those more enlightened circles customarily abound in
citizens of the world and friends of the human race. For
progressive persons have an odd weakness for the enemies
of their country; and twenty years of Opposition in the
Great War had left a strange affection for the French
implanted in Whig bosoms. But Palmerston was sadly
immune from those generous emotions, and Whig heads
shook nightly at Brooks's over his obduracy, so different
from the canonical orthodoxy of John Russell. In Cabinet
circles this divergence of doctrine was accentuated by his
firm treatment of refractory colleagues. For the *fait
accompli* was his favourite argument, tending to make
unwilling captives rather than loyal adherents. But, foreign
affairs apart, a further difference shadowed his somewhat
precarious collaboration with John Russell. For that eager
zealot was a fervid Churchman, prepared at any opportunity
to challenge Rome with Protestant gusto. His slightly
narrow affections were shared by Reform and the Reformation, while Palmerston had shown a dangerous breadth of
view in sectarian matters. His early opinions on the
Catholic question and his tenants' schools in Sligo pointed
a different way; the Canningite had lost a University seat for
his Catholic sympathies in 1831, and it was still feared that

his was a heart that beat no faster when warned of the Church in danger. So Palmerston, almost perceptibly separated from the elders of the Whig conventicle, preserved his association with the party to a large extent by the ties that united him to Melbourne.

There was much to be said for Opposition—friends, travel, entertaining, guns at Broadlands, and the Forest hounds. He was in his place when the House met and warned Peel that " there is a country as well as a House of Commons "—a warning frequent on the lips of minorities. But Palmerston was always aware of a world of Englishmen beyond Westminster—in omnibuses and trains, at meets and markets and quarter-sessions. Perhaps the unusual knowledge made him slightly indifferent to the nice delimitation of parties. Then he was off to Ireland with Lady Palmerston to see his property on the west coast and admire their growing harbour; and on the way home they viewed his slate quarry in Wales, which had hitherto displayed a wholly unsuspected capacity for absorbing capital without any proportionate return of slate. They missed the official rejoicings in November, which provoked a loyal poet to announce

> a little Prince at last,
> A roaring royal boy;
> And all day long the booming bells
> Have rung their peals of joy.

The Palmerstons were on a round of visits, returning to find Carlton Terrace dark and dinnerless because the steward was out and " the other servants who have no more heads than Pins would not take the liberty to open his letter." Then they went off to Derbyshire, where Em had her wedding-day, " the Anniversary of my marriage—two years that each deserve a flitch of bacon."

The prospect was delightful—first Broadlands, where he could hunt and shoot and thin plantations " as in the olden time," then Parliament with a Tory Government to bait, a summer tour through Germany and Austria, and a winter in Italy. Small wonder that an irreverent pencil in the new *Punch* depicted " Cupid out of Place ", at ease

beside his fire and using the last arrow from his sheaf of
protocols as a toothpick. But a young Tory relative, at
Broadlands in the first weeks of 1842, found that her host was
" bitter as usual and evidently cannot get reconciled to not
being longer Secretary, tho' he doesn't appear at all bored
from having a great deal to do, but he abuses every thing,
and every body connected with the Tories. Thinks Lord
Ashburton a rascal, Sir R. P. ditto; Lord Aberdeen ditto :
ditto : and so on." He abused the Tories to some purpose
in the next month, watching with the tempered enthusiasm
of a slightly sceptical Free Trader the first steps of Master
Robert in his ' Free Trade walk ' with Papa Cobden. His
own position was hardly uncompromising, since he was in
favour of a fixèd duty on imported corn; but it was only
justified for revenue purposes, and he dealt admirably with
the Protectionist *mirage*—

> " Independent of foreign nations for its supply of food !—
> a nation in which several millions of men live by foreign com-
> merce calling itself independent of foreign nations for the means
> of subsistence of its people. Why, Sir, those who depend on
> foreign commerce for the means by which they buy their bread
> are, to all practical purposes, as dependent on foreign nations
> for food as if the food which they bought was grown on a
> foreign soil. . . . Your fields may be filled with luxuriant
> harvests, and yet the face of the starving manufacturer may
> grow pale with fear of famine."

And he closed a speech, of which he thought well enough
to print copies for distribution, with a positively Cobdenite
peroration upon the blessings of free exchange.

Free exchange was, indeed, the very latest mode, as
up-to-date as Mr. Browning's slightly cryptic enquiries
for an absent Waring, first heard that year. For Mr.
Cobden, just elected for Stockport, glowered at the rosy
squires of 1842 from a back bench, and the public mind was
full of corn and sliding scales and rebates. As Palmerston
had made his first Free Trade speech in 1832, before the full
beauties of the doctrine were revealed to either founder of
the Free Trade church, his record was as good as most men's;
though ungrateful Free Traders could still remember that

he had once voted against hearing the Manchester Anti-Corn-Law Association at the bar of the House. His views on that, as on several other topics, were curiously advanced. Slavery abolition had drawn him into a long series of treaties at the Foreign Office; it was as much a crotchet of his as of Lord Brougham's, and they used to say in Cabinet that neither of them was quite accountable for his actions where the Black Man was concerned. That session another novelty engaged him, when he gave systematic support through all its stages to Lord Ashley's Mines and Collieries Bill, founding himself upon the strangely enlightened reasoning that work for boys in pits was wholly incompatible with education. Indeed, his zeal for education even inspired him to press for grants of public money in aid of singing classes. His sympathies found bolder expression in his avowal to John Russell that " I own I agree with Ashley about his Ten Hours Bill as far as children under a certain age are concerned. They are not free agents and seem entitled to protection against the combined cupidity of parents and masters."

But his main concerns in Parliament were more external. That winter a lonely figure on a flagging horse rode into Jellalabad with the dreadful news that Kabul was up, Burnes and Macnaghten murdered, the ladies either hostages or dead, and the little army strewn on the trampled snow along the freezing passes. Excited Tories blamed the Whigs; and Palmerston defended Indian frontier policy from the airy invective of Mr. Disraeli, sceptical of the Russian menace and innocent of a ' scientific frontier ' still nearly forty years away, whilst his delighted critic got a cheer from Peel, a word from " the mighty *Mister Cobden*," and Tory congratulations on being " one of the few who have broken lances with Palmerston and rode away in triumph." He found a more congenial topic in the decline of national prestige under the less heroic guidance of Lord Aberdeen. His own philosophy mingled with his complaints in a letter to a former colleague :—

" Our foreign affairs seem to have got upon a sliding scale, as well as the corn duties, and we are in that respect sliding

P

downwards by a very decently rapid Descent. Foreign nations, as was to be expected, take our professed love of peace even beyond the letter when they see the sincerity of our professions so abundantly proved by submission to everybody with whom we have any dealings. . . . Foreign governments will take the Hint, and will extort from us one after the other a great number of concessions which with a little firmness we never need have made; and some fine day, led on and encouraged by our want of proper spirit, they will drive us to the wall upon some point on which they will have gone too far to recede, and we shall have gone too far to be able to go back any further; then one or other party must submit to open disgrace; if as is probable it be the Foreign Government that yields . . . the country will find out, though too late, that much previous disadvantage and humiliation might have been escaped by making the same stand at the first steps which we shall then have made at the last; if on the other hand this nation shall become so cowed and spirit broken by the habit of submission as to prefer even a great indignity or real loss to the exertion necessary for Self Defence in War, then we shall cease to be really independent; and we must look out for some less timid Power who may kindly be disposed to take us under its protection. No doubt for valuable consideration we could prevail upon our dear Friend the Czar to take us under his wing and his Conditions would probably be acceptable to many, as he would most likely be satisfied with being allowed to relieve us from the sin of selling opium to the Chinese, and from the crime of attempting to defend our Indian Empire by civilizing Affghanistan."

Such irony was an asset in Opposition; and while John Russell was inclined to stay at home, Palmerston found himself welcomed as a leader of Whig *francs tireurs*, and wound up the Session with a grand denunciation of ministers for " living upon our leavings . . . like a band of men who have made a forcible entrance into a dwelling, and who sit down and carouse upon the provisions they found in the larder." Mr. Macaulay even urged him to write for the *Edinburgh*; but Palmerston preferred " if one has any good hits to make about the present state of foreign affairs . . . to reserve them for the House of Commons."

That autumn something snapped in Melbourne. They
rushed to Brocket and found him helpless. There was
a slow recovery; and Lady Palmerston wanted to keep it all
a secret, because it might harm the party, while Palmerston
wrote hopeful letters and reflected privately that his afflicted
brother-in-law " had for a long time past been in the habit of
eating and drinking too much, and taking exercise too little.
Bacon says a man ought to make exercise a religion, and be
punctual in the observance of it." These were devotions
that he never missed, getting his " rowing for two or three
hours before breakfast and also . . . bathing and swimming
in the Thames at the same time of day " in the full heat of
the Eastern Question. The patient mended slowly, coming
down to meals and even making little jokes about " a
runaway knock." A family circle of Cowpers and Palmerstons, Ashleys and Jocelyns gathered round him,
including that new sister-in-law in whom Palmerston could
find no fault but her being a foreigner. But what hope was
there of the ageing, broken man, who shuffled round the rooms
at Brocket, leading the party again? It was a blow to
Palmerston as well. For, Melbourne effaced, he was left
alone with Russell and the Whig zealots. There was no
breach. But he was already a trifle restless, when he
observed that " some of our party, Radicals and old Whigs,
are disposed to take their views of our foreign relations from
Ellice; God help them, say I. But they have a right to
choose for themselves; only I must claim for myself equal
liberty of judgment and action. And I happen to think
that I understand our foreign relations better than he
does. . . ." This sturdy confidence was scarcely likely to
accord for long with a sour orthodoxy; and he expressed it
with perfect freedom in the columns of the *Morning Chronicle*,
where Aberdeen's foreign policy was exhibited daily under
every form of ridicule. His journalistic exploits had teased
the Whigs in 1840; Majesty was provoked to anxious
questions; and even Melbourne hesitated to approve.
But Palmerston's press manœuvres were no secret. The
Morning Chronicle was widely known to be an instrument on
which he played at will; and Mr. Greville hailed him with

malicious glee as " a *magnus Apollo* of newspaper writers."
Whig pens were busy that autumn. For Mr. Macaulay,
momentarily escaped from the attractions of omniscient
conversation, displayed a novel tendency to

> hangs round Nurscia's altars
> The golden shields of Rome.

But Lord Palmerston's productions had a more immediate
interest, and a Whig conclave moved John Russell to
send a grave remonstrance. Palmerston replied with spirit,
expressing " readiness to co-operate with the party, and to
consult for the common advantage, but that he must in the
course of the Session take an opportunity of expressing his
own opinions upon the questions of foreign policy which
would arise." So, almost imperceptibly, he drifted towards .
independence.

But he was never lonely. A smiling lady made parties
for him, told them how wonderful he was and how dis-
loyal all his colleagues were. She gathered everyone.
Even Mr. Greville was asked down to Broadlands and
heard him denounce the American treaty in terms which
bore a delicious resemblance to the *Morning Chronicle*,
whilst an eager hostess, growing almost voluble, was very
nearly spiteful about Lord Clarendon, derided Melbourne
and John Russell for their excessive caution, and let him
see " through her graceful, easy manner and habitual
urbanity, how impatient they are of exclusion from office,
and how intolerant of any dissent from or opposition to his
policy or opinions." He was more impenetrable himself,
though the prejudices burned bright and steady behind his
" gay and gallant exterior." So they went talking out of
1842.

Another year of Opposition found them attentive on
Melbourne, who recovered slowly, and still hopeful of their
German holiday in the summer. But there was always the
Ashburton Treaty—he called it " the Ashburton capitula-
tion "—to be denounced; and he denounced it richly with
two lines of Virgil and a wealth of topographical detail,
finding its weakness on the slavery question peculiarly

distasteful. Then he was off on agriculture, applying the best modern arts of management to his own farms and reading books on gardens with a mild complaint that "these matters . . . are now become sciences." There were plans for a new flower garden at Broadlands and hopes of the new Methodist gardener who went preaching on Sundays, tempered by an uneasy fear that "he thinks too much of his sermons to be very successful in his garden." There were even hopes that year of a runner at Ascot; and the chains across the stable doors at Broadlands were padlocked more securely than ever. But the owner found time to raise a friendly voice in support of Lord Ashley's cherished bantling, the new Anglican Bishop of Jerusalem. He was heard on Irish questions also, stating a tolerably Liberal view, marred only by an inability to contemplate the application of legislative solutions to the Land problem. Perhaps a pupil of the economists was bound to utter rather gingerly "the somewhat absurd term 'fixity of tenure'"; and he wrote sardonically to Lansdowne that "no wonder the tenantry of Ireland are looking with eager anxiety to this Commission; they naturally expect that its Result is to be to transfer to them a Portion of what now belongs to their Landlords; a very natural object of desire." But he was prepared for some diminution of the Irish Church establishment and a corresponding endowment of the priesthood, "but not for making the Catholic Religion either the dominant one or an equally established one. Putting all doctrinal questions aside, I look on the Catholic Religion as a bad political institution, unfavourable to morals, to industry, and to liberty." Such cool Erastianism plainly belonged to the Eighteenth Century, and left him sadly averse from the more impulsive detestation of the Pope for his own sake, which was becoming fashionable. But the wide assortment of his views made it a shade unjust in the pugnacious Quaker, who took his seat that year as Mr. Cobden's Pylades, to write to an admiring family in Rochdale of Palmerston's "very clever speech, if there was no country; it would have been very well at a debating club." The year went out upon them all at Broadlands. Melbourne and the whole family were there

with the observant Mr. Greville, who noted that he seemed
" in pretty good force, more grave, more silent than
formerly." Melbourne lived in his memories now, and the
talk was mainly of old times. It had been an easy, pleasant
year for Palmerston, with a sufficiency of politics, two packs
of hounds to choose from (one of them with " seldom less
than fourteen or fifteen red-coats "), and a good chance of
birds in Yew Tree Wood.

But 1844 opened more briskly, with Mr. Bright in roaring
meetings and the League at its nine-millionth leaflet. Mr.
Gladstone served a laborious apprenticeship at the Board of
Trade ; ' Young England ' swore by young Disraeli ; and in
Cheyne Row Mr. Carlyle struggled with Cromwell, the
eternal truths, and the piano practice (no less eternal) of the
young lady next door. The Condition of England question
was momentarily obscured by the bulky figure of Mr.
O'Connell ; and Lord Palmerston watched Ireland shrewdly,
whilst his devoted lady informed callers at Carlton Terrace
that every step taken by Peel towards justice was Palmerston's
idea. Melbourne was there sometimes, with his sad make-
believe that he was still in politics, telling them all how he lay
awake half the night thinking how to advise the Queen when
next she sent for him to Windsor. But one afternoon they
had a more unusual visit. The Ten Hours Bill was in the
Commons, and two gentlemen from Lancashire called to
explain the conditions of child-labour in the cotton mills.
When they reached Carlton Terrace, Lady Palmerston was
waiting on the balcony, a carriage at the door ; and, late as
usual, Palmerston was dressing for his drive. To her despair
he saw them—" dressed like a youth of eighteen, and as
lively as a cricket "—in the big dining-room. A footman
aiding, they wheeled the chairs about in a wild representation
of textile machinery ; and Lady Palmerston, intruding, was
startled to observe her lord absorbed in these industrial
exercises. Her drive, it seemed, was lost beyond recall ;
but she could still smile and say how glad she was " to see
your Lordship has betaken yourself to work at last." So the
carriage waited ; the grave charade proceeded ; and the
eager missionaries made their convert.

The season was far from lively, since the Queen was scarcely visible, and there was Court mourning for the Prince's father, lately dead at Gotha.   The Czar came and gave a Cup at Ascot; and Palmerston, who heard the cheers on the course, reflected drily that " if we can purchase his good-will by civility, without any sacrifice of national interest, it would be folly not to do so."   But he could still inform the Commons that " influence abroad is to be maintained only by the operation of one or other of two principles —hope and fear.   We ought to teach the weaker Powers to hope that they will receive the support of this country in their time of danger.   Powerful countries should be taught to fear that they will be resisted by England in any unjust acts either towards ourselves or towards those who are bound in terms of amity with us."   How true was the observation of Mr. Raikes that he was " very little altered by time."

That year they got their foreign holiday.   He had been reading *Coningsby*—" well worth reading, and admirably written "—and most considerately sent a key of all the characters to his brother at Naples.   They could not get so far themselves, stopping at Brussels for the somewhat formal pleasure of two dinners with King Leopold.   Then they went off to Ems, where he endured improving conversation with a minister of Louis Philippe.   Frankfort was scarcely brighter, since he dined with a Rothschild and kept the funds steady with reassuring talk.   Berlin received him with the varied charms of a sententious painter, who shared Prince Albert's passion for fresco, and a walk with a Prussian minister, who talked on schools.   Slightly dispirited, he drank the waters at Wiesbaden, which gave him gout.   But in the intervals of this depressing ritual, which was performed in the best English company, he formed a favourable opinion of the Germans, " civil and obliging, good-natured and independent."   Partly recovered from their cure, they were at Berlin in October, dined at the Schloss, and were highly impressed by Frederick William IV., that vivacious Hohenzollern whose varied accomplishments were attributed by sympathisers to the Romantic movement and by *Punch* to Clicquot.   They were a little awed by Berlin, where a royal

mausoleum and a profusion of frescoes seemed to foretell an
age of art, while popular education indicated that " Prussia is
taking the lead in German civilisation; and as Austria has
gone to sleep, and it will be long before she wakes, Prussia
has a fine career open to her for many years to come." It
was, in 1844—*consule* Metternich and with Sadowa twenty-
two years away—a sage prediction. Then they saw sights at
Dresden, made a run into Austria, and came home to Peel
and corn and the unwearied eloquence of Mr. Bright.

1845 moved to a livelier measure. Palmerston was at
Broadlands " full of vigour and hilarity, and overflowing
with diplomatic swagger," insisting cheerfully to Mr. Greville
that " France with her colonies and America with her slaves "
were equally susceptible to British pressure. Well on in
Sybil, Mr. Disraeli bowed to his sovereign in black velvet
or thought out sharp things for the coming session; Sir
Robert Peel continued his occult reflections on Free Trade;
and Mr. Gladstone gave the first public exhibition of his
conscience with an inexplicable resignation over Irish
education, which left an irreverent newspaper observing that
" a lady's footman jumped off the Great Western train, going
forty miles an hour, merely to pick up his hat," while
Disraeli predicted hopefully that the strange man's career
was over. The House met; and Palmerston was soon deep
in the wrongs of Mr. Pritchard in the Pacific, with a general
desire for " a stout frigate on the station " and a passionate
insistence on the slavery question. He performed on the
Navy Estimates in the precarious dawn of steamships, and
his main anxiety was for the suppression of the slave trade
by the right of search. But coast defences found him in a
less Quaker mood and fully alive to the march of science;
fearing a sudden concentration of French troops by railway,
a dash of paddle-steamers, and a raid on Portsmouth, he
pleaded for more guns. Yet slaves were his ruling passion
that year; he had already received the humane distinction
of an address of thanks from the Anti-Slavery Society, and
one summer evening he even carried his Parliamentary
enthusiasm to the point of being counted out. He was
heard on Ireland as well, standing boldly for the transfer of

the superfluous endowments of the Irish Church to Catholic education, and explaining to Tiverton Dissenters that "to proselytise the Irish people and to convert them to Protestantism, is in the existing state of things impossible. Our only choice is between leaving six millions of men in comparative ignorance, and in consequent bigotry and superstition, or endeavouring to enlighten them, and at least to make them good Catholics if we cannot make them Protestants; and in making this choice we must not forget, as some men in their zeal seem to do, that Roman Catholics are Christians." He was at Broadlands when the House rose in August. They had the family as usual and Mr. Greville and the uneasy shadow of Lord Melbourne, who sat among them in his past. One of the company found that he "seems to bear on his face a perpetual consciousness of his glory obscured, and looks grave and stern, while he sits for hours in silence." Then they were off to the constituency, both caught colds at Tiverton races, and crossed to Ireland, taking the eternal slate quarry (with a distant prospect of a dividend two years ahead) on their way home through Wales.

That year the autumn rain fell heavily. The Palmerstons returned from Ireland, and the potato crop lay rotting in the ground behind them. Their Welsh slates gleamed in the steady downpour; and the roads in front of them wound into England across a dismal landscape, where the blackened crops of 1845 stood in the sodden fields, until the Duke could say in his vivid *staccato*, "Rotten potatoes have done it all; they have put Peel in his d——d fright." Peel's mental processes were not so simple; but the crop-failure brought the Irish famine, and famine brought Free Trade. A distracted Cabinet faced the Prime Minister's trio of searching questions—

" Shall we maintain unaltered,
" Shall we modify,
" Shall we suspend—the operation of the Corn Law? "

John Russell launched his Edinburgh letter in favour of unequivocal Free Trade; and *The Times*, after a famous

communication to ' Mr. Tonans in his den at midnight '
made, if not by a lady, at least by the most ladylike member
of the Government, Lord Aberdeen, announced that Peel
was a convert to Free Trade.

There was a sudden flutter. Peel resigned, John Russell
went to Osborne; and for a delirious fortnight England
. enjoyed the unusual spectacle offered by Leech's showman
to his bewildered client—" On your right you will perceive a
Prime Minister a Bolishing of hisself. And over your left
is another Prime Minister a Bolishing of the Corn Laws."
The Whigs hung, like Mahomet's coffin, between heaven and
Opposition in an ecstasy of private meetings. Could they,
would they take office to repeal the Corn Laws? One detail
intervened : the Whigs in power meant Lord Palmerston
at the Foreign Office. Osborne had already murmured
some apprehension at the prospect; the *Bourse* was nervous;
Guizot and Lieven shared a common fever; Louis Philippe
denounced him openly as " *l'ennemi de ma maison* ";
even the reigning Rothschild complained that " *il a l'incon-
vénient de faire baisser les fonds de toute l'Europe sans nous
en avertir.*" But there was nothing for it; the Foreign
Office was his freehold, and Palmerston must have the first
refusal. One Whig at least thought otherwise; and, fortified
by copious draughts of Mr. Ellice, the new Earl Grey came
up to town, resolved not to sit in a Whig Cabinet with
Palmerston as Foreign Secretary.

Meanwhile a minor comedy was played in Paris. French
politics consisted at the moment of a steady alternation of
M. Thiers with M. Guizot. Guizot, under the unremitting
tutelage of his Dorothea, was in; but Palmerston, mindful,
perhaps, of earlier bouts with Princess Lieven, had taken an
opportunity earlier in the year to show marked courtesy to
Thiers. So while the King despaired and Guizot dined with
desponding bankers, Thiers was in transports. A stranger
figure crossed the scene one evening, when Mr. Disraeli, in
Paris for the recess, left his hotel in the Rue de Rivoli, bound
for St. Cloud, to taste for one ambrosial evening the delicious
company of princes, the rich savour of diplomacy. There
was a concert at the Château—" very choice, as there was

no one but the Court." The King was gracious and less
inconsequent than usual. His resourceful guest improved
the proud occasion by a lecture of half an hour, delivered
" with delicacy, but without reserve," on the public virtues
of Lord Palmerston—his love of France, his frankness, his
disinclination to take litigious views. Then the accomplished monarch rose and, murmuring royally, " We must
not lose all the music," dismissed his interlocutor. But
Mr. Disraeli, in a pleased flutter, was asked to stay behind
after the concert. Then they conferred again. Majesty
had been thinking over . . . was much gratified to learn
. . . was prepared to welcome the returning Palmerston,
if he came back to office without *rancune*. But the royal
mind was most uneasy about the coming revolution which
was to start, it seemed, in Central Europe. Then (it was
almost midnight) Mr. Disraeli drove back to his hotel in a
pleasant glow. On the next day he sat down to report
the interview to Lord Palmerston in loving detail, with a
respectful hint that a few reassuring words in Parliament
might do good—perhaps a suitable question could be
managed, and Mr. Disraeli would be most happy to assist.
It was a slightly formal letter, since the two men were
strangers. But Disraeli was a friendly stranger, whose
glowing fancy envied Palmerston his red boxes and his
protocols. Did not *Endymion* long remember ' Lord Roehampton ' ? " He is the man. He does not care a rush
whether the revenue increases or declines. He is thinking
of real politics; foreign politics." It was delightful to
collect the confidences of crowned heads, to drop a hint,
to put in a word for Palmerston. Besides, if he could
smooth his path to the Foreign Office, was he not helping
the Whigs back to power and Peel to destruction? Lord
Palmerston replied politely to these unusual confidences,
was extremely obliged to his new correspondent, and remained " My dear sir, yours sincerely." There was no
intimacy, although a common hostility to Peel seemed for
an instant to unite the observant Whig with the Tory *bravo ;*
and the two vessels drew momentarily together on the
troubled sea of fiscal politics. For Disraeli was always a

privateer; and perhaps Palmerston, slightly buccaneering himself, admired his Jolly Roger.

But the event was decided in London, where a conclave of Whig magnates decided to repeal the Corn Laws with some measure of rating relief to land-owners by way of compensation. Then John Russell started to form his Cabinet. The anxious little man saw Palmerston at once, who explained his taste for private life and added firmly that the only place where he could be of the least service was the Foreign Office. Faintly apologetic, John Russell alluded to the impression—in his opinion, the unjust impression—that Palmerston was warlike, with a hint that if he felt embarrassed, he might perhaps prefer the Colonial Office. But Palmerston declined the bait; John Russell promptly offered the Foreign Office in due form; and he accepted. The train was fired. Lord Grey exploded with a flat refusal to serve in any capacity, if Palmerston was not displaced; a hint reached Palmerston, who cheerfully responded that Grey's obduracy supplied an additional reason for his own insistence; John Russell wrung despairing hands, resigned the Queen's commission and, in Disraeli's lively image, "handed back with courtesy the poisoned chalice to Sir Robert." So Peel was back at Christmas; Lieven and Guizot smiled contented smiles; the Queen breathed her relief; and the Prince was *seelenfroh* at last.

But 1846 opened in an excited buzz. Pledged to Free Trade, Peel's Cabinet rested on Whig support, while Tory mutineers plotted in corners. Disgusted squires heard Peel announce the last and most beneficent of his three apostasies; Disraeli, in a cold fury of denunciation, drawled his invectives; and Mr. Bright and Mr. Cobden intoned their richer hallelujahs. The Tory rebels found an unsuspected leader in Lord George Bentinck, one of those odd blends of the turf with personal rectitude, by which the foreign observer of English politics is periodically baffled; and with every party primed for acrid conflict they settled down to the ' sad, fierce session ' of 1846.

In the opening movement Palmerston maintained a

cautious silence. But he wound up a long debate on the
Corn Laws with an odd speech, of which he thought well
enough to print copies for distribution. He opened with a
defence of Peel on the ground that country came before
party, and proceeded to an attack upon Protection in his
familiar vein. Corn, he informed the cheering Whigs, was
no exception to the salutary rule. But revenue was needed;
and the cheers died away, as he exclaimed, " I am for a
moderate fixed duty." The puzzled Free Traders heard him
suggest a duty of 4s. or 5s., and their confidence was only
half restored by his closing declaration that if he must
choose between Free Trade and sliding-scale Protection, he
chose Free Trade. It was a singular pronouncement.
Always romantic, Mr. Disraeli diagnosed " diplomacy even
in debate; Lord Palmerston threw a practised and prescient
eye over the disturbed elements of the House of Commons,
and two months later, when a protectionist Ministry on
moderate principles (principles moderate and not fixed) was
not impossible, the speech of the noble lord was quoted by
many as a rallying point." His grasp of fiscal doctrine had
been secure enough since Dugald Stewart's lectures; and,
unlike most Free Trade champions, he had been making
Free Trade speeches continuously since 1832. But perhaps
Free Trade in 1832, with the genteel sanction of economists
and the aphorisms of Mr. Huskisson, was not quite the lively
exposition of the creed which prevailed in 1846, when Mr.
Bright and Mr. Cobden waved their roaring audiences forward into the Promised Land. Russell's announcement of
his Free Trade views in the Edinburgh letter had startled
many of the landed Whigs. Indeed, it found its warmest
advocate in Grey, against whose " ultra Free Trade Doc-·
trines " Palmerston had warned John Russell in 1844.
Free Trade appeared to flourish in precisely those Whig
circles which had done least to make Palmerston at home in
the party; and so, perhaps, he was not grieved to disappoint them, although he seemed to have little confidence
in his own proposal, writing to Disraeli, " I could not refrain
from affording one ' pitying tear to grace the obsequies ' of
fixed duty. Many would, I am persuaded, be glad to

revive it; but to all appearance its life seems entirely
extinct."

This strange manœuvre ended, he resumed his preparations for a return to the Foreign Office with a visit of
elaborate courtesy to Paris. The French were reassured
by the sight of a bland Viscount, who crossed drawing-
rooms to greet old enemies with a friendly hand and with
(more reassuring still) a perfect accent. Meals were a trifle
odd; he missed his coffee and hated banquets at midday
instead of his accustomed orange. But a delighted wife
reported that he was "quite a Lion." They dined at
Court; they dined with Guizot and his Lieven; and he
spent a whole day being driven round the new fortifications
by M. Thiers, the big top-hat gracefully inclined to catch the
martial explanations of the shorter hat beside him. One
night at dinner (Dumas was there as well) the rolling eye of
M. Victor Hugo was caught by Palmerston's red ribbon.
He found the wearer *un homme replet, petit, blond, qu'on dit
spirituel*, and thought his countenance *pleine, ronde, large,
colorée, rejouie et fine, un peu vulgaire*. They exchanged
commonplaces on the French climate and the Irish famine.
But Lady Palmerston was charming; their long romance
was known to the delighted poet, who concluded sagely that
*lord Palmerston appartient un peu à l'histoire et beaucoup au
roman*. Then they set off for London, leaving Paris loud
behind them with praise of *ce cher Lord Palmerston ;* and
even the exacting Dorothea confessing that his language was
très-mesuré et très-convenable.

Back in his place, he watched the Tory rebels hunting
Peel. His own silence was unbroken except for two words
on the innocuous topic of railway gauges. But there were
whispers of compromise on Free Trade. His faint plea in
March for a fixed duty might seem to make Carlton Terrace
a convenient focus of such slightly questionable activities.
The vital object with the Tories (and perhaps with Palmerston) was to get rid of Peel; and malicious Whigs breathed
rumours of "certain proceedings, very like intrigues,
principally hatched at Palmerston House." But his small
leader held firmly on his course; the Corn Laws were

repealed; and the Protectionists had nothing but revenge to hope for. They hunted Peel more savagely than ever. The ardour of the chase kept Mr. Disraeli at a white heat and even drew inarticulate sounds of abhorrence from the lips of infuriated squires. They killed in June; the Government was beaten; and John Russell was summoned once again. This time Lord Grey forgot his scruples; Melbourne looked on a little sadly, whilst a Whig Cabinet was formed without him; and Palmerston, his Free Trade faith restated in an echo of Peel's panegyric on Mr. Cobden, was back once more at his protocols in July.

VII

HE returned in 1846 to a changed world. Lord Palmerston was much the same. The smile, the springy step, the tilted hat, the cane, the small but manly whisker still told their cheerful tale of exercise and health even at sixty-one. The Foreign Office still commanded Downing Street with its sentry-box and its unimpressive chimneys; the clerks inside still wrote their lamentable hands, watered the ink, or punctuated in gross defiance of the rules of that mysterious art. Consuls were still illegible, foreign ambassadors importunate, and red boxes showered again like leaves in an autumn gale. But so much had changed. John Russell sat in the seat of Melbourne, a poor exchange for Palmerston's more manageable brother-in-law. Hardly a *roi fainéant* (his hail of little notes on policy and even on points of drafting repel the charge), Melbourne was an indulgent colleague, and accommodation with his Foreign Secretary was almost a family matter; besides, the two men had been Canningites together. Time had replaced him now with a less friendly figure. Thin-lipped and earnest, Russell was a small embodiment of Whiggery, an evening at Holland House incarnate. To unfriendly eyes his calendar seemed to consist of Whig anniversaries from 1688 to 1832, his meditations to require for their accompaniment a bust of Charles James Fox. Such perfect orthodoxy kept him a trifle prim. The Prime Minister flirted no cane; his hat was never tilted; he exchanged no friendly notes with the unhallowed Disraeli. Was he not Peace, Retrenchment, and Reform in his own person? Such perfection was hardly likely to accord for long with Palmerston, who wrote him genial letters full of Virgilian tags and lines from Horace and Surteesian tropes about hounds chopping hares in cover. The pair were strangely ill-assorted; their politics diverged, and even in physique—the one robust, the other small and frail—they differed widely. There was a friendly understanding; but colleagues gleefully explained that 1846 was not 1841, that Russell was not Melbourne, and that the Foreign Office was no longer to be an independent principality. The world, for Palmerston, was changed indeed.

The change reached higher still. Five years before he had served a small but cheerful sovereign, who rode out with him, laughed at his jokes, passed on his opinions to her uncle, and commanded him to sit for his portrait. That happy time was past. Slightly inscrutable and a shade stouter now, the little Queen had faded into a more decorous figure, which presided over a different scene. The tone was lower, the voices more subdued; the lights were not so bright; there was improving conversation; guests went earlier to bed. Something was dimmed; and as the bright past receded, it was observed that the monarch was unmistakably Victorian. And she was more besides. For something in the intervening years had taught her to surround herself with the mysterious divinity that hedges kings in Central Europe. Germans are always apt to be slightly mystical about monarchy; and the bewildering convolutions of the *Reich*, with its rich profusion of Electoral Princes, Prince-Bishops, Majesties, Serene Highnesses, and Excellencies, made for a nicely graduated hierarchy. For Germany was still the land of monarchy *par excellence*. A century before a German voice had murmured in a royal ear, " George, be a king "; and perhaps the small sovereign caught a private whisper of " Victoria, be a queen." It was a brave departure from the easier manners of the English throne. There were no more rides with ministers; the wheels of monarchy revolved far more impressively; and where once decisions had been taken on half a sentence from Lord Melbourne over his apple or one of Palmerston's diverting letters, patient Teutonic hands wrote endless memoranda. So the Queen submitted to her transformation; and the tiny, dancing figure of 1838 vanished in her new

Q

character. She had a right that bordered on the divine; she had five babies in the nursery; and she had a husband. The change was severe for Palmerston. That easy figure —equally at home in the world of *Jorrocks*, of *Sidonia* (did not the reigning Rothschild say of him, *Lord Palmerston est un ami de la maison—il dine chez nous à Francfort*?), of *Rastignac*—was somehow never quite in place with the Prince Consort. Those eager readings from Hallam's *Constitutional History of England*, that passion for geology, and those lonely outpourings on the Castle organ by evening light were strange indeed for him to contemplate. It was so long since Palmerston had improved himself. He was not given to mournful improvisations in the setting sun, and it may be doubted whether he had ever felt the fascination of a fossil. He dined; he rode to hounds; he played a graceful part in the world of manly sport and female accomplishment. But there was something slightly incongruous in his membership of the Royal Commission on Fine Arts, and the Prince's varied (but uniformly elevating) plans had more enthusiastic friends. The contrast was not lost upon the Queen. For there was little in Palmerston of those paler virtues which now compelled her admiration; and he remained a slightly distasteful reminder of her vanished past before the conquering advent of her husband. She had had her doubts of him even in Lord Melbourne's time, when they found some of his despatches " rather severe." His cool defiance of the elements in 1840 was most alarming, as well as singularly unkind to the poor, good King of the French. Had she not written more than once to check him—to say nothing of a discreet reminder, when it was all over, that she must see important Foreign Office drafts before they were despatched? So he had his warning.

Her transformation had provided him with a most disturbing spectacle in the five years of Tory rule. He watched the German predilection grow on her, even heard them call her ' Albertine '; and Lady Palmerston told Mr. Greville how wrong she was to insist on having the small Prince of

Wales gazetted ' Duke of Saxony.' But there was worse to come. So long as Albert opened Institutes, he remained a harmless (if not conspicuously amusing) pastime. But when he took to reading the Queen's papers, conferred with ministers, and pelted them with memoranda, things grew serious. Alone, he might perhaps have been ignored. But Albert was not alone. For he enjoyed the inexhaustible advice of Stockmar. So one more figure in the royal circle stood in vivid contrast with Palmerston. The two had been in friendly contact since the days when Stockmar was Leopold's factotum and Belgian business took him to the Foreign Office. Palmerston spoke respectfully of his powers —' one of the best political heads he had ever met with '— but their divergence was neatly pointed in Lord Melbourne's casual portrait of the industrious envoy : " An excellent man; he has rather a contempt of human affairs and means; a bad digestion." This watchful, dyspeptic figure leaned perpetually above Albert's shoulder or poured his sagacity into interminable letters to his attentive *Liebling*. The Prince had inherited this privilege from his wife's uncle Leopold, who corresponded vigorously in his own person as well; and events in England drew a constant stream of good advice from Brussels. This constellation of well-wishers might subject British policy to curious influences; indeed, they almost constituted a second Foreign Office. The Cabinet proposed; but the Queen disposed—after Leopold had dropped a judicious hint, Stockmar composed a memorandum, and the Prince another. It was an interesting variant of constitutional practice; and without enthusiasm Palmerston observed the unobtrusive but undoubted dawning of a Saxe-Coburg *camarilla.*,

That was, for him, the last and most fatal change of all. He was accustomed to advise the Queen; but now she had advisers of her own—and what advisers ! His respect was not compelled by the country of their birth. For Palmerston, more cosmopolitan than most men, had not yet learnt respect for Germany. His outlook on the world, acquired in early travel and his years of office, comprised a compre-

hension of the French, suspicion of the Russians, a strong
distaste for Austria, and a love of Italy. But somehow
Germany was outside the circle. It remained for him a
tangled territory of slightly ridiculous principalities, whose
statesmen laboured under the supreme disadvantage of
mostly doing as Metternich told them—and Metternich was
mostly wrong. Besides, however black the ink, he could
not read their dreadful *Schrift*. This disesteem of their
genus was deepened by an added drawback attributable to
their species. They uniformly came from Coburg, sharing a
common loyalty to the ducal house of Saxe-Coburg-Gotha.
The cautious progeny of Frederick the Serious had married
with a brave persistence, until it was impossible for any
statesman to take two steps in Europe without tripping over
their family ties. An uncle reigned in Brussels, united by
his second wife to Paris and by the memory of his first to
Windsor, where a nephew ruled as Consort, whilst another
filled the same honourable station more precariously at
Lisbon and a niece strengthened the French connection as
Duchesse de Nemours. These silken strands served to
unite Louis Philippe to the invisible directors of British
policy. For it was evident that the Coburg family circle,
no less than Belgian interests, must require eternal peace
between France and England. Indeed, the Queen's first
message, when Palmerston came back to office, was a
warning " *not* to oppose French influence in Spain and *not*
to attempt to get up an English party there." But such
exigencies are frequently embarrassing to ministers, and these
restraints were likely to sit uncomfortably on Palmerston.

Peel and Aberdeen had accommodated themselves to the
new atmosphere with marked success and were in consequence regretted as " irreparable losses " and " our valuable
Peel." But Palmerston was not quite easy. He had
prepared the way with a slightly laboured apologia submitted to the Queen through Melbourne in the previous
year, in which he dwelt almost tearfully on his love of
peace, adding with cheerful malice that his critics accused
his policy of " a *tendency* to produce war, and I suppose

they would argue that it was quite wrong and against all rule that it did not do so." Now he was back at work again in July, 1846. Almost his first official words were spoken on the slightly embarrassing occasion of a Reform Club banquet to Ibrahim Pasha, heir to Mehemet Ali and the hero of his Syrian campaigns. A military band played Turkish airs at dinner; and the delighted company, noting a bill of fare containing forty-nine items, agreed that Soyer had excelled himself. The *menu* was a monument of international tact. The soups alone were *à la Victoria, à la Comte de Paris,* and *à la Louis Philippe;* there were *Petits Pois à l'Anglo-Français, Charlotte Prussienne,* and (happy memory of 1840) *Grenadins de Bœuf à la Beyrout.* But the crown of the evening was a miracle of confectionery entitled *Crème d'Egypte à l'Ibrahim Pacha,* adorned with edible portraits of the Club's guest and his august father. Small wonder that the inspired *chef* was sent for and complimented by the delighted Highness. Lord Palmerston proposed 'Mehemet Ali and the prosperity of Egypt' with a cheerful reminiscence of ancient conflicts, and replied for 'Her Majesty's Ministers,' observing that "it was with no small satisfaction that they had seen the measures for which they had been turned out of office carried by the late ministry (Cries of 'Mr. Cobden ')."

Installed at the Foreign Office once again, he looked warily round Europe, shed a few perfunctory tears upon the grave of Poland just reopened in order to receive Cracow, and wrote a singularly prescient letter to John Russell—" Italy is the weak part of Europe, and the next war that breaks out in Europe will probably arise out of Italian affairs. . . . France and Austria would then fight each other in Italy, and France would have all the Italians on her side." So the first shadow of 1859 began to fall upon the screen. But Palmerston was drafting upon Egypt and Portugal and Spain (for there was still a Spanish question).

Then, in the first week of September, he plunged straight into the peculiar world where his sovereign and her consort pursued the milder forms of pleasure in the *Victoria and*

Albert. They sailed from Osborne on a chilly morning and ran for the Channel Islands. It was a trifle rough at first; but when they left the swell behind, " Bertie put on his sailor's dress," and *Punch* was able to delight a loyal public with a small Heir Apparent, " every inch a sailor," regaling an enormous Jack Tar with grog ' to drink Mama's health.' They made a call at Jersey; and the Prince, whose *forte* lay in detection of instructive resemblances, compared it to the Bay of Naples. He had already remarked the similarity of Perth to Bâle, of Birnam Wood to Thüringen, and of the Tamar to the Danube; and he was to live to find more than a touch of Paris in the view of Glasgow. His Queen, not to be outdone, was put in mind of Mayence by the Jersey orchards. Then they proceeded with the cruise. They saw Land's End; and Albert took all the gentlemen ashore for a delirious afternoon of mineralogy, returning loaded to the water's edge with specimens of serpentine. On the next day they scaled St. Michael's Mount, and Albert sketched and found a lot more stones with most exciting markings. Then Palmerston played truant with the Queen. They stayed on board, whilst Albert went ashore again in search of further geological adventure. The Corporation of Penryn came off in boats; and " I stepped out of the pavilion on deck with Bertie, and Lord Palmerston told them that that was ' The Duke of Cornwall.' " But Albert got them all ashore at Fowey and even down a mine, where " Albert and the gentlemen wore miners' hats," and Albert was happy knocking off specimens again. He had a strange capacity for enjoyment; his visible pleasure in a game of cards struck Mr. Greville, and Lady Palmerston once wrote a trifle faintly after two nights at the Castle, " Whatever he does amuses him." So they sailed happily up-Channel, detecting resemblances in every headland, whilst Albert talked to them or arranged his specimens. But they had graver topics. For at Penzance, Lord Palmerston received the staggering news that Louis Philippe had arranged a double marriage at Madrid and, abandoning the *rôle* of Napoleon for that of Louis XIV., erased the Pyrenees.

The prospect of this pleasing *imbroglio* had hung over Europe for years. A small Queen and a small Infanta were a sad temptation to ambitious dynasts. Louis Philippe, always a model parent, would welcome such an addition to his spreading family; indeed, Palmerston had suspected something of the kind so early as 1839. Unnumbered suitors eyed Madrid; French princes aired their charms; a Neapolitan uncle preened himself; the Coburgs pricked a hopeful ear; and a languid Spanish cousin, whom Palmerston dismissed as " an absolute and Absolutist fool," lounged in his corner. The French professed alarm at the prospect of a Coburg husband; for Coburgs had a dangerous aptitude for marrying queens. But the real danger was a French alliance, since a union of the two crowns in a single family was plainly inadmissible. That dreaded possibility had once caused an interminable War of the Spanish Succession; and when it was mentioned statesmen could still look grave and quote the Treaty of Utrecht. So Spanish politics proceeded briskly; riot succeeding riot; troops mutinied with pleasing frequency; and a bewildering succession of generals jingled spurs up ministerial stairs and down again, while promotion in the higher ranks of the Spanish army seemed almost to have reached the point of diminishing returns; and the two little ladies at the palace waited with dwindling patience for their bridegrooms. But Louis Philippe was more adroit than Louis XIV. Skirting the larger prize, he marked the younger sister for his son Montpensier. The well-meaning Aberdeen made diplomatic passes to exorcise the dynastic nightmare; and whilst his sovereign walked with Louis Philippe among the bright parterres of Eu, there was a compact. Something was said about the Coburgs, and Aberdeen was understood to promise that England would not press their suit at Madrid; but it was plainly agreed that Montpensier's marriage with the Infanta should be deferred until the Queen, her sister, had a husband and a nursery. The quest for both was still proceeding, when Palmerston returned to office in 1846. It was the old problem of his *Cristino* days, " England wishing

Spain to be independent, and France desiring to establish a paramount influence in Spain." He surveyed the candidates without enthusiasm, observing in the language of the kennels that " we . . . should see with pleasure a good cross introduced into the Royal Family of Spain." But he was not unduly exercised by the choice. A Coburg prince might serve his turn, though he was under no illusion that planting a Coburg at Madrid was tantamount to planting the Union Jack—" a third son of a German nobleman . . . he is only cousin to the husband of our Queen." So possibly, all things considered, one of the Spanish cousins would do quite as well. He was drafting freely in this sense before the summer holidays. But the French watched Madrid with a more fevered eye; for an excited diplomat had telegraphed three months before, ' *La reine est nubile depuis deux heures.*' So when Palmerston, in an incautious enumeration of Isabella's suitors, mentioned the Coburgs, they started wildly. Always suspect, he seemed convicted by the rash admission of favouring the dreaded candidate. It might, it could, it should be construed in the darkest sense; and the delighted French held a pretext for departing from the Eu agreement. With sudden stealth they proceeded to their counter-measures. The Spanish cousin was produced; his physique was really preposterous and, in a lover, his voice left much to be desired. But the Queen was young; supper was served at midnight; and a flurried girl accepted him. Meanwhile, her sister was betrothed to the manly figure of Montpensier; and a proud father at the Tuileries smiled in the knowledge that their children (and his grandchildren) might occupy the throne of Spain.

This news, arriving in Lord Palmerston's red box, came on board the *Victoria and Albert* at Penzance; and in Falmouth Harbour indignation poured from his sovereign's pen. It was *infamous*; it was *too* bad; and it was done in such a *dishonest* way. The missive, heavy with underlinings, sped to Brussels; and when the Queen of the French imparted her new felicity, she received from Osborne the tart rejoinder that the news filled the recipient with nothing but *surprise et un bien vif regret.*   The Whigs exploded with the most impressive reverberations.   Their historical parallels went off like minute-guns; and John Russell's post-bag was full of solemn reprobation.   Even Clarendon was angry, while Palmerston explained triumphantly that " we have been defeated by our timidity, hesitation, and delay . . . and we have all—I mean the whole Whig Party—been too much afraid of France.   Besides, we were not sure of our own Court, and we did not believe the French Government to be as tricky as they have shown themselves, and we thought we should have more time to act.   But Louis Philippe and Guizot, like practical and sagacious men, determined to knock us down at once, and make an apology afterwards if necessary to pacify us."   It was a salutary lesson for his colleagues, and he began to write more cheerfully of orders to the fleet.   After this, with Lansdowne indignant and John Russell using language that was positively strong, there could be no more nonsense about the preservation of Lord Aberdeen's precious *Entente Cordiale.*

But the effects of the singular event were felt in more exalted circles.   The Queen was angry; Albert was deeply pained by this departure from the truth; and Stockmar put his displeasure on paper at considerable length.   It gave them quite a new feeling for Lord Palmerston.   A month before they had found his drafts a shade alarming.   But at Falmouth his royal mistress " must do Palmerston the credit to say that he takes it very quietly, and will act very temperately about it."   Europe was loud with her reproaches. She grieved to say that the good King had behaved *very dishonestly.*   But though she grieved, she said so.   She wrote it to every branch of his ramifying family—to her uncle, to her poor dear Louise, and finally (in a letter which Palmerston gleefully recorded as " a tickler ") to the King himself, when that incautious monarch in a last effort at self-exculpation suggested, through his daughter, that *notre bonne petite Reine . . . ne voit maintenant les choses que par la lunette de Lord Palmerston,* dilating on the superior merits of Lord Aberdeen's instrument for young sovereigns.   This

was too much; and she plunged into a spirited defence of
Palmerston's despatches that would have done credit to an
Under-Secretary. For Lord Palmerston was more than
defensible—he was right and (better still) " quite ready to be
guided by us." One may doubt the readiness; but it was
something to have created the illusion. So the strange
trio drew together—the Queen, the unsmiling Prince, and
the bland minister. A common deception had united
them, and Stockmar almost seemed to bless their union.
They had suspected Palmerston so recently, had regarded
the pacific Clarendon as their one safeguard in the Cabinet.
But soon they saw Clarendon depart to the Viceregal Lodge
without a pang, and Palmerston was almost gilded with an
unexpected beam of royal confidence.

He had a busy autumn, " hunted about from Place to
Place, and swamped by Boxes of Despatches wherever I
have been." Before the year was out, they had to move
from 5 Carlton Terrace, to 4 Carlton Gardens, because their
landlord chose to marry. He managed to get down to Broadlands, where he had only a single day at his own birds. But
he enjoyed the unusual satisfaction of telling a French
minister that his sovereign had failed to keep his word,
while *Punch* endeavoured without particular success to rouse
public indignation with the spectacle of ' The Royal Fagin of
France instructing his Boys.' There was a satisfying crop of
problems—the usual civil war in Portugal, a protest to be
made (but not too loud) against the extinction of Cracow,
anxiety in missionary circles about French treatment of Tahiti,
and the interminable fighting round Montevideo, where an
Italian legion rode in red shirts across the *Banda Oriental*
behind a big, blonde man named Garibaldi. He even found
time for the more distant pleasure of " conveying to the
Khan through his envoy the conviction that England is as
large as Bokhara and quite as civilized and as strong."
Ministers still fumed about French duplicity, and Palmerston
wrote triumphant diatribes against Louis Philippe. Indeed,
his fervour woke old memories of invading legions and flat-
bottomed flotillas; and, chilled by the thought of paddle-

steamers lurking in French harbours, he composed a plea for the Militia and an improved system of coast-defences, to be financed by loans. But though such views commanded the warm approval of the Duke, the public mind was not greatly disturbed by the misdeeds of princes; and *Punch* drew Palmerston as a discouraged showman announcing ' Horrible Treachery, to which is added the Confiscation of Cracow ' and ' To be seen alive—the British Lion roaring ' to a crowd that was frankly apathetic. His sovereign, only half captivated, still found time to dissent from one of his drafts to Portugal—" she does not quite approve of the tone of it "—in the midst of the heavy correspondence entailed by her thoughtful endeavour to institute a medal for the Peninsular War whilst a few veterans still survived to wear it. So 1846 went out on Palmerston declaring sturdily that " I have no doubt that Louis Philippe hates me; but I am not ambitious of being *le bien aimé* of any French sovereign, and I care not for dislike which is founded on nothing but a conviction that I am a good Englishman, and that I see through, and will do my best to thwart, all schemes of foreign powers hostile to the interests of my country."

As 1847 opened, they were all explaining hard. The King explained the purity of his intentions to an attentive son-in-law from Brussels; his son-in-law passed on the explanation to a slightly less attentive niece at Windsor. M. Guizot explained himself away at preternatural length; Princess Lieven, a good Frenchwoman now, explained M. Guizot; and M. Thiers explained without superfluous gallantry that Princess Lieven was a fool and a liar, while Mr. Greville flitted delightedly about Paris, collecting explanations. Lord Palmerston informed a colleague that " the wish for the Coburgh Marriage originated with Christina and was real with her to the last; but I think it is also nearly certain that Louis Philippe and Guizot after we came in made use of this Desire of Christina's to endeavour to entrap us into something which they might be able to put their Finger

upon and to pronounce to be a Secret Intrigue which set
them free from all their former engagements and which
justified the immediate conclusion of the Montpensier Match."
He concluded bitterly that " the French have gained all they
wanted by deceiving us, and they wish to stand as well with
us as if they had acted like honest men." Indeed, when
France became placatory, he wrote to John Russell that
" Bresson talks of resuming the Entente as if it was a military
position that could be evacuated or occupied by word of
command," and more laconically informed his wife that " our
line must be sulk." So Lady Palmerston alarmed a guest
with the unpleasing prospect of settled hostility to France;
and the Duke, deep in Apsley House, concluded with an
angry grunt to Charles Arbuthnot that the whole Spanish
tangle was " damned stuff."

But it had proved a rare blessing to Palmerston. For it
snapped the threads of Aberdeen's embarrassing *Entente
Cordiale* and stung the Whigs into momentary loyalty to
himself. Even the Court, in the shock of losing its illusions
about the poor, good King, relaxed its first suspicions of
Palmerston; and for an instant, while Stockmar murmured a
benediction, he almost seemed secure in the approval of that
Eminence grise of Coburg diplomacy. But the gleam passed;
the watchful eyes were never off his papers; and an anxious
Queen was soon repeating her request " through Lord John
Russell and personally to see that the drafts to our Foreign
Ministers are not despatched *previous* to their being submitted to the Queen. Notwithstanding this is still done, as
for instance to-day with regard to the drafts for Lisbon. . . ."
He had his troubles with Russell as well, when the Prime
Minister got his first news of a particularly lively threat to
France from a scared colleague; and Peel in Opposition
shook an anxious head over such insubordination. Under
this tutelage, he pursued his course, confronting 'the Napoleon
of Peace ' in Spain, Morocco, Portugal, and even Switzerland;
keeping a brisk look-out on China, where " we must make them
all clearly understand, though in the civilest terms, that our
treaty rights must be respected, unless they choose to have

their seaports knocked about their ears"; watching the
unpromising dawn of Queen Isabella's married life, as that
spirited bride sought other consolations, wishing "in the
true spirit of inductive philosophy . . . to found her conclusions upon a great variety of experiments"; and observing in the pale dawn of Prussian constitutionalism—"If she
does go on, Germany will follow her, and sooner or later her
example must be followed by Austria"—the first hint of a
redder daybreak.

That summer there was a General Election, and once again
he smiled at Tiverton from the window of the Three Tuns.
The Radical butcher had brought down a Chartist candidate
for his particular delectation, and the town was in a pleasing
uproar. On nomination-day the town band called to fetch
him, and they marched him through the streets behind that
heartening thump and blare. A lively crowd was waiting at
the hustings, and the speaking began. After an interlude the
butcher proposed his man, denounced the cruel Poor Law,
dilated on the vast Bastilles where aged couples were separated, and enquired (to loud laughter from his lordship) what
the noble lord would say if he and Lady Palmerston were
treated so. The Chartist followed after a deft and (quite
superfluous) appeal by Palmerston for a fair hearing, speaking
for above two hours with occasional refreshment from a large
blue jug. After dwelling lovingly on Palmerston's Tory
origins, he perambulated history from the time of the Six
Acts, ranging from Ireland to Cracow by way of Turkey,
Belgium, Egypt and Afghanistan. Then Palmerston replied.
His hearers showed a disturbing tendency to interrupt; but
hardened to amicable shouts of "Ah, Cupid! sly Cupid!"
he stood smiling at them over his folded arms and found time
for an hour's denunciation of the Charter, together with a full
defence of his policy (as well as of his subscriptions to local
charities). The solemn ritual of a show of hands by the
whole crowd went strongly in the Chartist's favour. This
agreeable farce concluded, custom dictated an appeal to the
more select tribunal of the lawful electors. A poll was
formally demanded, and Palmerston made repeated efforts

to entice his adversary into the narrower arena. But he declined to " try his strength and test his principles," and Palmerston was safely re-elected by 117 Tiverton electors.

These exercises ended, he withdrew to Broadlands, where his reflections were mainly Italian. That month the white-coats marched into Ferrara in protest against the scandal of a reforming Pope, and Palmerston played with the notion of a mission to the Vatican, which might support the generous impulses of Pius IX. against the bayonets of Metternich. Besides, a British minister at Rome might (as he wrote to Russell) counteract the dangerous influences which had made the whole Irish priesthood advocate Repeal. The Queen was strangely favourable to the idea, was even prepared to sanction the despatch of a fleet to Italian waters " as a very proper measure to give countenance to the Sovereigns engaged in Liberal Reform, and exposed alike to the inroads of their absolutist neighbours, and to the outbreaks of popular movements directed by a republican party, and perhaps fostered by the Austrian Government." Such disrespectful language about the impeccable Metternich was extremely puzzling; but Palmerston received the unexpected allies with his accustomed calm.

He made closer contact with the royal opinions in September, when his Emily pursued her " dearest love " to Scotland with wifely warnings against sailing on Highland lakes—" those lakes are all so dangerous "—or swimming (at nearly sixty-three) out of his depth. But while she stayed behind " only employ'd like Robinson Crusoe in notching off the days and counting when I may *hope* to have you back again," he was behind the mists in attendance on his sovereign and her Prince. They were all at Ardverikie in a house profusely embellished with stags' horns and delineations of their noble wearers from the accomplished hand of Landseer. The country bore a comforting resemblance to Thüringen. But the weather was execrable and afforded ample opportunities for conversation.

The Prince, unnaturally exhilarated by his mother-in-law's birthday gift of " Statuettes of the Consoling and

Avenging Angels," was full of opinions when Lord Palmerston arrived. He had been passing a delightful holiday composing memoranda on German unity with Prince Charles of Leiningen, and in the course of these diversions they discovered a uniform distaste for Austria. Was not Austria "the main obstruction "? Did not the rigid form of Metternich stand at the end of every European vista? His tocsin sounded at the slightest movement, his bayonets were levelled at the least hint of change. How could Germany grow Liberal and free and strong under that shadow? England, perhaps, might play a helpful part, might even intervene to check Austrian intervention. This reasoning (it was the old lesson of Mr. Canning) had brought the Prince in the course of a few memoranda to Palmerston's conclusion, though not quite expressed in Palmerston's language, " that England's true position is to be the *Schutzmacht* of States whose independent development is sought to be impeded from without." Inspired by German aspirations, this logic was no less applicable to the case of Italy; and the Prince composed a stirring paper on the mission to the Pope urging the issue of a more than Palmerstonian circular warning the world that England would regard aggression against reforming states as a breach of the Treaty of Vienna. So they sat talking in the Highland drizzle, under the Landseers at Ardverikie; and the Prince found Lord Palmerston slightly deficient in principle, but apt to be worn down by a steady drip of argument. But one day they reached the burning topic of German unity, and there the Prince outstripped the minister. His memorandum was a lively denunciation of Austria—"a State composed less of German than of non-German elements, whose policy is governed by other than German interests and views" —followed by a plea for German unity under Prussian auspices. But Palmerston lagged sadly behind these leaping ideals; and in a somewhat limp reply he admitted the probability of Anglo-German friendship in face of Franco-Russian aggression, eschewed the topic of United Germany, and paused to explain at length to the Prince Consort (a convinced Free Trader) that a patriotic *Zollverein* was already

lamentably apt to maintain prohibitive import duties on
British goods, closing upon the view that British ministers
should " make every proper effort to persuade the States of
Northern Germany, who have not joined the Zollverein, to
continue to refrain from doing so." This was a dismal
ending. Indeed, it was almost painfully apparent that
Palmerston regarded Germany less as a nascent Power
than as a British market.

Then he returned to Emily, to the absorbing draft of his
instructions to Lord Minto who was to unfold the blessings of
freedom to a grateful Pope, to the Swiss papers which revealed
a highly unusual civil war between the Cantons by the
startled waters of the Lake of Zug, and to the new House of
Commons where the indomitable Mr. Urquhart, just returned
for Stafford after a busy decade spent in persuading working-
men that Palmerston persistently betrayed his country,
observed him with an eye of dark suspicion. The Queen
was restive, too, *again* remarking that the drafts have since
some weeks been sent to her *after* they were gone. He fenced
a little, explaining that the objectionable despatches were
mere statements of his personal opinions; although he was
slightly embarrassed by the ridiculous circumstance that he
had missed a Council through riding absently from Carlton
Gardens to the Nine Elms Station (for the Broadlands line),
and consequently failed to catch the Windsor train which
went from Paddington. But Majesty was unconvinced and
fought him stoutly on a draft to Portugal, which appeared to
involve a risk of war without the slightest consultation
either of herself or of the Cabinet; John Russell was
invoked; and, completely cornered, Palmerston withdrew.
Minto, a sturdy Palmerstonian, perambulated Italy, dis-
tributing constitutional principles from an ample cornucopia
and complying with requests for a few words by the words,
exceptionally few but rousing, *Viva l'Indipendenza Italiana*!
while Metternich watched uneasily and put more white-
coats into Lombardy, and a French fleet, ready to rescue
almost anyone from Austria, haunted Italian waters.

That autumn there was an odd scare of invasion, which

startled Wellington, although it left his countrymen mainly undisturbed. It found Palmerston writing anxious letters about dark nights and foggy days in the Channel, and memoranda on the Militia, with the gay reservation that " no doubt it would be most agreeable to a nation if its defence could be provided for by an army of angels, without any effort of its own, just as it would like its services to be provided for by some Aladdin's lamp, without any demand upon its own pecuniary resources." He even found time to turn Lord Minto to account for Irish purposes. Agrarian crime was rife in Ireland ; and whilst he wrote regretfully to the Lord Lieutenant that " the true remedy cannot in these days be applied, but if you *could* hang the Priest of the Parish whenever a murder such as these last was committed, I have a notion that lay Protestant life would be much more secure," he instructed Minto to advise the Pope that " a little good advice to the Irish priests on these matters would be well bestowed."

So 1847 faded on the Queen among her Christmas trees at Windsor, and Palmerston at work on boxes of Italian papers, and Melbourne murmuring in his chair. Beyond the sunset Garibaldi still trailed his *poncho* round the dusty streets of Montevideo, dreaming of Italy; and a dull-eyed Prince, escaped from Ham, seemed almost to have escaped from destiny itself, as he sat entertaining London dining-rooms in his muffled voice. But something stirred in Italy ; there was a faint *malaise* in France ; even Germany seemed restless. The scattered voices rose on the still air ; and a hint of thunder came across the silence, as the world slipped quietly into 1848.

That year the storm broke over Europe. At first there was a flicker of lightning below the skyline, as it felt its way into Italy and muttered round Milan and Naples. Then Paris flashed and thundered into revolution, and the echoes rolled across Germany. A gleam lit up the south ; and then, flash after flash, the northern states were caught by the strange glare. Baden, Bavaria, Hesse, Wurtemburg, Han-

R

over, Saxony, the Hansa Towns whirled in a witches' sabbath; Vienna joined the dance; and Berlin stumbled
heavily before the gale. The wrack went scudding across
Europe. King's, ministers, and thrones waved like a wheat-
field in the wind, with monarchs (in the gleeful image of
Carlyle) " running about like a gang of coiners when the police
had come among them," or sadly housed (in Mr. Disraeli's
shocked enumeration)—" the King of France in a Surrey
villa, Metternich in a Hanover Square Hotel, and the Prince
of Prussia at Lady Palmerston's."

But Palmerston had his private storm as well. That
winter the indomitable Urquhart prepared for his impeach-
ment; and one evening a faithful disciple launched upon the
House a terrifying motion of thirty counts against the odious
Secretary of State. Alluding freely to his treason, the indignant speaker deplored the national degradation in terms
that would have been scarcely excessive after a successful
invasion, with the Tower in flames and the Bank in ruins.
Speeches of 1829, despatches of 1830 were ransacked for
evidence of his infamy; but after the accusing voice had filled
twenty columns of *Hansard* an inattentive House was
counted out. The unwearied Anstey resumed a fortnight
later. That evening a French crowd was surging up a street
in Paris to break Guizot's windows; a nervous picket fired;
and the incautious shot ended the old King's reign. For the
crowd saw its dead, acclaimed the martyrs, and made barricades by torchlight; and the next morning brought the
Second Republic. But in the calm air of the House of
Commons Mr. Urquhart's spokesman was resuming his
indictment of Lord Palmerston for every variety of treason
and high misdemeanour. The gloomy picture was continued
—Poland betrayed, Circassia violated, Egypt coerced, and
(worst of all) the *Portfolio* disowned. He called for discovery
of official documents on a Gargantuan scale. This time he
was unchecked, and filled ninety-four columns of *Hansard*
in five hours. Responding a week later, Palmerston almost
repaid him in his own coin and in reply spoke fifty-seven.
The long review of his career reminded him of a drowning

man's vision of his past life. But his rejoinder, which was both precise and pointed, was far from jocular and closed with a full statement of his principles :

" I hold with respect to alliances that England is a Power sufficiently strong, sufficiently powerful to steer her own course, and not to tie herself as an unnecessary appendage to the policy of any other Government. I hold that the real policy of England—apart from questions which involve her own particular interests, political or commercial—is to be the champion of justice and right, pursuing that course with moderation and prudence, not becoming the Quixote of the world, but giving the weight of her moral sanction and support wherever she thinks that justice is, and wherever she thinks that wrong has been done. . . . It is a narrow policy to suppose that this country or that is to be marked out as the eternal ally or the perpetual enemy of England. We have no eternal allies, and we have no perpetual enemies. Our interests are eternal and perpetual, and those interests it is our duty to follow.''

This said, he sat down upon the sentiment of Mr. Canning that, with every British minister, the interests of England ought to be the shibboleth of his policy. It was the authentic voice of *Endymion's* admired ' Lord Roehampton,' still " thinking of real politics; foreign politics, maintaining our power in Europe.''

Europe in 1848 gave him enough to think of. Its landmarks vanished in the rising flood. France was submerged, leaving a dismal jetsam of discarded royalty on English beaches; the sharp outline of Austria dissolved in a haze of civil wars, and the nice equipoise of Germany ceased to exist. The view from England eastwards across the Continent was an unnatural void. The Czar remained, and there was still a king at Brussels. But Louis Philippe had bolted; Metternich was gone; and from Calais to the Russian frontier there was nothing left standing in the track of the storm. Even the sacred frontiers of 1815 were threatened, where Italians leapt hopefully at Austrian throats, and Danes scuffled with Germans in Schleswig-Holstein.

So Palmerston lived on in a changed world. But he had
more to face than a mere alteration of the diplomatic landscape, though that was grave enough. Few men are
adaptable at sixty-three; and the antics of Provisional
Governments were highly distracting for a minister accustomed to the grave rapier-play of Talleyrand and Nesselrode. Yet Palmerston managed the transformation, and
moved the new pieces on the board with his old skill. He
could contrive to write : " *Vive* Lamartine ! " though he
retained a sound conviction that " the French are Children in
regard to all serious affairs," together with a lively regret
that " the example of universal suffrage in France will set
our non-voting population agog, and will create a demand for
an inconvenient extension of the suffrage, ballot, and other
mischievous things." The new surge of national sentiment
presented novel problems. But he had inherited from Mr.
Canning a *penchant* for ' nations struggling to be free.'
Besides, Metternich had always disbelieved in nationalities ;
and Metternich (it was his firm conviction) was mostly
wrong. So Palmerston could define the principle of
nationality in the most modern language :

> " Providence meant mankind to be divided into separate
> nations, and for this purpose countries have been bounded by
> natural barriers, and races of men have been distinguished by
> separate languages, habits, manners, dispositions, and char-
> acters. There is no case on the globe where this intention is
> more marked than that of the Italians and the Germans, kept
> apart by the Alps, and as unlike in every thing as two races
> can be. Austria has never possessed Italy as part of her
> Empire, but has always held it as a conquered territory.
> There has been no mixture of races. The only Austrians have
> been the troops and the civil officers. She has governed it as
> you govern a garrison town, and her rule has always been
> hateful. We do not wish to threaten ; but . . ."

The lesson was plainly learnt and admirably repeated ;
and Palmerston, at sixty-three, faced the new world of
Lamartine and Mazzini with all the grace that had confronted
the old masters of classical diplomacy. The change was

vast; and ageing men find changes difficult. But Palmerston (it was his secret) never lost his youth.

The prospect, if he must confess the truth, was not unpleasing. He observed with sober pleasure " the sweep made of the Plotters of the Spanish Marriages; and what is most poetical in the Retribution is that they have all of them been themselves the active agents of their own Destruction." And it confirmed the feeling of a lifetime to know that Metternich was really wrong, even if it involved a call on him at the Brunswick Hotel in Hanover Square, or a visit later in the year to the Old Palace, Richmond Green, where the Prince was installed with his Princess and her parrots, and he found Mr. Disraeli calling in an ecstasy of high diplomacy. There were consolations in a *dénouement* where " Metternich and Guizot meet in exile in London . . . sovereigns like Louis Philippe drink unwholesome water and sour small beer at Claremont, instead of champagne and claret at the Tuileries." But he faced a graver peril, since the general disturbance threatened a general war. The main risk was, as he stated it, " that in defence of constitutional liberty in Italy, the French nation would rush to arms, and a French army would again water their horses in the Danube "; and he laboured to avert the outbreak. Writing to Lansdowne, he repudiated a pretentious policy—" We are not the arbiters of Europe nor a High Court of Justice to investigate disputes and adjudicate upon Contested Rights "—and he defined to Clarendon his simple method in pursuit of peace :

" It seems to me that the true Policy of Europe at present is to say as little and to do as little as possible, so as not to stir matters in France beyond their natural and existing Turbulence, and to watch events and to be prepared for them."

But it appears from the alarming figure of 29,000 despatches written or read by Palmerston that year that his policy of watchful waiting was far from passive. The effort was immense; but it succeeded, since Europe came through 1848 without a general conflagration.

So Palmerston sat drafting with an increasing passion for

plain sentences and blacker ink, and a frenzied admonition
to the gentlemen of the Foreign Office to " take more Pains
to form their letters distinctly." But he had graver im-
pediments, since his sovereign and her coadjutors were more
than ever disinclined to leave foreign policy to a mere Foreign
Secretary. She was rejecting drafts before the revolution.
Diverted by that cataclysm, which engulfed the poor, good
King, she was lost for a time in cries of sympathy. Letters to
Claremont, minglings of royal tears at Windsor, left little
time for her papers; even the stream of good advice from
Brussels was momentarily stifled by Leopold's faint shriek
that " the human race is a *sad* creation, and I trust that the
other planets are better organised, and that we may get there
hereafter "; and Albert, always so calm, was almost
hysterical in his appeal to Stockmar to " come, as you love
me, as you love *Victoria*, as you love *uncle Leopold*, as
you love your German Fatherland." Lord Palmerston
enjoyed the unusual respite and drafted on without royal
admonitions. He disliked the nest of exiled royalty at
Claremont; but he gave a little dinner for Guizot and Lieven
at Carlton Gardens and Mr. Greville thought the two ministers " would have shaken each other's arms off." Then
London enjoyed the mild distraction of an *émeute* of its own.
The Chartist threat impended, and the Government invoked
the Duke to make the military arrangements. He was at
Palmerston's one night, assuring a nervous diplomat that the
troops would be kept well out of sight. An April morning
dawned, and Lady Palmerston wrote " Revolution " in
her diary; the servants were all enrolled as Special Constables; and she retired to spend the day with Minnie, while
Palmerston went off to defend the Foreign Office. A meagre
issue of Service muskets and cutlasses had been made; and,
true to departmental habits, a dispute was raging between
two branches as to the command. But the fortress in
Downing Street was never tested. A wet afternoon put off
the Chartist *journée*; and Palmerston was left exulting over
" the Waterloo of peace and order," with a mild regret that
" the foreigners did not show; but the special constables

had sworn to make an example of any whiskered and bearded rioter whom they might meet with, and I am convinced would have mashed them to jelly." So Mr. Carlyle, out without his umbrella, went home by the Chelsea omnibus after noting the absence of traffic in the West End; and Em sent little notes to her " dear Harry " asking for leave to emerge from her place of refuge, and crept back to Carlton Gardens after dinner.

The echoes died away; and Majesty, a little calmer, found her pen again " to urge Lord Palmerston to keep her informed of what he hears, and of the views of the Government on the important questions before us. She now only gets the Drafts when they are gone." The dreadful winter faded, and in the springtime his sovereign found strength to refuse Palmerston a card for a Court Ball that he had the effrontery to ask for some envoy of the French Republic. The monarchy resumed its normal avocations; Albert addressed the Society for the Improvement of the Condition of the Labouring Classes; and the drafts were scrutinised once more. Lord Palmerston, intractable as ever, was deep in a Spanish escapade. A more than usually Palmerstonian draft to a highly Palmerstonian ambassador at Madrid was causing endless trouble. It had suggested bluntly that " it would be wise for the Queen of Spain . . . to strengthen the executive government by enlarging the basis upon which the Administration is founded, and by calling to her councils some of those men who possess the confidence of the Liberal Party." Smuggled somehow past John Russell, it provoked every variety of indignation. The Spaniards raged, since ministers are rarely friendly to suggestions of their imperfection; the British ambassador was very pardonably ordered to leave the country; the Queen was torn between disapproval of the draft and resentment of the insult to herself—" for in whatever way one may wish to look at it, Sir Henry still is *her* Minister "; the Whigs were helplessly indignant, angry gentlemen crowding into Mr. Greville's room to shake their heads and leave him bitterly convinced that " it will all end in nothing, as usual, and

Palmerston will not care a straw "; while Lady Palmerston
pleaded with him to throw over his ambassador, " because I
am afraid you should go & act the Knight Errant to screen
Bulwer if he is attacked—& really such a Man does not
deserve that you should put yourself in any scrape for him."
Knight-errantry on behalf of subordinates was in his habit,
and his defence of Bulwer in the House of Commons was a
fine demonstration of official loyalty.　But he was on his
own defence as well.　Besides, he had particular reasons for
resenting such unusually spirited action on the part of Spain,
which he confided to Clarendon, an old hand at *cosas de
España:*

"I have no doubt in my own Mind though I cannot allege
any tangible Reason for the Suspicion that this Fly-out of the
Spanish Govt. had been much encouraged, if not prompted,
by the Orleans Family & Ministry.　Louis Philippe & Guizot
saw that the Revolution & Republic would frighten Christina
& Narvaez and that Fear would drive them to seek closer
Connection with England; they also thought that to purchase
our support the Spanish Govt. might be disposed to make
some sacrifice of the Montpensier Interest; and to avoid this,
the best thing was to get up a Row between the Spanish & the
English Govts.; and as Glucksberg & young Talleyrand
Guizot's staff have been staying on at Madrid . . . Guizot had
good Tools to work with, and easy means of Communication
by Isturitz's Messengers.　Accordingly the Spanish Govt. first
gave us a Slap on the Face by sending back our Note & Despatch to see whether that would do; to that we said we were
not at all offended; they then determined to strengthen the
Dose & gave us a Stick on the lower Parts, & have assured us
it was meant as a Proof of Friendship & Esteem. . . ."

It was a reading of the case that did little to increase his
sympathy with the poor, good King at Claremont.

Claremont, indeed, was not inactive.　Palmerston was
always convinced that Guizot was *un austère intrigant.*
Even the gentle Russell wrote to Clarendon that " Louis
Philippe and Guizot grumble and intrigue like ungrateful
dogs that they are."　Guizot sat primly in the Lords to

hear Lord Stanley denounce Palmerston; the King and all his brood retained a fixed belief that he had caused their downfall; and what was easier than to impart this dark conviction to a sympathetic Queen? The watchful Greville thought as much—"I take for granted that they have persuaded the Queen that their ruin has been the work of Palmerston"—and so a fresh ingredient was added to Victoria's distaste for her Foreign Secretary. The world night see "Bulwer and Palmerston . . . triumphantly curveting about, completely smashing their antagonists in argument." But the Crown was veiled in clouds of disapproval.

Untaught, apparently, by his experience with Spain, the incorrigible minister next sought to warn the Portuguese against their own proceedings. The Queen protested to John Russell; Russell concurred, with the lame addition that "it is just to Lord Palmerston to say that his general course of policy has met with the warm approval of the Cabinet, and that the cases of difference of judgment have been rare exceptions"; and Lady Palmerston endeavoured to correct his ways with feminine wisdom:

"I am sure the Queen is very angry with you ! ! I am afraid you contradict her notions too boldly. You fancy she will hear reason, when in fact all you say only proves to her that you are determined to act on the line she disapproves, & which she still thinks wrong. I am sure it would be better if you *said* less to her—even if you *act* as you think best. I often think there is too much knight errantry in your Ways. You always think you can convince people by Arguments, & she has not reflection or sense to feel the force of them—therefore the strength of your Arguments & all the explanations you give only prove to her how deeply imbued you are with what she calls error, & how impossible it is for her to make any effect on you. I should treat what she says more lightly & courteously, and not enter into argument with her, but lead her on gently, by letting her believe you have both the same opinions in fact & the same wishes, but take sometimes different ways of carrying them out."

But the lesson was lost on him; and his sovereign was left complaining that " no remonstrance has any effect with Lord Palmerston."

Trying in Portugal and Spain, his escapades became more serious in Italy. The dreadful man appeared to be resolved upon " the establishment of an *entente cordiale with the French Republic* for the purpose of driving the Austrians out of *their Dominions.*" But how were all her friends at Claremont to return to Paris, if the Republic had England for an ally? She had already fought her hardest against sending an ambassador to Paris and was left protesting, when Palmerston made deft use of his favourite argument of the *fait accompli.* Indeed, he unceremoniously informed John Russell that " the Queen's objection to having an Ambassador from the French Republic . . . is not a feeling upon which the British Government can act." But now he positively proposed to make common cause with them in Italy. The royal protests rose on the summer air. It was a *disgrace,* a most iniquitous proceeding, made worse by the underhand manner in which it was done—" Lord Palmerston has as usual pretended not to have had time to submit the draft to the Queen before he had sent it off." The Prime Minister was lectured on the shocking consequences of his colleague's action : " It will be a calamity for ages to come if this principle is to become part of the international law, viz., ' that a people can at any time transfer their allegiance from the Sovereign of one State to that of another by universal suffrage (under momentary excitement).'" Russell was duly shocked by the dreadful hint of self-determination; but the royal rage was unabated. Even the air of Balmoral, first tasted in that autumn, failed to soothe it, although the landscape was reassuringly reminiscent of the *Thüringerwald* and abounded in points of geological interest. They sketched; they shot; they rode about on ponies. But, somehow, it was quite impossible to get Lord Palmerston out of their minds; and one day his mistress poured out all her distresses to John Russell—how she felt really she could hardly go on with his dreadful colleague, having no confidence in him, and being seriously anxious and uneasy for her country and for peace in general, hardly knowing from one day to another what might happen; how he had made trouble in Spain and got himself distrusted everywhere abroad by his prejudiced and one-sided views; what dreadful things he wrote—"always as bitter as gall"—and how she often felt quite ill from anxiety; and how delightful it would be, if they could only bring Lord Clarendon home from Ireland and send Lord Palmerston to Dublin in exchange. Lord John was soothing —he was aware of the royal grievances and felt the truth of all (or nearly all) that his plaintive sovereign said. But what was he to do? Lord Palmerston, he explained, was a very able man, entirely master of his office and of affairs, a very good colleague, never making difficulties about other questions, and even complaining—most unreasonably, Lord John felt sure—that other people interfered with his. As to the Queen's suggestion, he felt sure that Palmerston would make an admirable Lord-Lieutenant. But would he go? He might resent the change; and if he turned against the Government, it would be extremely awkward. His sovereign unwillingly agreed, with an unpleasant hint that one day she might have to tell him that she really could not put up with Lord Palmerston any longer. It was a novel doctrine of the Constitution. But the Prime Minister, untroubled by thoughts of the Glorious Revolution, took it just as his Queen could wish; and, for future guidance, she made a memorandum of their little talk.

The year wore on; and still the shadows of revolt flitted across the Foreign Office screen. Croats fought with Magyars; there was a Hapsburg abdication; the Holy Father scampered out of Rome with a mob at his heels. But the tide was falling now. *Bomba* resumed his kingdom; the King's troops marched stiffly into repentant Berlin; and France, abandoning the barricades for the sober exercises of a Presidential election, weighed the contrasted charms of a general, whom she knew too well, and of an unknown Prince. It was, for Palmerston, a most distracting season; even his Turkish papers asked for some unusual form of help that

Stratford Canning wished to give to an archæologist named Layard, deep in the refuse heaps of Babylonia; and a tired minister was glad of a birthday note from Em that autumn— " This is the most fortunate day of my life, the one to which I owe all my happiness, for it is your birthday." But 1848 ended at last; and the French elections brought the slight consolation of a Prince-President in place of the old King, as the name of Bonaparte was heard once more, and guests at the Elysée were received by a large moustache and a hesitating manner.

Then it was 1849, and the storm died slowly on the distance. The French were almost quiet now, though Austria still pitched on the long swell and the clouds hung low over the great plain of Hungary. So Palmerston was left with his reflections. Always a stout believer in the British system, he was more convinced than ever. For its timbers had withstood the tempest in which a dozen rivals foundered. His cheerful confidence breathes in a letter to a colleague :

" If Stanley and Aberdeen should twit us about the Austrian Govt. not having sent an Arch Duke to announce the accession of the Emperor, might we not reply that if this is so, and if their not having sent such a mission was owing to their dis-approval of our Foreign Policy, we have in the first place to say that the Business of an English Govt. is to pursue that course of Foreign Policy which on the whole they may think right; and not to attempt the impossible task of at all times and upon all subjects doing that which is most agreeable to all Foreign Governments. A man who in private life attempts to please everybody, invariably fails; and the Government of a great country would not be more successful in such an endeavour. But secondly without any want of Respect for the Austrian Govt. or Imperial family, we must say that if the case is as stated, we are sorry for the Austrian Arch Duke. For if he had come, he would have had a very distinguished Reception, which would have made his visit very agreeable to him; and he has lost that gratification; and in the next place it must at all times be an advantage to a foreign Prince, and particularly to an Austrian Arch Duke in the present state of the continent to visit England and to see with his own eyes, how Liberty may be combined with Loyalty, Freedom with public order, and how the Respect which is shewn by the Crown for the Rights of the Subject and for the enactment of the law produces corresponding Feelings on the Part of the People, and inspires them with similar Respect for the Rights of the Crown and for the Laws which secure the Liberties and the Property of all, from the highest to the lowest in the Land."

That was a proud conviction, which Palmerston shared with most of his countrymen. Had they not come through 1848 with a *fiasco* on Kennington Common and a running fight in Ireland? It had been the burden of his discourse to foreign statesmen for nearly twenty years; and when it was proved to demonstration, he would have been less than human—and far less than Palmerston—if he had kept a modest silence.

Now, more than ever, he was a European figure. Perhaps there were no others left. The waters of 1848 had submerged so many of his equals. The small survivors might represent a party, a successful insurrection, or a provisional *régime;* but Palmerston spoke in the name of England. England, to be sure, was not wholly unanimous in its approval of the impersonation. An angry Queen revised his drafts; reluctant colleagues twittered, though John Russell (cruelly diagnosed by Lady Palmerston as " obstinate and weak ") was limply loyal; and Aberdeen deplored his rash proceedings in endless speeches to the House of Lords. But the Queen's ideas were apt to come from Brussels or from Claremont or from a husband who could still avow himself to Stockmar a good German; and his critics were frequently no less exotic in their inspiration, since Guizot and Lieven occupied their abundant leisure in furnishing awkward points to Opposition speakers. England at large was more contented. There was a comfortable impression in the public mind that Palmerston was generally inclined to put down the mighty from their seats, and he had a way of dealing with his critics. Mr. Greville might conjecture hopefully that he was "more uneasy (as well he may be) than he ever was before"; but he admitted sadly that "in the House of Commons there will be nobody to attack Palmerston, and between those who won't grapple with him, and those who can't, he will come off unscathed, as he has always done"; and quite soon he was recording another "slashing, impudent speech, full of sarcasm, jokes, and clap-traps, the whole eminently successful."

There was an awkward moment early in the year, when the Cabinet became aware that he had been sending guns from Woolwich to the Sicilian rebels; and Russell took his delighted sovereign's pleasure "on the propriety of offering to Lord Palmerston to exchange the Foreign Office for the Lord-Lieutenancy of Ireland," with an English peerage and possibly the Garter. The royal pen was almost feverish, supposed Lord John to be convinced at last that Palmerston could no longer be retained with safety at the Foreign Office, and hoped that things might be so managed as to reflect the least possible discredit upon the Government and Lord Palmerston. They were. For Palmerston, who knew the value of an opportune retreat, concurred with all the pleasure in the world in a full apology to the indignant King of Naples. His colleagues breathed again; Lady Palmerston remarked delightedly to Stockmar that "everyone keeps what he has got"; Lady John's diary recorded "Queen disappointed"; and Albert, with a gesture of despair, addressed a public meeting in support of the Servants' Provident and Benevolent Society.

Early in the session he made a wise defence of secret diplomacy:

> "If a proposition to negotiate for a certain object were given out to be published, how could it be expected that a Government, which might have rejected an overture in the first instance, would be induced to reflect over and modify a first decision? Nail them down to a first objection, and you render accommodation impossible. Pit two popular assemblies one against the other, and you put out of the question all amicable adjustment."

Perhaps his reply to Mr. Cobden's motion in support of international arbitration was a shade less reasonable, since he was inclined to dwell upon the dangers to peace itself which must result if foreign Powers were permitted to suppose that "the manly spirit of Englishmen is dead"—to say nothing of the distasteful prospect of submitting British interests to foreign judges. But he argued intelligently upon the futility of arbitration in the absence of an international tribunal and of a system of international sanctions, by which its decrees might be enforced. Lord Palmerston need hardly be reproached for failing to foresee Geneva : at least he realised the aimlessness of unsupported Hague Tribunals. Indeed, his practical pursuit of peace had been neatly proved by a workmanlike proposal for a treaty with the United States providing "that in all cases of difference which may hereafter, unfortunately, arise between the contracting parties, they will, in the first place, have recourse to the (mediation) (arbitration) of some friendly Power ; and that hostilities shall not begin between them until every endeavour to settle their difference by such means shall have proved fruitless." The value of delay (a lesson elaborately learnt by Europe in 1918) and the peculiar relation of Great Britain to the United States were plainly realised by Palmerston in 1848. In the next year he encountered the no less modern shadow of disarmament, when the Prince-President in a New Year mood launched a remarkable proposal for the reduction of the French and British fleets. It was rejected, since the navy was the ark of the Palmerstonian covenant. Had he not been a Lord of the Admiralty within two years of Trafalgar ? Invasion never ceased to haunt his dreams. Besides, his country had no army ; and if the navy was reduced, how was she to cut a European figure ? Another vision swam into his ken, when the Prince-President murmured to Normanby that a Congress (a taste for Congresses tormented him through life) might resettle Europe. But Palmerston advised John Russell shrewdly that the world had changed since the great age of Congresses—then "nations counted for nothing, sovereigns submitted to the

decisions of the Congress, and its resolves became easily
law. But nowadays sovereigns count for little, and nations
will submit to no external dictation without the actual
employment of overruling force; and a Congress might not
find it easy to give effect to its resolutions without establish-
ing a European *gendarmerie*." Besides, it was certain to
raise awkward questions; and he was for giving " a civil
but declining answer."

On more immediate topics his views were equally defined;
and Aberdeen's alternatives were cheerfully dismissed as
" antiquated imbecility." The voice of Guizot was re-
peatedly detected behind those blameless hands. For the
' travell'd thane ' was " the natural Cat's Paw for such a
purpose." Lansdowne was instructed to maintain a brave
front over the Sicilian guns—. . . " never a more legitimate
Resistance to illegal Power . . . unjust, oppressive, corrupt
and tyrannical . . . hardly an Instance of the Rising of a
People against their Rulers, which stands upon . . . Stanley
will talk much of the King of Naples as one of our allies;
but such a term is slip-slop . . . ' the Right divine of Kings
to govern ill.' "

His main concern, however, was less simple. Among the
monsters left upon the shores of Europe by the receding tide
of 1848 was a Hungarian state. Its *personnel* consisted
mainly of the indomitable Kossuth, its history of a protracted rearguard action. It had made repeated efforts to
attract Palmerston's favourable attention. A Note, an
offer of ' most favoured nation ' treatment for British
imports, a military gentleman who called at Carlton Gardens
followed in quick succession. But Palmerston remained
wholly immovable in an attitude of almost unnatural correct-
ness, insisted that his Government " has no knowledge of
Hungary except as one of the component parts of the Austrian
Empire," referred the indignant patriots to the Imperial
ambassador as an appropriate channel of communication,
and read their Declaration of Independence " simply as an
interesting document." Unlike the Italians, Magyars struggling to be free left him unmoved. He had been stirred by

Italy to every variety of mediation. But Italy, perhaps, had stronger claims upon his sympathy. He had travelled there, knew Italian, and could share the aspirations of Italian patriots. But Austrian rule in Hungary was merely the oppression of one outlandish race by another slightly less outlandish; and his classical proclivities would scarcely be satisfied by a free Hungary. Besides, Italian problems demanded close attention, since a slip in Italy meant war between Austria and France; and peace, still more than abstract freedom, remained the goal of his interminable manœuvres. But Hungary had no such claims. Indeed, Hungarian independence might even constitute a menace to peace, since Austria, weakened by the secession of Hungary, became at once too light to counterweigh the impending mass of Russia—and Palmerston was never unaware for long of those impending domes against the sky. His distaste for Austria was always marked. He was scornful of "European China," with its solemn mandarins who nodded at the Ballplatz. He could write with eloquence upon "the greatest brutes that ever called themselves by the undeserved name of civilised men. Their atrocities in Galicia, in Italy, in Hungary, in Transylvania, are only to be equalled by the proceedings of the negro race in Africa and Haiti. Their late exploit of flogging forty odd people, including two women at Milan . . ." He was prepared to share the emotions of Mr. Browning's fugitive:

> That second time they hunted me
> From hill to plain, from shore to sea,
> And Austria, hounding far and wide,
> Her blood-hounds thro' the country-side,
> Breathed hot . . .

But there was always Russia. It would never do to resolve the Hapsburg empire into its component nationalities and leave the Czar to tower over Europe. Even "the revolutionary firebrand who now presides at the Foreign Office in Downing Street" (as he lovingly christened himself in emulation of the 'Lord Feuerbrand' of the angry Viennese) had his moments of reflection; and he could tell a sorrowing

s

emissary from Budapest that if the Austrian Empire " did not already exist, it would have to be invented." So he was deaf to Magyar blandishments. Then they became preposterous, offered to put a Coburg on the throne, to cede a Danube port to England, to form a Balkan League with Turkey under British auspices, to . . . But Palmerston was obdurate. Even when Russian troops marched heavily into Hungary to stamp out the dying embers, he made no move. Once only, at a later stage, he became active; but then his care was engaged by a graver matter than the sorrows of a problematic Hungary. For the routed patriots had fled to Turkey, and Czar and Emperor demanded their surrender from a scared Sultan. Now, Russia must never be permitted to dictate to Turkey. Had he not toiled from 1833 to 1840 to prevent it ? So he rushed gaily to the rescue, enlisted France in his singular crusade, carried " the Broadbrims of the Cabinet," sent reassuring warships to the Dardanelles " like holding a bottle of salts to the nose of a lady who had been frightened," put heart into the shrinking Sultan, and foiled the Czar. In later years, describing these manœuvres to a delighted deputation of Islington electors, he confessed in an idiom appropriate to his hearers that " a good deal of judicious bottle-holding was obliged to be brought into play"; and *Punch* promptly gratified his admirers with the rakish figure, check-waistcoated and redolent of the prize ring, of the Judicious Bottle-holder.

Perhaps the Crown was less obstructive. The Prince found other occupations. There was so much to think of—the code for Bertie's education, a new History Professor at Cambridge, and the first dawn upon that untiring mind of a Great Exhibition. But they devised a fresh system for the drafts, designed to relieve Majesty from the unpleasant necessity of taking decisions " within a few minutes as is now done sometimes " and Palmerston from his complaint that " She often keeps drafts a long time." There was another angry talk with Russell about his incorrigible colleague. But nothing came of it; and the Queen was left complaining bitterly to Peel, while Mr. Greville gloated over

the strange spectacle of " the Queen turning from her own
Prime Minister to confide in the one who was supplanted by
him; a Minister talking over quietly and confidentially
with an outsider by what circumstances and what agency
his colleague, the Minister for Foreign Affairs, might be
extruded from the Government; the Queen abhorring her
Minister and unable to rid herself of him; John Russell,
fascinated and subjugated by the ascendancy of Palmerston,
submitting to everything from him, and supporting him
right or wrong, the others not concealing from those they
are in the habit of confiding in, their disapprobation of the
conduct and policy of their colleague, while they are all
the time supporting the latter and excusing the former, and
putting themselves under the obligation of identifying themselves with his proceedings, and standing or falling with
him." The serpent of this Eden needed all his steadiness.
Radicals cheered him when he defied the Czar and Austria,
Tories and Whigs as he recoiled from Hungary and the
Mazzinian republic which French guns bombarded behind
the crumbling walls of Rome. But he was always sure of
one supporter, who promised to give a House of Commons
dinner for him, as " it tends to give a spirit and to keep the
party together, and induces our people to meet ! " Indeed,
she quite frightened Brougham, when that tangential critic
proposed to make an onslaught in the House of Lords, wrote
him indignant letters, and scared him into submission. So
his followers recognised the first of Palmerstonians, when
they proposed to have his portrait painted for Lady
Palmerston.

The skies of 1850 were no less clouded. His sovereign
frowned; heads shook in unison at Brussels, Claremont,
Osborne, and Vienna over his lightest act; Guizot and
Metternich moaned like distracted sibyls; and Lord
Aberdeen feared the worst with touching frequency. Even
his colleagues were a trifle apt to wring their hands over
Foreign Office papers which had not been circulated, without
reading those that they had received. But Palmerston sat

on among his boxes. He was extremely busy at the moment
with some claims on Greece. The case was trivial; John
Russell thought it "hardly worth the interposition of the
British Lion," and Lady Palmerston wrote to a friend that
"it will be of no importance, and is probably settled by this
time." So Athens, where a more than dubious minister
held office under a Bavarian king, cast no shadow. This
odd *régime* was free from any undue reverence for British
property. Incorporating a historian's field in the royal
garden, it had incorporated Mr. Finlay in his own *History
of Greece;* and its lighthearted subjects, in a darker mood,
had celebrated Easter by destroying a Jew's house. Un-
happily for Greece, the Jew, described impartially as Mr.,
M., Signor, or Don Pacifico, was a native of Gibraltar and
a British subject. Greek justice was not embarrassingly
prompt; and the claims (as claims are apt to) improved with
keeping. While Mr. Finlay's field from its modest purchase
price of £10 attained a value of £1,500, the inconspicuous
residence of Don Pacifico soared into thousands. The
furniture alone was worth £2,000, the contents £2,000 more;
but somewhere in the house, more precious still, some documents had perished, representing claims against the Portuguese Government, and these, it seemed, were worth no
less than £26,000 to the ' Rock scorpion.' Lord Palmerston
was sceptical of the figures. But Greek delays were most
annoying; he had a fleet bound homeward from the Levant
after its kindly mission of encouraging the Turks; and he
instructed it, on the way from the Dardanelles, to look in at
Athens, where the British Minister might find it helpful.
He was advised to "persevere in the *suaviter in modo* as
long as is consistent with our dignity and honour, and I
measure that time by days—perhaps by some very small
number of hours." Then he might try the effect of a
blockade, land some marines, or capture the Greek navy.
A gleeful Minister complied, blockaded the Piræus, and
seized shipping to the value of the British claims. But the
French, always chivalrous to England's enemies, flung themselves between the startled heirs of Pericles and their angry

creditor with an offer of *bons offices ;* and the Russians
scented a dark design to provoke a revolution at Athens.
There was a diplomatic flutter, French mediation, and
questions in the House of Commons. The Cabinet had
failed, as usual, to read their Foreign Office papers and were
committed. But Peel kept Mr. Greville in St. James's
Park for over half an hour, whilst he disapproved of Palmerston; and his indignant Queen sought her customary consolation and altered a despatch. There was the usual
misunderstanding, and his sovereign was left complaining
that "Lord Palmerston has *sent* off the draft *unaltered.*"
Explanations followed at enormous length—that he had
done nothing of the kind; that of her two amendments one
had been adopted, while the other had been slightly varied
by the Cabinet; that John Russell should have told her so;
that the messenger had only just caught the mail. But
nothing softened the asperity of her "scolding letter,"
with its stern insistence that "this must not happen again.
Lord Palmerston has a perfect right to state to the Queen
his reasons for disagreeing with her views, and will always
have found her ready to listen to his reasons; but she
cannot allow a servant of the Crown and her Minister to act
contrary to her orders, and this without her knowledge."

One night in the same month Lord Clarendon, on leave
from Dublin, dined at the Palace. The tactful guest had
hoped that dangerous topics might be avoided, since it was
particularly awkward for a possible successor to listen to the
royal litany of Palmerston's misdeeds. Dinner passed off
without mishap. But in the drawing-room the Queen, in
his indecorous metaphor, "exploded"; and when she
flagged, the Prince took up the tale. The evening proving
insufficient, Clarendon was asked to call again next day.
The Prince was angrier than ever, and talked, with trifling
interruptions, for two hours and a half. His anger ran to
patiently digested detail; and he abounded, in his quiet way,
in anecdotes of altered drafts, of foreign sovereigns outraged,
of the Queen humiliated by her utter helplessness. He had
been studying the Constitution; he knew it well, was

perfectly aware that policy must be approved by the nation.
But the nation, he was quite convinced, did not approve of
Palmerston. Nor did his colleagues. The rich catalogue
of his iniquities continued, until Lord Clarendon hazarded the
mild enquiry whether his royal host had ever put his views to
Palmerston himself. The Prince, it seemed, had done so
frequently, had always found him easy, good-humoured, and
extremely pleasant. But nothing had the least effect on
Palmerston's official conduct; he was completely unreliable;
and they had quite given up talking to him. Then they
found the Prime Minister so unhelpful. He supposed that
some etiquette united Cabinet colleagues. But Russell
must surely disapprove of Palmerston. Clarendon, perhaps,
might tell him of their views.

The interview concluded, Clarendon withdrew to the
Prime Minister and discharged his slightly embarrassing
cargo of royal grievances. It was extremely awkward.
John Russell, perfectly aware of Palmerston's shortcomings,
had no particular desire to part with him. His policy was,
in the main, acceptable. Besides, if he went, where would
he go to? Parties in 1850 were somewhat oddly arranged.
Four years before Peel and his staff had left the Tory forces
deep in the marshes of Protection, where they had floundered
under the leadership of Lord George Bentinck, and floundered
still (but slightly less) with Mr. Disraeli, while their Front
Bench gazed down at them with Peelite scorn from the
impeccable, if slightly lonely, heights of Free Trade. The
Whigs, apparently united, watched with complacency this
scene of Tory discord; but their own unity was gravely
threatened by a lively group of Radicals. Tories and
Radicals were both, it seemed, in search of leaders; and each
fleet made strenuous signals to the slightly buccaneering sail
of Palmerston. His Tory past, his patriotic airs, his horses,
and his gun endeared him to the squires; whilst eager
Radicals observed the friend of Italy, the enemy of tyrants,
and the steadfast liberator of slaves. The prospect of
encountering Palmerston in either capacity was a trifle
cheerless for John Russell. But he consulted Lansdowne

and spoke to Palmerston himself, who seemed prepared for a
transaction. Then he reported progress at the Palace.
First he depressed them with his colleague's merits—really a
most agreeable man, in close association with himself for
nineteen years, and such a spirited politician. He had
supposed (the embarrassed narrative proceeded) that if he
took a peerage and left Palmerston to lead the Commons,
the latter might consent to some exchange of offices. Indeed,
he had already indicated as much, confessing to John Russell
his regret that he had lost his sovereign's confidence—entirely
on grounds of policy, though not for personal reasons. An
eager voice asserted that her reasons were personal as well.
But the grave utterance of the Prince insisted that they were
grounds of policy. The Queen accepted the correction;
and the happy trio proceeded to discuss names for the Foreign
Office, so soon to be deliciously vacant. They must wait,
of course, until the session ended; then Palmerston should
go, out of harm's way, to the Home Office. A sudden doubt
assailed the Prince : might he not be dangerous as Whig
leader in the House of Commons? Lord John thought not,
reminded them that Palmerston was sixty-five, and " too
old to do much in the future." It had a reassuring sound.
Then the trio parted with airs of secrecy; and Albert made a
memorandum of it.

The session—if all went well, it was to be Lord Palmerston's
last session as Foreign Secretary—proceeded. They were
still deep in the Constitution, and Stockmar produced a
minute with an ominous conclusion :

" The least the Queen has a right to require of her Minister
is—

" 1. That he will distinctly state what he proposes in a
given case, in order that the Queen may know as distinctly to
what she has to give her royal sanction.

" 2. Having given once her sanction to a measure, the
Minister who, in the execution of such measure, alters or
modifies it arbitrarily, commits an act of dishonesty towards
the Crown, which the Queen has an undoubted constitutional
right to visit with the dismissal of that Minister."

The stern purpose gleams through the imperfect syntax. But Palmerston still laid about him: His sturdy distaste for the slave trade, which breathes in his hope that an Argentine dictator may fight Brazil and "give those profligate Slave Traders a sound thrashing," involved the Government in grave peril. A sharp attack was made upon the African squadron, maintained at great expense for the exclusive purpose of pursuing slavers; but it was repelled. He appeared in a sugar debate as the slaves' friend and a convinced Free Trader, and his reforming zeal even earned the commendation of a Buxton. The incorrigible man had one more brush with the Queen—this time upon a question of *personnel*—and left her gasping to John Russell that he was "really too bad and most disrespectful to the Queen; she can really hardly communicate with him any more; indeed, it would be better she should not."

Then the Greek affair exploded. The French ambassador was suddenly withdrawn from London, when his Government found Palmerston a shade inclined to supplement their mediation with a further use of force at Athens. Russia was shocked as well; and he detected a familiar touch in the manœuvre, which "savours much of the strategy of the *Tambour Major* of Paris, as I am told our old friend the Princess is called." For Lieven, strenuously revisiting the glimpses of the diplomatic moon, was active still. She was an Orleanist now for Guizot's sake, but ineradicably Russian; and Palmerston's head would be a welcome offering to either throne. There were the usual protests. The Prince was grave, and this time Lord John seemed really firm; Mr. Greville found him "very angry and therefore very stout." Palmerston must go; his policy would have to be defended, since "the Cabinet was as much to blame"; but then he must go. There was no attempt to gild the pill, since on reflection it seemed better that he should not lead the Commons. So he should be transferred without other consolation to the Colonial Office; but they must still wait, of course, until the session ended. The royal hearts beat high. Victoria sat happily beneath the trees at Osborne;

the children were catching butterflies; and Albert sipped his
Kissingen with an air that was almost lively. The precious
lily, grown for so long with so much care, was flowering at
last. Then an incautious hand essayed to paint it, and the
blossom fell.

The rash touch came from the hand of Lieven. Palmerston was always a trifle apt to suspect foreign influences;
but Mr. Disraeli was convinced in later years that " Lord
Aberdeen had planned the attack on Palmerston under the
inspiration of Madame Lieven and Guizot." Aching for
further triumphs, she impelled the Tories to a grand onslaught
in the House of Lords. This was still better than the distant
days of the Cottage Côterie, when a delighted King inclined a
royal ear by Virginia Water for details of the grand conspiracy *pour faire sauter M. Canning*. The day came;
and Palmerston was duly censured by the Lords. But the
effect upon John Russell was singular : he informed the
House of Commons that so long as the Whigs remained in
office, Palmerston would " act not as the Minister of Austria,
or as the Minister of Russia, or of France, or of any other
country, but as the Minister of England." This had a
strangely Palmerstonian ring. Could it be that his resolution had changed once more? Had the Lords' vote of
censure made a Palmerstonian of him? Russell had never
found much fault with his policy; and few Prime Ministers
could tolerate such interference from the peers. Had he not
introduced an unforgettable Reform Bill, and defied the
House of Lords himself? The Commons must decide;
and since an obliging Radical had given notice of·a vote of
confidence, they would.

While the world waited, Lady Palmerston received her
presentation portrait. The statesman was significantly
posed near a bust of Mr. Canning; and the accompanying
address was heavy with Whig signatures in admiration of
" the independent policy by which he has maintained the
honour and interests of this Country," whilst a group of
Radicals acknowledged in a grateful appendix his " noble
and constant exertions in the suppression of the Slave

Trade." Then the debate began. It opened on a Monday
and lasted the evening; but Palmerston said nothing. On
the next night he watched members bandying despatches and
quotations from the poets, and rose to speak a little before
ten. A full House was listening until nearly half-past two;
and before he sat down, he had (in Lady Clarendon's phrase)
" triumphed over a great mass of educated public opinion,
over that mighty potentate *The Times*, over two branches of
the Legislature, over the Queen and Prince, and most of the
Cabinet he sits in, besides all foreign nations."

It was a quiet speech, delivered without notes. He
opened with a deft denial of the proposition which he
fathered upon his critics, that " British subjects abroad must
not look to their own country for protection, but must trust
to that indifferent justice which they may happen to receive
at the hands of the Government and tribunals of the country
in which they may be," and passed to a survey of the Greek
claims. These were reviewed in lucid detail, with a solemn
rebuke (since it was no occasion for his ' Ha ha ' style) of
ill-timed humour—" It is often more convenient to treat
matters with ridicule than with grave argument; and we
have had serious things treated jocosely; and grave men
kept in a roar of laughter, for an hour together, at the poverty
of one sufferer, or at the miserable habitation of another;
at the nationality of one injured man, or the religion of
another . . . as if a man who was born in Scotland might be
robbed without redress; or, because a man is of the Jewish
persuasion, he is fair game for any outrage." Then he dealt
with the argument of false chivalry. (" Does the smallness of a
country justify the magnitude of its evil acts? . . . We
are to be generous to those who have been ungenerous to
you; and we cannot give you redress because we have such
ample and easy means of procuring it.") But he discerned
the wider purpose of the debate; and, in a broad sweep from
" the sunny plains of Castile and the gay vineyards of
France . . . to the mountains of Switzerland " and " from
the rugged Alps into the smiling plains of Lombardy," he
reviewed his European policy since 1830. It was an amazing

survey of twenty years of history. The old maxim of ' Spain
for the Spaniards ' was restated; his " little experimental
Belgian monarchy " was justified; the Italian mission of
Lord Minto was explained; and there was a wise word on
those " revolutionists of another kind; blind-minded men,
who, animated by antiquated prejudices, and daunted by
ignorant apprehensions, dam up the current of human
improvement; until the irresistible pressure of accumulated
discontent breaks down the opposing barriers, and levels
to the earth those institutions which a timely application
of renovating means would have rendered strong and
lasting." Then, returning to his opening theme, he perorated
briefly :

" I do not complain of the conduct of those who have made
these matters the means of attack upon Her Majesty's Ministers.
The Government of a great country like this, is undoubtedly
an object of fair and legitimate ambition to men of all shades
of opinion. It is a noble thing to be allowed to guide the
policy and to influence the destinies of such a country; and,
if ever it was an object of honourable ambition, more than
ever must it be so at the moment at which I am speaking.
For while we have seen, as stated by the Right Honourable
Baronet the Member for Ripon, the political earthquake rock-
ing Europe from side to side—while we have seen thrones
shaken, shattered, levelled; institutions overthrown and
destroyed—while in almost every country of Europe the conflict of civil war has deluged the land with blood from the
Atlantic to the Black Sea, from the Baltic to the Mediterranean; this country has represented a spectacle honourable
to the people of England, and worthy of the admiration of
mankind.
" We have shown that liberty is compatible with order;
that individual freedom is reconcilable with obedience to the
law. We have shown the example of a nation, in which every
class of society accepts with cheerfulness the lot which Providence has assigned to it; while at the same time every individual of each class is constantly striving to raise himself in
the social scale—not by injustice and wrong, not by violence
and illegality—but by persevering good conduct, and by the

steady and energetic exertion of the moral and intellectual faculties with which his Creator has endowed him. To govern such a people as this is indeed an object worthy of the ambition of the noblest man who lives in the land; and, therefore, I find no fault with those who may think any opportunity a fair one, for endeavouring to place themselves in so distinguished and honourable a position. But I contend that we have not in our foreign policy done anything to forfeit the confidence of the country. . . . I therefore fearlessly challenge the verdict which this House, as representing a political, a commercial, a constitutional country, is to give on the question now brought before it; whether the principles on which the foreign policy of Her Majesty's Government has been conducted, and the sense of duty which has led us to think ourselves bound to afford protection to our fellow subjects abroad, are proper and fitting guides for those who are charged with the government of England; and whether, as the Roman, in days of old, held himself free from indignity, when he could say *Civis Romanus sum*: so also a British subject, in whatever land he may be, shall feel confident that the watchful eye and the strong arm of England will protect him against injustice and wrong."

He had been speaking for four hours and thirty-five minutes. But Em, whose eyes had never left his face, thought it had lasted just an hour.

The debate ran on for two nights more. Mr. Gladstone, now the rising hope of the stern, if slightly bending, Peelites, spoke scornfully of a Foreign Secretary " like some gallant knight at a tournament of old, pricking forth into the lists, armed at all points, confiding in his sinews and his skill, challenging all comers for the sake of honour, and having no other duty than to lay as many as possible of his adversaries sprawling in the dust," though he found time for a glance of admiration at the speaker who " from the dusk of one day to the dawn of the next . . . defended his policy before a crowded House of Commons in that gigantic intellectual and physical effort "; Mr. Cobden emitted the stern note of Manchester; Peel wrapped himself in his impenetrable virtue, though not without confessing that Palmerston's " most able and most temperate speech . . . made us proud

of the man who delivered it"; John Russell leapt to the
rescue; and Mr. Disraeli kept them out of bed from two
o'clock till four on the last morning.   It was a pageant of
Victorian eloquence.   But Palmerston's spell remained unbroken, and the Government came through by forty-six.
   The effects were startling.   Friends rejoiced, and enemies
paid grudging tributes; even *The Times* prepared to trim;
and the Queen wrote ruefully to Brussels that " the House of
Commons is becoming very unmanageable and troublesome."
Whilst Em hung her new picture, the Radicals gave Palmerston a dinner at the Reform Club.   They had even con-
templated a demonstration at Covent Garden; but the more
select function was preferred.   The club-house was illumi-
nated; palms rustled in the hall; and the Guards band
played selections through an interminable dinner.   The
guest, received with the unusual tribute of ' Rule, Britannia,'
was in a mood of happy reminiscence.   His speech abounded
in echoes of his recent effort.   He recalled the arm of
England; he gloried in freedom; but he reminded them that
there was no need " to go, like knights-errant of civilisation,
forcing institutions on other countries."   It was a great
occasion; and as they streamed out into Pall Mall with the
music and the speeches in their ears, he owed it—and all his
·triumph—to the impulsive Lieven and her too obedient
peers.
   The Queen's hopes were fainter now.   But she could still
denounce him to John Russell and complain that " each
time that we were in a difficulty, the Government seemed to
be determined to move Lord Palmerston, and as soon as these
difficulties were got over, those which present themselves to
the carrying out of this removal appeared of so great a
magnitude as to cause its relinquishment.   There is no
chance of Lord Palmerston reforming himself in his sixty-
seventh year, and after having considered his last escape as a
triumph."   The prospect might be brief; but it was most
unpleasant.   So they went over it all again to Clarendon; a
Whig duke was summoned to Osborne and pelted with the
names of suitable posts for Palmerston's retirement; and

John Russell, goaded into action, made a last approach to his
alarming colleague, who received him with bland surprise.
Had he not faced his accusers and been triumphantly
acquitted? He was quite unconscious of the least disrespect
to the Queen, and sorry for it. But how could he resign?
His resignation would be groundless, even discreditable.
Lord John was quite disarmed, and dropped the subject.
The news caused grave concern at Osborne—" We expressed
our surprise that he had not made Lord Palmerston any
offer of any kind "—and, left to their unaided efforts, the
royal pair made a despairing attempt to discipline their
inseparable servant. Stockmar's unpleasant minute on the
whole duty of a minister was copied out (with slight improve-
ments of the syntax) and delivered as an ultimatum. Palmerston complied with the most irritating alacrity. Of course
the Queen should see the drafts, and the despatches too;
and, if necessary, the Treasury must allow him an additional clerk or so for the purpose. For a few weeks they
found him " exceedingly attentive and active, writing and
explaining to the Queen all that is going on." He even
interviewed the Prince, who found him strangely " low and
agitated." He was distressed by their complaints; the
dreadful imputation of disrespect towards the Crown quite
pained him; such conduct would be unworthy of a gentleman—towards the Queen, too, whose virtues he admired so
much. The smile had faded; he was positively shaky;
and Albert was almost moved by the sight of tears in those
aged eyes. But after his reprieve Palmerston could afford
to be pathetic. He was remaining with them after all, and
it was just as well to keep their favour; perhaps his mild
demeanour even betrays a touch of Em's judicious coaching.
But Albert was glacial, pointed sternly to his past misdeeds,
and demanded full disclosure in the future. For instance,
what did Palmerston propose to do if the Germans went to
war with Denmark over Schleswig-Holstein? The aged
figure recovered something of its elasticity, talked for an
hour, and never gave an answer: Lord Palmerston was
himself again.

His luck was in that summer—his critics foiled, Peel's fatal accident on the day after the great debate, and now the old King dead at Claremont. Mr. Greville, at Brighton, might conclude that "hardly more importance attaches to the event than there would to the death of one of the old bathing-women opposite my window." But Palmerston could write that "the death of Louis Philippe delivers me from my most artful and inveterate enemy." While Russell spent a lively autumn striking Protestant attitudes, he had his own diversions, though he found time to write a disrespectful letter to a colleague about "his Emptyness the Pope," and found an ingenious explanation of some awkward phrases used by his excited leader :

"I certainly wish that John Russell had not put into his Letter the words Insolent & Mummery, but I told Sheil that he should say to the Italians that Insolent means unusual & is synonymous with *Insolito*, and that the fair meaning & application of Mummery is that such is the real nature of Forms & Ceremonies of the Catholic Religion when introduced into the Protestant Ritual where they have no meaning & no foundation of Belief & Significance, as they have in their natural Places in the Ritual of the Church to which they belong. That the Passage does not imply therefore any Reflection on the Catholic Religion and is only a Reflection on those Protestants who introduce into the Service of our Church things which do not belong to it. A man might ridicule the use of Frenchified words in an English Discourse, without casting any slight upon the French Language; phrases and words which would be proper in a speech of Guizot's in the French assembly would be ridiculous affectation in the mouth of a Manchester Manufacturer in the House of Commons. This explanation seemed to tell, perhaps you might try it experimentally upon one or two of your Irish Catholics."

The diplomat in Palmerston obscured the Churchman, and John Russell's zeal evoked only the faintest echo from his colleague : one feels that Palmerston would never have chalked up ' No Popery ! ' on a door, or that, having chalked it, he would not have run away.

But his diversions were more secular. The Schleswig-Holstein question trailed its dreadful length across the scene. It was a problem on which diplomats could cite without a quiver an instrument of 1460, to say nothing of a treaty of 1720 and a protest of 1806. To be plain, the Duchies lay between Germany and Denmark, and both wanted them. Some inconclusive fighting was now ending in a labyrinth of protocols. The Court's opinions were quite unmistakable; since Albert, whose views were hardly Prussian enough for Stockmar, was more Prussian than most Englishmen, and his taste for German unity had always been pronounced. A difference on a draft provoked Palmerston to one of his rare discourtesies—" Is not the Queen requiring that I should be Minister, not indeed for Austria, Russia, or France, but for the Germanic Confederation? " A flaming page from Buckingham Palace repelled the scandalous insinuation—" the Queen does not wish her Minister to be Minister for Germany, but merely to treat that country with the same consideration which is due to every country on whose interests we mean to decide . . ." But the suspicion stayed in his mind (he once complained that Germany was " in her eyes and in those of the Prince the all-important part of Europe ") and the taunt in theirs; and in revenge for his un-German qualities they privately nicknamed him *Pilgerstein.*

One final lapse enlivened his relations with the Crown before the year was out. London was visited that autumn by General Haynau, who had attained a sinister celebrity for Austrian atrocities. An odd fancy moved him to inspect a brewery, where he was promptly mobbed by angry draymen. The Court, deep in the Highlands, throbbed with indignation; and Albert, with perfect justice, described the General's assailants as " illiterate." But Palmerston completely failed to share these generous emotions. Indeed, he seemed to feel that an opportunity had been missed and informed the Home Secretary that the clumsy mob, which merely tore the General's coat and pulled his long moustache, should have " tossed him in a blanket, rolled him in the kennel, and then sent him home in a cab, paying his fare to the hotel." The Austrians complained. But this cheerful mood was scarcely calculated to produce apologies, and Palmerston retorted blandly that the General should have stayed at home. The Queen revised the draft; but the Note had already been delivered. He explained at length, recounted instances of British generosity to fallen enemies, compared the General to several murderers of the day, and enumerated his atrocities, adding a trifle tactlessly that he was known as 'General Hyæna.' The Queen insisted; Russell was invoked; Palmerston threatened to resign and, since they seemed inclined to let him, withdrew his resignation together with the offending paragraph, leaving his sovereign rejoicing soberly that " Lord John has the power of exercising that control over Lord Palmerston, the careful exercise of which he owes to the Queen, his colleagues and the country, if he will take the necessary pains to remain firm. The Queen does not believe in *resignation* under almost any circumstances." Neither did Palmerston.

He was at Broadlands for the Christmas holidays of 1850. There was a slight lull in his drafting, and he was able to escape his dismal routine. Of recent years it had been papers all the morning, a look in on the party halfway through lunch to eat his orange, then more papers, and an evening ride. Now he even got a little hunting and saw something of his birds. But early in the new year the red boxes claimed him once again, and Em was left lamenting at Brighton—" Poor darling, I wish you had a little more leisure." She waited like a schoolgirl for the news that he was packing up to join her—" Let me know when you begin to open your carpet bags," and a few days later, " Whenever you write me word that you have opened your carpet bags, I shall make a bonfire on the Steyne." For her youth, like his, was quite imperishable; and one feels no surprise in catching her coy whisper to a grandson, at sixty-two: " Come back with me, Evelyn, to London; Poodle Byng has asked for a seat in my carriage, and I don't think Palmerston

T

will like it." Yet she was no sultana. Even Mr. Greville learned to wince at " a fresh correspondence with Lady Palmerston about *The Times* attacking her husband."

But whilst he drafted on in London or pressed Russell to build forts at Plymouth and raise " some dormant but partially trained force of the nature of a militia or *landwehr*," the Government was suddenly defeated. John Russell resigned with almost evident relief. Ten days of wild confusion followed. As *Punch* observed, " everybody went to call upon everybody. The hall porters were never known to have had such a time of it, but though knocking and ringing at doors continued throughout the whole day, nothing seemed to answer." The Tories were tried first and failed. The ball returned to Russell, who played it smartly to Lord Aberdeen ; and for a day or so the Whigs attempted a Coalition with the Peelites. Since their bereavement this accomplished group had joined the melancholy ranks of political widowhood. Their weeds were most becoming, and their fidelity was quite undoubted. Relics are often hard to please ; and though John Russell wooed discreetly, the projected Coalition failed. But whilst it lasted, Palmerston was gravely endangered, since the Crown was almost as much concerned with his exclusion as with the search for ministers. The Queen insisted on his removal from the Foreign Office ; Lord John concurred and seemed inclined to send him to Dublin or the House of Lords ; and Palmerston, who had refused to go, spoke moodily of retiring from business at his age. The Tories tried again ; and his shadow still perturbed the Court. For the unprincipled man had friends on both sides, and Albert was tortured by the horrid fear that " Lord Palmerston had often so much secret understanding with Disraeli that he might be tempted with the bait of keeping the Foreign Office." There had been mysterious overtures ; the Danish minister carried messages between them in diplomatic French ; and a shocked Tory warned his leader that the unhallowed union threatened the sacred cause of Protection, since Palmerston's prediction that " when you see the river Exe running up from the sea to Tiverton . . .

you may then look upon it that Protection is near at hand "
was scarcely a promising epithalamium for a Tory wedding.
But the Tories failed again; and as the Whigs returned, the
despairing Crown made one last effort to elude his services.
Lord John was warned, " but said he could not think for a
moment of resuming office and either expel Lord Palmerston
or quarrel with him. He (Lord John) was in fact the weakness and Lord Palmerston the strength of the Government
from his popularity with the Radicals." The Queen
insisted; and the unhappy little man promised to attempt the
dreaded transfer in the Easter recess. But Easter brought
no relief. For the Prime Minister had failed them once
again.

So Palmerston sat on. The Whigs still governed England
and denounced the Pope to their indifferent countrymen.
But the Exhibition saved them. That gleaming monument
of good intentions engaged the public mind, and England
hurried to Hyde Park. Lord Palmerston was at the opening
and watched the women kiss their hands to the old Duke, as
he walked round the building just in front of him. He found
an evening for a word on Papal Aggression in the House of
Commons; but his main concerns were much as usual. The
Foreign Office punctuated worse than ever; and in an
agonised appeal the Secretary of State implored his clerks to
" write to the Stationery Office for a sufficient supply of
Full Stops, Semi-colons, and Commas; but more especially
Semi-colons . . . I furnish these things out of my own
private stores when I have time to look over despatches for
signature, but I am not always sufficiently at leisure to supply
deficiencies." There was still Italy to think of, where he
found an unexpected ally. The weakness of a daughter's
eyesight had taken Mr. Gladstone as far as Naples, where he
saw something of King *Bomba's* prisons. The wary Peelite,
whose smooth black hair and downcast eye recalled a
Monsignor, was rarely impulsive. But the spectacle provoked him to a pamphlet of magnificent vituperation. He
saw Palmerston and confessed his error—" Gladstone and
Molesworth . . . say that they were wrong last year in

their attacks on my foreign policy; but they did not know the truth "—and the gleeful Minister, quick to detect a Palmerstonian touch, distributed the invective to every Government in Europe, with the stout corollary that an attempted refutation was " only a tissue of bare assertion and reckless denial, mixed up with coarse ribaldry and commonplace abuse of public men and political parties."

He had a brush with Mr. Cobden, still active in the cause of peace, explained that all his own misdeeds had never caused a war, and expressed a reasoned preference for sound defences. But the autumn was enlivened by a brighter figure. For Kossuth appeared in a triumphal blaze of popular receptions, and Palmerston was strongly inclined to meet him. The Queen was shocked; John Russell intervened; Lord Palmerston was firm upon his right to ask whom he chose to Carlton Gardens; the helpless Premier advised his sovereign " to command Lord Palmerston not to receive M. Kossuth," withdrew the advice, summoned the Cabinet, and managed by their collective weight to restrain his impetuous colleague. But Palmerston, though he refrained from the forbidden fruit, could not resist the gesture of a flourishing speech to a Radical deputation, which called to thank him for his Hungarian sympathies. They left spirited addresses, in which two Emperors were eloquently termed (in the idiom of Finsbury) " odious and detestable assassins," not to say " merciless tyrants and despots." This language incensed his sovereign still further. Fresh protests rained on Russell; but this time the Prime Minister, content with his slightly unexpected victory, was more indulgent. Palmerston was almost apologetic, complaining of inaccurate reports and the strange novelty of deputations; and Lord John defended him at length, urging that " every Minister must have a certain latitude allowed him which he may use, perhaps with indiscretion, perhaps with bad taste, but with no consequence of sufficient importance to deserve notice." Besides, there was " the importance of maintaining the popular confidence which Your Majesty's name everywhere inspires. Somewhat of the good opinion of the Emperor of Russia and other foreign Sovereigns may be lost, but the good will and affection of the people of England are retained." So one more opportunity had gone. The Queen made no attempt to hide her disappointment; Stockmar was gloomily convinced that " the man has been for some time insane "; and Lord John sought consolation in the absorbing details of a new Reform Bill. His perpetual *rôle* of " umpire between Windsor and Broadlands " was really most exacting; and a pleasant flavour of old times dwelt, for John Russell, in franchises and lists of boroughs and schedules.

The world was almost still that winter. Even diplomacy was scarcely stirring. Schleswig-Holstein unwound its latest coils like a sleepy dragon; and an odd question about the custody of Catholic churches in the East hung between France and Russia. The cloud was small—Palmerston deprecated argument upon " a matter in itself so unimportant," and wrote with truth that " this is a quarrel fitter for times long gone by than for the days in which we live "— but it grew in two years to be the Crimean War. The Prince-President, in 1851, had other interests. His term was ending; and private life (since he was a Bonaparte) held few attractions. The Chamber was obstructive. But he had a star; he had a Prefect of Police named Maupas; and (more important still) he had the army. He trotted through the mist on winter mornings to watch it drilling in the Champ de Mars and exchange a word with General Canrobert. He even made a rousing little speech with quite a military flavour, in which he undertook to say " *Je marche, suivez-moi !* " This spirited declaration caught Lord Palmerston's pugnacious fancy. For that watchful eye was fixed on Paris, where politics resembled nothing so much as a race. The republicans, the Orleans princes (though they were doubtful starters), and the President might soon be running neck and neck; and if he had to choose between them, there was much to be said for the Prince-President. He was a Bonaparte, of course; but, oddly enough, he seemed less likely than the others to give trouble to England. The Red Republicans

might make war on anyone, and they retained a foolish taste
for ancient projects of invasion. The Orleans princes, with
their martial airs, were even worse. Besides, they were
inseparable from the flavour of stale chicane, of Guizot, of
the Spanish Marriages. So Palmerston, on purely British
grounds, was faintly Bonapartist. His Paris ambassador
was not; quite to the contrary, Lord Normanby was
genteelly Orleanist. But Russell knew the Foreign Office
view; since Palmerston had written that " if the Reds were
to triumph or Joinville to succeed, we should have to sleep
with one eye open." So when he heard that the President
was past the post, Lord Palmerston was pleased and said so.

The troops were on the move in Paris before the sun
(it was the sun, amongst other things, of Austerlitz) rose on
December 2. A new constitution was proclaimed by breakfast time; the party-leaders were arrested in their bedrooms;
and by twelve o'clock they had the news in London over the
" wonderful Electric Telegraph." On the next day the
French ambassador called at the Foreign Office to ask Lord
Palmerston's opinion, and reported gleefully to Paris that he
approved. That night at Carlton Gardens they heard a
queer story of packing up at Claremont; and Palmerston
passed on the tale to his ambassador in Paris, with the blunt
conclusion that the Prince-President " was quite right . . .
to knock them down first," adding a sharp reproof of
Normanby's Orleanist connections, and a highly irreverent
description of the violated constitution as " the day-before-
yesterday tomfoolery, which the scatter-brained heads of
Marrast and Tocqueville invented for the torment and per-
plexity of the French nation." There was a Cabinet next
day; and they decided, in accordance with a note from
Osborne, that strict neutrality should be maintained in
Paris. Then Palmerston, with a wary eye on Claremont,
wrote to Normanby again, complaining of his Orleanist
tone; and when that dignitary called at the Ministry of
Foreign Affairs with a majestic intimation of his complete
neutrality, he was shocked to learn that Palmerston had
already approved the new *régime*. Bewildered and extremely

angry, he appealed to Russell against his chief. But a still loftier appeal remained. For he was a Phipps; and Colonel Phipps was Albert's secretary. So Lady Normanby composed a letter full of her husband's woes and sent it to his brother at Osborne. Another followed with a careful exposition of Palmerston's misdeeds, while Normanby himself plied the Prime Minister. Having prepared the ground by these discreet communications, he formally complained of Palmerston's official acts. The train was fired; Russell demanded explanations; soft hands were clapped at Osborne and restrained from livelier intervention by Stockmar, "certain that if Palmerston requires another thrust, his colleagues themselves will give it." Palmerston explained the *coup d'état*, explained the President, explained the Chamber, explained anything except his own proceedings. He sat up until half-past four to write it, and John Russell hardly improved its reception at Osborne by an avoidable delay of three days in transmission. Recalled to the point, Palmerston contended that his talk with Walewski had been unofficial and in no sense binding on the Government. But Russell had his case; he had always argued that the ground for dismissal must be some clear departure from the Cabinet's policy, and Palmerston's remark was plainly at variance with their system of neutrality in Paris. Armed with his reasons, he consulted no one, but dipped his pen at Woburn Abbey and informed his colleague that " no other course is left . . . than to submit the correspondence to the Queen, and to ask Her Majesty to appoint a successor to you in the Foreign Office," adding a trifle mirthlessly that if Palmerston would care to go to Ireland as Lord-Lieutenant, a British peerage was at his disposal. So Lord John made his own *coup d'état* as well.

The sequel was almost breathless. A sudden Cabinet was called, received the news, approved; Lord Granville, rushing into Mr. Greville's room, exclaimed, " Pam is out," and very nearly knocked him off his chair; the Prince sent dazed congratulations; Em wrote Lord John a furious letter, and Uncle Leopold at Brussels had the glad tidings just in time for Christmas that " *Lord Palmerston* is *no longer Foreign Secretary*—and Lord Granville is already named his successor ! " There was a *gaffe* about the seals. They waited for an hour at Windsor, where he was expected to attend and give them up. Faces grew longer. Was it all a dream? Did the dreadful man intend to retain office by force? Could he . . . then some one found them in a box, and contentment reigned once more. His young successor (Russell called him ' Granville the polite ') was charming. He had been extremely helpful about the Exhibition; and might not foreign affairs be conducted on the same lines? So—whilst a cheerful voice in London said, " Ah, how are you, Granville? Well, you have got a very interesting office "—they asked him to submit a comprehensive pro- gramme with an abundance of general principles; and if all went well, they might inaugurate a cooling rain of memoranda.

Em wrote the epilogue—

BROADLANDS,
Jan. 7th, 1852.

DEAREST FRED,

I know I have been an idle writer lately so I am going to make up for it now—& first to tell you of Valesky's visit here, which was most satisfactory—One thing surprised us and that was to find that John had used exactly the same expressions about the President's success as Palmerston on two several occasions, 1 on Wed^y the 3d at our House when he asked Valesky to dine with him the Friday after, when he dined with him & repeated very nearly the same things which Pal^n had—so that Valesky wrote to Turgot of those two satisfactory interviews in much the same terms as he did of Pal^{ns}—he also met G. Grey riding, who said much the same things—and Wood also on another occasion— therefore John must have forgotten all this when he accused Pal^n of approving the President without consulting the Cabinet since he had done just the same thing and so had Grey & Wood. In truth there was no reason why they should not, for the Cabinet never agreed not to give any opinion—nor was the subject ever brought forward in that shape.

When the Cabinet met on the 4th, it was upon the instructions to be given to Normanby (who had proposed to cease relations with the President)—telling him to keep on the best terms he could, to shew no coldness, and not to interfere with the internal affairs of France—but nothing was said of the course they were themselves to follow—The whole of John's attack was done in such a hurried manner that Palmerston could not himself remember exactly all the circumstances for he made no memorandums & conversed every day with Valesky, as at that time they met nearly every day,—and he was glad to refresh his memory of what he had said by talking over the circumstances with Valesky —he, P., had said namely this which Valesky repeated to Turgot—that as it appeared a rupture was imminent between the Parliament and President it was much better that the President should have succeeded. That it was better for the interests of France, as it would conduce more to a settled Govern^t, and that as it was better for France, it must also be so for the rest of Europe—how curious, it is that out of this simple and incontrovertible statement so much mischief should have arisen—but it is clearly an intrigue of Normanby Phipps and the Prince worked up by the deep disappoint^t of the Orleans overthrow, and the hopes which no doubt Normanby had helped to raise. . . .

By the next day her temper rose a trifle higher—

BROADLANDS,
Wednesday.

MY DEAREST FRED,

I believe I forgot to tell you in my letter yesterday that John had offered to Palmerston to go Ld. Lieut. to Ireland with a Peerage which he refused at once—it was in the letter which I mentioned yes^y among the facts of the case—John has behaved shamefully ill to Pal^n, and I suppose there never was such a case before of a man throwing over a

Colleague & a Friend without the slightest reason to give
for it.

No doubt the Queen & Prince wanted to get Palmerston
out & Granville in because they thought he would be pliable
& subservient and would let Albert manage the Foreign
Office which is what he had always wanted—you may think
it lucky therefore that the dream of United Germany &
the Sleswick-Holstein business are now pretty nearly over.

John has behaved like a little Blackguard giving in to their
plans and trying to put it upon a private opinion expressed
to Valesky (which bound the Govern^t to no course, and
left it quite unshackled).

The Times article to-day is full of false statements, for
there are no differences now between Pal^n & any Governments or any foreign ministers, nor are there any differences
at home.

We have often seen that many of his Colleagues were
jealous of him, but apparently they were all on the best
possible terms and there were no points in dispute.

I think the House of Commons will be very angry at this
Granville appointment—a young Lordling who has done
nothing but dance attendance on Albert & patch up differences amongst the Crystal Palace Commissioners, who has
whispered a speech or two about the Board of Trade & the
one at Paris in which he put forward his having passed his
holidays in his Father's Home at Paris & having married a
French woman.

He has a good deal of tact & is very courteous & those
are his real merits & that is what makes him so popular.

I am still vexed & provoked at the whole thing but I take
it much more calmly. It is so lucky for an effervescing
Woman to have such a calm and placid husband which no
events can irritate, or make him lose his temper.

    *   *   *   *   *   *

We have had a lovely day & very bright but cold, Georg^e
without her hat sitting under our great magnolia.

The best thing now that can happen in my opinion would
be the break-up of this Govern^t and to let the Protec-

tionists have a try. We should then see whether the land
could be relieved, whether there can be any duty on corn,
and what changes can be made—and I think it would be
fair enough to see that side of the question tried. . . .

She was still more explicit to Mrs. Huskisson :

" There never was such a *querelle d'Allemand*. . . . If one
looks for the real reason, there is nothing strikes one so forcibly as a Foreign Conspiracy. We know that Austria has
long been working very hard against Pal^n because she thinks
him to be a warm supporter of Constitutional Govern^{ts}.
Then all the little Princes of Germany follow Austria, &
then there is the family of Orleans at Clermont dreadfully
annoyed at the President's success, and at their Intrigue
with the Burgraves & Parliamentary party, with whom they
are in close Alliance, having so failed—for they were prepared to go off to Paris as soon as the President was put
into Vincennes. Think then what their disappointment
must have been when the President's Coup d'État cut in
just before theirs—and that all their Friends were put into
Vincennes instead of the President. To these elements of
conspiracy add Normanby who has behaved as ill as possible,
& who is constantly in Correspondence with Charles Phipps
his brother who is Secretary to Prince Albert and I think
you will guess how all this has arisen, but pray don't repeat
these latter hints as coming from me. . . ."

As he marked his trees at Broadlands, England repeated
' Palmerston is out ' in all its various tones. " Palmerston
is out," said Mr. Macaulay, " it was high time; but I cannot
help being sorry." For he had always admired his " knack
for falling on his feet," and never could believe that there
was " any scrape out of which his cleverness and his good
fortune will not extricate him." " Palmerston is out,"
echoed Mr. Bright in a less pleasant voice. " Cobden and I
have found him out years ago, but many simpletons have
fancied him a great friend of freedom abroad, though he
never did anything for it at home; and that all his bustling
diplomacy was a proof of England's influence on the Con-

tinent. . . . He is finished now as an official, unless he joins
Disraeli.''

So England murmured ' Palmerston is out,' and Bulwer
shrewdly called him " Mamma England's spoilt child. . . .
What a spirit he has ! cries Mamma, and smash goes the
crockery ! '' And with the smash still ringing in their ears
the streets were singing that

> Small Lord John has been and gone
> And turned adrift Lord Palmerston,
> Amongst the lot the only don,
> Who didn't take care of number one ;
> Out spoke Home Secretary Gray,
> I wish old Palmy was away.
> Aye, turn him out they all did say,
>   For he's the people's darling.

HOME OFFICE

I

DISMISSED but cheerful, Palmerston went out of town. His lady was extremely angry, and even he had warned John Russell with unusual asperity not to " imagine that I do not feel that just indignation at the whole transaction which the circumstances of the case must naturally inspire." He was at Broadlands in the clear winter sunshine of 1852. Mornings were free for shooting now; and he could ride to hounds or stroll round his plantations. The garden was a lamentable sight. For " it is a trial to a man to be left as much alone and unlooked after as the gardener of a Secretary of State necessarily is "; and the gardener (like the Secretary of State) was dismissed. A minister no longer, he savoured his new leisure. But the world, in the intervals of reading Mr. Disraeli's *Life* of his lost leader and wondering how he had managed to find five hundred pages in Lord George Bentinck, was lost in agreeable conjectures. Could Palmerston explain? Was there a place for him among the Radicals? Or would he join the Tories? Lord Clarendon informed a friend that " the open manner in which different parties are bidding for P. is not very respectful to his principles or consistency, but I hope they will be disappointed. At least it must be a long time before he could join the Protectionists whom he has so lately defied, or the Radicals with whom he has no real sympathy, even supposing, which I do not, that he could thus sacrifice his principles to his spleen." Lord John was unafraid, since he retained a heartening belief that his late colleague " has no hold in the country —but he has a hold on some 10 gentlemen of the H. of Comm⁸., who may make our position unpleasant." It was an odd conviction, with the *Morning Post* in daily eruption and the streets singing :

Whene'er doth meet the Parliament,
The Whigs to pot will straight be sent,
That humbug of a Government
    Won't live a moment longer.
Then Palmy he'll be at our head,
And keep the tyrants all in dread,
Austria and France will wish him dead
And for a milksop in his stead,
Haynau and the Russian Tsar
Will curse him in their realms afar.
And on their feelings it will jar
    To find old Palmy stronger.

The House met in February to hear the explanations, and Majesty was *very* curious *how* they will go off. They went off curiously indeed. "The personages," as Mr. Disraeli remarked with gusto in the debate, "were considerable, the subject important, and the audience were the assembled Commons of England." They heard John Russell, in the tone normally reserved for his most Roundhead doctrines, enunciate a strikingly Cavalier theory of ministerial responsibility—"that Minister is bound . . . to the Crown, to the most frank and full detail of every measure that is taken, and is bound either to obey the sanction of the Crown, or to leave to the Crown that full liberty which the Crown must possess, of no longer continuing that Minister in office." This stated, he recited the Queen's transcript of Stockmar's minute of 1850, which had required Palmerston to submit drafts and proposals for his sovereign's pleasure and, the royal will once ascertained, not to depart from it on pain of dismissal. Then the indictment travelled a familiar course—the *coup d'état*, the Cabinet's resolve (with royal sanction) to stand neutral, Palmerston's shocking avowal of sympathy to Walewski repeated in a despatch to Normanby, the vain demand for explanations, and the dismissal—and left the House confronted with the simple question " whether the Secretary of State was entitled, of his own authority, to write a despatch as the organ of the Queen's Government, in which his Colleagues had never concurred, and to which the Queen had never given Her Royal sanction."

Lord Palmerston was neatly trapped; for nothing short

of open dissent from the Queen's view of ministerial duty
would suffice to meet the charge. Russell had warned him
that the point would be taken against him; but Palmerston
confessed to someone afterwards that " somehow I did not
believe it." Besides, he was not prepared to argue with
the Queen. He could hardly tell the House of Commons, as
he wrote to Lansdowne, that " the paper was written in
anger by a Lady as well as by a Sovereign, and that the
Differences between a lady and a man could not be forgotten
even in the case of the occupant of a Throne; but . . . I
had no reason to suppose that this memorandum would ever
be seen by, or be known to, anybody but the Queen, John
Russell, and myself." Had not his system always been to
receive his sovereign's demands without indecorous dissent
and, when they seemed excessive, to ignore them? It had
served well enough for Foreign Office business; but once
stated in debate, her demands became unanswerable, unless
he was prepared to challenge them in public. He had
served the Crown too long to face that lively prospect,
since " I should have been bringing for decision at the bar
of public opinion a personal quarrel between myself and
my Sovereign—a step which no subject ought to take if he
can possibly avoid it; for the Result of such a Course must
be either fatal to him or injurious to the Country. If he
should prove to be in the wrong, he would be irretrievably
condemned; if the Sovereign should be proved to be in the
wrong, the Monarchy would suffer." He had prepared
instead a second Don Pacifico speech with a full vindication
of his public record. But his long achievement, even the
soundness of his views upon events in Paris, were quite
irrelevant to the charge and had to be abandoned. He
had drooped a little, as Lord John proceeded; and before
he had spoken two sentences of his defence, Mr. Disraeli felt
(with a creditable command of sporting imagery) that he
was " a beaten fox." There was a brave attempt at the
old manner; but it almost failed him. The facts were
handled rather gingerly—Walewski's story was " a somewhat high-coloured explanation of the result of a rather

U

long conversation," and his despatch to Normanby had
been a bare statement of his own opinion. The Radicals
forgot to cheer, as he detailed his approbation of the *coup
d'état*; but the House laughed when he seemed to convict
Russell and half the Cabinet of expressing precisely the
same opinions as himself, enquiring blandly whether " every
Member of the Cabinet . . . is at liberty to express an opinion
on passing events abroad; but the Secretary of State for
Foreign Affairs, whose peculiar duty it is to watch over
those events and to form an opinion—who is unfit for his
office if he has not an opinion on them—is the only man not
permitted to express any opinion at all; and when a foreign
Minister comes and tells him news, he is to remain speech-
less, like a gaping dolt, or as silent as the mute of some
Eastern Pasha." Then, assembling a few fragments of his
general defence and angling for Radical cheers with a word
on slavery, he sat down in a House that was largely unconvinced. For he had never faced the point.

The clubs, with their accustomed wisdom, said ' Palmerston is smashed '; a Peelite pitied him; and Mr. Disraeli,
at an evening party, told somebody in slightly condescending
retrospect that "there *was a* Palmerston." There was,
indeed. For in three weeks he had divided the House
against a Militia Bill, defeated the Government, and had
his unforgettable tit-for-tat with John Russell. Lady
Palmerston wrote almost apologetically that he " did not
intend to put out the Government." But Samson, it may
be conjectured, had a shrewd notion of his Parliamentary
strength. John Russell and his Government resigned, the
Prime Minister informing a colleague that " we go out on the
first blow, and do not wait to be kicked," while Palmerston
diagnosed a certain weariness of life in their sudden impulse
—" I must conclude that the Cabinet were glad to make use
of the Militia Question as a convenient Parachute to avoid a
ruder Descent and a more dangerous one . . . or at all events
if they thought the Difference between Regular and Local to
be one of vital Importance to them, and if they wished to
live and not to die, it is strange that they should not have

been able to get together more than 125 members of the House of Commons who thought the existence of a Ministry of more value than an eight o'clock dinner." John Russell saw his much-tried sovereign and informed her that Palmerston's action in defeating him was " most reprehensible," omitting to recall that it was just two years since he had told them that his victor was " too old to do much in the future." Then he resigned, advising with some malice that, as Lord Palmerston had no party, Lord Derby should be asked to form a Tory Government. So they parted from Lord John; but at least they were spared Palmerston.

The choice, as Derby hurried to the Palace, startled the Palmerstonians. But their man was not without prospects, since Mr. Disraeli had advised his leader that " it is everything for your Government that P. should be a member of it. His prestige in the House is very great; in the country considerable. He will not give you trouble about principles, but he may about *position*. He would not like to serve under me. . . ." The two had met at a party on the night before, and Disraeli dropped a hint to Palmerston. Derby was more explicit. He had warned the Crown that though he could not propose him for the Foreign Office in view of recent events and " what he might be allowed to call the ' well-known personal feelings of the Queen,' " he should ask him to be Chancellor of the Exchequer. There was a flood of royal warnings, and the Prince asked darkly whether he fancied he could keep his place for long with Palmerston leading the House of Commons. Lord Derby thought so, and the offer was made. It was his third chance of the Exchequer. Mr. Spencer Perceval had offered it in 1809; he had accepted it from Mr. Canning; and here was Derby promising that if he took it, he would find Mr. Disraeli an able, loyal lieutenant. Protection barred the way; for they must sink Protection if he came in. Derby demurred; might they not leave it open until the General Election? But Palmerston was firm, opposing " not the principle, but . . . the expediency of the imposition of any duty, under

any circumstances, upon foreign corn." He had other
reasons—he might have joined " a general union of parties,"
but a solitary enlistment in the Tory ranks was less attractive. His sovereign breathed again ; Mr. Disraeli went to
the Treasury ; and Palmerston was left writing that " this
new Government can hardly be of long Duration—it is too
much pledged to protect others to be able long to protect
itself."

It lasted long enough to reconcile him with the Whigs,
although he gave a friendly hand to the new Tory Foreign
Secretary, calling on Malmesbury, his old guardian's grandson, and repaying ancient debts with a survey of the state
of Europe. The main point, it seemed, was to keep well
with France, the main obstacle that France and England
both wished to predominate in the East " like two men
in love with the same woman." He told the beginner that
he could have " no idea . . . what a power of *prestige* England
possesses abroad," and warned him not to lose it. He
coached him in office business and advised insistence on
plain handwriting, with proper intervals between the lines,
adding that he would soon be struck with " a very curious
circumstance—namely, that no climate agrees with an
English diplomatist excepting that of Paris, Florence, or
Naples." But playing mentor to young Tory ministers was
an unsatisfying occupation ; and it was far from Palmerston's
intention " to enlist under Derby's banners. I do not think
highly of him as a statesman, and I suspect that there are
many matters on which he and I should not agree. Besides,
after having acted for twenty-two years with the Whigs,
and after having gained by, and while acting with them,
any little political reputation I may have acquired, it would
not answer nor be at all agreeable to me to go slap over to
the opposite camp, and this merely on account of a freak of
John Russell's, which the whole Whig party regretted and
condemned ; moreover, I am in no great hurry to return to
hard work, and should not dislike a little more holiday."
That year, indeed, he took a strange one on his land in
Ireland. Ecstatic tenants proclaimed their devotion to

" the British Empire and yer honour's family, and it's proud
we are to see ye in the Far West." There were triumphal
arches made of boughs festooned with red flannel and old
clothes. He saw his harbour and the row of lodging-houses
that he had built for summer visitors who never came.
' His honour's musicinier ' brought up his fiddle every evening
and played jigs; and his pockets were stuffed with preposterous petitions from ' abandoned orphans ' of fifty, from
' dissolute widows,' and one from a corpse asking his honour
to ' give me a coffin and bury me.' There had been no
evictions in the bad times; and he had more leisure now to
read the weekly letter from his bailiff.

Once they were back in London, his mornings were filled
with the mild labours of a committee on ventilation; but
his abundant leisure left time for thought on the party
situation. He was still a Whig, received a summons to
John Russell's conclave, and had a talk with him at one of
Lady Palmerston's evenings. But though they met as
friends, Palmerston was hardly disposed to serve under
him again. That year he was Steward at Tiverton Races,
and told them that " Johnny will not serve me that trick
again, for I will not again take office under him." Lord
John was growing flighty, acted on impulse, and left Palmerston reflecting that " the Whigs would be glad to be rid of
John Russell and to have me in his stead." The change
would not be easy; but the Court might relent; and for
the first time in his life he began to think of himself as
Prime Minister.

He was assiduous in the House, active as ever on Militia
and national defence, and even finding time for a word on
the preservation of the Crystal Palace and its treasures that
might be audible at Osborne. There was a dissolution in
the summer; and he went down to Tiverton again to sleep
at the Three Tuns in his own four-poster (for he was no less
particular in beds than in handwriting). He told them
stoutly that Protection " means practically taxing the food
of the many for the sake of the interests of the few "; he
contrasted British felicity with Continental discontents; and

he found a delicious apologue for the slow movement of reform in England—

"Now, in many parts of the Continent if an innkeeper wishes to recommend his inn, he hangs up a sign of ' The New White Horse,' or ' The New Golden Cross.' . . . Here, gentlemen, a contrary course is pursued, and, if the owner of a country alehouse wishes to draw custom, he hangs up the sign of ' The Old Plough New Revived.' There is at a place called Hanwell, not far from London, an inn to which gentlemen who were fond of pigeon-shooting used to resort to practise their skill. Well, what is the sign of that inn? It is ' The Old Hats.' Not that anybody was thought to prefer an old hat to a new one, but it was expected that gentlemen would come to ' The Old Hats ' in preference to ' The New Hats.' Now, a rival inn was set up, and what was its sign? Why, ' The Old Old Hats,' and much it profited by that superlative designation."

The apt interpreter of England proceeded to politics, to the Militia Bill, to a reminiscence of his own service, when a private had asked for leave because "the fact is that before I comed here I promised a young woman in my parish that I'd marry her, if so be as I surwived the campaign." As to his own prospects, he was slightly mysterious. The Chartist butcher was inquisitive as ever—

"Mr. Rowcliffe has asked me what Government I mean to join. Now, that is a question that must depend upon the future; but I will tell him what Government I do not mean to join. I can assure you and him that I will never join a Government called a Rowcliffe Administration. . . ."

—and the awkward question vanished in the ensuing laugh. But he could be definite enough against the ballot and " triennial, or, as they are sometimes called, triangular Parliaments." His particular scorn was excited by " sneaking to the ballot-box and poking in a piece of paper, looking round to see that no one could read it." For " a true Englishman hates doing a thing in secret or in the dark." Can it be wondered at that he was unopposed and Em, who read it all in the newspaper, never saw " anything better, so clever, so witty, so exactly all one could wish and *dans le fond* so conservative " ?

He found her waiting for him at Carlton Gardens when it was all over, prouder than ever of her husband. She had been seeing something of Azeglio, who brought her " Cavour, is that his name?—the Man we were to meet at Hatherton's. He is pleasing and intelligent looking—would it not be right to ask them to dinner Saturday, and any other few I can think of ? " She had seen Disraeli, too, who came and sat next to her at a party and told her that " they were watching the Election as the Egyptians did the Nile. . . . He is very fond of Eastern imagery." The Tories sent a journalist to sound him once again. Em had been telling everyone that he was quite unpledged, and Stanley scented " an old helmsman who would be very useful in taking an occasional spell at the wheel." This time he was to have the Home Office; but he preferred his freedom. For it was pleasantly filled. One horse had won six races for him and was to run at Goodwood. Besides, his own prospects were improving. John Russell was in evident eclipse, and he began to think where he should place him in a Palmerston Administration.

The summer of 1852 went out on his reflections. The prospect, on the whole, was most agreeable—the Whigs inclined to follow, the Tories deferential, even the Peelites primly attentive; Lord John touched with a vague discredit, and Lansdowne comfortingly old; the unwearied Urquhart cast from Stafford into outer darkness, and his faithful Anstey convinced at last of Palmerston's rectitude and ripening for the post (rewarding, but remote) of Attorney-General at Hong-Kong. The summer faded into autumn, and autumn was appropriately filled with manœuvres. John Russell clung to the Whig leadership. But Palmerston was in conference with a duke at Brocket and wrote at enormous length to Lansdowne. He made it plain that Russell was " infirm of Purpose, changeable in his views, and perpetually swayed by Influences which are known and felt only by their Results "; he was reminded of " what Horace Walpole, I think, somewhere says of John, Duke of Bedford, that he never was steadfast in any opinion unless it was one which had been instilled into him by somebody else, and which was at variance with his own previous convictions "; and no pleading would induce him to serve under him again.   These views, unsweetened, were conveyed to Russell, who obligingly consented to serve under Lansdowne; and Palmerston replied with sober joy that " John Russell's Decision does him Credit in every way. . . . I now for the first time begin to see Day Light through the mist which has of late obscured the political Horizon."

That year two veterans were buried, the old Duke and Protection. Mr. Disraeli pronounced orations over each, and Palmerston was in both processions.   Indeed, he played an active part in the obsequies of Protection. Fresh from the country, the victorious legions of Free Trade were slightly inclined to make their rivals eat the leek. This operation was distasteful to Palmerston, more tender of Tory feelings and with a preference for " a nearly unanimous affirmation of a great principle of domestic policy." The Peelites shared his taste; and an amendment was devised by Gladstone and Sidney Herbert, carried to Carlton Gardens, and moved by Palmerston in the debate. This milder declaration of the blessings of Free Trade was rich in rewards for its ingenious mover. The Government was saved; Windsor approved; the Tories bowed their thanks; the Peelites almost made him leader; and Palmerston basked in the unaccustomed sunshine. For an instant there was positively talk of Conservative reunion under his leadership in the Commons : at least it would relieve Mr. Gladstone from the distasteful necessity of serving under Mr. Disraeli. But the gleam passed. The Government was beaten on the Budget; Derby resigned; Lord Aberdeen was summoned and proceeded to combine Peelites and Whigs in a single comprehensive Cabinet.

The gossamer of Coalitions is woven by a thousand pro-

cesses of infinite delicacy; and while the looms were busy
with that filmy fabric at Argyll House and Chesham Place,
Lord Palmerston was in some jeopardy. They spoke of
him at Osborne, and all agreed that it would be imprudent
to omit him. Lord Aberdeen "had thought of Ireland for
him." The thought was not original. But Palmerston's
name had an unusual power of suggesting distant posts to
nervous Premiers. Lansdowne and Aberdeen, the 'Great
Twin Brethren' of the new constellation, both called at
Carlton Gardens and offered him *carte blanche*, with a slight
bias in favour of the Admiralty. But he declined, with a
friendly reminiscence of old times with Aberdeen at Harrow.
The tale reached royal ears; and, with an odd failure to
grasp British institutions, "we could not help laughing
heartily at the *Harrow Boys* and their friendship." Lord
Palmerston's refusal was highly natural, since he and
Aberdeen had differed too conspicuously on foreign politics
for an alliance to look anything but ridiculous. Then he
reflected. The past year had been brilliant—" I have . . .
been acting the part of a very distinguished tight-rope dancer
and much astonishing the public by my individual per-
formances and feats." The Whigs turned out, the Tories
saved, Free Trade affirmed were a respectable record. " So
far, so well; but even Madame Sacqui, when she had
mounted her rope and flourished among her rockets, never
thought of making the rope her perch, but prudently came
down to avoid a dangerous fall." What were the prospects
for a suitable descent? The Tories wanted him. "If I
had been a reckless adventurer, without principles to restrain
one, without friendship to care for, without character to lose,
such a course would have been a clear one." But what
would England say? What, if it came to that, would
Tiverton? So he must plainly alight among the Whigs
once more. As to a place, he had had his fill of the Foreign
Office already—" *j'y ai été*, as the Frenchman said of fox-
hunting." Why not the Home Office? "It does not do
for a man to pass his whole life in one department, and the
Home Office deals with the concerns of the country internally,

and brings one in contact with one's fellow-countrymen, besides which it gives one more influence in regard to the militia and the defences of the country." So his choice was made.

But would they ask again? An eager ally made sure that they did. For Em, whose anxiety for his return to office was even noticed at Windsor, wrote hurriedly to Lansdowne:

I thought you seemed very anxious yesterday that Palmerston should join this Government.—I am very anxious too as I think it would unite him again with all his own Friends —Pal^n had a courteous & friendly meeting with Ld. Aberdeen in the afternoon, but declined Office from the notion that by doing so he would subject himself to misconstruction—

Now I think that if you could speak to Pal^n again & urge him strongly to reconsider his determination that he might perhaps be induced to do so—We have heard that Clarendon is to have the Foreign Office and not Canning, & I know Palmerston thinks this gives a different Character to this Government & would therefore make him more inclined to accept—

Now these are my inmost thoughts & written to you as an old friend—If it is now too late and this letter is useless I trust you will burn it and mention it to no living soul—but if you are willing to try your influence with Pal^n and that it is yet time to do so—pray come here any time either to him or to me—but *never* let him know that I have written this—

If besides your opinion & advice which he so much regards you could be empowered to offer the Home Office I think this might tempt him—as it is the place he would always have preferred as he believes it is the Department in which he could do most good.

Believe me, dear Ld. L.
Yrs. ever sincerely,
E. PALMERSTON.

There was a breathless postscript—

I think you had better not answer this letter unless you can do so by the return of my Servant, as I should be afraid of its falling into P.'s hands.

Fair hands were busier than usual in the confection of that
austere Cabinet.   For while Lady Palmerston set her cap at
the Home Office, they were making terms with Lady John
for John's inclusion.   He was to lead the Commons; but
they wanted him at the Foreign Office.   She feared the
effort for him, and after a hard struggle they gave " their
words of honour as gentlemen that on the meeting of Parliament J. should leave the F.O. and not be asked to take any
other office."   So both the ladies had their way.   For Em's
move succeeded; and Palmerston secured the Home Office,
while she informed a friend that " after many negotiations
and many refusals from Palmerston he has at last been prevailed upon by Ld. Lansdowne to form part of the new
Govern^t."

II

A GOVERNMENT of Prime Ministers is the most impressive and least durable of structures; and in Lord Aberdeen's, whilst he, Lord John, and Palmerston formed a brief summary of English politics since 1828 (and provided Lieven with an irreverent comment on 'an incomprehensible Trinity'), the sober presence of Mr. Gladstone amongst his elders seemed to include a neat prevision of the remaining fifty years of Victorian history. They opened quietly, and Windsor almost smiled upon the slow unclosing of that singular bud. For though 'our admirable Peel' was gone, 'our excellent Aberdeen' remained. They were at the Castle to receive their seals in the last week of the old year; and whilst a princely eye observed that Palmerston was looking ill and walking with two sticks, a royal pen confided to an uncle, together with her good wishes for 1853, that the new Home Secretary was "terribly altered, and all his friends think him breaking."

He did not break that year, although his gout had been giving trouble. Instead, he took to the business of his new office with a rare gusto. He visited prisons, answered questions about water mains, closed burial-grounds, and abated smoke. He still wrote state papers; but now they were about the ventilation of cells. That eye, which had once watched Russia, was watchful still; but it was fixed upon the menace to public health presented by the London graveyards. He became the implacable enemy of intramural burial, enquiring blandly "why, pray, should archbishops and bishops and deans and canons be buried under churches if other persons are not to be so? What special connection is there between church dignities and the privilege of being decomposed under the feet of survivors? . . . and as

to burying bodies under thronged churches, you might as well
put them under libraries, drawing-rooms, and dining-rooms."
Smoke was his next quarry; he studied learned reports and
Jukes's patent, and made stern speeches about " a few,
perhaps 100 gentlemen, connected with these different
furnaces in London, who wished to make 2,000,000 of their
fellow-inhabitants swallow the smoke which they could not
themselves consume, and who thereby helped to deface all
our architectural monuments, and to impose the greatest
inconvenience and injury upon the lower class." For the
Eighteenth Century was without undue reverence for the
industrial magnates of the Nineteenth. He devised a system
for the grant of tickets of leave to convicts; and when his
strange son-in-law, Lord Shaftesbury, startled the House of
Lords with beneficent Bills on juvenile crime and mendicancy,
the Home Secretary was an apt pupil, and combined the
lessons of the Ragged Schools in a Youthful Offenders Act.
But he was not always equal to the march of progress. His
scheme " to put down beershops, and to let shopkeepers sell
beer like oil and vinegar and treacle, to be carried home and
drunk with wives and children," was somewhat rough-and-
ready temperance; and in refusing firmly to permit com-
binations of workmen to terrorise their fellows, he somehow
failed to recognise the latest flower of freedom. Mr. Gladstone's finance filled him with dark forebodings. A Succession
Duty was " wholesale Confiscation," and his objections were
confided to Lansdowne almost in *falsetto* :

> " Suppose a man to succeed to an estate giving a taxable
> income of £2,000 a year when his chances of life were 30 years;
> the value of his estate would be £60,000, 10 per cent. on £60,000
> would be £6,000, just equal to *Three times his income.*
>
> " How is such a man to pay? Is he to go to the Union
> House & hand over his Estate to the Treas^r till the amount
> is paid? "

But, for a man of sixty-nine, a Secretary at War of Peninsular
days, and a former colleague of Lord Liverpool, the Home
Secretary was amazingly enlightened. He even refused to

deal with the cholera by the simple expedient of appointing a national fast; and the shocked Presbytery of Edinburgh learned that, in his view, " the Maker of the Universe has established certain laws of nature for the planet in which we live, and the weal or woe of mankind depends upon the observance or neglect of those laws. One of those laws connects health with the absence of those gaseous exhalations which proceed from over-crowded human beings, or from decomposing substances, whether animal or vegetable. . . . Lord Palmerston would, therefore, suggest that the best course which the people of this country can pursue to deserve that the further progress of the cholera should be stayed, will be to employ the interval that will elapse between the present time and the beginning of next spring in planning and executing measures by which those portions of their towns and cities which are inhabited by the poorest classes, and which, from the nature of things, must need purification and improvement may be freed from those causes and sources of contagion which, if allowed to remain, will infallibly breed pestilence, and be fruitful in death, in spite of all the prayers and fastings of a united but inactive nation." The righteous were appalled, and the delighted heathen said that Lord Palmerston had treated Heaven as a foreign power.

But he earned unusual praise from Shaftesbury:

"I have never known any Home Secretary equal to Palmerston for readiness to undertake every good work by kindness, humanity, and social good, especially to the child and the working-class. No fear of wealth, capital, or election-terrors; prepared at all times to run a-tilt if he could do good by it. Has already done more than ten of his predecessors."

His new character charmed deputations and even found favour at Windsor. Lady Palmerston wrote that they were " very friendly and courteous now to P. as in olden times "; the Queen shared his alarms about the Militia; and in the autumn he was positively asked to Scotland. The invitation, it was true, owed something to Aberdeen's persuasion. But it was granted; and he left Em at Broadlands, " shorn of its

beams by your departure." She was quite worried by a bad
dream about trains; and when he reached Balmoral, a letter
followed him. For she came "poking in with my small
advice." The shy advice was sound—

> "Don't shut yourself up too much with your papers in
> your distant room. But remember you have only one week
> to remain there, so you should manage to make yourself agree-
> able and to appear to enjoy the society."

Perhaps he did. At any rate they had begun to talk to him
again; and one day when his Queen, anxious about strike
troubles in the North, asked, "Pray, Lord Palmerston, have
you any news?" the Home Secretary, whose interests were
more distant, answered a trifle absently, "No, Madam, I
have heard nothing; but it seems certain that *the Turks
have crossed the Danube.*"

It had come at last. For thirty years Europe had waited
for the Russian attack on Turkey to develop. The slow
hours of that interminable vigil had struck in 1833 and 1840
and 1849. But it was ending now. The Czar had murmured that the Turk was a sick man; the small cloud of
1851 had grown, until the whole diplomatic sky was filled
with trivialities about the Holy Places, and France disputed
'problems of keys, stars, doorkeepers, gardens, domes, and
outbuildings' with the Russians. These solved, the Russians
moved again. A special envoy from the Czar appeared at
Constantinople with the manners of an invading army; two
corps were mobilised behind him; and he demanded all that
diplomacy had laboured to avert for a generation—perpetual
alliance between Russia and Turkey on the terms of a Russian
protectorate over the Christians of the Turkish Empire.
Leech gauged affairs correctly when he drew a Czar (of slightly
heightened ferocity) inviting a convivial neighbour to 'finish
the Porte.' Upon this animated scene Lord Aberdeen's
diplomacy made helpless passes. There was a rain of
Notes, which somehow failed to damp the Russians; the
British fleet moved by uncertain stages from Malta to Besika
Bay; the new Emperor of the French, to whom the *rôles*

of eldest son of the Church and hereditary foe of Cossacks were
almost equally congenial, was an eager, and sometimes an
insistent, ally.   Uncertain doves of peace hovered between
London and Vienna.   But the Turks were firm; the fierce
ambassador withdrew; a Russian army passed the Turkish
frontier; and the protecting fleets of France and England
sailed up the Narrows of the Dardanelles and anchored off
Constantinople.

   Whilst England drifted into war, Lord Palmerston was
almost unnaturally well-behaved under the provocation of
the dismal succession of half-measures by which Lord
Aberdeen pursued his blameless ends.   His own views may
be imagined.   He was not likely to concur whole-heartedly
in " waiting timidly and submissively at the back door while
Russia is violently, threateningly, and arrogantly forcing her
way into the house "; he had his own opinion of " the
robber who declares that he will not leave the house until the
policeman shall have first retired from the courtyard "; and
the old Canningite insisted that " if Lord Liverpool's government had so acted in regard to the Provisional Government
of Spain, we should never have driven the French out of the
Peninsula."   But he expressed himself with extreme
discretion.   Even Mr. Greville had some difficulty in as-
certaining his opinions.   He was assiduous in canvassing his
colleagues.   From time to time there was a protest or a
proposal; and Lady Palmerston informed the world that " if
Palmerston had had the management of it, all would have been
settled long ago."   He corresponded assiduously (but never
insistently) with Clarendon, who had succeeded Russell at
the Foreign Office; and even Aberdeen admitted that
" Palmerston urged his views perseveringly, but not dis-
agreeably."

   These mysteries were slowly unfolded to the public mind.
Its interest was mild at first.   For other matters crowded on
its limited attention; and all, oddly enough, revived a
friendly memory of Palmerston.   There was a new Napoleon,
who might assemble a new Army of England at Boulogne.
But Palmerston was sound on home defence and wooden walls

and the Militia. The world was startled by a rising at Milan
and an attempt upon the Emperor at Vienna; distracted.
Austrian *gendarmes* had visions of the hated writing of Lord
Palmerston carried in the incautious felon's shoe; and there
were hoarse demands for the surrender of Mazzini and Kossuth, plotting securely in the London suburbs. But Palmerston was at the Home Office, and most unlikely to betray
a foreign refugee to please a foreign despot. As these
distractions faded, England became aware of the rich complications of the Eastern tangle—but in a simple form. A
gigantic Cossack threatened a small, but dauntless, Turk; a
palsied Cabinet, not improbably in Russian pay, delayed the
angry arm of England; and Palmerston was helpless. There
was a growing tendency in public meetings to demand " a
bold, energetic, far-seeing man at the head of affairs (loud
cries of ' Palmerston ')." Even his enemies assisted; Mr.
Urquhart, who saw Russian gold almost everywhere, now
saw it in Lord Aberdeen's pocket and *The Times* office; and
his invectives were repeated rather thickly by a strange
disciple named Karl Marx, who had other reasons for dis-
liking Russia. So the strange fever rose, as the black clouds
drove slowly across Europe. A modern hand has painted
the strange scene—" In a palace on the Bosphorus sat the
Sultan, a fleshy and irascible debauchee, usually intoxicated,
and always lethargic, surrounded by a group of Moham-
medan fanatics of whose plots to supplant him he was dimly
aware, and whose ability to rouse the fury of a priest-ridden
mob kept him in abject terror and peevish submission. In
England were public halls, crowded with respectable shopkeepers, evangelical maiden ladies, and stolid artisans,
enthusiastically proffering their lives and money in the service
of this obese little tyrant in a fez, whose name they could not
pronounce and whose habits of life were as unknown to them
as those of a prehistoric monster." And above the uproar
rose a strange conviction that Palmerston could put it right,
that he had stood—must always stand—for England. Oddest of all, he began to seem mysteriously younger than his
colleagues, who fumbled in their senile fashion with the knots

x

that he alone could cut. Yet Russell, Clarendon, and Graham were all younger men; and he was born in the same year as Aberdeen. But he became the embodiment of youthful gallantry; and for some occult reason, buried deep in the English heart, this wary, active, humorous old man of vast experience and limitless industry shared at sixty-nine the irresistible appeal of fearless midshipmen and gallant drummer-boys.

III

His first move in his new character was a trifle obscure. For months he had controlled his strong distaste for the Prime Minister's diplomatic methods, described by him in earlier days as " antiquated imbecility." Notes showered on Europe like a stage snowstorm on a starving heroine, until someone threatened to compose ' an Oriental romance to be called *Les Mille et Une Notes*,' and diplomacy seemed to have become a more than usually futile paper-chase. Lord Palmerston began to feel a cheerful doubt " whether the gold and silver age of Notes is not gone by, and . . . the age of brass and iron already begun." The public was frankly disrespectful; and Prince Albert wrote apprehensively to Stockmar that " the Palmerstonian stocks have gone up immensely, people saying that if he had been at the Foreign Office, he would by his energy have brought Russia to reason." A strong desire grew on him to " make an Example of the Red-haired barbarians, or, as Gray politely called them, ' the blue-eyed myriads of the Baltic Coast.' " But it was kept in check, whilst he filled boxes for Lord Clarendon with sketches of protocols, notes on the Dardanelles, and hints for his communications with the engaging Brunnow. He was more convinced than ever that " the Policy and Practice of the Russian Government in regard to Turkey and Persia has always been to push forward its encroachments as fast and as far as the apathy or want of Firmness of other Governments would allow it to go, but always to stop and retire when it has met with decided Resistance." It was the old problem of Russian aggression, which he had faced in King William's time and in the first years of the small Queen. He was still convinced that " if England and France make the Russian

307

Government clearly understand that the Russian troops *must* go out, the Russian Government will somehow or other find the way to make them go out "; and the arguments of 1833 and 1838 flowed from his pen. He fought his battle in the Cabinet with perfect loyalty, although he walked his horse along Pall Mall one afternoon and talked a little freely to Lord Malmesbury. His customary ally in these contests was, oddly enough, John Russell, who had acquired from long environment a slightly Palmerstonian tinge in foreign affairs.

. The silent wrestle in the Cabinet continued through the year. But the hard breathing of contending colleagues was scarcely audible outside. Then, in December, Palmerston's patience failed suddenly, when Lord John returned to his first love and projected a new Reform Bill. There were quarters where democracy was viewed as a private fancy of Lord John Russell's; and Em wrote angrily from Broadlands, "How hateful it is to hear of John Russell beginning again with his Reform Bill, and all to indulge his wretched Vanity!" Palmerston was on the drafting committee and jibbed almost at once. He might endure persistent errors of diplomacy; but Johnny's fads were really more than he could bear. Besides, he had warned the Prime Minister when he joined that he might differ on the question. Incompetence abroad was no concern of the Home Secretary; but Reform was almost a Home Office matter—he would have to defend it in the House of Commons and (worse still) at Tiverton. His main objections were to the lavish grant of seats to the large towns and to the broader franchise—" I cannot be a party to the extensive transfer of representation from one class to another. . . . We should by such an arrangement increase the number of Bribeable Electors and overpower Intelligence & Property by Ignorance & Poverty." He told Clarendon that he was not prepared to face interminable Reform debates " at his time of life," and startled him by the intimation, since nobody had yet heard Palmerston confess to a time of life. Writing to Lansdowne, he added one more reason to the formidable list—" I do not choose to be dragged through the dirt by John Russell." This was conclusive. His grounds were stated to Lord Aberdeen with a plain threat of resignation. Osborne heard the news and bore the blow with equanimity—" If Lord Palmerston has made up his mind . . . to leave the Government, there will be no use in trying to keep him in it." A business-like suggestion followed for getting his reasons in writing. But a misgiving stayed the princely pen : both for Reform's sake and the Queen's, should they not " balance the probable value of the modification with the risk of allowing Lord Palmerston to put himself at the head of the Opposition Party, entailing as it does the possibility of his forcing himself back on her as leader of that Party ? " There was so much to think of. Then Palmerston presented his ultimatum and resigned, even managing a graceful good-bye to Clarendon—" You have a hard task before you, and in Paddy's language I wish ' more power to your Honor.' " Em, informing callers in the best of spirits that " he is always in the right in everything he does," worked hard to bring him in again, sent Mr. Greville (a momentary convert) to see his colleagues, copied his letters, argued fine distinctions between objections of principle and objections of detail.

His Peelite colleagues, from whose Tory bosoms Reform was powerless to strike a spark, were strangely fluttered. They had not the least desire to be left alone in the Cabinet to face the ghosts of 1832, and they gazed longingly after the trim, retreating figure of Palmerston. Mr. Gladstone called at Carlton Gardens and sat for an hour. Eager Conservatives began to speculate upon his destination, Lord Derby's heir enquiring of Disraeli, " Will he lead the Commons under my father ? And in that event, you co-operating with him as joint leader, what becomes of Gladstone ? G. and his follower, S. Herbert, are to all appearance very strongly bound by personal ties to Palmerston. . . ." Then the Eastern sky darkened suddenly, as the Russians sank a Turkish fleet at anchor. England raged ; even the Cabinet prepared for war ; and in these changing winds

Palmerston's course was altered. His colleagues grew still more insistent, since a war without Palmerston was quite unthinkable; and he was more inclined to hear their pleas, since office, enjoyable at any time, was doubly attractive in time of war. The prodigal returned; Aberdeen received him with a note which he described as "grumpy and ungrammatical"; John Russell played the ungrateful part of the elder son, sulked and was heard complaining that "it would ruin anybody but Palmerston," while they assigned to his Reform Bill the *rôle* of fatted calf. The returning prodigal was bland; Em smiled more than ever; and the Prince, exasperated beyond all bearing by the hopeless illogicality of English public men, wrote to his sympathetic friend at Coburg that "the state of politics here has been quite *toll* . . . treachery is everywhere the cry. It is the Eastern question that has turned him out, and Court intrigues! *Uncle Leopold and I* have been his enemies. . . . Even *you* are attacked." Truly the English were all mad, and their bewildered student shook a rueful head at Windsor over his bitter confession that "one almost fancies oneself in a lunatic asylum."

The sequel was exciting. War still delayed. But England, in a war-time mood, began the hunt for traitors a little earlier than usual. It found them, with a happy instinct for sensation, in the highest places. Leader-writers wrote in dreadful whispers that "*there was a third key to the despatch box*" which conveyed the papers from the Minister to the Queen." There was a highly exciting story that somebody had bribed a patriot with £100 and a cask of sherry to suppress the true facts of Lord Palmerston's dismissal in 1851. The eager searchers found an occult power in the Privy Council and, growing still warmer, even located a "shadow behind the throne." Worse still, it was a foreign shadow; and with startling suddenness the Prince was unmasked as "the English representative of the Austro-Belgian-Coburg-Orleans clique, the avowed enemies of England and the subservient tools of Russian ambition." The storm raged in the newspapers for two months, whilst hoarser voices in the streets intoned in a preposterous litany how

> little Al, the royal pal,
> They say has turned a Russian.

His destiny was predicted in a lively chorus :

> We'll send him home and make him groan,
> Oh, Al ! you've played the deuce then;
> The German lad has acted sad
> And turned tail with the Russians.

A later verse betrayed the glorious incapacity of Englishmen in moments of strong emotion to distinguish between the different varieties of foreigners—

> Bad luck, they say, both night and day,
> To the Cobugs and the humbugs,
> The Witermbugs and the Scarembugs,
> And all the German horserugs;
> And the old bug of Aberdeen,
> The Peterbugs and Prussians.
> May Providence protect the Turks
> And massacre the Russians.

Even *Punch* regaled its readers with a princely figure of slightly sinister aspect skating perilously on the thin ice of foreign affairs. Provincial papers rumoured him impeached, arrested, and committed to the Tower; one version generously added the Queen to the number of the prisoners of state; and hopeful crowds waited on Tower Hill.

The victims bore the shock of this remarkable explosion, each in his own fashion. The Queen wrote at becoming length to Aberdeen, proposing the immediate conferment of the title of Prince Consort (once underlined) with precedence over all other princes (twice underlined) upon the husband of the Queen Regnant (with triple underlinings). The Prince composed a memorandum, in which the causes of his unpopularity were ably analysed. Stockmar responded with a luminous (if lengthy) study of the Constitution, as it related to Princes Consort. There was a tendency to blame Lord Palmerston; and that cheerful Banquo

haunted the royal table. Stockmar hinted as much; and
Mr. Greville almost credited a strange story which attributed
' the run upon the Prince ' to the French Emperor, Walewski,
and the Home Secretary. But it was most unlikely. For
Greville found much of the evidence for his conspiracy in
someone's story that Palmerston was making up a match
between the Emperor's cousin and Princess Mary of Cambridge. The tale was quite untrue, since the matchmaker
in that instance was the blameless Leopold. It was just
possible that Palmerston had called these spirits from the
vasty deep, when he resigned in mid-December. But the
storm omitted to subside on his return to office, and raged
far into February, when no motive remained to him for
further attacks upon the Court. For Palmerston was not
vindictive. Yet perhaps there was a smile at Carlton
Gardens for *Who's to Blame ?* and *Lovely Albert*. He made
no comment, apart from a denial that he had authorised a
highly abusive pamphlet or surrendered documents damag-
ing to the Prince, and an announcement in the *Morning
Post* that his resignation "had not the remotest connection
with anything on the part of the Court."

Guilty or innocent, he settled comfortably in again among
his colleagues, almost shocking Aberdeen with " a note just
as if nothing whatever had taken place " and writing to
Russell without a shadow of embarrassment about the
despotism of Trade Unions (" five of his men sway despoti-
cally a thousand ") and the danger of this influence in the
enlarged constituencies—" By letting in 100 or 150,000
workmen you would be giving great power to these agitating
but secret leaders whose objects are not such as *you* would
wish to promote." He was at Broadlands for a few days
early in 1854 with Mr. Greville and Azeglio. The Flahaults
were there as well. For he was extremely intimate with the
French of the new Empire. The Emperor was said to think
the world of him, and he was always talking to Walewski
at evening parties. He welcomed them, perhaps, because
they kept the Orleans out of France; and was he not
himself a martyr of the *coup d'état* ?

The war came slowly nearer. Mr. Kingsley heard that the Guards were going, and his blood boiled; the Queen stood on a balcony to see them go, and thought it "a touching and beautiful sight"; Mr. Carlyle heard that they had gone, and concluded that the human race was mad, while Mr. Tennyson beat a melodious war-drum and rejoiced that—

> the peace, that I deem'd no peace, is over and done,
> And now by the side of the Black and the Baltic deep,
> And deathful-grinning mouths of the fortress, flames
> The blood-red blossom of war with a heart of fire.

The Cabinet settled down to the details of Reform; Lord Palmerston was full of bland objections; and Aberdeen displayed an awkward tendency to resign. One night in March there was a dinner at the Reform Club in honour of a departing admiral. The coffee-room was hung with Allied flags, and Palmerston was in the chair. He proposed the Allied monarchs with becoming gravity, crediting Napoleon "with the greatest straightforwardness (great cheering), with the most perfect good faith (hear, hear) and the most singleminded sincerity (loud cheers)," and even commending the Sultan to his hearers as "a great reformer." He submitted with suitable emotion the armed forces of France and Great Britain—"the toast I am about to propose to you is, I will venture to say, entirely a new one since the days of the Crusaders"—and when he reached the guest of the evening, he was slightly jocular. His gallant friend had served in Portugal; and the egregious happenings incidental to Portuguese civil wars were retailed to an accompaniment of cheers and laughter. Was he not poked at in the shrouds by a Miguelite pikeman? And had he not disposed of an infuriated Portuguese with a deft parry and "a hearty kick and sent him down the hatchway (roars of laughter). Well, gentlemen, that victory was a great event (much laughter)—I don't mean the victory over the officer who went down (renewed laughter). . . ." The Reformers laughed till their sides ached. Then Palmerston took a more solemn tone, and passed to Syria. They

cheered his memories of 1840; and he closed upon a note
of cheerful confidence. The guest responded with Lord
Nelson's signal at Trafalgar, and a blunt failure to appreciate
the finer shades of Aberdeen's diplomacy—" I cannot say
we are at war, because we are still at peace (great laughter).
But I suppose we are very nearly at war, and probably
when I get into the Baltic, I'll have an opportunity of
declaring war (loud cheers, laughter, and a cry of ' Bravo,
Charley !).'' Graham, who followed him, discarded even
more of his Peelite reserve—" my gallant friend says, when
he goes into the Baltic he will declare war (laughter). I, as
First Lord of the Admiralty, give him my free consent so
to do (loud cheering).'' There were more toasts—the
Turkish minister, more admirals, the Chairman, and the
Club—and the Reformers parted for the night. But their
happy mood attracted a stern reproof. For Mr. Bright and
Mr. Cobden were lecturing their countrymen with the full
fervour of the Peace Society and that conviction of being
completely in the right which men derive from an almost
total absence of support. Read in his newspaper, the
speeches gave Mr. Bright a sleepless night; and when the
House met, he took Palmerston solemnly to task for his
disgraceful levity. But the Home Secretary was never less
inclined for a soft answer. Calling his critic, with a certain
lack of urbanity, " the honourable and reverend gentleman " (which brought Mr. Cobden to his feet in angry
protest), he informed him coldly that " any opinion he may
entertain either of me personally, or of my conduct, private
or political, is to me a matter of the most perfect indifference. . . . I therefore treat the censure of the honourable
gentleman with the most perfect indifference and contempt. . . . I will only say, in conclusion, that if he should
get himself elected a member of the Reform Club (an hon.
member : ' He is a member ')——Oh ! he is a member,
is he? a most unworthy member, I must say. . . .'' There
was an unusual asperity in his tone, which left even Mr.
Macaulay lamenting over his " want of temper, judgment,
and good breeding . . . He did himself more harm in three

minutes than all his enemies and detractors throughout the
world have been able to do him in twenty years." But
conscious virtue has a rare capacity to exasperate; and
Mr. Bright was nothing if not virtuous.

The war came in the last days of March; and as the
armies fumbled vaguely round the Black Sea, the country
was in transports. There was a national day of prayer;
the Queen denounced the Czar's sinful ambition to Aberdeen; and Britannia assumed her noblest aspect in cartoons
to keep a solemn vigil beside her arms. Palmerston's war-
aims were concisely stated to John Russell :

"My beau ideal of the war which is about to begin with
Russia is as follows: Aland and Finland restored to Sweden.
Some of the German provinces of Russia on the Baltic ceded
to Prussia. A substantive Kingdom of Poland re-established
as a barrier between Germany and Russia. Wallachia and
Moldavia and the mouths of the Danube given to Austria.
Lombardy and Venice set free of Austrian rule, and either
made independent States or incorporated with Piedmont.
The Crimea, Circassia, and Georgia wrested from Russia, the
Crimea and Georgia given to Turkey, and Circassia either
independent or connected with the Sultan as Suzerain."

It was a comprehensive programme. But for a moment
he turned aside to lay the uneasy ghost of Reform. An
icy House saw John Russell introduce his Bill in March;
the second reading was postponed; and after mutual
threats of resignation (and an admission by Palmerston
that he was "not adverse to improvement in our representative system, and . . . quite ready to consider at any
time any scheme which may have that object in view with
a sincere purpose of correcting any defects which that
system may still contain ") Lord John consented to forgo
the pleasures of Reform for one more session.

Then they were deep in martial business. Maps were
brought out; and they proceeded to "the experiment of
carrying on a war by means of Cabinet Councils," as it was
acidly described by John Russell a few months later. Faced

by the bulk of Russia, they had greater difficulties than
Napoleon in 1812, since neutral states now covered every
land frontier, and they were reduced to a dismal survey of
the maritime extremities of that insensitive colossus. The
fleet, which had sailed from the Reform Club, was bound
for the Baltic; and in the south an attack upon Sebastopol
was under discussion so early as January. Lord Palmerston, though departmentally aloof, was in his element. He
still answered questions on reformatories and the sale of
fireworks. But the Home Office was soon producing proposals for a Turkish loan, maps of the Crimea, a Prussian
plan for fortifying Constantinople in the Parisian fashion,
and every variety of diplomatic expedient for Clarendon's
guidance. He was impressed in March with " the advantage
of a great attack on the Crimea "; by June he was an
eager advocate; and in July he pressed his colleagues to
" stick to our plan & be steady to our Purpose & that is
to go to the Crimea." His advocacy earned from Mr.
Gladstone " the thanks I offered at an earlier period, for the
manner in which you urged—when we were amidst many
temptations to far more embarrassing and less effective
proceedings—the duty of concentrating our strokes upon
the heart and centre of the war at Sebastopol "; and, from
the British point of view, there was much to be said for
his opinion. True, a Russian naval base was not the heart
of Russia. But the destruction of Russian sea-power in the
Black Sea was a sensible objective which would, if reached,
reduce the naval burdens of Great Britain in eastern waters,
and protect the northern shores of Turkey; and Palmerston
was justified in his prediction that " we should be able
materially and at once to reduce our naval expenditure if
the Russian Black Sea fleet were destroyed or in our possession; and, holding the Crimea and Sebastopol, we could
dictate the conditions of peace in regard to the naval
position of Russia in the Black Sea." His prophecy was
less judicious—" sixty thousand English and French troops,
with the fleets co-operating, would accomplish the object
in six weeks after landing, and if this blow were accom-

panied by successful operations in Georgia and Circassia, we might have a merry Christmas and a happy New Year."

They landed in September; and Leech's tar asked unforgettably, "May me and Jim Grampus have a liberty day ashore, to go a shootin' with them sojers?" They shot, indeed, along the dismal road from Eupatoria to the Redan. But its depressing milestones—the Alma, Balaklava, Inkerman—passed slowly by. There was no merry Christmas and a most unhappy New Year, as the Crimean winter shut down on the freezing trenches. Rumours of hospital deficiencies and imperfections in the "hospital spring wagons jargonically called ambulances" began to creep into the Home Secretary's correspondence. But his chief concern was with *haute politique*, with terms of treaties, with the fate of the Crimea after the war, and all the diplomatic detail of the interminable negotiation which was the strange accompaniment of that curiously half-hearted war. He cheerfully defined the limits of a new Poland, disposed of Russian provinces, and at one moment urged that it would be " worth while, if we have the means of doing so, to take at least nominal possession of the Russian territory on the north-west coast of America, and so forestall the Bargain between Nicholas and the Yankees." The strange ally at Paris filled his mind; and once that year he was the subject of Imperial conversation, when Albert visited Boulogne, inspected troops, and puzzled his host by an unwillingness to smoke. The Emperor had enquired a trifle innocently what were the Queen's objections to Lord Palmerston—he had always found him *très-bon pour lui*. The Prince replied that he could see no reason for the Emperor's gratitude—" the only thing I knew was that he hated the Orleans family, and *que cela pourrait bien être pour quelque chose* in what appeared *bonté pour lui*." Napoleon, with a laudable thirst for information, asked why Palmerston disliked the Bourbons; and Albert obliged with a full narrative of Franco-Spanish policy since 1835, to which the Emperor, who " seemed to know very little about that whole contest," listened with awe. Then he explained the *imbroglio* of 1851, Lord Palmerston's dismissal, his methods, principles, and taste for intervention, and just where it differed from Mr. Canning's speech in 1826. The Emperor seemed strangely unaware of what Mr. Canning said in 1826; but as he wished to know, Albert explained. It was, it seemed, a turning-point in history—the Holy Alliance. . . . Then there was more and more to be explained, until the happy guest, in a full flow of explanation, felt quite like Stockmar. But Palmerston, in spite of everything, was dining at St. Cloud before the year was out. Emily went with him; and in the bright dawn of the Second Empire they saw the blue and silver of the *Cent-gardes*. They had not been in Paris since he dined with all the solemnities of the last *régime* in 1846 and drove round with little M. Thiers to see the fortifications. But now he went out shooting with the Emperor, or watched the thin smoke of that cigarette rise slowly on the languid talk. A low voice behind a big moustache came to him, with its refrain of operations for next year, of *remaniement territorial*, and the best way to disappoint the Austrians. There was the Empress, too, with her slanting eyes; and the more he looked at her, the prettier she seemed. Then they went back to London and, just to complicate affairs, prepared to move from Carlton Gardens into Piccadilly.

A greater move impended, since Lord John, more unaccountable than ever and resigning on an average four times a year, was permanently on the point of breaking up the Cabinet. Baulked of Reform, he burned with an unnatural ardour for the efficient prosecution of the war and became a sounding-board which echoed every popular complaint to his disgusted colleagues. First, he insisted on the departmental amputation of the Colonies from the War Office, judging correctly (though in defiance of tradition) that the Secretary of State for War might be relieved in war-time from the administrative problems of the Windward Islands and British Honduras. The bold change was promptly effected, with a slight awkwardness due to the fact that the existing staff was sagely transferred to the

new Colonial Office, leaving a distracted duke to create a
new department and organise a war. The year wore on;
and England, having exhausted the fascinations of the
search for scapegoats, turned to look, as its way is, for a
leader. John Russell caught the popular refrain; and his
fancy now was Palmerston. Perhaps a speech, which Lady
Palmerston described as " so courteous and so kind to that
wayward Johnny," was not without effect; and Palmerston
replaced Reform as Russell's panacea. Nothing would
satisfy him now but Palmerston for war minister in charge
of the combined departments of the Secretary at War and
Secretary of State for War. The duke must be displaced;
the situation needed " a man who, from experience of
military details, from inherent vigour of mind, and from
weight with the House of Commons, can be expected to
guide the great operations of war with authority and
success. There is only one such person. . . ." But Aberdeen, with a slight tenderness for the struggling duke,
demurred; he even urged that Palmerston was old. Russell
retorted that " the vigour of his mind and body " repelled
the base suggestion. Lord Palmerston received the news
with some complacency. He was not disposed to deny
that " the change . . . would be well received both at
home and abroad "; and as for his age, he did not feel
at all disqualified by that. But Russell must really not
break up the Government. So Palmerston put the crown
gently by. There was a sultry Cabinet, in which John
Russell mourned for his lost Reform Bill, threatened to
resign, and then (to everyone's surprise) resigned. Lord
Aberdeen whimpered at length to Windsor. If Russell
went, there was no alternative to Palmerston as Leader of
the House of Commons. The Queen assented. But Lord
John withdrew his resignation—he had been talking to
Panmure, who had convinced him that the moment was
inopportune.

So, after a brief winter session, in which Mr. Bright
uttered his exquisite lament for Colonel Boyle—" the
stormy Euxine is his grave; his wife is a widow, his children

fatherless "—the year 1854 went out. Russell went off to
Paris, leaving his sovereign most indignant over " the practice of the Queen's different Cabinet Ministers going to
Paris, to have personal explanations with the Emperor."
Refreshed by this diversion, he returned and, noticing that
Mr. Roebuck had given notice of a motion to enquire into
the conduct of the war, resigned again. This time, however, it was final. There was a Cabinet; Palmerston
" admitted that somehow or other the Public had a notion
that he would manage the War Department better than
anybody else," did not expect to do it half so well as the
Duke of Newcastle, and consented to try, with the leadership of the House of Commons. Mr. Roebuck's motion
was debated; Palmerston, for the defence, briefly defended
Coalitions in the abstract, and maintained a striking silence
as to the Crimea. The Government was beaten by 157;
the Cabinet resigned; and Derby was summoned to the
Palace.

His future colleagues were discussed, and they reached
the invariable topic of Lord Palmerston. The country
called for him quite unmistakably; a strange letter from
the Tuileries even insisted that he and Clarendon were vital
to the Anglo-French alliance; and no Government could
live without him. Derby was patronising. The public
might believe in him; but Derby thought him " very deaf
as well as very blind, . . . seventy-one years old, and . . .
in fact, though he still kept up his sprightly manners of
youth, it was evident that his day was gone by." But the
French and the newspapers had a taste for him. So, by
Disraeli's leave, he might lead the House of Commons as
Lord President of the Council. The dotard, interviewed,
gave signs of life, stipulating that Lord Clarendon, whom
he could handle, should be retained at the Foreign Office,
while Gladstone and Sidney Herbert must be included
somewhere. But his conditions were not satisfied; the
aged indispensable declined to join; and Derby failed.

Then Russell took his place on the roundabout, a royal
hand recording in an anguished memorandum that " it was

very important that it should not appear that the Queen
had any personal objection to Lord Palmerston. . . . The
Queen might write such a letter to Lord John as would
record the political reasons which led to her determination."
The letter was composed, with the discreet addition that
" it would give her particular satisfaction if Lord Palmerston
could join in this formation." Once more Lord Palmerston
was most obliging, would gladly serve with Russell if others
would—especially if Clarendon stayed at the Foreign Office.
But others would not; and John Russell failed.

The cup was almost drained. One drop remained; and
Palmerston was asked to try his hand. He tried; the
Whigs accepted; the Peelites struggled with their scruples,
refused to join, consulted Aberdeen, wavered, and yielded.
The Government was formed; and on February 6, 1855,
Lord Palmerston kissed hands, Prime Minister at seventy.

Y

PRIME MINISTER

I

THE goal was reached at last; and on a winter's day in 1855 Lord Palmerston sat quoting Virgil almost thoughtfully (if slightly wrong) and writing to his brother—" A month ago if any man had asked me to say what was one of the most improbable events, I should have said my being Prime Minister. Aberdeen was there, Derby was head of one great party, John Russell of the other, and yet, in about ten days' time they all gave way like straws before the wind, and so here am I, writing to you from Downing Street, as First Lord of the Treasury." Such straws required a wind indeed for their removal; but the gusty air of war-time blew too hard for them. The thoughtful Aberdeen became a figure of fun, the stately Derby a slightly incalculable grandee; and Russell's chronic resignations bore an unpleasant look of weakness. One figure still preserved its outline, where Lord Palmerston, smiling and seventy, sat trimly on the Treasury Bench or strolled across the Horse Guards to a Cabinet. The House was grateful for his smile; colleagues remembered a decisive voice, the friendly pressure of an arm insisting, as they went down the Duke of York's steps together, that Sebastopol could be invested and that invested places ultimately fell, or a bland enquiry, on the news that Mr. Cunard had lent his steamships, for his Christian name. " Samuel," replied a puzzled colleague. " *Sir* Samuel," said Lord Palmerston.

A cheerful minister is a rare boon in time of war. Nothing dismayed him : even Raglan's victories failed to shake his courage. And as the news grew blacker, he became " *l'inévitable.*" ' It was unfortunate,' as in the case of *Endymion's* great chief, ' that he had been a member of the defunct ministry, but then it had always been understood that he had always disapproved of all their measures. There was not the slightest evidence of this, but everybody chose to believe it.' · The Court was almost friendly now. John Russell had replaced him in disfavour, and Stockmar told someone that the Queen disliked him less. For the war had roused her to strange heights, and his passion for England had now a royal echo. So he acceded, while the country cheered and the Queen almost smiled. But pleasure was not universal, where Mr. Bright confided angrily to his Journal: "Palmerston Prime Minister. What a hoax! The aged charlatan has at length attained the great object of his long and unscrupulous ambition. He is believed in by a shallow portion of the public, and he has had the advantage of a 'cry' from a portion of the Press, but it passes my comprehension how the country is to be saved from its disasters and disgrace by a man who is over seventy years of age, who has never been known to do anything on which a solid reputation could be built, and whose colleagues are, with one exception, the very men under whose Government everything has been mismanaged." Mr. Cobden even aged him a trifle, and informed a friend abroad that "all men of the age of seventy-two, with unsatisfied ambitions, are desperadoes"; while Mr. Disraeli, whom the nation's choice had left extremely bitter, broke out to a great lady about "an impostor, utterly exhausted, and at the best only ginger-beer, and not champagne, and now an old painted pantaloon, very deaf, very blind, and with false teeth, which would fall out of his mouth while speaking, if he did not hesitate and halt so in his talk, here is a man which the country resolves to associate with energy, wisdom, and eloquence." It was, to Mr. Disraeli, tormented almost beyond bearing by the honeyed cup of office brushed maddeningly past his lips, wholly inexplicable. But such doubts were rare in 1855. England had tried a galaxy of Elder Statesmen, "governed for two years by all its ablest men, who, by the end of that term, had succeeded, by their coalesced genius, in reducing that country to a state of desolation and despair. ' I did not think it would

have lasted even so long,' said Lady Montfort." But it
was over now. The nation's needs were simpler, and its
dreams were filled with a neat, whiskered, pugilistic figure,
who believed in England and might give the Czar a bloody
nose. It was just five years since Lord John had told them
that he was " too old to do much in the future."

He opened boldly. Russell, to everyone's surprise, consented to run his diplomatic errands in the Conference,
which sat interminably at Vienna and played a rather disregarded treble to the bass that still boomed before Sebastopol. The House of Commons was informed that he
proposed to amalgamate the two War Secretaries in a single
War Department, to merge the Ordnance in the army, set
up a board for naval transport, and send commissions to
the Crimea for the reform of supply and sanitary services.
This said, he made a bold appeal for the reversal of the
House's vote in favour of a Parliamentary enquiry :

> " We all remember the old case of that young monarch of
> England who, in meeting a body of discontented subjects, and
> finding that they had lost their leader, rode boldly up to them
> and exclaimed, ' You have lost your leader, my friends; I
> will be your leader,' so I should say to the House of Commons,
> if they will agree not to appoint this Committee, the Govern-
> ment will be their Committee. . . ."

The move was deft. But critics were still unsatisfied;
and Palmerston did not improve his chances by a flourishing retort a few nights later to some comments on family
influence in the army—" Talk to me of the aristocracy of
England ! Why, look to that glorious charge of the cavalry
at Balaklava—look to that charge, where the noblest and
the wealthiest of the land rode foremost, followed by heroic
men from the lowest classes of the community, each rivalling
the other in bravery, neither the peer who led nor the
trooper who followed . . ." But the House was sceptical;
and to escape defeat, he granted the enquiry. This unavoidable concession pained his Peelite colleagues, and the
tender consciences of Graham, Gladstone, and Sidney
Herbert were tormented into resignation. They went;

and, for their pains, the country thought them slightly
casuistical deserters, whilst *Endymion* retained a disrespectful recollection of 'that band of self-admiring geniuses,
who had upset every cabinet with whom they were ever
connected, in hopes of a return on the shoulders of the
people, though they were always the persons of whom the
people never seemed to think.' Their places were refilled
by Whigs of more sober paces, John Russell even joining
the team in a rare burst of magnanimity, and Lady Palmerston reporting that the new man at the Treasury was
" thought to be much more satisfactory than Gladstone's
sophistry and eloquence and long-winded orations."

The war went on. That winter ' General Février turned
traitor,' and the Czar died of his own climate. Lord
Palmerston slaved at his papers in a comforting supremacy.
The Whigs were docile; the Radicals inclined for union in a
Liberal Party; and John Russell was safe among the protocols at Vienna, with the tame prospect of a return to the
House of Lords " with an olive branch round his Temples."
In this agreeable air Palmerston's views about the Crown
were changing. He wrote to Clarendon about the " value
in matters of so much importance to have the superior
Deities on our side "; he found a letter from the Queen
" eminently characteristic of the writer, full of good sense
and decision "; he even—*quantum mutatus ab illo*—paid
tributes to the Prince's gifts to callers wholly unconnected
with the Palace. They were still nervous of him, and a
cautious mistress asked quite anxiously for " those accts.
from him of the *Cabinets* which he used to give her and to
which she attached so much value as they enabled her to
follow exactly the *business* proceedings and discussions of
the govt." For though the hand that soothed them was
often the graceful hand of Clarendon, the voice was still
the voice of *Pilgerstein*. But he was strangely altered, and
Clarendon gave a shrewd reading of the change :

> " He has no colleagues to fear or to upset; he has attained
> the object of his ambition; he can't act upon his impulses at
> the F.O.; he is more immediately responsible to Parliament

than he ever was, and he is proud of having, as he thinks,
overcome the repugnance of the Court. The Queen must,
therefore, not persist in thinking him the Palmerston of old.
He has put off the old man and has become a babe of
grace. . . ."

It was almost millennial; and he sat reading princely
memoranda on the Eastern Question (at the rate of ten
volumes *folio* per annum) with an indulgent eye.

His life was an exhausting round of War Office meetings,
maps, mortars, Minié rifles, the House for half the day and
half the night, sometimes an evening ride, and then his
papers—endless drafts from Clarendon, and box after box
filled with the strange accumulations of a war. There
were experiments by gunmakers; the curator of a Belgian
museum wrote to impart the secret of Greek fire; the
French were doing something with " suffocating shells";
and there was Dundonald's plan. Miss Nightingale wrote
firmly about relief for Jewish refugees from Russia; someone thought that sulphur might be obtained from the
Dead Sea; and Panmure was extremely trying, his chief
arriving at a pained conclusion that " his Head has evidently
been turned by the Concentration of Departmental authority
in his Person." Behind it all remained the eternal problem
of effectives—" we *must* reinforce our army; we *cannot*
stand being driven out of the Crimea; we *cannot* stand seeing our brave fellows killed off by a set of Russians ten of
whom killed are not equivalent for one Englishman."
Then he was off to Windsor, when the Emperor came; and
they held a council of war in his apartments (last occupied
by the poor, good King) expressly to dissuade Napoleon
from administering the *dernier coup de main* in person.
For the phrase (it was Clarendon's) had struck his fancy;
and the Imperial mind was haunted by equestrian visions
of himself triumphant in the East, whilst Eugénie nervously
consulted fortune-tellers, and Allied statesmen devised the
most compelling reasons why he should stay at home. They
held another council on the evening of the Emperor's birthday, royally celebrated by a drive to Sydenham to see the

Crystal Palace, where the fountains failed to play. He met another royal visitor that year when, fiercely moustachioed and "startling in the extreme," King Victor Emmanuel made his *entrée*. That rolling eye surveyed the Windsor scene, alarmed his hostess, and quite fascinated the small Prince of Wales. The King told someone that Palmerston "*parle comme les Lombards ; il me fait peur—il me fait peur.*" But the terrifying linguist had his uses. For when he got his Garter, the Queen desired the oath to be comprehended by her latest Knight (who, as one lady said, was the only member of the Chapter who seemed as if he would have the best of it with the Dragon); and so Lord Palmerston wrote it all out for him in Italian.

He still found time for a fling at *Bomba* in the old manner—three line-of-battle ships to anchor opposite the palace, half an hour for a boat to take a letter ashore, an hour for the reply, and half-an-hour for the boat to return with it—and if the fleet brought off his political prisoners, so much the better. Indeed, he was urging Clarendon to spare a trifle from the Secret Service money towards a fund raised by Panizzi for their rescue. He wrote on everything—on the utility of Euclid to aspiring diplomats, on the preponderance of Cambridge men in posts of legal eminence, and on a most unlikely recruit for the diplomatic service—" If you wanted for Vienna or Constantinople a man of ability and not belonging to the present diplomatic body, there is Disraeli ready to your hand; and barring any little objection to the wife, I take it you could not well have a better agent."

· Once he assumed the Colonial Office *ad interim* to spare a colleague's health; and though his eyes were riveted on the Crimea, he could still survey the world in his old fashion. The Americans incurred his grave displeasure. He disliked their diplomatic manners, and the old abolitionist despised them for their slave-owning—" I take it they are mere swaggering Bullies. If however they should push matters to extremities . . . we have a deeply piercing Blow to strike at their Southern States if ever we should be at war

with them. Freedom to the Slaves proclaimed by a British
Force landed in the South would shake the Union to its
Base." The other hemisphere engaged him, when the
indefatigable de Lesseps in the first dawn of his long effort
proposed a highly unprecedented canal from Port Said to
the Red Sea at Suez. Lord Palmerston was elaborately
sceptical and full of deterrents—the certainty of loss, the
risk of blowing sand filling the channel, vast working costs,
and all the reasons which crowd upon objectors to large
projects. But his repugnance lay still deeper, since he
saw a revival of the old menace of 1840, an independent
Egypt under French control : " It was natural that the
Partisans of French Policy should consider it an object of
great Importance to detach Egypt from Turkey in order
thereby to cut off the easiest Channel of Communication
between England and British India . . . to interpose
between Syria and Egypt the Physical Barrier of a wide
and deep Canal defended by military works, and the political
Barrier of a strip of sand extending from the Mediterranean
to the Red Sea granted away to, and occupied by a Company of Foreigners." He had a sudden vision of a ship
canal lined with war steamers, Egypt revolted from the
Turks and " a dependency of France," a war, a rush from
Toulon, the canal closed to Great Britain and open to the
French, a *coup de main* on Aden, French cruisers in the Red
Sea, Mauritius lost, and possibly a dash at the Australian
gold-diggings.

But for the moment a more present war absorbed him.
The long siege dragged to its slow conclusion, and the
diplomats droned their interminable *obbligato* at Vienna.
As the parallels crept nearer, an uneasy feeling grew that
gains made in the field might be lost at the green tables of
diplomacy. The negotiation ended obscurely; and on its
failure Russell became a scapegoat and resigned. Then the
French began to lose their fervour. The Queen sent rousing
letters to the Emperor. But France remembered suddenly
that he had said " *L'Empire c'est la paix* "; and strange
influences worked in Paris, where Morny and Walewski

were both buying for the rise. Palmerston was firm (Lord Clarendon found him positively "rabid"); he stood in cartoons exhibiting a large siege-mortar as "the English pacificator," and finally assured his ally that Great Britain would fight on with Turkey alone in a stout conviction that "England must stand upon her own Bottom, trust to her own Resources and while taking advantage of foreign alliances as long as they last not reckon upon their permanent continuance, nor make her own safety or the maintenance of her own Interests depend upon anything but her own Strength, Energy and Courage." His sovereign was no less spirited, informing Clarendon "what *her own* feelings and wishes at this moment are. They *cannot* be for peace *now*, for she is *convinced* that this country would *not* stand in the eyes of Europe as she *ought*. . . ." She was quite a Palmerstonian now. They had been at Paris in the summer and found the Emperor more charming than ever "on all subjects—EVEN the *most* delicate, viz. the Orleans Family." So the old suspicions faded; and with a strange reversal of 1851 Queen, minister, and Prince-President seemed to come together in the dance. But, in spite of brave Queen and gallant Premier, the war died slowly down; and in the opening weeks of 1856 it ended.

In the first silence of the peace, while the diplomatists hurried to Paris for the Conference, Lord Palmerston closed his career as a war minister. He had come in to win a war. The war, indeed, had ended when it was half won. But he had brought England somehow through the dark winter of 1855, when hope burned low and an old man of seventy showed the solitary light of his cheerful energy. That service, if he had rendered no other, was substantial. But his positive achievement was far from negligible. For the old Peninsular Secretary at War found England in 1855 fighting with the same military machine which he had left in 1828. Forty years of peace and the Duke had left it a trifle rusty. But the same wheels revolved with the same groans that he had listened to, when news came in from Portugal and he danced with Lady Cowper at Almack's.

He laid ungentle hands upon it, dismissing ruthlessly, strangely accessible to new ideas, and even promoting that *fine fleur* of England in war-time, a railway manager. Panmure was warned not to " let departmental or official or professional prejudices and habits stand in our way; we must override all such obstacles." Every variety of Cerberus was boldly faced; and he left in the field an army of 80,000 men, clothed and equipped, in admirable health, and resting upon a transport service that was almost modern. Its victories were few. But British victories are rarely won in the second year of British wars. Besides, victories depend on generals; and Mars, in the higher ranks, was singularly unpropitious. For Palmerston's generals, like his War Office, dated from Waterloo. Leech could depict the application of " a sperity old woman to look after things in the Crimea—no objection to being made a Field Marshal, and Glory not so much an object as a good salary "; whilst even a minister, writing of the higher command, proposed " to remove that elderly gentlewoman from the position she ought never to have occupied." Generals take time to find; the First Republic, with the guillotine to help it, searched for three years before it found Napoleon; and Palmerston had less than twelve months. A depressing array of Peninsular veterans, diversified by General Simpson with " his shiney forehead, his red button of a nose, his *ailes de pigeon*, his circular abdomen, and his general appearance of a major of militia or a stockbroker *en retraite*," would paralyse most thunderbolts of war. England in 1854 had hoped that Palmerston was Chatham. Judged by the test of 1855, he was not. But—without Clive, Wolfe, and Hawke—was Chatham?

II

THE war was over; and the diplomacy of Europe hurried England, slightly protesting, into peace. War, for an instant, had seemed quite congenial. It revived exciting memories to cheer the bearded Guardsmen and to sing,

Cheer, boys, cheer! our Queen shall hear our story;
Courage, brave hearts, shall bear us on our way. . . .

How wonderful it was to see the Queen presenting medals to the noble fellows on the Horse Guards Parade; and there was quite a vogue (mostly for baritones) of heroic midshipmites and imperishable drummer-boys. But war, it must be confessed, was a slightly unnatural interlude in that comfortable age. The 'smooth-faced rogue' had leapt, at Mr. Tennyson's summons, from his counter; but, war once ended, he leapt back again. Peace was their element; and, to its gentler accompaniment, the reign resumed.

The Queen retained her people's hearts. For the age was nothing if not loyal. But they had eyes for another figure, where Lord Palmerston stood smiling at her elbow. That was a reign as well. It held its court at Cambridge House, where Emily wrote out the cards and Fanny and Minnie were called in to address the envelopes. A tide of broughams set towards Piccadilly, checked at the gate, and set down at the big door. They trooped upstairs past the official portrait of Lord Palmerston looking so stern beside his boxes, and found him smiling at the top with Em beside him, "her head held high, always very smart and sparkling, and looking so well in her diamonds." The big rooms were full of people : for all parties met at Lady Palmerston's. Whigs elbowed Radicals and Tories; ambassadors

rode on the flood; and editors abounded. Then, as the
talk died down, the tide receded; and they were left alone
with the candles and the stiff Empire chairs. Palmerston
would say, " Well, my love, how well you have managed it
to-night "; and Em would answer, " Yes, really, we never
had a nicer party; you seemed to please everybody."

England submitted happily to the strange rule of its
contrasted dynasts. The Queen was still the Queen,
though she was stouter now, and something of her power
to please had faded with her youth. For her youth was
almost gone. But Palmerston's endured at seventy-one.
The white hat became a talisman, where it jogged on horseback through the crush in Piccadilly bound for the House
of Commons, or stood full of papers beside him on the
Treasury Bench. He sat for hours, buttoned tightly into
his frock-coat; the gloved hands were quite still; and the
Prime Minister stared at the table absently, while Mr.
Gladstone showered refinements on the House or Mr.
Disraeli explored the obscurer chambers of his scorn.
Yet, even on the longest night, the speech always came—
the air of bland surprise, the simple argument, the little
joke. Mr. Disraeli might complain a trifle sourly of " the
jolly tone in which our Prime Minister laughs at the public
and both Houses of Parliament, and even himself " and
" the rollicking air with which he performs his cajolery."
It was easy to write of him as " a sort of Parliamentary
grandpapa " with his " wallet of small pleasantries of an
excruciating kind," even to call him " a gay old Tory of
the older school, disguising himself as a Liberal and hoaxing
the Reform Club." But his majorities knew better. The
bright eye, the whisker, and the witticism—who could
resist them, though sometimes the eye was tired, the
whisker had a deep, unnatural bloom, and the witticism
was very mild indeed? They adored him, when he poked
simple fun at City companies; Academicians laughed; even
the Royal Literary Fund forgot its woes. Guests found an
easy host, who made young members welcome at Cambridge
House or fluked at billiards on the Broadlands table (and

made a point of winning if Lady Palmerston was by).
Harrow saw him dismount outside the Headmaster's
house on Speech day and comb the short grey hair with a
little pocket-comb as he walked into Hall, and knew that
he had trotted the twelve miles from Hyde Park Corner
inside the hour. He was at home on race-courses; and
Tiverton observed a lordly figure in a green cut-away and
a white top-hat approached by Mr. Rowcliffe with more
deference than usual for a trifle towards the Tradesmen's
Plate, a friendly hand thrust into a trouser-pocket emerging
with a long silk purse, the gold rings pushed aside, and
sovereigns genially counted out into a Chartist palm.
Small wonder that the Tiverton Volunteers assembled in a
field by the railway station to give him a salute. But he
could be less majestic, when a porter ordered his cigar to
be put out in a waiting-room, discovered who the unknown
smoker was, apologised, and was rewarded by, " I took
you for an honest man, but I find you are only a damned
snob." This easy, smiling *revenant* from Almack's ruled
the age of Trollope. Leech's ' pretty girls ' clustered in
mid-Victorian drawing-rooms, while their papas downstairs
swore by Lord Palmerston; and as the first Forsyte was
getting on in business, the Regency lived on at Cambridge
House.

The reign of Palmerston (for it was hardly less) opened
in time of war. But in 1856 it passed into the milder light
of peace-time. Peace, indeed, was not quite welcome at
its first appearance; Tenniel's lion listened suspiciously at
the key-hole of conference chambers, and Leech's John Bull
accepted with evident distaste his ally's invitations to wear
an olive-branch in his button-hole and come out to see the
fireworks. For England, after twelve months of organising
victory, would have been glad to win some; and Palmerston
concealed the same emotion under more statesmanlike forms.
Besides, the Russians must be taught their lesson, or all the
struggle would be wasted. But Clarendon went off to Congress; the diplomats streamed into Paris; and Mr. Greville

followed, still in pursuit of news and marching, like an
eager general, to the sound of the guns.   The Congress was
disappointing, as peace conferences are.   For the French
usurped the British privilege of chivalry towards fallen
enemies and displayed an irritating aptitude to see the
Russian point of view, while Cavour, with the fine inconsequence of nations struggling to be free, kept raising the
Italian Question at the oddest moments.   But Turkey was
made secure; the Black Sea was neutralised; and the
Czar's Black Sea fleet ceased to exist in law as well as fact.
There have been worse treaties after better wars.

The world resumed; and Palmerston industriously surveyed the scene, with cheerful intervals in which he could
inform a colleague that " we came down here this afternoon
and mean murder to the partridges to-morrow." His
running comment upon Europe suggests the rather worldly
head of a slightly unruly college; though sometimes, perhaps, it was more forcible than any common-room—" What
a tricky rogue this Walewsky is," and " Prokesh is a low-
minded strolling player, a village attorney turned into a
diplomatist, and Thouvenel is an accomplished follower of
Loyola, burning within him with intense hatred and jealousy
of England and an unvarying desire to humble and thwart
us whenever and wherever he can, but always putting
forth the *patte de velours*."   He could be still more emphatic
on occasion—" It really will become a Question whether
King Otho should be allowed to continue to be the Curse
of the Greek People.   He was put upon the Throne to do
them good, but he is their Malignant Demon instead of their
presiding Angel.'   But Palmerston was more than trenchant.   For as the French began to veer, he diagnosed the
finer shades of policy with a rare delicacy :—

" It is quite evident that our marriage with France will
soon end in a separation on account of *Incompatibilité de
mœurs* : & it is mortifying & disgusting to find our dear friend
the Emperor so little to be trusted. . . . After all, when we
consider the different private interests of England & France,
the different characters & habits of the two nations, we ought

z

rather to be thankful at having got so much out of the
Alliance, and at having maintained it so long than to be sur-
prized or disappointed at its approaching end.   It may still
exist in name, and be useful to us for some purposes & on
some occasions, but we must trust to our own Policy and to
our own means for carrying us through the difficulties which
from time to time we may have to deal with."

The old whip still held the reins; but now his touch
was moderated by an ideal assistant.   For there was a joint
control of foreign affairs.   But this time he shared it with
the Foreign Office, not with Stockmar.   The drafts came in
from Clarendon in an unending stream, and " old habit
leads one to tinker a Note or a Despatch as often as one
reads it."   He saw the diplomats, reported loyally to his
Foreign Secretary, or sketched a bold reply.   But a judicious
hand across the way in Downing Street often endorsed upon
his letters :

" Will you make a Dft. to Bruce & to Cowley out of Ld. P.'s
note but in softened language.

C."

That was the secret.   Palmerston was still in charge.   But
the deft despatch, the mild remonstrance, and the reassuring
note to Windsor came from Lord Clarendon.
      The Prime Minister stood at his desk in Cambridge
House behind a parapet of boxes.   He saw Cavour and
told him " that he might say to the Emperor that for
every step he might be ready to take in Italian affairs
he would probably find us ready to take one and a half ";
he wrote with slight irreverence upon the capacity of the
late American ambassador for expectoration and with
genuine emotion on his successor's taste for introducing
compatriots at Court in unsuitable attire;   Naples kept
him in almost continual effervescence;   and one day he
saw a caller with a strange proposal to form a company
with Sir Moses Montefiore, purchase the Balaklava railway,
and lay it down from Jaffa to Jerusalem.   He was still
firm against the Suez Canal, warning the Pasha of Egypt

that he would end as Viceroy of M. de Lesseps, or a French *Préfet*, or possibly a companion in captivity of Abd-el-Kader. But he had an eye for modern transport-routes, when he wrote that " the real Communication with India must be by a Railway to Constantinople and from Broussa or some other point opposite Constantinople down through Asia Minor to the Head of the Persian Gulph " : a prevision of the Baghdad Railway in 1856 is creditable to any man of seventy-two.

The round went on. Sometimes he welcomed it, when his brother died on leave from the Legation at Naples and he begged Clarendon to " deal with me as to public business as usual. In cases of this kind unavoidable occupation is indeed a Relief to the Mind." The work was incredible in its variety. There was a little war in Persia, where that Russian outpost threatened Herat once more; and Naples faced him with the eternal doubt whether a Murat or a republic would be *Bomba's* best successor. But his main concerns were Russian. For the execution of a highly complicated treaty afforded unlimited opportunities for chicane. Frontiers were meticulously delimited; Bolgrad became a name of terror in diplomacy; and an angry minute from the Prime Minister ejaculated that " the Russian Govt. is acting in all things like the most incorrigible Ticket of Leave man who begins robbing and cheating in every Direction the moment he is let out," whilst a suggested arbitration by the blameless Leopold was heartily rejected on the ground that " it would be Threadneedle Street to a China Orange against us—he would give it for the Emperors as sure as Eggs is Eggs."

At home the skies were clearer; and Mr. Greville eased his conscience with the confession that " I myself, who for so many years regarded him politically with the greatest aversion and distrust, have come to think him the best minister we can have and to wish him well." Palmerston, he thought, might stay in office as long as he lived, unless the unforeseen disturbed the public mind. But England in 1856 settled, far from the unforeseen, into the deep,

central calm of the Nineteenth Century and was not easily
disturbed. Even Mr. Browning's *Men and Women* failed to
disturb it. It read Charles Reade, listened to Mr. Thackeray
lecturing on *The Four Georges,* and waited for the next
instalment of *Little Dorrit.* It did not mind a war in Persia,
provided that it stayed there. It rather enjoyed the
Rugeley poisonings of the atrocious Palmer and was frankly
delighted, when the Prime Minister suggested to a harassed
deputation from the town, who wished to change its name,
that they should take his own; and it was less exercised
than Lord Shaftesbury by the iniquity of bands that positively played on Sundays in the Parks. He warned Lord
Palmerston, who countenanced the enormity and spoke with
the most distressing levity on the subject in the House of
Commons. But his resourceful son-in-law obtained a letter
from the Archbishop; and awed by this missive, the Prime
Minister silenced the bands, while Shaftesbury (ascetic even
in his triumph) waited behind drawn blinds in Grosvenor
Square for an ungodly crowd to break his windows. His
hold on Palmerston was odd. In early days it had taken
the older man into the lobby in support of factory legisla-
tion; it tutored him in social reform when he was at the
Home Office; and now it led irreverent critics to term
Shaftesbury the 'Bishop-Maker.' He had wondered, not
without trembling, what Palmerston's Church appointments
would be like, sorely afraid that they "will be detestable.
He does not know, in theology, Moses from Sydney Smith.
The vicar of Romsey, where he goes to church, is the only
clergyman he ever spoke to. . . ." It was a dreadful
prospect. Why, the Prime Minister had only just heard of
the Tractarians; and how, in this benighted state, could he
ward off the dreadful menace of Popery? But Shaftesbury
was Minnie's husband, and Minnie was Em's daughter. So
Palmerston was quite content, when Church patronage was
in question, to follow meekly after his Evangelical shep-
herd; and while his mentor rejoiced to someone that the
Dissenters would shortly join the Church, an unsympathetic
peer replied that the Churchmen would shortly leave it.

In Parliament his course was easy. The Opposition was
half-hearted; Tories were disinclined to attack a ministry
that had won a war, and Peelites were uncertain whether
they were still Peelites. John Russell was in Italy, and
Mr. Gladstone was in his library with one eye on his place
in Homer and the other on Mr. Disraeli's in the Tory Party.
Someone at Broadlands reported that he was determined to
restore Helen of Troy's reputation, and Lady Palmerston
answered reminiscently, " Well, you know, people used to
abuse Melbourne because he said Mary Magdalene was not
near so bad as she was represented." All the world seemed to
stand aside for Palmerston. Even *The Times* was friendly
now, and he exchanged notes with Mr. Delane. Windsor itself
was wreathed in smiles. He got the Garter for the peace
treaty and thanked his sovereign without a touch of irony
for her enlightened views and unvarying support; he conferred with perfect gravity on the new title of Prince
Consort; and he attended with becoming emotion the confirmation of the Princess Royal—" Ah, ah ! " he told a
colleague, " a touching ceremony, ah, ah ! " The idyll was
surprising; and, more surprising still, it seemed to last.

Another year unfolded. The Prime Minister's gout was
worse than usual; and he was reduced to crutches in his
room at Broadlands, while Persigny was out shooting his
pheasants. But as *Lady Montfort* said, ' all prime ministers
have the gout '; and he was soon promoted to two sticks,
and then to London. There was unpleasant news from
China, where the incorrigible Chinese were more Chinese
than ever. The last movement of the Persian war had left
his head full of Russian designs in Central Asia and a stout
conviction on the subject of Kabul and Kandahar that
" sooner or later those two Places must become the outposts
of British India." And he was soon discussing the designs
for Netley Hospital with Miss Nightingale. The lady was a
shade severe. But it was never one of his axioms that the
soldiers were always right. Besides, they wrote lamentable
hands—" the officers of the Army are apt in general to

write like kitchen maids." So he passed on her views to
Panmure. A Foreign Office box brought odd reports from
Paris. The Emperor, it seemed, had been talking in his
quiet way about a new partition of North Africa—Egypt for
England, Morocco for himself, and Tunis for Victor Emmanuel. For that incalculable pencil hung poised above
the map or traced experimental frontiers in the beguiling
smoke of cigarettes. But Palmerston was unenthusiastic.
He had never wanted Egypt " any more than any rational
man with an estate in the north of England and a residence
in the south would have wished to possess the inns on the
North Road. All he could want would have been that the
inns should be well kept, always accessible, and furnishing
him, when he came, with mutton chops and post-horses."
It was a sober taste; and his ambassador was instructed to
head off the Emperor's roving fancy, whilst he warned
Clarendon that " this conquest of Morocco was one of the
secret aims of Louis Philippe, and is one of the plans
deposited for use, as occasion may offer, in the archives of
the French Government." For he retained a stout belief
that Frenchmen were always Frenchmen, unable to forgive
Trafalgar and Waterloo and quite unchanging in their aims.

But his immediate troubles lay in the House of Commons.
John Russell pointed, like an uneasy setter, towards Reform;
the Liberals were a shade listless; and the Radicals were
frankly hostile; while Mr. Gladstone, weary of privateering
as a Peelite, drifted back towards the Tories and caused
a most unpleasant accumulation of talent in Opposition.
Combining with Disraeli (and appearing with him in *Punch*
as " The Balancing Brothers of Westminster ") he made an
onslaught on the Budget. But the China war was a more
favourable fighting ground. For the lorcha *Arrow* was a
less creditable representative of the British *raj* than Don
Pacifico himself. That lively vessel flew the British flag
in the China seas. Its right to do so had expired with its
licence; but the glorious emblem still fluttered at Fong
Ah-Ming's mast-head when the Chinese police boarded him
in search of pirates, hauled down his flag, and carried off

the crew. Hong-Kong protested and, when Commissioner Yeh complied imperfectly, proceeded to bombard Canton in the Queen's name. Excusably annoyed, Yeh offered a reward of thirty dollars for each British head; and there was war. The issues were congenial to Mr. Cobden, who detected without undue difficulty that his countrymen were wrong and moved a vote of censure. Tories, Radicals, and Peelites seemed to draw together; and an anxious watcher at the Palace, who had once counted votes for Lord M., studied the prospect with something of her old alarm and frankly winced at the thought of the Opposition. On the last night of the debate Gladstone was lofty, while Disraeli scoffed at the new Liberal programme—" No Reform ! New Taxes ! Canton Blazing ! Persia Invaded ! " The Prime Minister, whose gout was reinforced by a bad cold, was poor—" very dull in the first part, and very bow-wow in the second "—and they were beaten by sixteen. Lord Shaftesbury, alone with his Journal, found a still darker explanation—

" Such a coalition was, perhaps, never before seen or imagined. Cobden, D'Israeli, and Gladstone, all combined to turn out Palmerston, and obtain office. J. Russell, ever selfish, came as an unit to the confederacy.

" I did not expect it. Hoped and believed that God having employed P. as an instrument of good, would maintain him. But His ways are inscrutable. To my own influence over future Ecclesiastical appointments (should Palmerston continue in power), I foresee the termination. They will say that my advice led him to the nomination of the several clergymen, that this exasperated Gladstone, and gave rise to the effort and the coalition. . . ."

He dissolved at once, and England plunged into the General Election of 1857. The public mind was clear. It saw the issue in the simple form of *Punch's* cartoon—Derby and Cobden as two preposterous mandarins bearing down upon a manly figure dressed as a British tar, that sucked the Prime Minister's legendary straw and rolled its sleeves up. Chinese

affairs were reduced to the simple formula of Palmerston's
address at Tiverton—"an insolent barbarian, wielding
authority at Canton, had violated the British flag, broken
the engagements of treaties, offered rewards for the heads
of British subjects in that part of China, and planned their
destruction by murder, assassinations, and poisons." The
plea was powerful; but it was hardly needed. For the sole
question which confronted candidates was, 'Are you or are
you not for Palmerston?' Their appeals, as Mr. Disraeli
wrote, were "made in favour of a *name*, and not a *policy*";
although the name was, perhaps, a policy in itself. The
elections were practically a *plébiscite* on Palmerston, and
the answer was unhesitating. For the tide submerged
his critics. Cobden and Bright both vanished in the flood;
even Manchester denied its School; and Mr. Borrow,
deep in a footnote to an appendix of *The Romany Rye*,
paused to exclaim that Palmerston "is indeed the sword
and buckler, the chariots and the horses of the party,"
but urged him to dismiss his colleagues. Lord Shaftesbury
was quite scared by his popularity; and Mr. Disraeli warned
his countrymen in vain against "the Tory chief of a Radical
Cabinet." For he returned to power, while Mr. Bright and
Mr. Cobden explored the shades, both more convinced than
ever that their countrymen were wrong.

His reign resumed, while Majesty made tender enquiries
after his health, and he wrote almost complacently that "it
is a great satisfaction and a great support to us all to have
the Court so friendly." Had not Clarendon been telling
her, as the royal head nodded assent, how badly she had
always wanted a strong minister and how hard it would be
to find a successor if anything were to happen to Palmerston?
For "nobody," as Mr. Greville wrote, "cares any longer
for John Russell; everybody detests Gladstone; Disraeli
has no influence in the country, and a very doubtful position
with his own party." He towered above them all, indomitable relic of an almost legendary past. Almack's,
Lord Liverpool, the Duke, the Canningites, Talleyrand and
his manœuvres, Mehemet Ali, Louis Philippe—all the old

rivalries had faded, as time removed each figure from the
scene.   Mr. Croker followed his master into a world where
there was no more gossip; and Lieven died that year in
Paris, though she had long been almost spectral, lost years
before in the turmoil of the Russian war, writing reproach-
fully to Em, " *Vous aimez les Turcs ; c'est un goût comme
un autre,*" and last seen in '53 behind her screens murmuring
" *C'est détestable, et tout pour* a few Grik Prists." They
were all gone.   But Palmerston persisted bravely.   When
the House met, he positively moved the Army Estimates
for the first time since 1828, because his Under-Secretary
had not yet had time to learn his business; and Parliament
seemed to obey him in an admiring silence—" scarcely a
semblance of opposition to anything that he proposes;
a speech or two here and there from Roebuck, or some stray
Radical, against some part of the Princess Royal's dowry,
but hardly any attempt at divisions."

But Nana Sahib broke the silence.   London was at its
gayest.   Even the Court was bright, with the young Fritz
arrived from Berlin to woo the Princess Royal, and Leopold
with his pretty Charlotte destined for her Archduke, and the
dark perfection of Castiglione, who was seen everywhere
that season.   But India throbbed with a strange fever,
and in the dusty glare of 1857 odd tales ran through the
villages, as runners flitted by and the tale of the greased
cartridges spread and spread.   The sepoys rose, and names
of Indian cantonments—Meerut, Cawnpore Lucknow—
acquired a hideous significance.   Across the world a comfortable nation called for revenge; and mutineers roped to
the muzzles of avenging guns hovered before its angry eyes.
Lord Palmerston was prompt in despatching Sir Colin
Campbell.   But his calm exasperated nervous colleagues.
Indeed, he was convinced at first that the Mutiny would end
by strengthening British control of India.   The surmise
was just.   But his sovereign danced with impatience, when
he seemed a trifle slow in calling out reserves.   She warned
him volubly of the danger of inadequate forces : for they
were all Palmerstonians now.   Yet he despatched 30,000

men in three months and rejoiced his countrymen with the sombre pleasures of a day of national Fast and Humiliation, which brought the Queen (in Mr. Tenniel's fancy) to her knees in a ring of kneeling widows, praying a little grimly, " O God of Battles ! steel my soldiers' hearts ! "

His work went on. The oddest things appeared in Foreign Office boxes. Napoleon proposed a general post in Northern Europe, which would leave Schleswig-Holstein to the Prussians; and in a moment of rare abnegation Lord Palmerston refused the Faroe Islands. Then he was off upon Reform :

" My Belief is that notwithstanding the slight stir got up about changes in our Representative System by a small minority here and there at the recent Elections the Country at large, including the Great Bulk of the Liberal Party, do not want or wish for any considerable changes in our Electoral System, and certainly do not wish for that particular change which the Radical Party cry out for, namely, the admission of a lower Class than the Ten Pounder . . . and I am decidedly of that opinion myself. . . .

" Besides it must be remembered that changes in our Electoral System are not an End, but a Means to an End. Before 1830 there were a great many things in the State of our Laws which the Commercial & Manufacturing Communities wanted to have altered. . . . But almost all these things have now been altered. The Ends have been attained, & the Means now possessed have been found sufficient. . . . The men who wish for this are those who cannot sway the Intelligent & the Possessors of Property, and who think that they could wield for their own advantage the lower Classes whom they want to have let in to vote. . . .

" My general notion is that votes might be given to officers of certain Ranks or perhaps of all Ranks in the Army & Navy, to all Barristers & Attorneys, to all graduates of universities, to all Medical Men registered as such & so on. I should be quite ready to give County votes to all occupiers of Houses rated at Twenty Pounds; & it might be worth considering whether a man in a Borough changing from one house to another in that same Borough might not immediately retain his vote instead of waiting as I believe is now the case for a twelvemonth.

"All this is a Bill of Fare that would fall far short of satisfying the appetite of our Radicals, but we must remember that we live under a Monarchy, fortunately for us, and if we intend that Monarchy should continue we should not run wild after Institutions and arrangements which essentially belong to that unhappy system of social organisation called a Republic."

But the great event that summer was the French visit, when the *Reine Hortense* steamed up the Solent and two smiling Majesties stepped ashore at the Osborne landing-stage. "Good Osborne," as its *châtelaine* wrote, "in no way changed its unpretending privacy." There was a little dance one night; and perhaps they had more pony-carriages than usual. But in the intervals of these rustic pleasures—so "quiet and *gemüthlich*"—the gentlemen transacted a good deal of business For Palmerston and Clarendon came down from town, the former with a shrewd suspicion that "the Emperor's notion of an Anglo-French alliance is that we should be the Canister & he the Dog to whose Tail it is tied." They had a long and most successful conference upon an outlying portion of the Eastern Question. Alone with Palmerston, Napoleon opened his design for reconstructing Scandinavia (with Holstein and Kiel for Prussia), and found him almost sympathetic. But the Prime Minister was more obtuse when he proposed to instal the Spaniards in Morocco. For Palmerston "observed that Spain could neither conquer nor hold it, and that this Idea implied a bloody war," refraining with his usual courtesy from stating that he held strong views upon the ownership of Tangier. The Prince Consort, fresh from the first use of his new title at Charlotte's wedding to her Maximilian, had further bouts of the Imperial conversation and learnt that Palmerston was sometimes a shade severe with Persigny, that it would be simple for the Mediterranean to become *un lac Européen*, that Denmark would go so well with Sweden, and that the treaties of 1815 were sadly out of date. Then the visit closed; and the Emperor wrote one of his most charming letters from the Tuileries, leaving Palmerston convinced that "nobody can come into personal Intercourse with the Queen & Prince without being impressed with the same Sentiments." A fortnight later the *Victoria and Albert* passed the breakwater at Cherbourg, which somehow managed to remind the Queen of Ehrenbreitstein. They were expected. For there had been official correspondence (in the course of which Palmerston gaily informed the Foreign Office that "Her Majesty writes a 'Look' at Cherburg and not a 'Lark')"; and international courtesies abounded. Then they returned, more Palmerstonian than ever, to call for returns of warships building and in commission, of work on the forts at Portsmouth, and the rate of recruiting for the Indian Mutiny.

Lord Palmerston sustained the burden, waved off an offer of Belgian troops for India, wrote on telegraph routes, a money crisis in the City, recruiting, *Bomba*, and transit through Egypt, with a cheerful aside for the Shah of Persia—"It is impossible to give the Shah the Garter, he is more deserving of the Halter"—and another on the destinies of the United States :

> "These Yankees are most disagreeable Fellows to have to do with about any American question; they are on the spot, strongly, deeply interested in the matter, totally unscrupulous and dishonest and determined somehow or other to carry their Point; we are far away, weak from Distance, controuled by the Indifference of the nation as to the Question discussed, and by its strong commercial Interest in maintaining Peace with the United States . . . I have long felt inwardly convinced that the Anglo-Saxon Race will in Process of Time become Masters of the whole American Continent North and South . . . it is not for us to assist such a Consummation, but on the contrary we ought to delay it as long as possible."

He shocked a colleague in the autumn by commanding cheerfully, "While you are shaving or taking a walk or ride turn over in your mind what will be the best thing to do as to the future government of India." Lord Clarendon wrote, almost with a gasp, that "he has a jolly way of looking at disasters." That, perhaps, was why they valued him in 1857 and the Queen "was full of the evil consequences of his dying or resigning to the country and herself." For while Colin Campbell moved towards Lucknow and ears were strained to catch the first faint rise and fall of the marching pipes, Lord Palmerston sat on sedately at Cambridge House. He was writing to the Office of Works about the iniquity of iron hurdles in the Park. They were unsightly, kept people off the grass, confined them to the gravel paths, reduced their pleasure, and were, in fine, an intolerable nuisance. Somewhere across the world a dusty remnant heard the pipes at Lucknow. But Palmerston was still denouncing hurdles with undiminished calm. There have been worse pilots to weather storms.

The storm subsided in 1858, though it still muttered in the distance. Perhaps the Government was a trifle shaken. The Liberals were restless; Mr. Bright informed the Speaker that he wanted the Tories in, because a Tory Government would create a Radical Opposition; and even colleagues found the Prime Minister a little failing—he seemed to sleep so much in Cabinet and even on the Treasury Bench, where a tilted hat secured him from irreverent eyes. But there was an easy feeling that "Lady Pam's parties and the opening of Parliament" would mend it all. Before the House met, Palmerston went down to Windsor, where they were in a flutter of preparation for Vicky's wedding. One night that week a waiting crowd stood in a Paris street. A Lancer escort clattered up; a carriage checked outside the Opera; and three bombs crashed into the road. The Emperor escaped; but Orsini's exploit had a strange echo. Meanwhile, they married Vicky in the Chapel Royal; and Palmerston walked just behind the Queen with the Sword of State, and shook hands with her when it was all over.

Then the session opened. Their chief business was the Government of India. The Company was in discredit after 1857, and ministers proposed a transfer to the Crown. The Bill was piloted by Palmerston, who cheerfully observed

that Chartered Companies were better suited to the simpler
exigencies of governing some North American wilderness,
where their chief functions " should be to strip the running
animals of their fur and to keep the bipeds sober." This
task accomplished, he turned to face the new problem of
the French. Beyond the Channel Orsini's bombs had started
an odd ferment. For those engines were discovered to have
been made in Birmingham, discussed in Soho, and thrown
by conspirators just arrived from England. The French
protested; Walewski read indignant Notes; and the
Moniteur printed the extremely eloquent, but highly undiplomatic, views of angry officers upon the assassins cherished
by perfidious Albion. Lord Palmerston had felt from the
beginning that something must be done. He asked " why
if the French find it necessary to expel dangerous Foreigners
from France, do they not send them to America instead of
shipping them to England," and was inclined at first to take
power for a Secretary of State to deport alien conspirators,
subject to control by a secret committee of each House.
Then they declined upon the mild provisions of a Bill
promoting conspiracy to commit murder abroad to the rank
of felony. He introduced the Bill himself; and Mr. King-
lake, still haunted after nearly twenty years by the blonde
memory of Miss Howard and more convinced than ever of
the depravity of his successful rival at the Tuileries, took a
strong patriotic line, defied the French, and urged the
House to yield to nobody, while Mr. Warren, who had
delighted novel-readers with *Ten Thousand a Year*, spoke
at tremendous length and solemnly exclaimed ' *Nolumus
leges Angliæ mutari.*' But the debate left the Prime Minister
convinced that " our Conspiracy Bill will do well." On the
next night John Russell joined the critics, arguing with
imperfect logic that the existing law was a sufficient deterrent
and that no conceivable deterrent would suffice for political
fanatics. But, with a sudden change of parts, he raised
the patriotic banner against Palmerston and declined to bow
the knee of England to a foreign despot. The Tories were
more friendly; the first stage was carried by two hundred

votes; and the Bill proceeded. Outside the tumult
deepened; *The Times* was chilly; *Punch* joined the patriots;
and England was manifestly disinclined to amend her law
in deference to Paris. The India Bill went smoothly on its
way. But walking from the House one night a Law Officer
warned Palmerston that, like a consul in a Roman triumph,
he should be followed by a slave to remind him that his
ministry was mortal : the joke, as became an Attorney
General, was grim. On the next day the House resumed
the Conspiracy to Murder Bill. The Prime Minister was
almost apologetic; the Radicals moved an amendment;
Mr. Gladstone, with a shocked denial that his country
sheltered assassins, borrowed the Palmerstonian lyre and
eloquently claimed the privilege of " discussing questions
of English law upon English grounds and English considera-
tions "; Mr. Disraeli took his opportunity, extracted himself
gingerly from his previous attitude, and marched the Tory
cohorts into the lobby with a motley array of Radicals
and Peelites, to defy the Emperor. For they were all
Palmerstonians now. The House was loud with stolen
thunder; the lesson of *Civis Romanus* had been learnt too
well; and Palmerston was out by nineteen votes.

III

THE sudden deposition of her lord plunged Lady Palmerston into the deepest indignation. She was at St. Leonards when the blow fell, and her pen ran protests—they had behaved abominably; the issue was " merely a sham reason and an excuse used by the Crafty to catch the fools "; and she felt comfortably sure that the cry would soon be ' Palmerston and no base Coalitions.' Oddly enough, it was not. For the Tories took office; and the dictator, as dictators sometimes are, was curiously effaced. He was assiduous in the House; all the old interests—the slave trade, the iron hurdles in the Park, the unnatural secrecy of the ballot—were actively maintained in Opposition. But the magic failed to work. The Prince Consort even wrote a Memorandum on the subject :

> "A House of Commons, having been elected solely for the object, and on the ground of supporting Lord Palmerston personally (an instance in our Parliamentary history without parallel), holds him suddenly in such abhorrence, that not satisfied with having upset his Government, which had been successful in all its policy, and thrown him out, it will hardly listen to him when he speaks. . . . The man who was without rhyme or reason stamped the only *English* statesman, the champion of liberty, the man of the people, etc., etc., now, without his having changed in any one respect, having still the same virtues and the same faults that he always had, young and vigorous in his seventy-fifth year, and having succeeded in his policy, is now considered the head of a clique, the man of intrigue, past his work, etc., etc.,—in fact, hated ! "

It was a strange enigma. Yet war-records frequently evaporate in time of peace; and Palmerston's was, in some degree, a war-time reputation. His own party was hope-

lessly divided, and two tides of feeling drew Liberals away
from Palmerston. For while stout Palmerstonians, returned in 1857 as ' Liberal-Conservatives,' recoiled in
horror of Reform towards the Tories, the Radicals, to
whom his name was an emblem of reaction, found a congenial leader in John Russell. Meanwhile assiduous
negotiators pursued the sober joys of Liberal reunion,
while Lady Palmerston explained that he retained " a
great affection for John," and the air was thick with allega-
tions of treasonable dealings with the Tories. The rival
leaders met by elaborate accident in someone's room. A
shower of rain came on, and they drove home in the same
brougham. The clubs enjoyed the matchless topic. But
extremely little came of it. For the party still voted half a
dozen ways at once, and Mr. Disraeli uttered his famous
apologue of the earthquake—" a rumbling murmur, a groan,
a shriek, distant thunder; and nobody knew whether it came
from the top or the bottom of the House. There was a rent,
a fissure in the ground. Then a village disappeared. Then
a tall tower toppled down. And then the whole of the
Opposition benches became one great dissolving view of
anarchy ! "

Palmerston had a more rewarding autumn. For in
November, to everyone's surprise, he went to Compiègne
with Lord Clarendon. He had maintained his intimacy
with the French ambassador, slightly to the disgust of his
Conservative successor. But it was going rather far for
two ex-ministers to accept Napoleon's invitation; and
Palmerston kept clear of Brooks's to avoid awkward
questions and even sent Delane an explanation. Whig
ladies wrote to his companion expressing grave relief that
" it was not one of the riotous parties when ladies defend
fortresses and mounds, and gentlemen pull them by the
feet to make them lay down their arms, for your young
companion P. would probably have joined in that fun
too." This was denied him. Indeed, it rained too hard
for shooting; and they were reduced to playing football
in a gallery and mounted quadrilles in the riding-school,

A A

while the Emperor (as became a former paladin of the
Eglinton Tournament) performed equestrian feats with a
lance. Then the weather cleared, and each sportsman's
gun was loaded by four alarming figures in cocked hats,
while Lancers in full uniform (only slightly impeded by their
spurs) beat coverts to the sound of bugles; and in these
opulent surroundings they pursued the Imperial birds, with
an irreverent suspicion that they were released from traps
beneath the Imperial gun. He sat next to the dark Mathilde
at dinner; but she made little of him, and he ate steadily.
The Emperor talked a good deal of Italy, explained the
Roman Question, and told Palmerston that the true basis
of the franchise was to confine it to married men. One
day there was a hunt in pelting rain. The party assembled
in a miscellany of mufflers and greatcoats. But Palmerston,
at seventy-four, appeared in the full panoply of pink and
top-boots, waving off wraps with the proud exclamation,
' *Rien ne perce un habit rouge.*' So the gallant figure passed,
indomitably English, across the bright stage of the Second
Empire.

Then he returned to England and the Liberal Party.
Reform was on the *tapis*—" John Russell, I hear, wants
to add a million to the existing voters. This would be
very much to swamp property and intelligence. . . . He
at length deems Bright a dangerous man. I suppose
this means that he thinks him a dangerous ally, because
he is losing his hold upon the country by unmasking his
revolutionary yearnings." These had impressed him deeply.
For that month he wrote to Lansdowne asking for a sub-
scription to enable someone to convert the *Statesman* into
an anti-Radical daily paper. Its object was " to show that
Bright's real wish is to assimilate our Constitution to that
of the United States of America "; and he wrote feelingly
of his " republican notions," adding that Panmure,
Clarendon, and he were all subscribing. Such was the
chilly welcome accorded by the right wing of the Liberal
Party to its left.

The new year opened in the stir of the Emperor's cold

words to the Austrian ambassador and Victor Emmanuel's eloquent allusion to the *grido di dolore* of Italy. Palmerston privately averred himself " very Austrian north of the Alps, but very anti-Austrian south of the Alps "; he should " rejoice and feel relieved if Italy up to the Tyrol were freed from Austrian dominion," and he met the Azeglios at dinner and asked Panizzi to bring Poerio and Settembrini, freed at last from *Bomba's* dungeons, to dine at Cambridge House. The Queen and Prince were frankly Austrian, while Tory diplomacy fluttered uneasily above the impending conflict, proliferating special missions, formulæ, and diplomatic sedatives of every kind. But the Austrians lost their patience and, with it, Lombardy. An ultimatum to Turin gave Count Cavour his war and Napoleon his *casus belli*. Once more there was a crash of Austrian bands, a gleam of Austrian bayonets in dark Italian streets; Mr. Gladstone, on his way home from Corfu, noted guns in Vicenza station, troops parading at Verona, and pickets at street-corners in Milan; and, deep in Vienna, Metternich uttered a spectral groan. The French were moving; and the *képis* swung through the rice-fields, where the Emperor, twisting his big moustache and smoking his cigarette on horseback, contrived at last to be Napoleonic and led an Army of Italy to war.

Another move for peace was more successful. The Tories, beaten on Reform, dissolved in April; and Palmerston went down to Tiverton once more, survived the customary ritual, and even left a banquet at the local Athenæum to celebrate the coming of age of a supporter's daughter in a glass of Irish whisky, which by a singularly happy choice formed part of her birthday presents. The elections over, he was at Brocket, where an odd letter from Disraeli found him. It opened almost in a whisper—" I address you in our ancient confidence. Consider well the views I am taking the liberty of placing before you "—and blandly proposed that Palmerston should combine with the Tories, control their foreign policy, and bring in his own Reform Bill, which might be " as conservative as you please." But he declined politely. Returned to town, he found the Liberals victorious but still disunited. Hasty *pourparlers* changed the scene. The obliging Granville trotted between the rival leaders, and they consented " to put an end to the notion that there are jealousies and ill feelings " by leaving the dread choice to chance—or, rather, to the Queen. For each consented to serve under whichever of them she might summon to form a Government. Even the Radicals were understood to be propitious; John Russell had been seeing Bright in the interests of unity; and as the French marched eastwards from Magenta, Radicals and Whigs trooped to a party meeting. A pleasing chance assembled it at Willis's Rooms, where Lady Patronesses of a bygone age had ordered the nightly festivities of Almack's. These shades now echoed to the deeper music of Liberals in conclave. The leaders both announced their perfect concord; Bright blessed their union; and on a scene familiar to a younger Palmerston he watched—not Lieven now, or Lady Cowper—but the formation of the Liberal Party. Rejoicing in its sudden unity (and with a wise resolve to act before it faded), it put out the Government. Azeglio was in the lobby; and when the figures were known, the diplomatic hat went up, the diplomatist himself into the arms of the French. *attaché.* Lord Palmerston walked out in buttoned coat, top-hat, and gloves; and there were further outcries of delighted Latins, where Italy acclaimed her friends.

But things were not so simple. Derby resigned. Majesty, bewildered by the Liberal feud, sent for Lord Granville, warning him with something of the old distrust of " the effect likely to be produced on the Continent by Lord Palmerston's name, if he had the direction of the Foreign Affairs." For Albert was deep in memoranda on the Italian Question; the French menace was lucidly exposed in endless letters to Stockmar, to Berlin, to Leopold; the drum of German unity was bravely beaten and Prussia recalled to its supreme duty to " be German, be *Volksthümlich.*" But Palmerston, alas! was recognised at Windsor as " out and out *Napoléonide*, maintains France to be in the right on all

points, the object a useful one, of driving the Austrians
out of Italy, and does not recognise any right on the part
of Prussia to interfere in the affair." Besides, he knew no
history. So they preferred Lord Granville, who had been
so very helpful with the Exhibition; and two gracious, but
identical, letters requested Palmerston and Russell to serve
under him. Invariably obliging (and with a shrewd notion
that Granville would fail), Lord Palmerston consented, if
he might lead the House of Commons. Granville agreed
and went off hopefully to Russell. Lord John consented
also, if Palmerston went to the Lords as Foreign Secretary
and he might lead the Commons. This coincidence of their
tastes was fatal. For Palmerston declined his elevation,
and Granville resigned the Queen's commission. So there
was nothing for it, and she summoned Palmerston.

He complied with alacrity; and by the end of June the
first Liberal Government was formed. John Russell, at
his own request, was accommodated at the Foreign Office,
excluding Clarendon. There was a bodyguard of Whigs.
But a friendly letter from Cambridge House waited at
Liverpool for Mr. Cobden, just returned from the United
States. He learnt from it that " Mr. Milner Gibson has
most handsomely consented to waive all former difficulties,
and to become a member of the Cabinet. I am most
exceedingly anxious that you should consent to adopt the
same line, and I have kept open for you the office of President
of the Board of Trade, which appeared to me to be the one
best suited to your views, and to the distinguished part
which you have taken in public life." They met in town,
and Cobden was quick to admit that the Prime Minister's
offer had been both manly and magnanimous. But he could
not accept. Had he not steadily denounced Lord Palmerston
for years? There was a laugh, and the Prime Minister
observed that personalities ought never to be remembered
for three months. Besides, if Cobden disliked secret diplomacy, why not join the Cabinet, where such matters were
decided? The tribune was embarrassed; but still his
armour held. " Why are you in the House of Commons? "

asked his host. " Upon my word, I hardly know," was the
reply. There was a louder laugh, and Palmerston enquired
why, being in, he should not go on. He wished to include
the advanced Liberals, and who else would fill the part?
There was Milner Gibson; but Bright had made himself
impossible by his wild speeches—" it is not personalities
that are complained of; a public man is right in attacking
persons. But it is his attacks on *classes* that have given
offence to powerful bodies, who can make their resentment
felt." For Bright had been thundering against the Lords.
The talk went on at Cambridge House. The Premier
plied the wary tribune, but without success. They parted
on the best of terms; and as the visitor moved to the door,
his host said, " Lady Palmerston receives to-morrow evening
at ten," and Mr. Cobden answered, " I shall be very happy
to be allowed to present myself to her." So Mr. Milner
Gibson went to the Board of Trade, and Mr. Cobden went
to Cambridge House.

But Palmerston secured a more elusive quarry. For
Mr. Gladstone, after a fluttering return to Toryism, a
Homeric interlude as High Commissioner of the Ionian
Islands, and an ambiguous homecoming, wavered once
more towards Palmerston. He still retained a dubious
vision of Tory reunion; but he dined with Whigs. He
had voted in the last division with the outgoing Tories.
But when Palmerston took office, he reflected that Italy
was in danger, that Russell and Palmerston were of his
way of thinking on Italian matters and, this strange reasoning concluded, he positively insisted on the Exchequer.
So Palmerston in 1859 assembled every element of Liberalism
—the Whigs, the Radicals, and (less simply classified) Mr.
Gladstone—and, by a pleasing irony, the Liberal Party was
founded at Almack's by that ancient beau.

IV

ONCE more the reign of Palmerston resumed; and passers-by in Piccadilly saw the grey horse amble through the gates of Cambridge House, as the Prime Minister rode down to Cabinet in Downing Street. The trim figure buttoned in the tight frock-coat sat nightly on the Treasury Bench under a tilted hat, or stirred, drew off its gloves, and rose to poke a little fun across the table at Mr. Disraeli in the perpetual winter of his discontent. Perhaps the hand fumbled a little now to hide his spectacles. But the voice was clear; and someone found him looking like " an old admiral cut out of oak, the figurehead of a seventy-four gun ship in a Biscay squall," where he sat squarely among his colleagues. They flanked him—Whigs, Radicals and Peelites; John Russell almost mellow now, the hard smile of Sidney Herbert, and Mr. Gladstone with his straight black hair, filling Disraeli's mind with unpleasant thoughts of Jesuits. The Cabinet, perhaps, fulfilled *Endymion's* recipe for a Whig Government—" at least a couple of men who had been prime ministers, and as many more who thought they ought to be." But the Prime Minister, in Clarendon's phrase, " held a great bundle of sticks together "; and England was excusably less interested in his subordinates than in the smiling figure which sucked its weekly straw in *Punch* and even drew from the austere Bagehot the unwilling confession that he had " the brain of a ruler in the clothes of a man of fashion." For, less isolated than of old, he was never less Palmerston.

His first concerns were appropriately European. He came in at midsummer. That month the French won Solferino, and the Austrians trailed off to wait for them still further to the east behind the big guns of the Quadrilateral. Lord Palmerston, urging his sovereign without success to make Mr. Bright a Privy Councillor, elicited a shocked refusal founded on " his systematic attacks upon the institutions of the country." But he turned sharply at the news from Italy. The armies halted; a carriage rolled along a dusty road between the lines; two Emperors sat talking in a hot room at Villafranca; and in the summer dusk Franz-Joseph signed a hurried treaty that ceded Lombardy but kept Venetia under

> The cursed flag of the yellow and black.

Cavour was raving; and the Queen wrote with a faint complacency that she was " less disappointed with the peace than Lord Palmerston appears to be, as she never could share his sanguine hopes that the ' *coup d'état* ' and ' the Empire ' could be made subservient to the establishment of independent nationalities, and the diffusion of liberty and constitutional government on the Continent." There were long faces at Turin; but Russell clung to his old opinions—" I do not wish to see either the Tedeschi or the Galli drinking the waters of the Po. Let the Italians govern their own affairs—that is my motto." An easy Pope took snuff and murmured helplessly to Mr. Odo Russell : " *Povere noi !* what is to become of us with your uncle and Lord Palmerston at the head of affairs in England? " They both made such extraordinary speeches —he always read them. Then there was Mr. Gladstone, who was so lamentably imposed upon about the prisoners at Naples; and Mr. Cobden, too, though he was always such a friend of peace and must be very fond of animals— he had wished His Holiness to write to Spain about the bull-fights.

Others besides the Pope were anxious. Osborne had watched Napoleon's progress with a nervous eye. Had he not struck down Austria? And was not Austria the right arm of Germany? This year on the Mincio, he might soon be on the Rhine. But the new Cabinet was sadly obtuse. Three ministers at least were deep-dyed

Italians; a colleague noted " Johnny and Pam like twins,
too much united on foreign affairs, for with Gladstone as
their ally they are inclined to meddle too much in Italian
affairs." It was an odd triumvirate; and Mr. Gladstone
made a strange coadjutor for the two old gentlemen. Yet
he was sound enough on Italy to satisfy the most Italian.
For when Palmerston got home one night, he heard a
speech of Gladstone's echoing from Em, " sprouting as
she read by candle-light." So Osborne watched with
grave distaste, concluding gloomily that Palmerston was
quite incorrigible—spite against Austria took him to any
length—while Mr. Gladstone had written dreadful things
about the King of Naples, and Italy was John Russell's
latest fad. But could they not see that the Emperor would
soon be master of the whole Continent? It seemed so
simple; and soon the Queen was objecting to Foreign
Office drafts in the old fashion. But they were Russell's
now; and there was no Prime Minister for her to appeal
to except Lord Palmerston, who shared his colleague's
heresies and seemed resolved that British policy should
win for Italy the victory that France had left half won.
But what was Italy, with Prussia mobilising and the *Reich*
in danger? It was most uncomfortable. Stockmar was
far away; all their old fears revived; and they poured out
their troubles to Clarendon—" Her old feeling against Palmerston is quite returned, and she spoke with bitterness of him
and Lord John. ' I can't say I am happy, because I am
not. I live in constant dread. . . . I have given up arguing
with Lord Palmerston, and now I only protest. Lord John
has not written a single dispatch that I did not wish he had
abstained from writing. . . .' " It was a sad predicament.
Frontal attack was hopeless; but they did their best by
writing privately to Granville, who was slightly embarrassed
by these royal confidences, but sent private reports of
Cabinet proceedings with the advice that Majesty would
do well to be kind to Russell and should " appear to communicate frankly with the Prime Minister." Lord Palmerston refused to abstain from active intervention in the

affairs of Italy. He advised the disputants at length
and with a strong Italian bias, holding that silence would
reduce Great Britain " to the rank of a third-class European
State." So Lord John was far from silent; the royal
pen worked havoc with his drafts; the Prime Minister
was highly indignant and wrote a paper " on the abstract
question of giving advice," sent it to Osborne, and took
the train after it. When he arrived, the Queen was " much
agitated and did not feel equal to discuss the matter with
him." She left him to the Prince, who argued the point.
There was a Cabinet, when Russell read out her minutes
" fast and low," and Palmerston " spoke for Johnny, and
bitterly as regarded the Court." But their colleagues
stood by the Queen, declined to accept the view that she had
acted beyond the Constitution, and felt a chivalrous regret
that she had been unnecessarily annoyed.

They passed a restless autumn, with Palmerston at his
old habit of private talks with the French ambassador,
while John Russell sat at Abergeldie pelting Balmoral
with odious memoranda, and the Prime Minister wrote
firmly that " if your Majesty's meaning is that Viscount
Palmerston is to be debarred from communicating with
Foreign Ministers except for the purpose of informing them
officially of formal decisions of the British Government,
Viscount Palmerston would beg humbly and respectfully
to represent to your Majesty that such a curtailment of the
proper and constitutional functions of the office which he
holds would render it impossible for him to serve your
Majesty consistently with his own honour or with advantage
to the public interest." There was a tame reply.

But Palmerston was not the victim of his French ally,
whose mind he shortly diagnosed as " full of schemes as
a warren is full of rabbits, and, like rabbits, his schemes
go to ground for the moment to avoid notice or antagonism."
He turned a wary eye on French projects in Morocco,
writing at length upon the danger to navigation of a cross-
fire in the Straits; and he fully shared the emotions that
rang from Mr. Tennyson's lyre that year—

True we have got—*such* a faithful ally
That only the Devil can tell what he means.
Form, Form, Riflemen Form !
Ready, be ready to meet the storm !
Riflemen, Riflemen, Riflemen form !

So he revelled in Volunteers, instructed Mr. Gladstone in
the dreadful details of invasion, and projected lines of
forts behind the dockyard towns.

But in the intervals of other business he encountered
something graver. For he met the Gothic Revival in its
severest form. In these years a noble impulse among
architects was covering England with reproductions of
the mediæval antique, of which the Law Courts are the
stateliest, the Randolph Hotel at Oxford not the least
worthy example. New public buildings were assiduously
fortified against the light artillery of the Fourteenth Century,
while some bore ineffaceable traces of the more spiritual
purpose for which their originals had been constructed.
So town halls disguised themselves as churches, and local
Justices performed their work lit by the dim illumination
of *meurtrières*. This revolution in design was not accomplished without controversy. But the banner-bearers of the
Goths was warmed by a deep moral purpose and the perusal
of forbidding contributions to a professional journal named
the *Ecclesiologist*. None among these built truer or wrote
more rousing pamphlets than Mr. Gilbert Scott; and when
a competition was announced for the new Government
offices, he was serenely uplifted by the opportunity of
covering the intervening space between Downing Street
and Palace Yard with spires and gables and bastilles.
He designed a Foreign Office in the vein of his exquisite
town hall at Halifax and got the commission. The Tories
were in office, and the Opposition made some unworthy
capital of their choice. Lord Palmerston professed particular indignation at the prospect of a Gothic Foreign
Office, preferred the Italian style, and spoke with genuine
emotion of " that street of palaces, Pall Mall." For that
ancient child of the Eighteenth Century preferred the

ordered decencies of frieze, capital, and *piano nobile* to
the horrid confusion of the Gothic. The Government
went out, and chance left Mr. Scott at his critic's mercy.
The Prime Minister summoned the architect, told him that
he would have nothing to do with this Gothic style, felt
sure that he could do the Italian just as well, and requested
him (with a bland unawareness of the enormity of his request)
to prepare drawings in the Italian manner. The purist
started, and went home to think. But his reflections were
assisted by a subsequent suggestion (made in the Premier's
most paternal manner) that he should be associated with a
classical colleague. Every corbel in his system revolted
at the thought. He went to Yorkshire, thought hard of the
Venetian Byzantine, and produced a Foreign Office worthy
of the Doges. Then he saw Palmerston again, who was still
more emphatic against Gothic, called his latest blend
" neither one thing nor t'other—a regular mongrel affair,"
and squarely demanded an Italian building. The wretched
architect went off to Paris, looked at the Louvre, and built
the Foreign Office in the hateful style, barely consoled by
Mr. Ruskin's generous admission that he had done quite
right. Such was Lord Palmerston's slightly devastating
contact with the arts.

The century rolled forward into 1860, taking Palmerston
into the decade of *Atalanta* and *Dolores*, where Mr. Browning's *Caliban* addressed his *Setebos* in the most unheard-of
language and *Sister Helen* melted her waxen man before
a widening circle. These changes almost touched him.
For Mr. Rossetti was dining one night with Em's son,
William Cowper, whom Palmerston had loyally promoted
to the Office of Works. A nervous hostess asked him
how they could improve the little house in Curzon Street.
The big head turned heavily round the room; and the
gilt pelicans cowered beneath their candlesticks, the roses
on the watered wall-paper quivered in their blue bows.
Then their tremendous guest pronounced his sentence :
they must begin by burning everything they had. They

reeled.   But though the drawing-room retained its imitation
Sèvres (by Minton), they did up the staircase with a Morris
paper and put a lovely little bit of glass by Mr. Burne
Jones into a window on the stairs.   So the breath of change
on William Cowper's stairs fanned Palmerston's old cheek.

That year he lost his faith in the French Emperor beyond
recall.   The forts at Cherbourg had been bad enough.
But French armour-plate and ironclads completed his
disillusion; and he settled comfortably down to a race of
armaments, in which his *Warrior* was matched against
Napoleon's *Gloire*, and heavy guns grinned out to sea
from shore emplacements as fast as Mr. Whitworth and
Sir William Armstrong could deliver them.   He spoke
quite sternly to the French ambassador, and revealingly
informed his shrinking Chancellor of the Exchequer that he
had had two great objects in his life—" one the suppression
of the slave trade, the other to put England in a state
of defence."   England was not unwilling, since her elusive
ally invited close attention.   The cool appropriation of
Savoy and Nice as a *pourboire* from Italy caused grave
alarm; and there were darker stories of designs on the
Balearic Islands and draught-horses under requisition at
Châlons and anti-British leaflets in French barracks.

The long tapestry of Italy wound slowly off the loom
that year, not without aid from England.   An anxious
couple at the Castle wrote almost with a groan to Brussels
that " though we modify matters as much as we *can*, we
can't entirely keep our Ministers (*the two*) from doing something."   Their ministers insisted grimly on their perfect
right to give advice.   But Majesty could still correct their
manners and compose a tearful protest to Lord Palmerston
against Lord John's unpardonable insinuation that she
was no friend of freedom.   Lord Palmerston assumed to
perfection the bland airs of a peace-maker and was soon
back in favour on the strength of his impeccable suspicion
of the French—" Lord Palmerston is *very stout and right*
about our neighbour."   A visitor to Osborne was told that
" they are both pleased with his civility and attention,"

now contrasted (by a strange irony) with the less pleasing
manners of John Russell and—novel ingredient in the
royal troubles—Mr. Gladstone's tantrums.

That year the May moon rose over Quarto, and the
Thousand sailed for Sicily. Before the month was out,
they held it; while *Bombino* sat at Naples, telegraphing
five times in twenty-four hours for the Pope's blessing
(and receiving the last three blessings by wire from an
exasperated cardinal without reference to the Holy Father).
The roaring ran before Garibaldi into Palermo, across the
straits, along the gleaming coast, right into Naples. The
tapestry was moving faster. Victor Emmanuel marched
into Papal territory, destroyed the shadow of an army,
and displaced the shadow of a power; John Russell composed an eloquent despatch, which covered the Italian
revolution with the respectable Whig precedent of 1688;
and his sovereign wrung helpless hands over what someone
called " offhand despatches and random shots by our leader
Robin Hood and his colleague Little John." But Palmerston remained irrevocably genial, condoling with her on a
move from Scotland to meet the Princess Royal with the
cheerful moral that " of all the gifts which good fairies were
in the habit of bestowing on their favourites, that which
would have been the most desirable would have been the
power which the Irishman ascribed to a bird, of being in two
places at one and the same time." But though he exchanged
voluminous apprehensions of invasion with the Prince
Consort, he refused a K.C.B. to General Bruce, who had
been so invaluable to Bertie on his tour through Canada.

Lively abroad, the year was almost livelier for Palmerston
at home. It opened with interminable Cabinets on Mr.
Gladstone's finance. That edifice rested upon a singular
foundation. For Mr. Cobden, with official status, had
passed the winter months in Paris, deep in amateur
diplomacy. He saw the Emperor and explained the blessings of Free Trade; he saw M. Fould and pressed upon
his shrinking mind the fact that British imports would
not ruin France; he saw M. Rouher and plunged into the

exciting details of an amended tariff. At intervals he
reappeared in England, took refreshing draughts of Mr.
Gladstone's fervour, or was slightly chilled by Palmerston's
absorption in the news of rifled cannon ordered by the French,
a rumoured contract for ten thousand tons of iron plating,
or a still darker tale of flat-bottomed boats at Nantes.
Then he returned to Paris and was lost to sight in a whirl
of conferences, schedules, public dinners, drafts, and all the
fierce joys of commercial negotiation. But they got a treaty
signed at last; and the Cabinet was busy on it in the first
weeks of 1860. Gladstone was ardent; but he found the
Prime Minister slightly neutral, although he had approved
the plan, read long reports from Mr. Cobden, and wrote
kindly, when the long effort seemed to tell upon his health,
that " the climate of Paris is perhaps better than that of
London, but then the French physicians are less in the
habit of curing their patients than ours are."

The Cabinets went on; and Mr. Gladstone unfolded the
impressive details of his Budget. Outside, the air of
expectation was almost operatic. The Chancellor looked
thin, and faces fell. He coughed, and Brooks's reeled.
He took to his bed, and Tories were seen whispering in
corners. But he rose invincibly and spoke for four hours,
" aided by a great stock of egg and wine." The treaty
was announced and he said a word of solemn exultation
over the open grave of Protection; the paper duties were
abolished; and (more novel still) the Income Tax was graduated. It was the triumph of Free Trade, and Mr. Gladstone
triumphed with it. The Prince wrote to Stockmar that
he was " now the real leader of the House," and Napoleon
received a copy of the speech with thanks appropriate
to a masterpiece. But the triumph was not uninterrupted.
For Lord John insisted upon interposing a Reform Bill on
the anniversary of his first glorious exploit in 1832. But
Palmerston recorded drily that he " was listened to without
any marks of approbation on the one hand, or of disapprobation on the other." For the Tories asked for nothing,
the Radicals for more, the Whigs for less. The flower

drooped in this depressing air. Somehow John Russell
and Reform were a dispiriting combination; and before
the unwanted blossom fell, a grieving hand had plucked
it, and the Reform Bill was withdrawn.

The Budget had a more exciting life. The Treaty of
Commerce passed, and an Academician painted the stately
scene for the Speaker (though Mr. Bright commented
rather bitterly upon the group—"the Cabinet was on the
Treasury Bench, Palmerston speaking, Cobden and I
up behind Ministers as if we were supporters, which we
are not. On the Table 'French Commercial Treaty'
lying open as if the glory of Palmerston's Government,
when Cobden and I know he did all he dared to make the
Treaty miscarry"). But the repeal of the paper duties
had a livelier passage. Lord Palmerston had never liked
the plan, fought it at length in Cabinet, and even informed
the Queen that if the Lords rejected it, "they will perform
a good public service." This view was imparted to Lord
Lansdowne. But as the day came near, the Prime Minister
was inclined to "doubt the Prudence of starting at the
present moment a nice Question of Functions and Privileges
between the two Houses of Parliament"; and Lansdowne
was informed that "my own opinion is that the House of
Lords has a perfect Right to do what Lord Monteagle
proposes; but there are strong opinions that the Exercise
of that Right would not be advisable; and it is probable that
it would lead to some motion in the House of Commons
which it would be very embarrassing for the Government
to know how to deal with; and on the whole I have come to
the Conclusion that for many Reasons it is desirable that the
motion should not be carried."

The Lords were less discreet; and so was Em. For when
the Bill came on, she was in the gallery, hoping loudly
that they would throw it out. A little careless of their
powers in relation to money Bills, they did. Gladstone
was angry, and his mood was not relieved by his leader's
easy consolation—"Of course you are mortified and disappointed, but your disappointment is nothing to mine,

who had a horse with whom I hoped to win the Derby,
and he went amiss at the last minute." Foul play was
suspected in both instances (his *Mainstone*, third favourite,
was scratched that year); but while the Cabinet was loud
with Mr. Gladstone's vows against the Lords, his chief had
no resource but riding down to Epsom for a glimpse of his
other runner finishing 'somewhere about tenth.' The
Tories, in a nervous flutter, sent Malmesbury to see him
with assurances of their support against the Radicals.
Once more the Cabinet debated; but when he breathed
vengeance and Restoration precedents, Mr. Gladstone found
Palmerston "keen and persevering," with an awkward
tendency in the House to prompt Russell, as he rose to speak
with a whisper of, " You won't pitch into the Lords." They
framed a sounding set of resolutions upon the Commons'
privileges, which the Prime Minister moved in a tone of
almost tender reproof of the peers' vagaries, while Mr.
Gladstone sounded a sterner note and Mr. Bright, alluding
meaningly to Pym and Selden, sniffed with solemn joy
the smoke of future conflicts.

But Mr. Gladstone's troubles were not ended. For he
burned with various fires. Less stern, perhaps, than the
sepulchral dignity of his later phase (he was remembered
in that year as " quite enthusiastic about negro melodies,
singing them with the greatest spirit and enjoyment, never
leaving out a verse, and evidently preferring such as ' Camp
Down Races ' "), he was unquestionably austere. Deriving
an ascetic pleasure from even the slightest deprivations—
" Lost my Savings Bank Monies bill; my *first* defeat in a
measure of finance in the H. of C. This ought to be very
good for me; and I earnestly wish to make it so "—he was
nowhere more austere than upon questions of public expenditure. For he wore, a trifle consciously, the mantle of
Sir Robert Peel; and Palmerston's alarming taste for
national defence drove him almost to distraction. Most
Chancellors would rather balance a Budget than launch an
ironclad; and it was excruciating for Mr. Gladstone to hold
the purse for Palmerston. As the new forts began to frown

B B

along the coast, the Chancellor of the Exchequer frowned more sternly still. From frowns he passed to argument, to endless memoranda, and (not infrequently) to resignation. But Palmerston was quite immovable, confiding brightly to the Queen how much he " hopes to be able to overcome his objection, but if that should prove impossible, however great the loss to the Government by the retirement of Mr. Gladstone, it would be better to lose Mr. Gladstone than to run the risk of losing Portsmouth or Plymouth."

So Mr. Gladstone at the Treasury wrote despairing papers, and

> all day long the noise of battle roll'd
> Among the mountains by the winter sea.

Lord Palmerston maintained his point and went briskly about his business in an avalanche of drafts, despatches, colleagues, trainers, ambassadors, and journalists. One night, indeed, he was compelled to speak in defence of the diversity of his company, when a determined critic drew the most sinister conclusions from the presence of Mr. Delane at Cambridge House, to say nothing of his former leader-writer, Mr. Robert Lowe, who now sat in minor glory on the Treasury Bench. The Prime Minister was bland. He had had the pleasure—frequently—of meeting Mr. Delane, who had done him the occasional honour of mixing in society under his roof. So, for the matter of that, had Mr. Disraeli. But neither undertook the least engagement, except to make themselves agreeable during their stay—and how admirably they fulfilled it. Such urbanity (he had the secret of it from the Eighteenth Century) is not easily penetrated; and as he smiled round the House, the imputation was bowed gracefully downstairs. But he had a more expansive manner, which he kept for suitable occasions. He opened Mechanics' Institutes with *aplomb ;* and once a crowd was waiting on Leeds platform to see his train go through. An engine whistled; carriage windows rolled by; and brakes shut down. There was a rush towards the door, where a friendly old gentleman appeared to be amused by the forest of hands thrust up for him to shake; and presently the deep voice made a little speech. It was quite like the audacious methods of Mr.

Lincoln, speaking that year from Yankee railroads in his Presidential campaign.   So Palmerston, in the first dawn of a new day, made friends with newspapers and speeches from railway-carriages, while Mr. Greville closed his Journal for the last time, and England glided into 1861.

That year he was heard frequently on Army and Navy Estimates.   But the Channel ports seemed to receive additional protection, when he was installed Lord Warden of the Cinque Ports.   This dignity vacated his seat at Tiverton.   So they returned him unopposed after a brush with Rowcliffe, followed by handshakes in the Mayor's parlour.   Even the Chartist butcher's heart was touched by a Prime Minister, whose golden sovereign had been the first given in the Lobby towards the testimonial to Sayers for his victory over Heenan; and the voice of *Punch* acclaimed *John Palmerston* to a familiar air, rendered by Tom Taylor :—

AIR—" *John Highlandman*."

An Irish Lord my JOHN was born,
Both Dulness and Dons he held in scorn,
But he stood for Cambridge at twenty-one,
My gallant, gay, JOHN PALMERSTON !
    Sing hey, my brisk JOHN PALMERSTON !
    Sing ho, my blithe JOHN PALMERSTON !
    Let Tory and Radical own they're none
    To compare with my jaunty JOHN PALMERSTON.

Thanks to tact and temper, and taste for the trade,
For twenty years in office he stayed,
Let who would be Premier, it seemed all one,
So his Sec.-at-War was JOHN PALMERSTON.
    Sing hey, &c.

There he did his work, for chief after chief,
Till the Tory party it came to grief;
And the Treasury Bench when the Whigs they won,
Who was Foreign Sec. but JOHN PALMERSTON !
    Sing hey, &c.

Since then years thirty and one he's seen,
But no mark they've left on this evergreen;
Still the first in his place when Debate's begun,
And the last to leave it is PALMERSTON.
    Sing hey, &c.

With his hat o'er his eyes, and his nose in the air
So jaunty, and genial, and debonair
Talk *at* him—*to* him—*against* him—none
Can take a rise out of PALMERSTON.
    Sing hey, &c.

And suppose his parish register say
He's seventy-seven, if he's a day;
What's that, if you're still all fire and fun
Like METHUSELAH, or JOHN PALMERSTON?
    Sing hey, &c.

How to marshal a House of Commons fight,
How to punish DIZZY, or counter BRIGHT,
How Deputations ought to be done,
Who can teach so well as JOHN PALMERSTON?
    Sing hey, &c.

Agricultural meetings he holds by the ears,
Through their facings puts Hampshire Volunteers,
Or with ROWCLIFFE takes up the gloves for fun,
This elderly evergreen, PALMERSTON.
    Sing hey, &c.

He'll resist the gale, or he'll bow to the storm—
He'll patronise BRIGHT, or he'll chaff Reform—
Make a Shafts'bury Bishop, or poke his fun
At original sin, will JOHN PALMERSTON.
    Sing hey, &c.

Of the Cinque-Ports, Warden he's made at last,
And fears of invasion aside are cast;
There's never a Mounseer son of a gun
Can come over *you*, my JOHN PALMERSTON.
    Sing hey, &c.

Since the days of the Patriarchs ne'er was seen
A head so grey with a heart so green;
And when, if ever, his day is done,
There'll be tears from *Punch* for JOHN PALMERSTON.
    Sing hey, &c.

He was seen everywhere—at Harrow in the drenching
rain to lay a foundation stone, at Windsor, where they
talked about the settlements on Princess Alice (soon to

be bound for Hesse-Darmstadt), at Broadlands in the congenial company of Mr. Delane, or riding round the forts on the south coast with an officer who was mildly astonished by the Prime Minister's eight hours in the saddle. His work continued without notable variations. There was still Mr. Gladstone to be humoured. He had resigned a dozen times over the forts, and he was still resigning. Indeed, his cheerful leader told Delane that he had set the study chimney at Broadlands on fire with Mr. Gladstone's resignations. They had a tussle over his proposal to repeal the cherished paper duties in the new Budget, and Gladstone recalled " a fierce discussion, in which Lord Palmerston appeared to me to lose his temper for the first and only time." He swallowed it at length, but with a stout refusal to stake his Government's existence on Mr. Gladstone's fiscal fad. His Government, indeed, rested upon an odd foundation. For the Tories, startled by dark forebodings of Mr. Bright, promised support to Palmerston if his impulsive colleagues actually resigned. Mr. Disraeli told the Prince as much at Windsor, adding (for he could rarely resist a historical allusion) that no minister since Mr. Pitt had been so powerful as Palmerston might be with Tory backing. But the kindly offer was hardly needed, though Palmerston politely acknowledged " the honourable and patriotic motives " which had prompted the Opposition. For that accomplished whip kept his uneasy team together (though Mr. Delane refused a place in it that summer); and the Broadlands chimney still smoked with Mr. Gladstone's wasted resignations.

But he had other colleagues. For Lord John was restless, too, irked by his craving for Reform (*Punch* viewed him as a small schoolboy perpetually cramming an enormous hobby-horse into an inadequate play-box) and troubled by a sudden taste for going up to the House of Lords in order to relieve the burden of his work. At the first intimation of this desire Lord Palmerston was slightly incredulous and blandly informed the Queen that he " would think himself doing better service by recommending the House of Lords for Mr. Gladstone." But the taste grew upon John

Russell; and he took the strange promotion in the summer, leaving Palmerston alone in the lower House among the restless voices of the future. Yet the change was not without its consolations; for the Prime Minister became " the representative of the Foreign Policy of the country " on the Treasury Bench, and Russell (though an earl) still kept the Foreign Office. Their views on policy abroad were quite harmonious. For Russell leant on Palmerston's vast stores of information. Both suspected France, and both were ardent in the cause of Italy—a rueful Prince once termed them with gloomy jocularity " the two ' Old Italian Masters.' " It was a sober passion, confined at first to a taste for seeing the Austrians expelled. Palmerston would have preferred two kingdoms in the peninsula, since the southern state with its enormous seaboard was more likely to have British leanings. But that year facts (and Garibaldi) reconciled him to a single kingdom of United Italy, slightly endeared to him by the circumstance that the change seemed uncongenial to France. There was still more to be thought of, with the French in Syria and the Spaniards in Tetuan, a chance of the Pope at Malta, and an odd notion that the Turks might sell Herzegovina to Victor Emmanuel to be exchanged with the Austrians for Venice.

But that year another problem dawned upon them, as the scattered shots rang out in Charleston harbour and Fort Sumter answered the Confederate guns. The brunt fell upon Russell. But Palmerston, after half a century of official life, was not without an attitude towards the Americans. It was composed of many elements. His view of the Republic was always coloured by his strong distaste for slavery, which had found its way into his consideration of most American questions; but it was particularly lively, when the State Department seemed to interpose some patriotic pedantry about the Right of Search between a British cruiser and the beneficent operation of examining a slaver. True, the dispute was almost settled now. But the slave-trade, which had been his whole life's abomination, was carried on under the shelter (however irregularly obtained) of the American flag; and Palmerston could not forget their slaves. So, by an odd irony, the cause of abolition coloured his view of the United States of Mr. Lincoln. Their diplomatic manners, too, did little to increase his favour. A studied truculence, however service-able in winning the Irish vote, was not the way to Palmer-ston's affections; and in face of this discouragement he had laboured through an endless negotiation on the Bay Islands Question. The raiding activities of unchecked filibusters had made unwelcome additions to his correspondence, although he felt little doubt of the ultimate absorption of Central (and even South) America by his informal kinsmen. But the *trait* that most forfeited his favour was the prompt and invariable recourse of almost every Secretary of State in his offical experience to a threat of war. Lord Palmerston was a shrewd judge of threats of war. He had heard them without perturbation from almost every Continental states-man of two generations. A long procession—Metternich, Thiers, Louis Philippe, Guizot, Persigny—had passed before him, clenching fists. His life-long response had been a placid invitation to proceed, followed in almost every instance by an angry glare, a lowering of hands, and then—with relaxing features—an amicable negotiation. It was his method to disbelieve in threats; and perhaps American diplomacy had been a shade too prodigal of them to command his entire respect.

In the first stages of the Civil War he steered a course of impeccable neutrality through the problems of belligerent status, privateering, and blockade. The tone of Mr. Seward, an epitome of Palmerston's worst fears about the State Department, made him slightly uneasy; and he warned Russell that " it is not at all unlikely that either from foolish and uncalculating arrogance and self-sufficiency or from political calculation Mr. Seward may bring on a conflict with us," with a wary addition as to the defence of Canada. In consequence, perhaps, he wrote with rather wicked glee of " the defeat at Bull's Run or rather at Yankee's Run," from which he drew the scarcely justified conclusion that

" the Unionist cause is not in the hearts of the mass of the population of the North . . . the Truth is, the North are fighting for an Idea chiefly entertained by professional politicians, while the South are fighting for what they consider rightly or wrongly vital interests." The diagnosis was unsound; but few Englishmen would have disputed it in 1861.

He was already thinking of the need for cotton and pressed the Board of Trade to give attention to the problem. As the war drifted on and Russell's drafts began to abound in claims and consular annoyances and all the minor 'incidents,' which form the joys and sorrows of a neutral, he still clung to his attitude : " Our best and true policy seems to be to go on as we have begun, and to keep quite clear of the conflict between North and South." He called sometimes at the Confederate offices in Suffolk Street, Pall Mall, and a cautious forecast of the future once found its way into a minute to the Foreign Office :

" It is in the highest Degree likely that the North will not be able to subdue the South, and it is no doubt certain that if the Southern Union is established as an independent state, it would afford a valuable and extensive market for British manufacturers. But the operations of the war have as yet been too indecisive to warrant an acknowledgment of the Southern Union."

There is little trace in the judicious terms of this highly confidential document of that malignant determination to destroy the Republic at all costs, with which Palmerston is sometimes credited in American fancy.

Five weeks later he had, if he desired to do so, his opportunity. For it was known in London that the United States sloop *San Jacinto*, Captain Wilkes, had stopped the British steamer *Trent* one day out from Havana and removed four Confederate passengers by force. That night a boy in Suffolk Street, Pall Mall, saw Palmerston come to the Confederate office and confer with Judge Mann, of Georgia. The two men stood in front of a large map of the United States. The boy was listening, and their talk seemed to run on the course of future naval operations. New York and Philadelphia were mentioned as points of attack for a British squadron; and there was even talk of some combined operation with General Johnston's army, which would result in the capture of Washington—and then (the Prime Minister was speaking) 'France and England will be in a position to demand the immediate cessation of the war and to exercise a rightful influence in regard to the terms of peace." It was a strange confabulation; and the boy's story leaves it far from clear whether the Judge or Palmerston did most of the talking. For while Palmerston might listen to the eager suggestions of a Southern gentleman, he was unlikely to discuss the movements of a British fleet with foreigners. He had a First Lord of the Admiralty; he had a Cabinet as well, which met later in the week to consider the disturbing news. The Law Officers and counsel to the Admiralty attended, advising that the forcible seizure of Confederate passengers was illegal. They had considered a point of the same kind a few days earlier, when a Federal warship seemed to be lying in wait for the Confederate envoys in British waters, and had advised on that occasion that belligerents were perfectly entitled to search neutral ships on the high seas for enemy despatches and (as Palmerston reported to the Queen) " if such are found on board to take her to a port of the belligerent, and there to proceed against her for condemnation." A slight confusion on the point of law had led him on that occasion to inform Delane that the warship was entitled " if the Southern men and their despatches and credentials were found on board, either to take them out, or seize the packet and carry her back to New York for trial." But the Law Officers had, in fact, advised that " she would have no right to remove Messrs. Mason and Slidell and carry them off as prisoners, leaving the ship to pursue her voyage." The distinction was important. For that was precisely what Captain Wilkes had done, seizing his prisoners in mid-ocean without waiting for a Prize Court. The cases manifestly differed, and the two views were perfectly consistent.

The Cabinet resolved " to demand reparation and redress "
and adjourned for Russell to prepare a draft despatch, while
Palmerston reported to the Queen, adding that an egregious
general in the Northern army was proposing to enlist the
French as allies in the ensuing war with England by a
fantastic offer to restore French Canada to Napoleon. On
the next day they met again; and Russell's draft was
" softened and abridged," slightly to Mr. Gladstone's relief.
The draft went off to Windsor, where the Prince was far from
well. He had been ailing all that winter. An inspection
of the new buildings at Sandhurst in the pouring rain did not
assist; and he had dragged himself to Cambridge for a night,
where Bertie was increasingly restless. Back at the Castle,
he found himself *recht elend ;* and when the draft arrived
from Russell, he was completely out of sorts. Still hunted by
his inexorable duty, he was up and reading in the dark
winter morning under his green lamp. He read the draft
despatch for Washington. It seemed a little meagre;
and though his hand was weak and chilled, he framed an
answer for the Queen to send to Russell and took it to her
room at eight o'clock, exclaiming pitiably, " *Ich bin so
schwach, ich habe kaum die Feder halten können.*" He never
held another; for it was his last memorandum. It suggested
thoughtfully that words should be inserted expressive of a
hope that Captain Wilkes had acted without orders or had
misunderstood them, but held firmly to the point that
reparation must be made.

The Cabinet redrafted the despatch and even abated something of the Prince's firmness. There were no doubts. For
Granville, reporting on the reception of the royal amendments, informed the Queen that " Lord Palmerston thought
them excellent "; and she reminded him a few weeks later
of " the observations upon the Draft to Lord Lyons, in which
Lord Palmerston so entirely concurred." Such acquiescence
on his part shows plainly that he was not set on war. For the
amended draft offered a relatively honourable way of escape
to the Americans; and if Palmerston really desired a war, he
was unlikely to part so lightly with his *casus belli.* Yet the

excited fancies of the time evolved in American minds a
slightly feverish mythology of a bellicose Prime Minister,
who suppressed a legal opinion, drafted a stiff despatch and,
when a wiser hand revised it, threatened to resign, whilst a
mob broke palace windows. The truth was less exciting;
there were no resignations and no broken windows. The
despatch went off, and the Guards sailed for Canada. But
Mr. Cobden, a connoisseur of warlike intentions, was not
deceived :—

> " I do not believe in war. Palmerston likes to drive the
> wheel close to the edge, and show how dexterously he can
> avoid falling over the precipice. Meanwhile he keeps people's
> attention employed, which suits him politically. . . .
> " Palmerston ought to be turned out for the reckless expense
> to which he has put us. He and his colleagues knew there
> could be no war. . . ."

Meanwhile, there was a pleasing tension. John Russell
studied Alison on the War of 1812; Mr. Delane rode to
St. James's Park and watched a battery clank by *en route*
for the St. Lawrence; at the White House the President
informed a caller rather languidly *à propos* of the *Trent*
case, " Oh, that'll be got along with "; and Mr. Tenniel's
Britannia, looking her very best, waited for Lincoln's
answer by the breech of a big gun. It came; the prisoners
were released; and Mr. Lowell was left singing rather
resentfully,

> It don't seem hardly right, John,
> When both my hands was full,
> To stump me to a fight, John—
> Your cousin, tu, John Bull.

That year a minor transatlantic problem faced them,
when the long-suffering holders of Mexican bonds succeeded
in interesting Paris and Madrid in their sorrows. Morny,
who had quite a feeling for a M. Jecker, was more than
usually attentive; the Emperor revived his ancient dream
of a European monarchy in America; and Spain toyed with
the pleasing notion of chastising her rebellious colonists.

At first there was a risk of single-handed intervention by the Spaniards; and Russell, with a lively vision of American resentment and fresh trouble with filibusters in the West Indies, hastily acceded to a Convention of London, by which the three Powers agreed on common action, but with a healthy reservation against forcible interference " in the internal affairs of Mexico." Late in the year they saw the tall mountain behind Vera Cruz come up against the sky; and when the ships stood in, they landed—Spaniards in force, a battalion of Zouaves, and some red Marines. But far behind them, in the silence and decorum of the Tuileries, Napoleon was unfolding his peculiar plan. To end the tangled promiscuity of Mexican politics he proposed to create an Emperor of Mexico; and for the post he had chosen from the *Almanach de Gotha* Franz-Joseph's brother, Maximilian, a mild young man of mainly botanical interests, who was married to Leopold's dark Charlotte. The Austrians insisted upon British approval; and a private request from the Tuileries reached Palmerston, who stoutly refused it. Quite undismayed, his resourceful correspondent satisfied all tastes by informing Palmerston that the scheme was dropped, while gratifying Vienna with the news that Palmerston approved, though he abstained from written avowals out of respect for American susceptibilities and " certain sections of British opinion, notably the School of Bright." A few months later the agreeable farce concluded with discoveries of the common deception and an unpleasant tendency on the part of the French at Orizaba to insist upon priority for the financial claims of M. Jecker; and Great Britain withdrew from Mexico with elaborate gestures of disapproval, leaving the future to Maximilian and Bazaine and Juarez and a firing-party.

A shadow quite as dark hung over Windsor in the last weeks of 1861. For the Prince was plainly very ill indeed. Lord Palmerston was at the Castle; and he was most uneasy, pressing them to call in another doctor. Then he was back at home with the most dreadful gout, still urging further medical advice on Windsor. He wrote

continually to Phipps, with a kindly solicitude that the
Prince should not be worried by too many strange faces
round his bed. He seemed to rally; but the Prime
Minister still wrote three times a day. One night the
news was grave, and Palmerston looked so white at dinner
that Em was quite alarmed. That night he wrote to
Phipps, almost unable to face the dreadful prospect—" in
all its bearings too awful to contemplate. One can only
hope that Providence may yet spare us so overwhelming
a calamity." But the end came. The Queen was widowed,
almost incredulous to the last, and left staring blindly at a
life, a sentence, almost a vocation of widowhood. The
Prime Minister was deeply shocked. He had been very
ill himself; Em was extremely anxious; and there were
positively rumours of his death. Besides, a death at forty-
two upsets a man of seventy-seven; and in the shock
all memory of old contentions faded. He had come to think
better of the Prince; and the Prince, in later years, seemed
to think almost well of him, even sharing some of his opinions.
For Albert could be genially " glad to see . . . that you
keep up the steam about our Defences." But that was
over now. The Queen sat dazed at Windsor, while Palmerston urged her with kindly pressure towards the quiet
of Osborne and wrote with unusual feeling that he had
" read with deep emotion your Majesty's letter . . . every
word of which went straight to the heart." For the old
man was deeply grieved. Then 1861 faded, and beyond
the lighted windows of Osborne the Solent swung drearily
in the grey winter light.

At first his sympathy appeared to touch her; the Prince
of Wales had written : " I cannot tell you how touched my
mother was by your kind and sympathising letter." But
other influences crowded upon her. Her memory was
full of Albert, of Albert hard at work, Albert devoted to
the cause of peace—peace, above all, with Germany. His
wishes had become her law. For now she had no object
except to follow every wish of Albert's. She tried hard

to remember them; and they all came back to her—the
causes that he had worked for, and his precepts, and his
adversaries. She was soon writing tearfully to Russell
that "one of his most anxious wishes was to see the two
great kindred nations, England and Germany—to which
we both belonged—understand each other and act together
—and it will be one of the Queen's most sacred duties to
watch over these interests—and she feels sure Lord Russell
will readily do what he can to bring about this desirable
state of things!" She could not quite write that to
Palmerston. His views had often failed to coincide with
Albert's; and old memories surged up unbidden of dreadful
wrangles with an earlier, more contentious Palmerston,
until a visitor to Osborne could record that "she retains
some of her husband's feelings about Pam and John, and
this is increased as regards the former by recollection of great
enmity between them at one time, although I believe both
the men have entirely forgotten and forgiven it."

The feeling grew upon her, and she began to dread a
visit from the Prime Minister. Leopold arrived from
Brussels with a slight tendency to take possession and
frequent references to his devotion to the Prince. He
trotted discreetly about London seeing stray ministers,
and wrote to Palmerston at length about the dark designs
of France on his beloved Belgium; for that rather easily
agitated fly on the wheel of European policy was rarely
still. Then he informed her that "all your most devoted
servants, Granville *à la tête*, are very desirous that you
should see Palmerston, that no appearance of coolness
should exist, as it would weaken the Cabinet; and it is
undoubtedly your own interest for the sake of having
no difficulties, as well as that of the country, that Pilgerstein
and his people should not be upset." The driven lady
yielded, and a day was fixed for his audience at Osborne.
The Prime Minister had really been very ill. His eyes gave
trouble in the year before (someone had seen him " wearing
a green shade, which he afterwards concealed," and looking
"like an old retired *croupier* from Baden "); and the gout

had crippled him. But he was better now, and started off from Broadlands in the slightly unseasonable attire of a brown greatcoat and light grey trousers, with blue studs in his shirt and a pair of green gloves. Perhaps he robed discreetly for his interview; at any rate the royal Journal found no fault with his demeanour. They were both nervous. Palmerston could hardly speak for his emotion, and the Queen could see how much he felt her loss. They talked of it together. Then the old man was fatherly and spoke of Bertie, said that he was "*the* difficulty of the moment," and how important it was that he should marry. The Queen was quite surprised, and "would hardly have given Lord Palmerston credit for entering so entirely into my anxieties." Then the interview concluded; and she was soon inviting him to stay. His sympathy was real. For he was shocked by the death of a younger man, pitied her loneliness, and took a parental tone with Bertie, warning him with perfect gravity against "the allurements of fortune, position, and social temptation." When the House met, he uttered a judicious threnody upon the Prince, observing that "as far as the word 'perfect' can be applied to human imperfection, the character of the late Prince deserved the term." The Queen relented slightly and asked Russell to return a letter which the Prince had written in the bad old times of 1850 about Palmerston's delinquencies. But duty called; the memory of Albert urged; and she was soon pressing him for a settlement of Schleswig-Holstein upon lines congenial to Prussia.

Home politics were less absorbing, though Mr. Cobden made his annual onslaught on the hated forts, together with an ingenious suggestion for a limitation of naval armaments to be arranged with France on lines familiar to a later generation. But the future still held Washington Agreements deep in its mists, and Palmerston in 1862 replied succinctly that "unfortunately man is a fighting and quarrelling animal; and that this is human nature is proved by the fact that republics, where the masses govern, are far more quarrelsome, and more addicted to fighting,

than monarchies, which are governed by comparatively
few persons "—in fine, that Mr. Cobden was a dreamer.
He met the same contention in a milder form, where Mr.
Gladstone fought his endless battle with the Estimates.
They sparred abundantly—eight quarto pages from the
Prime Minister, twelve in reply from the Chancellor, and then
a rapid fire on either side.

The war went on beyond the Atlantic.   British neutrality
was strenuously maintained, though Palmerston supplied a
vivacious interlude on the news that a Northern general
had authorised his troops to treat as ' women of the town '
all persons guilty of insulting behaviour.   He seemed to
recognise the shade of Haynau and shocked the American
minister with an indignant protest in his early manner—
the offending order left it, he said, " difficult if not impossible to express adequately the disgust which must be
excited in the mind of every honourable man. . . . If the
Federal government chooses to be served by men capable
of such revolting outrages, they must submit to abide by
the deserved opinion which mankind will form of their
conduct."   The tone was sharp.   But Palmerston was
rarely tender where he suspected cruelty.   Besides, he had
been writing sharp letters for half a century.   There was
an angry scuffle; Russell was nervous; as the dust subsided,
the American minister relieved his feelings with a taste of
adjectives which, though restrained, was forceful; and
Palmerston was left explaining.

That summer *Alabama* slipped away to sea after a tangle
of mischances, in which the Prime Minister was not concerned.   Launched as *Enrica*, known to official correspondence by the mysterious name of *Number 290*, she fitted out
at Liverpool and was successively the object of American
suspicions, consular enquiries, diplomatic representations,
and finally of a case submitted by the Foreign Office to the
Law Officers that arrived too late.   The ship escaped.
But while she was taking in her guns in the Azores, the
Cabinet considered a draft from Russell directing all colonial
ports to detain her; but the proposal was dismissed.

They faced a larger question, when Palmerston in June

declined to offer mediation. In the same month a minute
to the Foreign Office showed him equally distinct upon the
conditions necessary for recognition of the South :

"We ought to know that their separate Independence is a
Truth and a Fact before we declare it to be."

But as the year went on, pressure began to come from
Paris. For the Emperor, deep in his Mexican adventure,
was keenly alive to the utility of Southern sympathies
and eager for intervention. Busy Confederates flitted
between Paris and London; there were uneasy hints that
Napoleon might appear single-handed as the saviour of
the South; and Palmerston began to veer. In July Mr.
Gladstone found that the Prime Minister " has come exactly
to my mind about some early representation of a friendly
kind to America, if we can get France *and* Russia to join ";
in August he was thinking of a move in the autumn; and
in September news from the front appeared to indicate
that Washington or Baltimore might fall—" If this should
happen, would it not be time for us to consider whether in
such a state of things England and France might not address
the contending parties and recommend an arrangement
upon the basis of separation? " Russell leapt at the notion
and proposed to intervene at once and, if mediation were
refused, to recognise the South. Lord Palmerston was less
impulsive, preferring to wait in order to associate Russia
in the proposed mediation and to see the results of fighting
still in progress. But such delays were not for Mr. Gladstone,
who steamed in triumph down the Tyne, entranced with
the music of cheers, steam-whistles, and guns, and in the
unaccustomed incense informed a Newcastle audience
that " Jefferson Davis and other leaders of the South
have made an army; they are making, it appears, a navy;
and they have made, what is more than either, they have
made a nation." Perhaps a note from Palmerston, which
gave a slightly summarised account of the position, misled
him. Perhaps the music of

> Honour give to sterling worth,
> Genius better is than birth,
>   So here's success to Gladstone

C C

proved too much. Yet the mistake was easy, since British ears were attuned to the cries of 'nations struggling to be free.' But policy moved far more slowly. There was a pause, while colleagues wrote lengthy memoranda (and at least one dissented publicly from Gladstone). But Palmerston was still waiting for "some more decided events between the contending armies." The pause continued; and the news of Antietam arrived. The South began to flag. There was a cross-fire of memoranda in the Cabinet, which left Palmerston "very much inclined to change the opinion on which I wrote to you when the Confederates seemed to be carrying all before them, and I am very much come back to our original view of the matter, that we must continue merely to be lookers-on till the war shall have taken a more decided turn." The Tories and Clarendon both shared his view; and when the French proposed to intervene, he let his colleagues riddle the project under the angry eyes of Gladstone and Russell. So Palmerston toyed warily with intervention and withdrew.

His caution was no less on Mexico, where the unwearied Leopold pressed hard for recognition of his deserving son-in-law, so soon to be an Emperor. But while Maximilian stared at the Adriatic from the big windows of Miramar, Palmerston was quite immovable. He had no taste for Mexican adventure. For there was work enough for a Prime Minister while the Civil War dragged on, and trouble brewed in Poland, and the French sentries paced uneasily in Rome. But he found time for an indignant minute, when the Admiralty rejected Dr. Livingstone's advice upon medical stores for issue to cruisers on the West Coast: "So the reports of ignorant and jealous medical men at home who form their judgment upon theory are taken to overrule the practical experience of Dr. Livingstone, who has administered the medicine with remarkably successful result. If this is not red-tapeism, I know not what is." So Palmerston sat on among his boxes; and soon it was 1863.

The wild miscellany of his work continued—a gay note

to Russell on the Greek succession, acquainting him that
the Prime Minister would be " sorry to see a Hen Leuchtenberg on the perch from which we have excluded the cock
bird "; a gentleman who called to explain the blessings
of monarchy in Mexico; a friendly line to Minnie Shaftesbury, enclosing five thousand pounds and insisting on his
right to pay his half of her son's start in the world; a grave
essay for Leopold, explaining with a wealth of historical
illustration the drawbacks of Napoleon's predilection for a
general Congress to resettle everything; a call from Mr.
Lowe, who wanted to resign because he found promotion
slow; the never-ending talk in Parliament; and mountains
of red boxes.　Appearing for an instant in the *rôle* of Baron
Haussmann, he found time for a speech about the Thames
Embankment and its impressive prolongation in Queen
Victoria Street. He saw the Prince of Wales marry his
pretty Alexandra in St. George's Chapel and dropped a tear
at sight of the Queen watching wistfully in black from a
gallery. He dined the happy couple at Cambridge House,
was off to Scotland, made a speech at Glasgow as Lord
Rector, and was acclaimed all the way down the Clyde in
triumph on a paddle-box. At Edinburgh he scaled Arthur's
Seat, and in spite of gout found the ascent much what it
used to be when he lodged with Dugald Stewart sixty years
before. An old maid of Mrs. Stewart's was still alive,
and he called on her for copious recollections of ' young
Maister Henry.'

　He was not failing yet, and his pen could still do justice
to the scoundrelly slave-traders in Brazil : " The Conduct
of the Brazilian Government resembles that of a Billingsgate
fishwoman seized by a Policeman for some misdeeds. She
scolds, and kicks, and swears, and raves, and calls on the
mob to help her, and vows she won't go to the Lock-up
House . . . but when she feels the strong gripe of the
Policeman, and finds he is really in earnest, she goes as quiet
as a lamb, though still using foul-mouthed language at the
corner of each street." Scandal assaulted him that year,
and Mr. Delane even heard it " set to filthy tunes and sung
in the streets." For Palmerston, at seventy-eight, was

young enough to have a scandal. But when an eager
tale-bearer brought the delicious morsel to Disraeli for
Opposition use, that hollow voice exclaimed : " For God's
sake, do not let the people of England know—or he will
sweep the country." And a provincial poet could still
address him in slightly exhausting stanzas :

> Perennial blossom of a nation's hopes,
>   Guardian of England's honour and her fame,
> Friend of the people. . . .

or more topically,

> Old, with a heart as young as when at first
> In life's arena thou didst head the van . . .

The ode even included Em—

> the honoured partner of thy lot,
> The sharer of thy cares and of thy fame.

So Palmerston sat enthroned above the mid-Victorian
scene. It was *Dundreary's* year, when Mr. Tennyson in
an ecstasy of ethnology informed a listening world that

> Saxon and Norman and Dane are we,
> But all of us Danes in our welcome of thee,
>   Alexandra !

These gaieties seemed to afford a slight distraction from
the gloomy spectacle of the American war. Officially
the tension was less severe, though Palmerston retained
his old conviction that the States could never reunite.
Alabama pursued her lively course; and Lairds were
building, to the order of a gentleman in Paris, two remarkably
unpleasant vessels, whose bows were embellished with an
underwater ram seven feet in length. These soon became
a focus of feverish American diplomacy; and Russell, with
Palmerston's concurrence, detained them at the port. As
Lairds were reticent, the ships were seized; but since the
point of law was doubtful, Palmerston proposed the helpful
expedient of purchasing them for the British navy. The
magic of Gettysburg began to work, and his attitude

to Southern advocates in Parliament became politely discouraging.

His work that year was full of echoes. The Poles flung into insurrection; and an echo of old talks in 1831 came on the wind, when a young Foreign Secretary had met anxious patriots, felt vaguely sorry for them, but remembered from lessons learnt in Lieven's drawing-room that the Czar must not be tried too far. His line was still the same. He was less tender of the Czar, perhaps; but he was equally insistent on the sanctity of the Treaty of Vienna. It seemed a useful way of tempering Napoleon's ardour. For, as in 1831, the French were still mysteriously devoted to the Poles; and England followed at a cautious distance, although the Queen was terribly alarmed at the French language and proposals respecting Poland and thinks, "*we* must, on NO account, let ourselves be dragged into what *may* be a war with Germany." Lord Palmerston, it seemed, had used most alarming language and left her shuddering at the very thought of "*what*, if we are not *very* careful and very guarded in our expressions to France, we may find ourselves plunged into." The gentle Granville soothed her and reported a Cabinet, where Palmerston had been cautious on the question, though Russell was inclined to plunge. The Polish cause, indeed, was always Whiggish. The Whigs had pressed him hard to intervene in 1831; and now he let Russell pour his indignation into essays of enormous length delivered to the Russians. They did (he hoped) no harm; they did (the world could see) no good. But they helped to satisfy the overflowing moral sense of England in 1863, and kept pace with Napoleon's chivalry. For it was always judicious to attach a restraining Sancho Panza to that Quixote. A solitary excursion into Polish affairs might do endless harm; but with England at his elbow, his tone was more subdued. The part that England played to France was played, on a smaller stage, by Palmerston to Russell. His taste for Poles was always of the mildest; and when Majesty was nervous of a draft of Russell's, she expressed a significant hope that it should be seen by

Palmerston. The Poles struggled blindly on; the conscience of Europe stirred uneasily on paper; but when the French proposed a general Congress, England refused almost rudely. So the piece ended with the old dying fall; and silence shut down once again on Warsaw.

But though the air was old, some of the instrumentalists were unfamiliar; and as Palmerston sat in his place, a peculiarly strident note fell on his ear from Berlin, where an odd minister named von Bismarck defied his Parliament in Cromwellian attitudes. Lord Palmerston was not impressed. He even wrote a disrespectful minute to the Foreign Office about " the crazy minister at Berlin," and added that the Prussians would be well advised not to provoke Napoleon—" In the present state of the Prussian army, its system of drill, formation and movement the first serious encounter between it and the French would be little less disastrous to Prussia than the Battle of Jena." The forecast was injudicious. But Palmerston might be excused for overlooking Moltke, still in the shadows. The Horse Guards were not yet convinced; and he could write to Russell that " all military men who have seen the Prussian army at its annual reviews of late years have unequivocally declared that the French would walk over it and get without difficulty into Berlin." For it was still the slightly unregenerate army of Wrangel and Bonin. Almost as long as he could remember Prussia had been completely futile, a deferential satellite of Vienna; and after a lifetime spent in contemplation of the aimless monarchy of Frederick William IV. it was excusable to miss the first stirrings of *Realpolitik*. Besides, he had never really understood Germany. For there had been no Germany for him to understand.

It swam into his ken that year, when a king died in Denmark and bequeathed the Schleswig-Holstein Question with the fresh complication of a disputed succession. Here was another echo; and it rang in his ears with a rustle of old drafts of 1850, of ancient arguments on the Elbe Duchies, German pretensions, Danish claims, and all the wandering voices that haunted that wilderness of protocols.

The air had quavered on for years, with the Germanic Confederation in a plaintive minor and an accompaniment of
good advice from England. The Danes made constitu-
tions of every shape—with Schleswig, without Holstein,
with both and neither. A shifting dance of separation,
local autonomy, and reunion perplexed observers; and
while the King of Denmark assiduously rearranged his
embarrassing possessions, the German Diet moodily proclaimed that one or both of them formed part of Germany.
Early in 1863 it threatened violence, unless the King
withdrew his latest constitution. At this stage someone
raised the question in a miscellaneous debate, and Palmerston replied. He made a little joke about the instrument
of 1460; he insisted that " it is an important matter of
British policy to maintain the independence and integrity
of the Danish monarchy," with a frank admission that the
Germans were entitled to see a suitable form of government
in Holstein. But he denied their rights in Schleswig altogether, deplored the use of force, and told a story about
Talleyrand. Then he grew graver, painted a general conflagration, unmasked the German object—" the dream of a
German fleet and the wish to get Kiel as a German seaport "
—and uttered a warning :

> " The honourable Gentleman asks, what is the policy and
> the course of Her Majesty's Government with regard to that
> dispute. As I have already said, we concur entirely with him,
> and I am satisfied with all reasonable men in Europe, includ-
> ing those in France and Russia, in desiring that the independ-
> ence, the integrity, and the rights of Denmark may be main-
> tained. We are convinced—I am convinced at least—that if
> any violent attempt were made to overthrow those rights and
> interfere with that independence, those who made the attempt
> would find in the result, that it would not be Denmark alone
> with whom they would have to contend."

Designed to warn the Germans from a dangerous course,
the hint, with its odd personal reservation, was almost
guarded. But Prussia did not take hints. Perhaps,
indeed, the age of hints was over.

The speech was grave, but hardly so grave as later eyes have found it. It stated a strong conviction, but without announcing that Great Britain would treat an invasion of Denmark as a *casus belli*. That Palmerston did not regard it as a threat of war is plain from his own note to Russell six months later :

> " Schleswig is no part of Germany, and its invasion by German troops would be an act of war against Denmark, which would in my clear opinion entitle Denmark to our active military and naval support. But you and I could not announce such a determination without the concurrence of the Cabinet and the consent of the Queen."

But in July there had been no Cabinet; the Queen was not consulted on his statement; and her silence after the speech was made shows that one eager student of the problem did not regard it as a pledge. For she was watching anxiously; and while Schleswig-Holstein puzzled Europe, those dismal Duchies darkened her relation with the Prime Minister.

She had dreaded him at first. But he almost won her with the reality of his sympathy and his fatherly concern for Bertie; and he made such a " kind and feeling speech " on the Vote for the Memorial that she wrote to thank him and sent a volume of the Prince's speeches. She was quite concerned about him when Mr. Disraeli was at Osborne, hoped that no crisis would be forced on the Government, and said Lord Palmerston was grown very old. Mr. Disraeli said that his voice was as loud as ever. " Yes, and his handwriting," she cried, almost with pride, " did you ever see such a handwriting? So very clear and strong ! Nevertheless I see in him a great change, a very great change. His countenance is so changed." Here was a tone that she had rarely used. She leant upon him now, wanted him in the House of Commons, and deplored his absences. When the Vote for the Exhibition buildings went astray (and Mr. Disraeli, always a trifle apt to think of a Parliamentary debate in terms of a cavalry charge,

reported his despairing effort " with a few aides-de-camp.
My marshals even deserted me . . ."), she wrote with
genuine concern to Cambridge House that " Lord Palmerston's unavoidable absence had much to do with it. . . .
The Queen hopes Lord Palmerston is better." But Schleswig-Holstein rose like a cloud between them.

Her view of it was easy to guess. She moved through
the mazes of the question as easily as Mr. Browning through
the square at Florence—

a Hand,
Always above my shoulder, pushed me. . . .

Her guidance in the matter was more than usually plain.
Could she not remember a loved voice exclaiming over
The Times, " *Wieder ein ganz infamer Artikel gegen Preussen;
er wird ungeheuren Schaden thun* " ? A visit to Coburg in
the summer revived her deepest feelings. She had warned
the Cabinet before she left against Danish perfidy. But
the sight of Germany strengthened her conviction. The
King of Prussia came to see her; and Granville reported
her " up in her stirrups, very German, and determined, if
necessary, to resist the Prime Minister." She revealed her
mind to Gladstone in the autumn. Not yet averse to
Palmerston, she still preferred his judgment to Russell's,
but disclosed " an immense interest in Germany, her
recollections of the Prince's sentiments being in that, as in
other matters, a barometer to govern her sympathies and
affections." They spoke of Schleswig-Holstein, " in which
she is intensely interested, because the Prince thought it a
case of great justice on the side rather opposite to that of
Palmerston and the Government policy. She spoke about
this with intense earnestness, and said she considered it a
legacy from him."

She was so lonely now. Stockmar was dead; and she
clung almost convulsively to Albert's wishes. Soon she
was urging them " *most* strongly to do *nothing* without
consultation with the other *Powers,* but *especially* with
Germany." What could a minister's opinion avail against
such ghostly counsel? So they drifted—the Queen, her

memories, the Danes, Lord Palmerston, and Bismarck—
into 1864.

As the year opened, they were all deep in their natural
avocations—the Prussians moving troops, the Queen composing a memorandum for the Cabinet to show that Denmark was quite in the wrong, Russell issuing invitations
to a Conference, and Palmerston writing with perfect
freedom to his sovereign that he could " quite understand
her reluctance to take any active part in measures in any
conflict against Germany, but he is sure your Majesty will
never forget that you are Sovereign of Great Britain, and
that the honour of your Majesty's Crown and the interests
of your Majesty's dominions will always be the guide of
your Majesty's conduct, as they must always be of your
Majesty's responsible advisers." He added genially that
" the Minor States of Germany are entitled to every just
consideration, but they have no exclusive privilege of
violence, injustice, perfidy, and wrong," making the point
a little plainer on the next day by writing to substitute
" peculiar " for " exclusive." For he was fastidious even
in invective. A stern reply informed him that her concern
for peace was purely British and that " no feeling for.
Germany could ever make her view of an international
question otherwise than as it might affect the interests of
the people of England." Lord Granville hurried off to
Broadlands, found him extremely gouty and rather irritable, and extracted a comforting assurance " that there
was no question whatever of England going to war," adding
in his report to Osborne that the Prime Minister's gout was
not unconnected with his tone in correspondence. A little
calmer, she addressed a positive rebuke to Ernst Coburg,
but provoked a further instalment of Lord Palmerston's
opinions by her comments on a draft despatch. He told
her roundly that the Germans were " acting like a strong
man who thinks he has got a weak man in a corner," and
that every impartial and right-minded man in her dominions
thought the same. But the despatch was amended by the

Cabinet; and the soft-footed Granville, known as ' Puss '
to some at least of his colleagues, sent a satisfactory account
to Osborne. For this monument of tact employed himself
in endless tip-toeings from Downing Street to Osborne,
pressing the royal view discreetly and armed with authority
to use the Queen's name " whenever he thinks it may be
useful." Her anxieties were dreadful. For though she
was sometimes sure of Russell, " Lord Palmerston alarms
him and overrules him "—and the Prime Minister had
made his opinions far too plain. They were unlikely to
find favour with a sovereign who wrote that month to a
daughter in Berlin: " My heart and sympathies are all
German. I condemn the Treaty of '52 completely, but
once signed we cannot upset it without first trying (*not* by
war) to maintain it, and this adored Papa would have felt
and did feel. . . ." Yet she could still express relief at
Palmerston's avoidance of a winter crossing to the Isle of
Wight, " as she dreaded his catching cold, or bringing on
a fresh attack of gout, when all his strength and vigour are
required to meet the fatigues of the Session."

His views were clear enough. But as the guns went off
in Schleswig and the Danes backed towards the redoubts
of Düppel, he was frankly disinclined for war unless the
French would join, since he could hardly oppose a British
army of 20,000 men to 200,000 Austrians and Prussians.
The French were far from helpful. England's desertion
in the case of Poland still rankled; and M. Drouyn de
Lhuys had concluded with gloomy malice *de l'attitude qu'il
a observée dans l'affaire de Pologne, que, dans les contestations
internationales où il est appelé à élever la voix, il entend
écarter absolument la pensée d'appuyer par des actes ses
efforts diplomatiques.* The solitary bait to draw the French
was Rhenish Prussia. But Palmerston was indisposed to
cast it, since that acquisition would endanger Holland,
Belgium, and ultimately Great Britain. So he inclined to
caution, with a large output of Russell's most eloquent
despatches, while the guns boomed before the Danish lines
and Bismarck commented a little brutally on *la productivité*

du Foreign Office. But things were slightly easier at Windsor, though he alarmed his sovereign by announcing that his blood would boil if Austrian warships were to pass up-Channel to attack the Danes. Indeed, premonitory symptoms began to appear, when Russell smuggled off a telegram proposing a joint Anglo-Franco-Russian naval demonstration in the Baltic to encourage Denmark. The Queen was desperate and wrote helplessly to Leopold about " the conduct of those two dreadful old men." But her elderly tormentors were effectually restrained by the ensuing Cabinet (and left a little rueful by their lack of "colleagues like those who sat in Pitt's "), though Palmerston broke out again a few weeks later with a cheerful intimation to the Austrian ambassador—" not as between an English minister and the Austrian ambassador, but as between Palmerston and Apponyi "—that if an Austrian squadron should pass the coast, a stronger British squadron would shadow it with suitable instructions. He added blandly that this communication was not a threat, but simply " a friendly reminder of consequences which might follow a possible course of action." This was a frank defiance of the Cabinet —he reported candidly to Russell that " I felt so little satisfied with the decision of the Cabinet on Saturday, that I determined to make a notch off my own bat." The run was scored; for though the Cabinet was deeply shocked and withheld its confirmation, the Austrians bowed to the warning and waited respectfully off Deal.

But in the spring the firing died away. The Danes were beaten, and diplomacy assembled in London to give a decent form to the *fait accompli*. The Queen was still disturbed. The Prime Minister advised the strictest caution in her *entourage* as to expressions of opinion on Danish matters; and an angry note informed her uncle that " Pilgerstein is gouty, and extremely impertinent in his communications of different kinds to me." That sage informed her that he was writing by the same messenger " to Pilgerstein. I do it rarely, but I know that it generally makes an impression on him; he is to be feared." The

impression, in this instance, may be doubted, since his
letter insisted bluntly that " my beloved niece the Queen "
was " by no means partial to Prussia." Lord Palmerston
knew better. Her public actions had been impeccable;
but she had made no secret of her sympathies. That
shadow fell between them now, although he retrieved a
little of his position in the summer by appearing " very
sensible, wonderfully clear-headed and fully alive to the
extreme dangers of the situation." But she had suffered
agonies; and they could wrangle quite in the old manner
over a Church appointment, with the Prime Minister writing
tartly of " a reference of a recommendation by one of your
Majesty's responsible advisers to the judgment of your
Majesty's irresponsible advisers," and the Queen in arms
again and mounted on her dignity and more surprised than
ever at the tone of Lord Palmerston's remarks. But she
could still " rely implicitly on Lord Palmerston to prevent
any hasty and ill-advised reduction in our Army or Navy ";
and they united in disapproval of Mr. Gladstone's perilous
approach to manhood suffrage.

Mr. Gladstone, indeed, was something of a trial that
year. His sudden declaration on Reform provoked an
amiable thunderbolt from Cambridge House. All the old
arguments were repeated—the perils of democracy, the
electorate submerged in a flood of pauper ignorance, the
control of working men by Trade Union leaders—concluding with a friendly menace : " Your speech may win
Lancashire for you, though that is doubtful, but I fear it
will tend to lose England for you." Gladstone replied at
length, construed his pledge with all its Gladstonian reserves
and qualifications, and almost defiantly reprinted it in
pamphlet form. He was as troublesome as ever on Estimates. For Palmerston retained his faith in the pacific
virtues of armaments; he had described the purchased
rams as " peace-keepers " and informed the Foreign Office
(with a happy side-glance at a terrifying buffalo known to
the natives as a ' peace-maker,' whose hide someone had
given him) that " our Peace Makers are our Armstrongs and

Whitworths and our engineers." But Gladstone pelted
him with letters on economy, receiving massive answers on
the Volunteers, embodying the stern reproof : " If I have
in any degree been fortunate enough to have obtained some
share of the goodwill and confidence of my fellow countrymen, it has been because I have rightly understood the
feelings and opinion of the nation. . . . Of that popularity
I sincerely wish you the most ample share." But when
the Tories pressed on Schleswig-Holstein, Palmerston could
still ask genially for " a great gun to follow Disraeli—
would you be ready to follow him ? " The need was sore.
For Mr. Disraeli had charged home, and the Prime Minister
after a rather weak defence took refuge in the marvels of
Gladstonian finance. The Government scraped through by
eighteen votes; and after the division he was seen dis-
appearing up the stairs in the direction of the Ladies'
Gallery. It was three in the morning. But Em was waiting for him; and in the summer dawn the old lovers
embraced.

The House was arduous that year, although the crowd
in Palace Yard cheered him as he went down to speak on
Denmark. An Under-Secretary in a scrape still brought
him into action (and left a young relation wondering " why
did old Pam sacrifice himself for him, and why did he not
accept his resignation? He is too quixotic about his
friends. . . .") His life outside the House was still more
varied. He saw Confederate emissaries and exasperated
them by the bland emptiness of his replies; he soothed an
excited Southern deputation with the sedative lyric,

> They who in quarrels interpose
> Will often wipe a bloody nose.

He was at Stafford House, when all the world met Garibaldi. The Queen was gravely concerned at the old
guerillero's triumph. Even the Cabinet debated what to
do with Garibaldi. " Do? " said a cheerful Premier.
" Oh, let's marry him to the rich Miss ——." Someone
objected that he had a wife. " Oh, then," said Palmer-

ston, "we'll get —— to explain her away." Can it be
doubted that his eye fixed Gladstone?

But London was not enough. He was off speech-making
in the provinces, opened a railway in the Midlands, unveiled
a statue in the West, and spoke in Yorkshire. That autumn
he was eighty; and on his birthday the Prime Minister
started from Broadlands by an early train, rode round the
forts at Portsmouth, and was home by six o'clock of an
October evening. But he was older now. The smile was
brave, but the old face was growing tired. His papers
were a perpetual torment, and reading someone's writing
was "like running Penknives into one's Eyes." Even at
Tiverton, when he went down to see the races, they began
to find the green coat rather rusty, and the white top-hat
began to age. But in one pair of eyes he was still as young
as ever, where Em folded a letter from him and put it with
the rest—recording innumerable trains to be met by the
barouche if fine, by the chariot if wet—and wrote her
answer, a little shaky now, to "My dearest love."

So one more year—his eighty-first—opened serenely.
The House met in February, and one night the Speaker
came to dinner. His host began with two plates of turtle
soup, an ample plate of cod and oyster sauce, a *pâté* and
two singularly greasy *entrées*; then he grew serious and
attacked a plate of mutton, a slice of ham that struck his
guest as "the largest and, to my mind, the hardest slice
of ham that ever figured on the table of a nobleman,"
concluding with a portion of pheasant. The Speaker was
alarmed and, meeting the Prime Minister at his levée,
expressed an anxious hope that he was taking better care
of himself. "Oh! I do indeed," replied that cheerful
portent. "I very often take a cab at night, and if you
have both windows open, it is almost as good as walking
home."

Lord Palmerston, at eighty, governed his country still.
A new world was waiting; and he used to say, "Gladstone
will soon have it all his own way; and whenever he gets

my place, we shall have strange doings." The stir was
in the air. Almost, as Mr. Bright had said, they could
hear the beating of its wings. Once more the little wind
that runs before the day breathed across England; and
an age was ending, as engineers at Sheffield consecrated
the new sanctities of Trade Unions with the new tyranny
of force and 'rattening.' Beyond the sea Prussians and
Austrians began to glare at one another in Schleswig-
Holstein; Moltke was studying the railways that led to
Sadowa; and in the autumn Bismarck called on a bewildered Emperor at Biarritz and heard the big Biscayan
rollers pounding the coast below the Villa Eugénie, as they
talked of Venice. The stage was slowly clearing for Sedan.
But Palmerston sat on. He was not particularly averse to
a strong Germany. Russia must be resisted somehow,
and why not by Prussia? As to the Duchies, " it was the
Wolf and the Lamb from the beginning, and no wonder
that two wolves were too much for one lamb . . . and
the two wolves having grabbed up what they wanted
would hardly be expected to give up their prey out of a
mere sense of what may be called posthumous justice."
The harm was done, and the prey might just as well be
swallowed by the Prussians, although he glanced a shade
maliciously at the Queen's new concern for Schleswig-
Holstein—" The fact is, as far as the Queen is concerned,
that so long as the injustice committed appeared calculated
to benefit Germany and the Germans, it was all right and
proper; but now that an example is about to be set of
extinguishing petty states like Coburgh, her sense of right
and wrong has become wonderfully keen, and her mind
revolts at the idea of consequences which grow naturally
from the proceedings she approved of." That shadow had
quite come between them now and his " strong anti-German
feeling " stayed in her mind. Before the year was out, she
wrote a cruel epitaph to Brussels :

" . . . poor Lord Palmerston, alias Pilgerstein. It is very
striking, and is another link with the past—the happy past—
which is gone, and in many ways he is a great loss. He had

many valuable qualities, though many bad ones, and we had, God knows ! terrible trouble with him about Foreign Affairs. Still, as Prime Minister he managed affairs at home well, and behaved to me well.   But I *never* liked him, or could ever the least respect him, nor could I forget his conduct on certain occasions to my Angel.   He was very vindictive, and *personal* feelings influenced his political acts very much.   Still, he is a loss. . . .''

But as 1865 slipped past, he could still write comfortingly on the navy, and the new forts at Quebec (in case the Americans gave trouble), and the nonsense talked by Irish members about Tenant Right—he called it ' Landlord's Wrong '—and the troublesome affair of Sir Alexander Cockburn's peerage, on which she yielded with quite a charming statement that she was " naturally at all times unwilling to refuse to accede to measures which her Prime Minister informs her are important, either for the support of the Government or for the transaction of business in the House of Lords."

That year he had other pastimes.   There were Cabinets on Estimates, which Mr. Gladstone found " almost as rough as any of the roughest times "; and warnings to be sent to Mr. Gladstone about his Church opinions; and Estimates settled " at the dagger's point."   But though the struggle swayed in Downing Street, he was loyal to his odd subordinate.   He told Lord Shaftesbury that " Gladstone has never behaved to me as a colleague in such a way as to demand from me any consideration." But he did his best to keep him in the University seat at Oxford (with a sly conviction that " he is a dangerous man; keep him in Oxford, and he is partially muzzled; but send him elsewhere, and he will run wild "). And Gladstone could forgive him a great deal for his service to Italy.   That year, indeed, when it was all over, he wrote to Panizzi :

" *Ei fu!* Death has indeed laid low the most towering antlers in all the forest.   No man in England will more sincerely mourn Lord Palmerston than you.   Your warm heart,
D D

your long and close friendship with him, and your sense of
all he had said and done for Italy, all so bound you to him
that you will deeply feel his loss; as for myself I am
stunned. . . ."

But Parliament sat on, and the Prime Minister was still
in his place. Perhaps he was not there so often now.
The Tories whispered that he had begun to fail and only
looked in for a few minutes to say a word or two and keep
his name in the newspapers. But they still caught his
voice distinctly and did their best to laugh, when he made
his little jokes. There was one (young Thomas Hardy
heard it from the Strangers' Gallery) about Mr. Lowe
taking a low view. . . . But he was quite eloquent when
Mr. Cobden died, and breathed a pious sentence on the
opinions of Dugald Stewart and Mr. Huskisson, his own
sponsors in the Free Trade faith. One July afternoon he
made a formal little speech about the services rendered by
members in Private Business : it was his last. That
month the House dissolved, and he was off to Tiverton for
one more brush with the indomitable Rowcliffe. There
was the usual handshake afterwards, and the crowd at
the hustings found that his voice had its old strength.
Once more the country voted on the simple issue of ' Pam
for Premier,' with an added impulse from the strange
stirrings of Mr. Gladstone's new democracy. The verdict
was unaltered ; and the reign of Palmerston continued.

THE last fight was won, and the old champion went into the country to wait for his eighty-first birthday. Alone of all the things he had waited for—the coach from Harrow, a seat in Parliament, office, Emily Cowper, the fall of Metternich, his tit for tat with Johnny Russell, the Premiership, news from Sebastopol, the end of Mr. Gladstone's speeches—it never came. He was not well that year. Even Majesty, far away among her memories in Coburg, had been solicitous; but she got little by her enquiries beyond his humble duty, thanks for her gracious mention, and a sturdy assertion that he " deems it a duty which he owes to your Majesty, to do his best to maintain that health which is essential for the performance of the duties of the post which your Majesty has been graciously pleased to confer upon him."

They were all at Brocket, and he was more than usually charming. There were two young couples in the house; and as he watched them, he drew Em's arm into his own and said so sweetly : " Here we are, three pairs of lovers." But he was looking ill; and something of his exhaustion crept into a reply, when they were looking at the stars one night, and someone expressed a wish to visit them in the hereafter. He thought it possible, but inclined to the opinion that there would first be " a time of repose after the action and fatigue of this life."

So the summer passed away, and the leaves fell. He was no better. One morning in October, with Parliament and the autumn Cabinets in prospect, he was gravely testing his strength, when a chance witness at a window saw a Prime Minister of eighty cross the drive without his hat, deliberately climb a railing twice, and go into the house

again. He was still bravely talkative when Em's eye was
on him, quoted Virgil, even told them a story of his fatal
proclivity for stone-throwing seventy years before at
Harrow; but as the old man told it, his laughter was a trifle
uncontrolled and showed a touch of weakness. He still
worked at his papers, writing to colleagues, urging Mr.
Gladstone to overcome his invincible repugnance to the
expenditure of public money and sanction an increase of
establishment at the Privy Council Office (although he had
his own moments of economy, and declined to spend £20,000
on a house at Copenhagen for the Prince and Princess of
Wales). He kept a singularly watchful eye upon the
Fenians, proposed to send an additional regiment of cavalry
to Ireland, was eloquent upon the merits of that arm in
agrarian disturbances, shrewdly opined that "a Fenian put
suddenly on horseback . . . would not be a cavalry
soldier," and was cheerfully prepared to override the
Commander-in-Chief in Ireland who "has been accustomed
to walk over everything and everybody opposed to him."
Was it not half a century since Palmerston had broken
his first lance with a Commander-in-Chief? He worked on
at his red boxes, pressing the War Department to improve
the defences of Quebec and maintain adequate supplies of
munitions in Canada; and eight days later, on October 11,
he was writing to Black Rod, offering the somewhat threadbare consolation on the defeat of a relative that "casualties
will happen in Parliamentary warfare, and it is not always
the most deserving that heads the Poll," and blandly
refusing the Bath on the ground of his imperfect knowledge of the claims of candidates. The letter was as brisk
as usual : he never signed another.

On the next day (it was a Thursday) Lady Palmerston
found him poorly; but they drove out together. Autumn
was drawing on, and he came home with a cold. Easy
as ever, he "was 1½ hours undressing and dawdling, and
would take his bath as usual." The lapse was fatal, and
he almost died that night. But he was still alive on Sunday,
making little jokes about his medicine. Beyond the Tweed

a royal letter-writer sat at Balmoral and conveyed the sad intelligence to a beloved uncle. She showed a mild regret, but bore the impending blow with calm, resolved sedately to send for Lord Russell if the worst happened, and was gratified to think that she would not need to hasten her departure by more than three or four days. This said, she plunged into bright memories of " *our dear Verlobungstag,* 26 years ago ! " Lord Palmerston had other thoughts that day, since one of his doctors felt the moment opportune for a vigorous exposition of the truths of revealed religion. Propounded in the form of questions, these elicited from the Prime Minister a brief, but gratifying, affirmative. " Oh certainly," he said; and to a further enquiry, " Oh surely." That succinct reply to ill-timed ardour must always seem, in the perfection of its courtesy, the last word of the Eighteenth Century.

Refreshed by these debates, he rallied upon a wild dietary of mutton and apple tart. He breakfasted on Monday off mutton chops and a half-glass of old port, expressing a gentle wonder that he " should have lived so long without discovering what a good breakfast it is." But he wavered on the next day, although the news of royal enquiries could still elicit a murmur of : " It is very kind of her Majesty; I am much better." The autumn day was fading, as he lay waiting in the room at Brocket, still waiting—with only two more days to wait—for his eighty-first birthday. It was a quiet room, where his poor weary Emily sat waiting also; until it fell silent on the morning of October 18, 1865, and the last candle of the Eighteenth Century was out.

AUTHORITIES

GENERAL

Ashley, Evelyn. *Life of Viscount Palmerston*. 2 vols. 1879.
Ashley, Evelyn. *Life of Viscount Palmerston, 1846–1865*. 2 vols. 1876.
Bulwer, Sir H. Lytton. *Life of Viscount Palmerston, 1784–1846*. 3 vols. 1870–4.
Francis, G. H. *Opinions and Policy of Viscount Palmerston*. 1852.
Lorne, Marquis of. *Lord Palmerston*. 1892.
Marx, Karl. *Story of the Life of Lord Palmerston*. 1899.
Ritchie, J. E. *Life and Times of Viscount Palmerston*. 2 vols. 1866.
Sanders, Lloyd C. *Life of Viscount Palmerston*. 1888.
Trollope, Anthony. *Lord Palmerston*. 1882.
[No references are given for citations from these authorities.]

PRELUDE

I.

THE YEAR 1784.

Boswell, J. *Life of Johnson* (ed. Birrell). 1901. VI.
Gibbon, E. *Miscellaneous Works*. 1796. I.
Graves, A., and Cronin, W. V. *History of the Works of Sir Joshua Reynolds*. 4 vols. 1899–1901.
Lecky, W. E. H. *History of England in the Eighteenth Century*. 1913. V.
Macquoid, P. *The Age of Satinwood*. 1908.
Reynolds, Sir Joshua. *Discourses*. 1842.
Walpole, Horace. *Letters* (ed. Toynbee). 1905. XIII.
Ward, H., and Roberts, W. *George Romney*. 2 vols. 1904.
Wright, T. *Works of Gillray*. 1851.
Wright, T. *Caricature History of the Georges*. 1867.

BIRTH.

[All previous writers, following Ashley's *Life*, have stated that Palmerston was born at Broadlands. The absence of any baptismal entry at Romsey Abbey suggested doubts of this tradition; and a search revealed that he was baptised on November 23, 1784, at St. Margaret's, Westminster. This evidence of a London birthplace is corroborated by the discovery of a pedigree in the Broadlands Papers, which states that he was born in Park Street. It appears from the Westminster Rate Books that his father was at that time in occupation of No. 4, Park Street, Westminster (now No. 20, Queen Anne's Gate), of which he subsequently acquired a lease from Christ's Hospital.]

II.

THE TEMPLE FAMILY.

Dictionary of National Biography, s.v. Sir William Temple (1555–1627), Sir William Temple (1628–1699), Sir John Temple (1600–1677), Henry Temple, 1st Viscount Palmerston (1673–1757).

2ND VISCOUNT PALMERSTON.

Boswell, J. *Op. cit.* V. 88, VI, 66.
Croker, J. W. *Correspondence.* 1885. I. 17.
D'Arblay, Madame. *Diary and Letters* (ed. Barrett). 1893. I. 110.
Dictionary of National Biography, s.v. 2nd Viscount Palmerston (1739–1802).
Fonblanque, E. B. de. *Life and Correspondence of Rt. Hon. John Burgoyne.* 1876. 389.
Gibbon, E. *Letters.* 1896. I. 50, 283.
Graves, A., and Cronin, W. V. *Op. cit.*
Miller, Lady. *Poetical Amusements at a Villa near Bath.* 1775. I. 12, 52–7, 60–3.
New Foundling Hospital for Wit. 1784. I. 51–9.
Walpole, Horace. *Catalogue of Royal and Noble Authors* (ed. Park). 1806. V. 327–8.
Walpole, Horace. *Letters* (ed. Toynbee). 1904. IX. 134, 146, 202, 269, 283, 376; X. 222; XII. 366; Supplement II. 148.

III.

CHILDHOOD.

1. UNPUBLISHED SOURCES.

Palmerston. *Letters to His Mother* (seven bundles).   Broadlands Papers.

> First letters.   Tour in 1794.
> Christmas letter.   French and Italian letters.
>   Tax on hair powder.

2. PUBLISHED SOURCES.

See authorities for I.

Browning, O. *Despatches of Earl Gower, together with the Diary of Viscount Palmerston in France during July and August, 1791.* 1885.
Minto, Countess of. *Life and Letters of Sir Gilbert Elliot, first Earl of Minto :* 1751–1806. 18, I. 97–8, 105–6, 111, 123, 135, 147, 157, 166–7, 204, 277, 281, 298, 311–2, 326, 331, 337, 364, 393; II. 6.
Walpole, Horace. *Letters* (ed. Toynbee). 1905. XIV. and XV.
Windham, W. *The Windham Papers.* 1913. I. 98.
Young, Arthur. *Travels in France* (ed. Betham-Edwards). 1913.

IV.

HARROW.

1. UNPUBLISHED SOURCES.

Harrow School MS. Bill Books : 1791–9 and 1800–2. Vaughan Library, Harrow.

.

Harrow Speech Bills : 1780–1829. Vaughan Library, Harrow.
Palmerston. *Letters to His Mother.* Broadlands Papers.

Arrival at Harrow.
Cake and cross bows.
Verses on the Nile.
Ferret.

War news.
Monitor.
Earliest mention of Eton *v.*
Harrow (May 29, 1796).

2. PUBLISHED SOURCES.

Howson, E. W., and Warner, G. T. *Harrow School.* 1898. 65,
165, 171.
Minto, Countess of. *Op. cit.* I. 107; III. 13.

EDINBURGH.

1. UNPUBLISHED SOURCES.

Palmerston. *Letter to Lord Pelham,* July 1, 1802. B.M. Add.
MSS. 37726, 18.
Letters to His Mother. Broadlands Papers.

Mrs. Dugald Stewart.
Chemistry.
Debates.

Reading.
Poodle.
Highland tour.

Palmerston. *MS. Notebook* (Political Economy) 1802–3. Broadlands Papers.
Temple, W. *Letters to Lady Palmerston :* July 23, 1801 ; June 1
and July 14, 1802. Vaughan Library, Harrow.

2. PUBLISHED SOURCES.

Dictionary of National Biography, s.b. Dugald Stewart (1753–
1828).
Minto, Countess of. *Op. cit.* III. 220, 231, 233, 235, 246, 255.
Stewart, Dugald. *Lectures on Political Economy.* 2 vols. 1855–6.

CAMBRIDGE.

1. UNPUBLISHED SOURCES.

Palmerston, 2nd Viscount. *Letter to Pitt.* October, 1798. *Record
Office.* Chatham Papers, 165.
Palmerston. *Letters to His Mother.* Broadlands Papers.

Nobleman's gown.
Wine and furniture.
Debating society.

Napoleon.
Sister's portrait.
Wales.

Palmerston. *Letters to Hon. E. Temple* (one bundle). Broadlands
Papers. (Volunteer captain, 1803).
Letters to Hon. F. Temple (one bundle). Broadlands
Papers.

" Cantab."

Pitt-Fox debate.

St. John's College. *MS. Admission Book.*
St. John's College. *Portraits of Dr. Craven and Dr. Wood.*

2. PUBLISHED SOURCES.

Baker, T. *History of the College of St. John the Evangelist.* 1869.
II. 1090.
Dictionary of National Biography, s.v. James Harris, 1st Earl of
Malmesbury.

Malmesbury, Earl of. *Diaries and Correspondence of First Earl of Malmesbury.* 1844. IV. 412.

Minto, Countess of. *Op. cit.* III. 118, 233, 343–4, 380.

Mullinger, J. B. *St. John's College.* 1901.

Smith, G. C. M. *Lists of Past Occupants of Rooms in St. John's College.* 1895.

V.

FIRST ELECTIONS.

1. UNPUBLISHED SOURCES.

Palmerston. *Letter to Lord Hardwicke.* October, 1806. B.M. Add. MSS. 35424, 72.

Letters to Hon. F. Temple. Broadlands Papers. November 6, 1806. (Horsham Election).

2. PUBLISHED SOURCES.

Byron, Lord. *Hours of Idleness, s.v. Granta, a Medley.* 1807.

Creevey, T. *The Creevey Papers* (ed. Maxwell). 1912. 75–7.

Wright, T. *Works of Gillray.* 1851.

ADMIRALTY.

1. UNPUBLISHED SOURCES.

Palmerston. *Letters to Hon. F. Temple.* Broadlands Papers. 1809. (Prospect of War Office.)

2. PUBLISHED SOURCES.

Airlie, Mabell, Countess of. *Lady Palmerston and Her Times.* 1922. I. 33–9.

Hansard. *Parliamentary Debates.* 1808. February 3.

Malmesbury, Earl of. *Op. cit.* IV. 387.

WAR OFFICE

I.

ARMY ADMINISTRATION.

Fortescue, J. *History of the British Army.* 1915. IV. 871–916.

Wheeler, O. *The War Office, Past and Present.* 1914.

II.

1809.

1. UNPUBLISHED SOURCES.

Palmerston. First letter. *Record Office.* W.O. 4. 305.

General letters. *Record Office.* W.O. 4. 208.

Militia circular. B.M. Add. MSS., 35677, 72.

Compassionate List. B.M. Add. MSS., 35648, 370.

Knighton. B.M. Add. MSS. 37309, 327.

2. PUBLISHED SOURCES.

Creevey, T. *Op. cit.* 129.

1810.

1. UNPUBLISHED SOURCES.

Palmerston. Dispute with Commander-in-Chief.
B.M. Add. MSS. 38194, 1–16.
B.M. Add. MSS. 38245, 154–283.
B.M. Add. MSS. 38246, 11, 13.
B.M. Add. MSS. 38361, 3–10, 154–191, 195–232.
Letters and minutes. *Record Office.* W.O. 4. 210.

2. PUBLISHED SOURCES.

Hansard. *Parliamentary Debates.* 1810. February 26; March 1, 14, 23.

1811.

1. UNPUBLISHED SOURCES.

Palmerston. Army Chaplains. *Record Office.* W.O. 4. 345.
General letters. *Record Office.* W.O. 4. 211–3.
Verses. *Lady Cowper's Album.* Broadlands Papers.

2. PUBLISHED SOURCES.

Airlie, Mabell, Countess of. *Op. cit.* I. 28.
Creevey, T. *Op. cit.* 148.
Hansard. *Parliamentary Debates.* 1811. March 4, May 23.
Lieven, Princess. *Diary* (ed. Temperley). 1925. 163.
Minto, Countess of. *Life and Letters of Sir Gilbert Elliot, First Earl of Minto :* 1807–14. 1880. 331.

1812.

Creevey, T. *Op. cit.* 157.
Hansard. *Parliamentary Debates.* 1812. February 22, March 23.

1813.

1. UNPUBLISHED SOURCES.

Palmerston. Invalid Office dispute. B.M. Add. MSS., 38151, 249; 38379, 233.
Greek Light Infantry, B.M. Add. MSS., 36543, 113.

2. PUBLISHED SOURCES.

Hansard. *Parliamentary Debates.* March 1, 8, 15; June 23.
Wellington, Duke of. *Supplementary Despatches.* 1861. VIII. 73.

III.

1814.

Creevey, T. *Op. cit.* 189–204.
Hansard. *Parliamentary Debates.* June 24; July 11 and 13.
Wellington, Duke of. *Supplementary Despatches.* 1862. IX. 154–157.

1815.

1. UNPUBLISHED SOURCES.

Palmerston. General letters. *Record Office.* W.O. 4. 221–2, 345.
Invalid Office dispute. B.M. Add. MSS. 38379, 233.

2. PUBLISHED SOURCES.

Anon. *New Whig Guide.* 1819.
Creevey, T. *Op. cit.* 205–239.
Croker, J. W. *Op. cit.* I. 58, 256.
Hansard. *Parliamentary Debates.* June 2, 15; July 8.
Parker, E. S. *Sir Robert Peel.* 1891. I. 168.

IV.

PARIS IN 1815.

Airlie, Mabell, Countess of. *Op. cit.* I. 95–7. (Palmerston's letter of August 30, 1815, misdated September, 1821.)
Croker, J. W. *Op. cit.* I. 61–71.
Metternich, Prince de. *Mémoires, Documents, et Écrits Divers.* 1880. I. 210, 322; II. 525.
Palmerston, Viscount. *Selections from Private Journals of Tours in France in 1815 and 1818.* 1871.
Phillips, W. Alison. *The Confederation of Europe.* 1914.
Wellington, Duke of. *Supplementary Despatches.* 1864. XI. 98–9, 175–7.

V.

1816.

1. UNPUBLISHED SOURCES.

Palmerston. Irish staff. B.M. Add. MSS. 38264, 69.
  French tour. Broadlands Papers, Letters to Hon. E. Temple.

2. PUBLISHED SOURCES.

Fortescue, J. *Op. cit.* 1923. XI. 33.
Hansard. *Parliamentary Debates.* February 14, 26.

1817.

1. UNPUBLISHED SOURCES.

Palmerston. Bridge tolls. B.M. Add. MSS. 38267, 71.

2. PUBLISHED SOURCES.

Hansard. *Parliamentary Debates.* March 10; May 8, 12; June 19.
Parker, C. S. *Op. cit.* I. 256.

1818.

1. UNPUBLISHED SOURCES.

Palmerston. Watchword. B.M. Add. MSS. 38566, 85–7.

2. PUBLISHED SOURCES.

Creevey, T. *Op. cit.* 272.
Fortescue, J. *Op. cit.* 1923. XI. 54.
Greville, C. C. F. *Journal of the Reigns of King George IV. and King William IV.* 1875. I. 6–7.
Hansard. *Parliamentary Debates.* March 2, 3, 6.
Palmerston, Viscount. *Selections from Private Journals of Tours in France in 1815 and 1818.* 1871.
Wellington, Duke of. *Supplementary Despatches.* 1861. XII. 711–8.

1819.

1. UNPUBLISHED SOURCES.

Palmerston. Patronage. B.M. Add. MSS. 38194, 46.

2. PUBLISHED SOURCES.

Creevey, T. *Op. cit.* 296.
Egan, P. *Life in London.* 1820 (ed. 1904). 206–16.
Greville, C. C. F. *Op. cit.* I. 22.
Hansard. *Parliamentary Debates.* May 7, December 2.

1820.

1. UNPUBLISHED SOURCES.

Cowper, Lady. *Letters to Hon. F. Lamb.* Broadlands Papers.
 August 17. (Queen Caroline.) November 23. (Lord Cowper.)
Palmerston. Cambridge patronage.
 B.M. Add. MSS. 38194, 61.
 B.M. Add. MSS. 38194, 66.

2. PUBLISHED SOURCES.

Creevey, T. *Op. cit.* 296–8; 305–339.
Croker, J. W. *Op. cit.* I. 157–179.
Egan, P. *Op. cit.* 96–9; 190–1; 231–46; 264–5.
Greville, C. C. F. *Op. cit.* I. 24–7.
Hansard. *Parliamentary Debates.* May 16; June 2, 14.
Lockhart, J. G. *Life of Sir Walter Scott.* 1837. IV. 366.

1821.

1. UNPUBLISHED SOURCES.

Cowper, Lady. *Letters to Hon. F. Lamb.* Broadlands Papers.
 May 3. (Hume and reduction.)
Palmerston. Army reductions. B.M. Add. MSS. 38289, 159.
 Refusal of peerage. B.M. Add. MSS. 38194, 83.

2. PUBLISHED SOURCES.

Creevey, T. *Op. cit.* 359, 363.
Croker, J. W. *Op. cit.* I. 196.
Greville, C. C. F. *Op. cit.* I. 43.
Hansard. *Parliamentary Debates.* March 12; April 6, 30.

1822.

Creevey, T. *Op. cit.* 383.
Croker, J. W. *Op. cit.* I. 219, 224–6, 230–1, 247, 250.
Greville, C. C. F. *Op. cit.* I. 55.
Hansard. *Parliamentary Debates.* March 12, 20.
Yonge, C. D. *Life of Lord Liverpool.* 1868. III. 212.

VI.

1823.

1. UNPUBLISHED SOURCES.

Palmerston. Dispute with Commander-in-Chief. B.M. Add.
 MSS. 38370, 164–232.

2. Published Sources.

Croker, J. W. *Op. cit.* I. 244.
Hansard, *Parliamentary Debates.* March 6, April 30, May 7.
Leveson-Gower, F. *Letters of Harriet, Countess Granville.* 1894.
    I. 234.
Monypenny, W. F. *Life of Disraeli.* 1910. I. 32, 39.
Morley, J. *Life of Gladstone.* 1903. I. 20.
Phillips, W. Alison. *George Canning.* 1903. *passim.*
Temperley, H. *Foreign Policy of Canning.* 1925. 35–42, 81.

1824.
    Creevey, T. *Op. cit.* 419, 429–30.
    Croker, J. W. *Op. cit.* I. 257.
    Hansard. *Parliamentary Debates.* April 9.

1825.
1. Unpublished Sources.

Cowper, Lady. *Letters to Hon. F. Lamb.* Broadlands Papers.
    June 7. (Palmerston at Windsor.)
Palmerston. Hunting. B.M. Add. MSS. 19242, 270.
    Election. B.M. Add. MSS. 36461, 389.
Stapleton, A. G. *MS. of December* 16, 1856. Stapleton MSS.
    [Communicated by H. W. V. Temperley by consent of E. P.
    Stapleton.] (Canning and Palmerston's Stock Exchange
    speculation.)

2. Published Sources.

Fortescue, J. *Op. cit.* XI. 88.
Hansard. *Parliamentary Debates.* March 4, 15.
Monypenny, W. F. *Op. cit.* I. 78.

1826.
1. Unpublished Sources.

Cowper, Lady. *Letters to Hon. F. Lamb.* Broadlands Papers.
    February 1. (Cambridge Election.)
Palmerston. Irish crops. B.M. Add. MSS. 35653, 109.

2. Published Sources.

Airlie, Mabell, Countess of. *Op. cit.* I. 132.
Croker, J. W. *Op. cit.* I. 321.
Hansard. *Parliamentary Debates.* February 28, March 10,
    December 11.

1827.
    Croker, J. W. *Op. cit.* I. 362.
    Hansard. *Parliamentary Debates.* February 19.
    Wheeler, O. *Op. cit.* 111.

VII.
1827.
1. Unpublished Sources.

Cowper, Lady. *Letters to Hon. F. Lamb.* Broadlands Papers.
    April 24, May 1, June 12. (Offer of Exchequer.) August 10.
    (Conversion to Canning.)
Palmerston. *Letters to Lord Lansdowne.* Bowood Papers. 1828.
    December 21, 28; January 5. (Yeomanry.)

2. PUBLISHED SOURCES.

Creevey, T. *Op. cit.* 465.
Croker, J. W. *Op. cit.* I. 364, 391.
Greville, C. C. F. *Op. cit.* I. 137.
Lieven, Princess. *Op cit.* 164 n.
Sanders, Lloyd C. *Lord Melbourne's Papers.* 1889. 108.
Wellington, Duke of. *Correspondence.* 1871. IV. 91.
Wheeler, O. *Op. cit.* 114.

1828.

1. UNPUBLISHED SOURCES.

Palmerston. Formation of Government. B.M. Add. MSS.
38754, 132; 38754, 152–5.
Slavery. B.M. Add. MSS. 38756, 44.
Resignation. B.M. Add. MSS. 38756, 146–204.

2. PUBLISHED SOURCES.

Croker, J. W. *Op. cit.* I. 404, 423.
Greville, C. C. F. *Op. cit.* I. 126.
Hansard. *Parliamentary Debates.* January 29; February 22,
26; March 10.
Lieven, Princess. *Op cit.* 165.
Maxwell, Sir H. *Life of Wellington.* 1899. II. 210.
Robinson, L. G. *Letters of Dorothea, Princess Lieven.* 1902. 132.
Wellington, Duke of. *Correspondence.* 1871. V. 339, 397, 453.

INTERLUDE

I.

1828.

Creevey, T. *Op. cit.* 497–8, 505.
Croker, J. W. *Op. cit.* I. 378, 409.
Disraeli, B. *Whigs and Whiggism* (ed. Hutcheon). 1913. 31,
290.
Lieven, Princess. *Op. cit.* 165.

II.

Creevey, T. *Op. cit.* 501.
Hansard. *Parliamentary Debates.* June 2, 27.
Lieven, Princess. *Op. cit.* 159.

1829.

1. UNPUBLISHED SOURCES.

Lieven, Princess. *Letters to Palmerston.* Broadlands Papers.
June 15, 1829; June 5, 1830.

2. PUBLISHED SOURCES.

Airlie, Mabell, Countess of. *Op. cit.* I. 162–71.
Butler, J. R. M. *Passing of the Great Reform Bill.* 1914. 71.
Creevey, T. *Op. cit.* 541, 546.
Greville, C. C. F. *Op. cit.* I. 156, 189, 191, 209, 213, 241.
Trevelyan, G. O. *Life and Letters of Lord Macaulay.* 1897. I.
161.
Wellington, Duke of. *Correspondence.* 1877. VI. 293.

E E

1830.

1. Unpublished Sources.

Cowper, Lady. *Letters to Palmerston*. Broadlands Papers. January.   (Presents from Paris.)

2. Published Sources.

Creevey, T.   *Op. cit.*   553.
Croker, J. W.   *Op. cit.*   I. 431 ; II. 56, 64.
Greville, C. C. F.   *Op. cit.*   I. 199, 250, 277, 282.
Lieven, Princess, and Grey, Earl.   *Correspondence* (ed. Le Strange). 1890.   I. 416.
Hansard.   *Parliamentary Debates.*   February 16, March 10.
Trevelyan, G. O.   *Op. cit.* I. 198.

III.

Airlie, Mabell, Countess of.   *Op. cit.* I. 173.
Butler, J. R. M.   *Op. cit.*   97–105.
Croker, J. W.   *Op. cit.*   II. 63.
Greville, C. C. F.   *Op. cit.*   II. 6, 7, 9, 32.
Parker, C. S.   *Life and Letters of Sir James Graham.*   1907.   I. 84.
Lieven, Princess.   *Op. cit.*   165–9.
Morrah, H. A.   *The Oxford Union.*   1923.   46.
Praed, W. M.   *Political and Occasional Poems* (ed. Young).   1888. *s.v.   The New Order of Things.*
Robinson, L. G.   *Op. cit.*   249.
Trevelyan, G. M.   *Lord Grey of the Reform Bill.*   1920.   236, 243, 379.
Wellington, Duke of.   *Correspondence.*   1878.   VII. 281, 328.

FOREIGN OFFICE

I.

Training :
(*a*) Lord Malmesbury.   *Supra.   Prelude,* IV.
(*b*) Princess Lieven.   *Supra.   War Office,* VIII;   *Interlude,* II.
(*c*) War Department.   *Supra.   War Office, passim.*
(*d*) Canning.   *Temperley, H. W. V.   Op. cit., passim.*
           Temperley, H. W. V., in *Cambridge.*
           History of British Foreign Policy.   1923.   II. 60, III.
           Phillips, W. Alison.   *Canning.*   1905.   III, 119.

1830

II.

(*a*) First Negociation.

Unpublished Sources.

Lieven, Princess. *Letter to Palmerston*. Broadlands Papers. November 19.
Palmerston. *Letter to Princess Lieven*. Broadlands Papers. November 20.

(b) BELGIUM.

Creevey, T. *Op. cit.* 605, 628.
Hall, Major, J. *England and the Orleans Monarchy.* 1912. 12–48.
Omond, G. W. T., in *Cambridge History of British Foreign Policy.* II. 119–54.
Trevelyan, G. M. *Op. cit.* 258–9.
Trevelyan, G. O. *Op. cit.* I. 235.

(c) GENERAL.

Croker, J. W. *Op. cit.* II. 80.
Hansard. *Parliamentary Debates.* December 6.

1831.
(a) GENERAL.
1. UNPUBLISHED SOURCES.

Cowper, Lady. *Letter to Lady Ashley.* Broadlands Papers. (Undated. Melbourne's opinion of Reform.)
Melbourne, Viscount. *Letters to Palmerston.* Broadlands Papers. October 10. (Differences on Reform.)
Palmerston. *Letter to Lord Lansdowne.* Bowood Papers. (Undated.)
　　　Election Address. B.M. Add. MSS. 36466, 315.
　　　Letter to Dr. S. Butler. April 20. Church patronage. B.M. Add. MSS. 34588, 32.

2. PUBLISHED SOURCES.

Butler, J. R. M. *Op. cit.* 221, 288, 319–20, 324.
Creevey, T. *Op. cit.* 368.
Croker, J. W. *Op. cit.* II. 139, 140–1.
Greville, C. C. F. *Op. cit.* II. 147–8, 211–9, 225.
Hansard. *Parliamentary Debates.* February 18; March 3; August 11, 12.
Morley, J. *Op. cit.* I. 71.
Russell, R. *Early Correspondence of Lord J. Russell.* 1913. II. 27.
Sanders, Lloyd C. *Op. cit.* 1889. 143.
Trevelyan, G. M. *Op. cit.* 281, 295–6, 301, 313.
Trevelyan, G. O. *Op. cit.* I. 246.

(b) BELGIUM.
1. UNPUBLISHED SOURCES.

Leopold, King. *Letter to William IV.* Broadlands Papers. July 24.
2. PUBLISHED SOURCES.

Hall, Major J. *Op. cit.* 48–102.
Omond, G. W. T. *Loc. cit.*
Stockmar, Baron. *Memoirs.* 1872. I. 144–233.
Trevelyan, G. M. *Op. cit.* 260.

(c) ITALY.
1. UNPUBLISHED SOURCES.

Strong, C. F. *Palmerston and the Dawn of Italian Independence.*

2. PUBLISHED SOURCES.

Guedalla, Philip. *The Second Empire.* 1923. 63–5.
Hall, Major J. *Op. cit.* 64–5.
Metternich, Prince de. *Op. cit.* V. *passim.*

(d) POLAND.
1. UNPUBLISHED SOURCES.

Grace, W. F. F. *Great Britain and the Polish Question.*

2. PUBLISHED SOURCES.

Askenazy, S., in *Cambridge Modern History.* 1907. X. 445–74.

1832.

(a) GENERAL.

Butler, J. R. M. *Op. cit.* 331, 355, 372, 384–402.
Creevey, T. *Op. cit.* 590, 604.
Doyle, J. (H. B.). *Up and Down.* (Caricature). May 18.
Froude, J. A. *Carlyle's Early Life.* (Ed. 1896.) II. 305.
Greville, C. C. F. *Op. cit.* II. 229–30, 245–6, 254–7, 290–5.
Hansard. *Parliamentary Debates.* May 14, August 7.
Praed, W. M. *Op. cit. s.v. A Cabinet Carol.*
Torrens, W. M. *Memoirs of Viscount Melbourne.* 1878. I. 408.
Wellington, Duke of. *Correspondence.* 1880. VIII. 426.

(b) BELGIUM.
1. UNPUBLISHED SOURCES.

Palmerston. *Letter to Lord Lansdowne.* Bowood Papers. September.

2. PUBLISHED SOURCES.

Hall, Major, J. *Op. cit.* 108–144.
Praed, W. M. *Op. cit. s.v. An Epistle from an Old Electioneerer to a Young Secretary.*
Raikes, T. *Journal.* 1858. I. 35, 68, 80.
Wellington, Duke of. *Correspondence.* 1880. VIII. 423.

(c) ITALY.
1. UNPUBLISHED SOURCES.

Strong, C. F. F. *Op cit.*

2. PUBLISHED SOURCES.

Hall, Major J. *Op. cit.* 103–108.
Metternich, Prince de. *Op. cit.* V. 373–381, 481.

(d) GERMANY.

Hansard. *Parliamentary Debates.* August 2.
Metternich, Prince de. *Op. cit.* V. 383–97.

1833.

(a) GENERAL.

Creevey, T. *Op. cit.* 610–1.
Croker, J. W. *Op. cit.* II. 200.
Greville, C. C. F. *Op. cit.* II. 339, 342; III. 20.
Hansard. *Parliamentary Debates.* February 15, April 2, August
    15.
Lieven, Princess, and Grey, Earl. *Op. cit.* II. 484, 490–1.
Victoria, Queen. *Girlhood of Queen Victoria, Diaries.* (Ed. Lord
    Esher. 1912. I. 72–4.

(b) RUSSIA.

Greville, C. C. F. *Op. cit.* II. 357–8.
Hall, Major J. *Op. cit.* 145–70.
Lieven, Princess. *Op. cit.* 168, 185.
Robinson, L. G. *Op. cit.* 332, 339.

(c) SPAIN AND PORTUGAL.

1. UNPUBLISHED SOURCES.

Palmerston. *Letter to Hoppner.* August 12, 1832. Lisbon
    refugees. B.M. Egerton MSS. 2343.

2. PUBLISHED SOURCES.

Artagan, B. de. *Carlistas de Antaño.* (Barcelona.) 1910.
Borrow, G. *Bible in Spain.* (Ed. Burke.) 1905. 173–4, 235.
Clarke, H. Butler. *Modern Spain.* 1906. 72–102.
Edmundson, G., in *Cambridge Modern History.* 1907. X. 310–
    339.
Greville, C. C. F. *Op. cit.* I. 209.
Hall, Major J. *Op. cit.* 181.
Maxwell, Sir H. *Life and Letters of Lord Clarendon.* 1913. I.
    72, 77.
Temperley, H. W. V. *Op. cit.* 377–381.

1834.

(a) SPAIN AND PORTUGAL.

Bourgeois, E. *Manuel Historique de Politique Etrangère.* 1906.
    III. 115–129.
Clarke, H. Butler. *Op. cit.* 102–5.
Greville, C. C. F. *Op. cit.* 82.
Maxwell, Sir H. *Op. cit.* 73, 83.
Metternich, Prince de. *Op. cit.* V. 458, 640.

(b) GENERAL.

1. UNPUBLISHED SOURCES.

Lieven, Princess. *Letters to Lady Cowper.* Broadlands Papers.

2. PUBLISHED SOURCES.

Creevey, T. *Op. cit.* 618.
Dino, Duchesse de. *Memoirs, 1831–5.* (Translated.) 1909. 34,
    67, 74–5, 93–4, 135, 155, 210.
Disraeli, B. *Coningsby.* 1844.

Disraeli, B. *Whigs and Whiggism.* (Ed. Hutcheon.) 45.
Froude, J. A. *Op. cit.* II. 450–1, 475.
Greville, C. C. F. *Op. cit.* III. 57, 126, 149.
Hansard. *Parliamentary Debates.* March 7, 26; May 9; June 2.
Lieven, Princess. *Op. cit.* 41.
Metternich, Prince de. *Op. cit.* V. 643.
Morley, J. *Op. cit.* I. 114.
Praed, W. M. *Op. cit.* *s.v. The False Report* and *Ode to a Noble Lord.*

III.

1834–5.

Borrow, G. *Op. cit.* 137–9.
Creevey, T. *Op. cit.* 647.
Greville, C. C. F. *Op. cit.* III. 155, 210, 253.
Hertslet, E. *Op. cit.* 24–5, 61, 73–4, 78–9, 220–1.
H., J. *The United Administration.* (Caricature.)
Malmesbury, Earl of. *Memoirs of an Ex-Minister* (one-vol. edition). 1885. 45.
Praed, W. M. *Op. cit.* *s.v. The Contested Election.*
Raikes, T. *Op. cit.* I. 239.
Rosebery, Earl of. *Miscellanies.* 1921. I. 219.
Russell, Lord J. *Early Correspondence.* II. 72–3, 107.
Sanders, Lloyd C. *Op. cit.* 268.
Torrens, W. M. *Op. cit.* II. 153–5.

IV.

1835.

1. Unpublished Sources.

Melbourne, Viscount. *Letters to Palmerston* (eleven bundles). Broadlands Papers. June 11. (Poles for Spain.) June 29. (King's censure.)
Palmerston. *Letters to Lansdowne.* Bowood Papers. November 6, 1832. (King on Denman's appointment.)

2. Published Sources.

Clarke, H. Butler. *Op. cit.* 107–124.
Creevey, T. *Op. cit.* 649.
Greville, C. C. F. *Op. cit.* III. 203.
Hansard. *Parliamentary Debates.* June 24, August 10.
Lieven, Princess, and Grey, Earl. *Op. cit.* III. 119.
Maxwell, Sir H. *Op. cit.* I. 106.
Metternich, Prince de. *Op. cit.* VI. 34.
Mowat, R. B., in *Cambridge History of British Foreign Policy.* 1923. II. 169.
Sanders, Lloyd C. *Op. cit.* 333–4.
Stockmar, Baron. *Op. cit.* I. 348.

1836.

1. Unpublished Sources.

Lieven, Princess. *Letter to Lady Cowper.* Broadlands Papers. (Appearance of Louis Napoleon.)

Melbourne, Viscount. *Letters to Palmerston.* Broadlands Papers. January 7. (Urquhart and *Portfolio.*) February 17, 29; May 15. (Circassia.) April 27. (Victoria's marriage.)
Palmerston. *Letter to Melbourne.* Broadlands Papers. January 7. (" *Ellice*inations.")

2. PUBLISHED SOURCES.

Disraeli, B. *Whigs and Whiggism.* 289–94, 308.
Greville, C. C. F. *Op. cit.* III. 325.
Guedalla, Philip. *Op. cit.* 87–9.
Sanders, Lloyd C. *Op. cit.* 337–340.

1837.

Disraeli, B. *Whigs and Whiggism.* 363, 406.
Doyle, T. (H. B.). *Martyrdom of St. Sebastian.* (Caricature.) March 30, 1837.
Greville, C. C. F. *Op. cit.* III. 403.
Hansard. *Parliamentary Debates.* March 10.
Metternich, Prince de. *Op. cit.* VI. 172.
Victoria, Queen. *Letters.* 1907. I. 80.

V.

1. UNPUBLISHED SOURCES.

Cowper, Lady. *Letters to Palmerston.* Broadlands Papers. October 11, 16. (Visit to Brighton.)
Melbourne, Viscount. *Letters to Palmerston.* Broadlands Papers. October. (Visit to Brighton.) November 17. (Queen refers Leopold's letter to Melbourne and Palmerston.)

2. PUBLISHED SOURCES.

Airlie, Mabell, Countess of. *Op. cit.* I. 193–4.
Creevey, T. *Op. cit.* 666, 668, 672.
Greville, C. C. F. *Op. cit.* III. 407.
Greville, C. C. F. *Journal of the Reign of Queen Victoria :* 1837–1852. 1885. I. 23, 31.
Victoria, Queen. *Girlhood.* I. 200–1, 205–6, 223, 225–7, 246.
Victoria, Queen. *Letters.* I. 112.

1838.

(a) GENERAL

1. UNPUBLISHED SOURCES.

Melbourne, Viscount. *Letters to Palmerston.* Broadlands Papers. September 23. (L. Napoleon's passport.) Undated. (Melbourne and Palmerston consulted on royal dinner-lists.)

2. PUBLISHED SOURCES.

Creevey, T. *Op. cit.* 678.
Greville, C. C. F. *Op. cit.* (2) I. 55, 63–4, 66, 117–8, 159.
Strachey, L. *Queen Victoria.* 1921. 59–96.
Victoria, Queen. *Girlhood.* I. 251, 256, 261, 267, 279, 293, 298, 384.
Victoria, Queen. *Letters.* I. 136–8, 144.

(b) EASTERN QUESTION.

1. UNPUBLISHED SOURCES.

Melbourne, Viscount. *Letter to Palmerston.* Broadlands Papers.
  November 1. (Queen requires map of Asia.)
Nesselrode. *Note disclaiming aggressive designs.* October 20.
  B.M. Add. MSS. 36469, 279.
Palmerston. *Note to Pozzo on Russian agents.* November 20.
  B.M. Add. MSS. 36469, 301.
    Letter to Lansdowne on Egyptian Policy. Bowood
    Papers. June 17.
    Letter to Hobhouse on Russia in Central Asia. Brough-
    ton Papers. November 14. (India Office.)
Wellington, Duke of. *Memorandum on Afghan Expedition.*
  November 21. Broughton Papers. (India Office.)

2. PUBLISHED SOURCES.

Forbes, A. *The Afghan Wars.* 1896. 1–17.
Hall, Major J. *Op. cit.* 219–37.
Muir, Ramsay. *The Making of British India.* 1915. 306–319.
Russell, Lord J. *Op. cit.* 223.
Torrens, W. M. *Op. cit.* II. 272–5.

1839.

(a) GENERAL.

1. UNPUBLISHED SOURCES.

Melbourne, Viscount. *Letter to Palmerston.* Broadlands Papers.
  February 4. (Pronunciation of ' guarantee.')
Palmerston. *Letter to Hobhouse on Annexation of Aden.* January.
  Broughton Papers. (India Office.)

2. PUBLISHED SOURCES.

Greville, C. C. F. *Op. cit.* (2) I. 178, 242–3.
Hertslet, E. *Op. cit.* 33–6.
Maxwell, Sir H. *Op. cit.* I. 144.
Praed, W. M. *Op. cit. s.v. The Treasury Bench.*
Victoria, Queen. *Girlhood.* II. 89, 94, 107, 114, 144–5, 149, 154,
  159, 178.
Victoria, Queen. *Letters.* I. 186.

(b) BEDCHAMBER PLOT.

1. UNPUBLISHED SOURCES.

Bundle in Broadlands Papers containing (1) three drafts of Queen's
  final letter to Peel; (2) Melbourne's working draft of Cabinet
  Minute of May 11.

2. PUBLISHED SOURCES.

Ashley, M., in *The Times.* January 27, 1926.
Victoria, Queen. *Girlhood.* II. 168, 175–7.
Victoria, Queen. *Letters.* I. 197–215.

(c) EASTERN QUESTION.

Bourgeois, E. *Op. cit.* III. 145–58.
Driault, E. *La Question d'Orient.* 1909. 144–8.
Hall, Major J. *Op. cit.* 237–58.
Mowat, R. B., in *Cambridge History of British Foreign Policy.*
    II. 161–74.

(d) AFGHANISTAN AND CHINA.

Forbes, A. *Op. cit.* 18–34.
Moriarty, G. P., in *Cambridge History of British Foreign Policy.*
    II. 199–209, 215–9.

(e) PALMERSTON'S MARRIAGE.

1. UNPUBLISHED SOURCES.

Lieven, Princess. *Letters to Lady Cowper.* Broadlands Papers.
Palmerston. *Letter to Lord Lansdowne.* Bowood Papers. December 12.

2. PUBLISHED SOURCES.

Airlie, Mabell, Countess of. *Op. cit.* II. 30–40.
Victoria, Queen. *Girlhood.* II. 260, 275.
Victoria, Queen. *Letters.* I. 255.

1840.

(a) GENERAL.

1. UNPUBLISHED SOURCES.

Melbourne, Viscount. *Letters to Palmerston.* Broadlands Papers.
    January 13. (Order of Coburg.) March 24. (Naples.)
    March 24. (Aberdeen's question.)
Palmerston. *Letter to Lansdowne.* Bowood Papers. April 25.
    (Maine boundary.) *Letter to Russell.* Broadlands Papers.
    June 30. (Napoleon's remains.)
Palmerston, Lady. *Letter to Mrs. Huskisson.* December 20,
    1839. ('Quite a pleasure to look at him.') B.M. Add. MSS.
    39949, 170.

2. PUBLISHED SOURCES.

Airlie, Mabell, Countess of. *Op. cit.* II. 41, 44–5.
Hansard. *Parliamentary Debates.* April 9.
Maxwell, Sir H. *Op. cit.* I. 181.
Strachey, L. *Op. cit.* 109.
Victoria, Queen. *Girlhood.* II. 236, 291, 316–7, 321.

(b) EASTERN QUESTION.

1. UNPUBLISHED SOURCES.

Lieven, Princess. *Letter to Lady Palmerston.* Broadlands Papers.
    December 17. (Congratulations.)
Melbourne, Viscount. *Letters to Palmerston.* Broadlands Papers.
    July. (Palmerston's resignation.) August 8. Spencer's
    warning.) August 25. (L. Philippe, "a good deal of
    Jemappe." September 14. (Narrow margin of Cabinet sup-
    port.) September. (Leopold's anxiety.) September 30.

(Enclosing memorandum from Prince Albert.)   December 14.
(Warning to send despatches to Queen before issue.)
Palmerston.   *Letter to Hobhouse* (" the Cossack and the Sepoy ").
July 14.   Broughton Papers.   (India Office.)
Palmerston, Lady.   *Letter to Lord Beauvale.*   Broadlands Papers.
(Fall of Acre " nuts to us.")

2. PUBLISHED SOURCES.

Bourgeois, E.   *Op. cit.*   III. 159–176.
Driault, E.   *Op. cit.*   149–157.
Greville, C. C. F.   *Op. cit.*   (2) I. 117–8, 303, 308–9, 312, 318,
320–359.
Guedalla, Philip.   *Op. cit.*   32–3, 116–23.
Hall, Major J.   *Op. cit.*   258–316.
Hodder, E.   *Life of Lord Shaftesbury.*   1886.   I. 238–41, 310–9.
Martin, Sir T.   *Life of the Prince Consort.*   1875.   I. 95.
Maxwell, Sir H.   *Op. cit.*   I. 185, 212.
Melbourne, Lord.   *Papers.*   460–92.
Mowat, R. B.   *Op. cit.*   175–182.
Robinson, G.   *David Urquhart.*   1920.   104–19.
Russell, Lord J.   *Op. cit.*   II. 238–9.
Russell, Lord J.   *Later Correspondence.*   (Ed. Gooch.)   1925.
I. 6, 15.
Sokolow, N.   *History of Zionism.*   1919.   I. 121–132.
Victoria, Queen.   *Op. cit.*   I. 290, 300, 304, 311–5.

1841.

1. UNPUBLISHED SOURCES.

Melbourne, Viscount.   *Letter to Palmerston.*   Broadlands Papers.
July 7.   (Royal command portrait.)
Palmerston, Lady.   *Letter to Mrs. Huskisson.*   August.   (' Prince
of a fairy tale.')   B.M. Add. MSS. 39949, 190.

2. PUBLISHED SOURCES.

Airlie, Mabell, Countess of.   *Op. cit.*   II. 46–50, 61.
Greville, C. C. F.   *Op. cit.*   (2) I. 363–4; II. 5, 37.
Hansard.   *Parliamentary Debates.*   May 18.
Melbourne, Lord.   *Op. cit.*   419.
Torrens, W. M.   *Op. cit.*   II. 363–4, 391.
Victoria, Queen.   *Op. cit.*   I. 329.

VI.

Airlie, Mabell, Countess of.   *Op. cit.*   II. 69–70.
Hansard.   *Parliamentary Debates.*   September 17.
Lee, Sir S.   *King Edward VII.*   1925.   I. 5.

1842.

1. UNPUBLISHED SOURCES.

Palmerston.   *Letter to Lansdowne.*   Bowood Papers.   November
4.   (Principles of foreign policy.)   *Letter to Macaulay.*
August 29.   Contributing to *Edinburgh Review.*   B.M. Add.
MSS. 34632, 118.

2. PUBLISHED SOURCES.

Cowper, Countess. *Earl Cowper.* (Privately printed.) 1913. 5.
Forbes, A. *Op. cit.* 70–125.
Greville, C. C. F. *Op. cit.* (2) II. 75, 98, 104–7, 131.
Hansard. *Parliamentary Debates.* February 16, July 1, August 10.
Monypenny, W. F. *Op. cit.* II. 127–9.
Morley, J. *Life of Cobden.* 1881. I. 171.
Russell, Lord J. *Op. cit.* (2) I. 54.
Torrens, W. M. *Op. cit.* II. 379, 381.
Victoria, Queen. *Op. cit.* I. 470–1.

1843.

1. UNPUBLISHED SOURCES.

Palmerston. *Letter to Lansdowne.* Bowood Papers. November 13. (Irish Land.)

2. PUBLISHED SOURCES.

Greville, C. C. F. *Op. cit.* (2) II. 217.
Hansard. *Parliamentary Debates.* February 2, March 21, June 23, July 12.
Russell, Lord J. *Op. cit.* (2) I. 67.
Trevelyan, G. M. *Life of John Bright.* 1913. 117.

1844.

Greville, C. C. F. *Op. cit.* (2) II. 230, 233, 244–5.
Hansard. *Parliamentary Debates.* August 7.
Hodder, E. *Op. cit.* II. 19–21.
Raikes, T. *Op. cit.* II. 445.

1845.

Disraeli, B. *Endymion.* 286.
Greville, C. C. F. *Op. cit.* (2) II. 264, 267, 289, 298, 322–3, 345–7, 351.
Greville, C. C. F., and Reeve, H. *Letters.* 1924. 124–5.
Hansard. *Parliamentary Debates.* February 4; March 31; April 24; June 13, 25.
Martin, Sir T. *Op. cit.* I. 312.
Monypenny, W. F. *Op. cit.* II. 249, 338–41.
Morley, J. *Gladstone.* I. 279.
Russell, Lord J. *Op. cit.* (2) I. 83–107.
Trevelyan, G. M. *Op. cit.* 132, 139.

1846.

1. UNPUBLISHED SOURCES.

Palmerston, Lady. *Letter to Lord Beauvale.* Broadlands Papers. (Visit to Paris.)

2. PUBLISHED SOURCES.

Greville, C. C. F. *Op. cit.* (2) 88, 388, 393–4.
Hansard. *Parliamentary Debates.* March 27, June 29.
Hugo, Victor. *Choses Vues* (ed. Nelson). 95.
Monypenny, W. F. *Op. cit.* II. 372–3, 377.
Raikes, T. *Op. cit.* II. 455.
Russell, Lord J. *Op. cit.* (2) II. 74.

(a) GENERAL.
1. UNPUBLISHED SOURCES.

Palmerston. *Letter to Russell.* Broadlands Papers. October 18.
  (Bokhara.)

2. PUBLISHED SOURCES.

Fagan, L. *The Reform Club.* 1887. 75–81.
Greville, C. C. F. *Op. cit.* (2) II. 65, 322, 345.
Hansard. *Parliamentary Debates.* August 17.
Hertslet, Sir E. *Op. cit.* 79.
Martin, Sir T. *Op. cit.* I. 77, 85–6, 95, 122, 191.
Maxwell, Sir H. *Op. cit.* I. 177.
Strachey, L. *Op. cit.* 122–4.
Victoria, Queen. *Girlhood.* II. 242, 296.
Victoria, Queen. *Leaves from the Journal of Our Life in the
  Highlands.* 1868. 203–15.
Victoria, Queen. *Letters.* II. 79–82, 103, 126, 132.

(b) SPANISH MARRIAGES.
1. UNPUBLISHED SOURCES.

Palmerston. *Letter to Lansdowne.* Bowood Papers. September
  28.

2. PUBLISHED SOURCES.

Clarke, H. Butler. *Op. cit.* 204–6.
Greville, C. C. F. *Op. cit.* (2) II. 413, 409–24.
Hall, Major, J. *Op. cit.* 368–405.
Martin, Sir T. *Op. cit.* 341–73, 503–16.
Mowat, R. B., in *Cambridge History of British Foreign Policy.* II.
  192–8.
Russell, Lord J. *Op. cit.* (2) I. 116–24.
Stockmar, Baron. *Op. cit.* II. 181–205.
Victoria, Queen. *Letters.* II. 113, 116, 119–20, 122–5.

1847.
1. UNPUBLISHED SOURCES.

Palmerston. *Letter to Lansdowne.* Bowood Papers. January 14.
    (Spanish Marriages.)
  Letters to Clarendon. Clarendon Papers. Septem-
    ber 23. (Invasion scare.) November 13. (Irish
    priests.)

Palmerston, Lady. *Letter to Beauvale.* Broadlands Papers. (Queen's first message to Palmerston and " Our line must be sulk.")

Palmerston, Lady. *Letter to Palmerston.* Broadlands Papers. September 3. (Visit to Scotland.)

2. PUBLISHED SOURCES.

Greville, C. C. F. *Op. cit.* (2) III. 14, 18, 28, 30–4, 55, 62, 64.
Hearnshaw, F. J. C. In *Cambridge History of British Foreign Policy.* II. 288–303.
Martin, Sir T. *Op. cit.* I. 424–49.
Russell, Lord J. *Op. cit.* (2) I. 173, 248–54, 308.
Snell, F. J. *Palmerston's Borough.* (Tiverton.) 1894. 77–87.
Victoria, Queen. *Leaves.* 57–8.
Victoria, Queen. *Letters.* II. 138, 143, 151–2, 157–8, 160–1.

1848.

1. UNPUBLISHED SOURCES.

Palmerston. *Despatch to Stratford Canning.* B.M. Add. MSS. 38979, 411. (Layard's Excavations.)
Letters to Clarendon. Clarendon Papers. March 9. (' The sweep made of the Plotters. . . . The true policy of England. . . .') April 22. (' The French are Children. . . .') May 30. (' I have no Doubt in my own Mind. . . .')
Letter to Lansdowne. Bowood Papers. April 3. (' We are not the arbiters of Europe. . . .')
Palmerston, Lady. *Letter to Mrs. Huskisson.* B.M. Add. MSS. 39949. (Chartist Riot.)
Russell, Lord John. *Letter to Clarendon.* Clarendon Papers. March 21. (' L.P. and Guizot grumble and intrigue. . . .')
Strong, C. F. *Op. cit., passim.*

2. PUBLISHED SOURCES.

Airlie, Mabell, Countess of. *Op. cit.* II. 116–7, 119, 122.
Froude, J. A. *Carlyle's Life in London.* (Ed. 1891.) I. 460, 468.
Greville, C. C. F. *Op. cit.* (2) III. 154, 157, 170, 173–4, 186, 194.
Hansard. *Parliamentary Debates.* February 8, 23; March 1; June 5.
Hearshaw, F. J. C. *Loc. cit.* II. 304–18.
Hertslet, E. *Op. cit.* 69, 78.
Martin, Sir T. *Op. cit.* I. 480; II. 33, 49, 64, 111.
Metternich, Prince de. *Op. cit.* VIII. 18.
Monypenny, W. F., and Buckle, G. E. *Op. cit.* III. 176, 192.
Russell, Lord J. *Op. cit.* (2) I. 296; II. 6.
Victoria, Queen. *Leaves.* 65.
Victoria, Queen. *Letters.* II. 172, 175, 202, 204, 208, 212–5, 221, 224–231–3.

1849.

I. UNPUBLISHED SOURCES.

Palmerston. *Letters to Lansdowne.* Bowood Papers. January
    28. ('If Stanley and Aberdeen should twit us. . . .')
    March 6. (Sicilian rising.) June 25. ('Guizot and Madame
    Lieven . . . putting Aberdeen up. . . . Cat's Paw.')
Palmerston, Lady. *Letter to Palmerston.* Broadlands Papers.
    April 17. (House of Commons dinner.)

2. PUBLISHED SOURCES.

Greville, C. C. F. *Op. cit.* (2) II. 260, 271–2, 276–7, 289–91,
    293.
Hansard. *Parliamentary Debates.* February 2, June 12.
Martin, Sir T. *Op. cit.* II. 56, 168, 174, 203, 224.
Russell, Lord J. *Op. cit.* (2) I. 348–9, 351–2; II. 5.
Simpson, F. A. *Louis Napoleon and the Recovery of France.*
    1923. 40–3.
Sproxton, C. *Palmerston and the Hungarian Revolution.* 1919.
    passim.
Stockmar, Baron. *Op. cit.* II. 366.
Victoria, Queen. *Letters.* II. 250–2, 263.
Walpole, S. *Life of Lord John Russell.* 1889. II. 52.

1850.

I. UNPUBLISHED SOURCES.

Palmerston. *Letters to Lansdowne.* Bowood Papers. March 27.
    (The Queen's "scolding letter.") July 14, 1851.
    (Germany "the all-important part of Europe.")
    Letter to Clarendon. Clarendon Papers. October
    23 ("His Emptyness the Pope.") November 9.
    ("Profligate Slave Traders.") November 13.
    (Interpreting Russell on Popery.)
Palmerston, Lady. *Letter to Clarendon.* Clarendon Papers.
    Undated. (Don Pacifico speech.)
Palmerston, Lady. *Letter to Mrs. Huskisson.* B.M. Add. MSS.
    39949, 264. February 7. (Greek claims.)

2. PUBLISHED SOURCES.

Curzon, Earl. *Modern Parliamentary Eloquence.* 1913. 64.
Fagan, L. *Op. cit.* 83–91.
Greville, C. C. F. *Op. cit.* (2) III. 311–2, 315–9, 324–5, 333, 362,
    364.
Hansard. *Parliamentary Debates.* May 31, June 20. 24–8.
Martin, Sir T. *Op. cit.* 269–76, 281–2, 287, 307–10, 327.
Maxwell, Sir H. *Op. cit.* I. 311–2.
Monypenny, W. F., and Buckle, G. E. *Op. cit.* III. 259.
Russell, Lord J. *Op. cit.* (2) II. 66–78.
Victoria, Queen. *Letters.* II. 277–82, 288–90, 296–8, 301, 306,
    309–16, 319–25.
Walpole, Sir S. *Op. cit.* II. 56, 63, 133–7, 141.

1851.

(a) GENERAL.

1. UNPUBLISHED SOURCES.

Palmerston, Lady. *Letters to Palmerston.* Broadlands Papers. January. (Brighton.)

2. PUBLISHED SOURCES.

Airlie, Mabell, Countess of. *Op. cit.* II. 121.
Greville, C. C. F. *Op. cit.* (2) III. 365.
Hansard. *Parliamentary Debates.* March 18, June 17.
Hertslet, Sir E. *Op. cit.* 81.
Maxwell, Sir H. *Op. cit.* II. 337.
Monypenny, W. F., and Buckle, G. E. *Op. cit.* III. 278.
Russell, Lord J. *Op. cit.* (2) II. 87.
Snell, F. J. *Op. cit.* 73.
Victoria, Queen. *Letters.* II. 354–63, 377, 380–1, 392–400.

(b) DISMISSAL.

1. UNPUBLISHED SOURCES.

Palmerston, Lady. *Letters to Beauvale.* Broadlands Papers. January 7, 8, 1852.
Palmerston, Lady. *Letter to Mrs. Huskisson.* January 9, 1852. B.M. Add. MSS. 39949, 266.

2. PUBLISHED SOURCES.

Greville, C. C. F. *Op. cit.* (2) II. 420, 426, 431, 433, 435.
Guedalla, Philip. *Op. cit.* 206–22.
Guedalla, Philip. *1851* in KERRY, EARL OF. *The Secret of the Coup d'État.* 1924.
Martin, B. Kingsley. *The Triumph of Lord Palmerston.* 1924. 56, 72.
Martin, Sir T. *Op. cit.* II. 411–28.
Maxwell, Sir H. *Op. cit.* I. 339.
Russell, Lord J. *Op. cit.* (2) I. 270; II. 83–101, 110.
Simpson, F. A. *Op. cit.* 163–7.
Stockmar, Baron. *Op. cit.* II. 459.
Trevelyan, G. M. *John Bright.* 197–8.
Trevelyan, G. O. *Op. cit.* II. 250, 300.
Victoria, Queen. *Letters.* II. 404–28.

HOME OFFICE

I.

1852.

1. UNPUBLISHED SOURCES.

Clarendon, Earl of. *Letter to Reeve.* Clarendon Papers. January 2. (Palmerston's position.)
Palmerston. *Letter to Clarendon.* Clarendon Papers. February 23. (Fall of Russell Govt.)
Palmerston. *Letter to Lansdowne.* Bowood Papers. October 24. (Russell's position.)
Palmerston, Lady. *Letter to Sir W. Temple.* Broadlands Papers. March 5. ('P. did not intend to put out Govt.')

Palmerston, Lady *Letter to Lansdowne.* Bowood Papers. De
    cember 22. (P. and Home Office.)
Palmerston, Lady. *Letter to Mrs. Huskisson.* B.M. Add. MSS.
    39949, 271. Undated. (P. ' prevailed upon.')

2. PUBLISHED SOURCES.

Airlie, Mabell, Countess of. *Op. cit.* II. 142–3, 145, 150–3.
Greville, C. C. F. *Op. cit.* (2) III. 448; (3) I. 2, 4, 14, 21.
Hansard. *Parliamentary Debates.* February 3, April 29.
Malmesbury, Earl of. *Op. cit.* 237–8.
Martin, B. K. *Op. cit.* 72.
Martin, Sir T. *Op. cit.* II. 426.
Monypenny, W. F., and Buckle, G. E. *Op. cit.* III. 343–4,
    380–1, 411.
Mount Temple, Lady. *Memorials.* (Privately printed.) 1890.
    45–7.
Morley, J. *Gladstone.* I. 433.
Russell, Lord J. *Op. cit.* (2) II. 93, 117.
Snell, F. J. *Op. cit.* 74.
Victoria, Queen. *Letters.* II. 438, 440, 445, 447–8, 488–92, 504,
    511, 516.

II.

1853.

(a) HOME AFFAIRS.

1. UNPUBLISHED SOURCES.

Palmerston. *Letters to Lansdowne.* Bowood Papers. April 22.
    (Succession Duty.) August 14. (Smoke abatement.)
Palmerston, Lady. *Letter to Mrs. Huskisson.* B.M. Add. MSS.
    39949, 290 April 11. (Court 'very friendly and courteous.')
Palmerston, Lady. *Letter to Palmerston.* Broadlands Papers.
    September 17. (Balmoral.)

2. PUBLISHED SOURCES.

Balfour, Lady F. *Life of George, fourth Earl of Aberdeen.* 1923.
    II. 178.
Greville, C. C. F. *Op. cit.* (3) I. 106.
Hansard. *Parliamentary Debates.* August 8.
Hodder, E. *Op. cit.* II. 444.
Victoria, Queen. *Letters.* II. 520, 523, 536, 548.

(b) FOREIGN AFFAIRS.

1. UNPUBLISHED SOURCES.

Palmerston. *Letters to Clarendon.* Clarendon Papers. Vol. 1853,
    passim.

2. PUBLISHED SOURCES.

Driault, E. *Op. cit.* 166–74.
Greville, C. C. F. *Op. cit.* (3) I. 50, 55, 95.
Hearnshaw, F. J. C., in *Cambridge History of British Foreign Policy.*
    II. 340–58.

Martin, B. K. *Op. cit. passim.*
Simpson, F. A. *Op. cit.* 220–37.
Victoria, Queen. *Letters.* II. 553.

III.

RESIGNATION OF 1853.

1. UNPUBLISHED SOURCES.

Palmerston. *Letters to Clarendon.* Clarendon Papers. May 22.
    (' Policy and Practice of Russian Govt.') Septem-
    ber 12. (' Red-haired Barbarians.') December
    15. (Resignation.)
    Letters to Lansdowne. Bowood Papers. December
    8, 14, 23, 24, 25.

2. PUBLISHED SOURCES.

Airlie, Mabell, Countess of. *Op. cit.* II. 138.
Greville, C. C. F. *Op. cit.* (3) I. 112–20.
Malmesbury, Earl of. *Op. cit.* 307–8.
Martin, B. K. *Op. cit., passim.*
Martin, Sir T. *Op. cit.* II. 524, 534.
Maxwell, Sir H. *Op. cit.* II. 29.
Monypenny, W. F., and Buckle, G. E. *Op. cit.* III. 527–9.
Morley, J. *Gladstone.* I. 490.
Russell, Lord J. *Op. cit.* (2) II. 123–9, 151.
Simpson, F. A. *Op. cit.* 241, *n.*
Victoria, Queen. *Letters.* II. 567–75.

1854–5.

1. UNPUBLISHED SOURCES.

Palmerston. *Letters to Clarendon.* Clarendon Papers. January
    16, 22; March 4, 7; July 24. (Crimea.) September 3;
    October 11. (Hospitals.) August 29. (Alaska.) November
    19, 21, 24. (P. in Paris.)
Palmerston, Lady. *Letter to Palmerston.* Broadlands Papers.
    August 8. (' That wayward Johnny.')

2. PUBLISHED SOURCES.

Fagan, L. *Op. cit.* 93–105.
Greville, C. C. F. *Op. cit.* (3) I. 126–8, 134, 229–37.
Hansard. *Parliamentary Debates.* March 13, 1854; January 29,
    1855.
Martin, B. K. *Op. cit., passim.*
Martin, Sir T. *Op. cit.* II. 538–65; III. 34, 111–2.
Morley, J. *Cobden.* II. 154.
Morley, J. *Gladstone.* I. 491, 494, 526–36.
Russell, Lord J. *Op. cit.* (2) II. 130–1, 136–7, 160–1, 174–8, 180,
    182.
Strachey, L. *Op. cit.* 176–8.
Trevelyan, G. M. *Op. cit.* 233–4.
Trevelyan, G. O. *Op. cit.* II. 374.
Victoria, Queen. *Letters.* III. 17, 25, 28, 73–8, 86, 102–31.

F F

PRIME MINISTER

I.

1855.

1. Unpublished Sources.

Nightingale, Florence. *Letter to Palmerston.* Clarendon Papers. October 4. (Jewish refugees.)

Palmerston. *Letter to Lansdowne.* Bowood Papers. June 30. (Panmure's ' head turned.')

Letters to Clarendon. Clarendon Papers. February 8, 10. (Russell for Vienna.) April 26. (Suffocating shells and Dundonald.) May 6. (Evening ride.) May 21. (" The superior Deities.") June 17, July 15. (Suez Canal.) July 4. (Disraeli as ambassador.) July 15. (Queen's letter ' full of good sense.') July 29, August 2. (Secret Service money for Neapolitan prisoners.) September 28. (U.S.A. and slavery.) 1856, January 9. (England to fight alone.)

Palmerston, Lady. *Letter to Sir W. Temple.* Broadlands Papers. April 23. (' Gladstone's sophistry.')

2. Published Sources.

Disraeli, B. *Endymion.* Chap. 100.

Douglas, Sir G., and Ramsey, Sir G. D. *The Panmure Papers.* 1908. I. 403 and *passim.*

Greville, C. C. F. *Op. cit.* (3) I. 220, 303.

Guedalla, Philip. *Op. cit.* 251–7.

Hamley, Sir E. *The War in the Crimea.* 1900.

Hansard. *Parliamentary Debates.* February 16, 19.

Martin, Sir T. *Op. cit.* II. 249; III. 245–59.

Maxwell, Sir H. *Op. cit.* II. 50, 63, 73–5, 88–9, 92–4, 106–7.

Monypenny, W. F., and Buckle, G. E. *Op. cit.* III. 567.

Morley, J. *Cobden.* II. 177.

Morley, J. *Gladstone.* I. 537–45.

Reddaway, W. F., in *Cambridge History of British Foreign Policy.* II. 377–86.

Russell, Lord J. *Op. cit.* (2) II. 174.

Simpson, F. A. *Op. cit.* 282–353.

Trevelyan, G. M. *Op. cit.* 241.

Victoria, Queen. *Letters.* III. 177, 198, 207.

II.

1856.

1. Unpublished Sources.

Clarendon, Earl of. *F.O. Minute on Palmerston's draft.* Clarendon Papers. December 18.

Palmerston. *Letters to Clarendon.* Clarendon Papers. January 5. (Otho.) April 3. (Jaffa-Jerusalem railway.) April 30. (Cavour.) June 25. (Americans at Court.) August 14. (Baghdad railway.) August 25. (Death of Sir W.

Temple.) October 17. (Russia, 'ticket of leave man.')
October 18. (Leopold an arbitrator.) October 31. (F.O.
drafts.) November 26. (Prokesch and Thouvenel.) December 10. (Anglo-French alliance.) December 14. (Walewski.)
December 18. (Suez Canal.)

2. PUBLISHED SOURCES.

Airlie, Mabell, Countess of. *Op. cit.* II. 43, 171–2.
Buckle, G. E. *Op. cit.* IV. 15.
Dasent, A. I. *John Thaddeus Delane.* 1908. I. 229, 237–8.
Fitzmaurice, Lord E. *Life of Lord Granville.* 1905. I. 136,
    172–222.
Hodder, E. *Op. cit.* II. 505; III. 31–2, 55.
Mount Temple, Lady. *Op. cit.* 56–8.
Reddaway, W. F. *Loc. cit.* 387–95.
Snell, F. J. *Op. cit.* 75, 94–5.
Victoria, Queen. *Letters.* III. 237–8, 249.

1857.

1. UNPUBLISHED SOURCES.

Palmerston. *Letter to H. Reeve.* September 27. (Fast Proclamation.) In the author's possession.
    Letters to Clarendon. Clarendon Papers. January
    16. (Kabul and Kandahar.) March 15. (The
    Court 'friendly.') March 29. (Schleswig-Holstein.) April 2. (Faroe Islands.) April 26.
    (Reform and Republic.) July 27. (The Queen's
    'Lark' at Cherbourg.) August 3. (Anglo-
    French Alliance.) August 16. (Tangier.)
    August 20. (Queen and Prince.) September 8.
    (Govt. of India.) September 29. (Belgian troops
    for India.) December 8. (Shah of Persia.)
    December 29. (U.S.A.)

2. PUBLISHED SOURCES.

Borrow, G. *The Romany Rye* (ed. Knapp). 364.
Buckle, G. E. *Op. cit.* IV. 73–4, 87.
Buckler, F. W., in *Cambridge History of British Foreign Policy.*
    II. 422–9.
Douglas, Sir G., and Ramsay, Sir G. D. *Op. cit.* II. 332–3, 373.
Greville, C. C. F. *Op. cit.* (3) II. 94–5, 109–10, 117.
Hodder, E. *Op. cit.* III. 40, 43.
Malleson, G. B. *The Indian Mutiny of* 1857. 1898.
Martin, Sir T. *Op. cit.* IV. 93–122.
Maxwell, Sir H. *Op. cit.* II. 140, 150, 157.
Victoria, Queen. *Letters.* III. 290, 312.

1858.

1. UNPUBLISHED SOURCES.

Palmerston. *Letters to Clarendon.* Clarendon Papers. January
    19, 23; February 9. (Conspiracy to Murder Bill.) March
    27. Bright's plans.

2. Published Sources.

Buckle, G. E. *Op. cit.* IV. 110.
Fitzmaurice, Lord E. *Op. cit.* I. 288.
Greville, C. C. F. *Op. cit.* (3) II. 160.
Guedalla, Philip. *Op. cit.* 268–71.
Hansard. *Parliamentary Debates.* February 8, 9, 12, 19.
Martin, Sir T. *Op. cit.* IV. 161–3.

III.

1. Unpublished Sources.

Palmerston. *Letter to Lansdowne.* Bowood Papers. December 4.
(Bright and *Statesman.*)

2. Published Sources.

Airlie, Mabell, Countess of. *Op. cit.* II. 169–70.
Buckle, G. E. *Op. cit.* IV. 152.
Cowper, Countess. *Op. cit.* 87.
Dasent, A. I. *Op. cit.* I. 302–3.
Greville, C. C. F. *Op. cit.* (3) II. 185, 188, 190, 193, 199–200, 215–6.
Malmesbury, Earl of. *Op. cit.* 422, 455.
Maxwell, Sir H. *Op. cit.* II. 167–9, 174.
Victoria, Queen. *Letters.* III. 382.

1859.

1. Unpublished Sources.

Palmerston. *Letter to Panizzi.* B.M. Add. MSS. 36719, 160.
April 1. (Poerio and Settembrini.)

2. Published Sources.

Buckle, G. E. *Op. cit.* IV. 235–7.
Fitzmaurice, Lord E. *Op. cit.* I. 325–6, 330–41.
Greville, C. C. F. *Op. cit.* (3) II. 248–50.
Guedalla, Philip. *Op. cit.* 277–88.
Malmesbury, Earl of. *Op. cit.* 488, 492.
Martin, Sir T. *Op. cit.* IV. 389, 434, 449.
Maxwell, Sir H. *Op. cit.* II. 183.
Morley, J. *Cobden.* II. 226–33.
Morley, J. *Gladstone.* I. 623–8.
Snell, F. J. *Op. cit.* 71–2.
Trevelyan, G. M. *Bright.* 281.
Trevelyan, G. M. *Garibaldi and the Thousand* (cheap edition). 121.
Victoria, Queen. *Letters.* III. 438–45.
Walpole, Sir S. *Op. cit.* 305–9.

IV.

Bagehot, W. *English Constitution* (ed. 1902). 170.
Fitzmaurice, Lord E. *Op. cit.* I. 349–67, 486.
Martin, Sir T. *Op. cit.* IV. 463.

Maxwell, Sir H. *Op. cit.* II. 193.
Morley, J. *Gladstone.* II. 19.
Russell, Lord J. *Op. cit.* (2) II. 234.
Scott, Sir G. *Personal and Professional Recollections.* 1879.
    176–201.
Victoria, Queen. *Letters.* III. 446, 455–7, 463, 474.

1860.
1. UNPUBLISHED SOURCES.

Palmerston. *Letter to Lansdowne.* Bowood Papers. May 17.
    (Paper Duties.)

2. PUBLISHED SOURCES.

Greville, C. C. F. *Op. cit.* (3) II. 290, 310.
Hansard. *Parliamentary Debates.* May 7, July 6.
Lee, Sir S. *Op. cit.* I. 111.
Malmesbury, Earl of. *Op. cit.* 522, 524.
Martin, Sir T. *Op. cit.* V. 55–7, 99–100.
Maxwell, Sir H. *Op. cit.* II. 197, 220.
Morley, J. *Cobden.* II. 241–86.
Morley, J. *Gladstone.* II. 21–38, 42–8.
Trevelyan, G. M. *Garibaldi and the Thousand.*
Trevelyan, G. M. *Bright.* 284.
Victoria, Queen. *Letters.* III. 492, 509, 519.
Walpole, Sir S. *Op. cit.* II. 323–8.

1861.
1. UNPUBLISHED SOURCES.

Palmerston. *Minute to Layard (F.O.).* B.M. Add. MSS. 38987,
    301. October 20. (Recognition of Southern States.)
Mexican Documents :
    1. *Russell to Crampton.* September 14 and 23, 1861. Record
        Office, F.O., Spain. (Danger of Spanish intervention and
        filibusters.)
    2. *Mulinen to Rechberg.* October 15, 1861. Wiener Staats-
        archiv : Berichte aus Paris. (Palmerston asked to
        approve Max.)
    3. *Apponyi to Rechberg.* February 15, 1862. *Ibid.* (Palmer-
        ston's refusal.)
    4. *Mulinen to Rechberg.* November 3, 1861. *Apponyi to
        Rechberg.* February 15 and 28, 1862. *Ibid.* (Napoleon's
        deception—" School of Bright.")

2. PUBLISHED SOURCES.

Adams, E. D. *Great Britain and the American Civil War.* 1925.
    passim.
Dasent, A. I. *Op. cit.* II. 12, 21, 26–7, 36–7.
Fitzmaurice, Lord E. *Op. cit.* I. 405.
Guedalla, Philip. *Op. cit.* 321–7.
Lee, Sir S. *Op. cit.* I. 122–3.
Martin, Sir T. *Op. cit.* V. 273, 285–7, 403, 416–26, 428, 434–5,
    437.

438 PALMERSTON

Maxwell, Sir H. *Op. cit.* II. 244, 254.
Morley, J. *Cobden.* II. 389.
Morley, J. *Gladstone.* II. 39–40, 73–5.
Mount Temple, Lady. *Op. cit.* 51.
Newton, A. P., in *Cambridge History of British Foreign Policy.* II. 488–507.
Newton, Lord. *Lord Lyons.* 1913. I. 48, 60.
Putnam, G. H. *Abraham Lincoln.* 1909. 88.
Putnam, G. H. *Memories of My Youth.* 1914. 205–11.
Russell, Lord J. *Op. cit.* (2) II. 273–4, 279, 281.
Snell, F. J. *Op. cit.* 93.
Taylor, T. *John Palmerston,* in *Punch,* April 6, 1861.
Victoria, Queen. *Letters.* III. 539–40, 545–8, 568, 593–8, 606.
Walpole, Sir S. *Op. cit.* II. 345.

1862.

1. UNPUBLISHED SOURCES.

Palmerston. *Minutes to Layard (F.O.).* January 18. B.M. Add. MSS. 38988, 40. (Livingstone's Medicine.) June 17. B.M. Add. MSS. 33988, 165. (Southern independence must be " a Truth and a Fact " before recognition.)
Mexican Documents :
   Leopold to Maximilian. September 29, October 27. Wiener Staatsarchiv. *Maximilian to Leopold.* November 3. *Ibid.* (P. refusing support.)

2. PUBLISHED SOURCES.

Adams, E. D. *Op. cit.*
Fitzmaurice, Lord E. *Op. cit.* I. 406–7.
Hansard. *Parliamentary Debates.* February 6.
Lee, Sir S. *Op. cit.* I. 123–4, 126.
Maxwell, Sir H. *Op. cit.* II. 257, 267–8.
Morley, J. *Gladstone.* II. 48–51, 73–86.
Newton, A. P. *Loc. cit.* II. 507–21.
Russell, Lord J. *Op. cit.* (2) II. 323, 327–8.
Victoria, Queen. *Letters.* (2) I. 7, 11–5, 18, 23–5, 33.
Walpole, Sir S. *Op. cit.* II. 349–50, 353–6.

1863.

1. UNPUBLISHED SOURCES.

Grace, W. F. F. *Great Britain and the Polish Question in* 1863, *passim.*
Palmerston. *Minutes to Layard (F.O.).* February 6. B.M. Add. MSS. 38989, 43. (Brazil.) June 27. B.M. Add. MSS. 38989, 147. (Bismarck and Prussian army.) *Letter to Russell.* Broadlands Papers. (' Hen Leuchtenberg.')

Mexican Documents :
   Bourdillon to de Pont. March 4. Wiener Staatsarchiv. (Interview with P.)
   Arrauquoiz to de Pont. September 11. *Ibid.* (P. and American separatism.)

2. Published Sources.

Adams, E. D. *Op. cit.*
Buckle, G. E. *Op. cit.* IV. 392.
Dasent, A. I. *Op. cit.* II. 65, 79.
Fitzmaurice, Lord E. *Op. cit.* I. 446, 453.
Gilpin, H. *Miscellaneous Poems.* 1863. s.v. *To Lord Palmerston.*
Guedalla, Philip. *Op. cit.* 343–50.
Hansard. *Parliamentary Debates.* July 23.
Hodder, E. *Op. cit.* II. 149.
Lee, Sir S. *Op. cit.* I. 160, 162.
Martin, Sir T. *Op. cit.* V. 229.
Morley, J. *Gladstone.* II. 97–8, 102, 116.
Russell, Lord J. *Op. cit.* (2) II. 334.
Victoria, Queen. *Letters.* (2) I. 66–7, 83, 97, 102, 115.
Walpole, Sir S. *Op. cit.* II. 388.
Ward, Sir A. W., in *Cambridge History of British Foreign Policy.*
    II. 522–73.

1864.

1. Unpublished Sources.

Leopold, King. *Letter to Palmerston.* Broadlands Papers. June
    15. (' My beloved niece . . . by no means partial to Prussia.')
Palmerston. *Minute to Layard* (*F.O.*). B.M. Add. MSS. 38990,
    328. October 23. (' Our Peace Makers are our Armstrongs.')

2. Published Sources.

Buckle, G. E. *Op. cit.* IV. 405.
Cowper, Countess. *Op. cit.* 119.
Fitzmaurice, Lord E. *Op. cit.* I. 457, 463–5.
Hertslet, Sir E. *Op. cit.* 79.
Morley, J. *Gladstone.* II. 119, 128–30, 138–9.
Origines Diplomatiques de la Guerre de 1870–1871. 1910. I. 36,
    234.
Snell, F. J. *Op. cit.* 95.
Trevelyan, G. M. *Bright.* 330.
Victoria, Queen. *Letters.* (2) I. 138–47, 150–4, 163–8, 181–9,
    219, 223, 236, 239, 244.
Ward, Sir A. W. *Loc. cit.* 573–82.

1865.

Buckle, G. E. *Op. cit.* 422–3.
Hansard. *Parliamentary Debates.* April 3, July 4.
Hodder, E. *Op. cit.* III. 187–8.
Malmesbury, Earl of. *Op. cit.* 607.

1865.

Morley, J. *Gladstone.* II. 140, 142, 151–2.
Russell, Lord J. *Op. cit.* (2) II. 315.
Snell, F. J. *Op. cit.* 99.
Victoria, Queen *Letters.* (2) I. 248–9, 256–62, 279; II. 62.

V.

ILLNESS AND DEATH.

1. UNPUBLISHED SOURCES.

Palmerston. *Letter to Sir A. Clifford* (last letter).   Private letter
    book, 1865.   Broadlands Papers.   October 11.
    Letter to Layard.   September 12.   B.M. Add. MSS.
    38992, 19.   (Copenhagen house for Prince of
    Wales.)
Palmerston, Lady.   *Letter to W. Cowper.*   Broadlands Papers.
    (Chops and old port.)

2. PUBLISHED SOURCES.

Airlie, Mabell, Countess of. *Op. cit.*   II. 174–6.
Cowper, Countess. *Op. cit.*   135–6.
Hodder, E.   *Op. cit.*   III. 185–6.
Mount Temple, Lady. *Op. cit.*   58–60.
Victoria, Queen. *Letters.*   (2) I. 272, 278.

INDEX

INDEX

Lightning Source UK Ltd.
Milton Keynes UK
UKHW012000120123
415233UK00001B/136